THE AUSTRIAN COMIC TRADITION

Edited by John R. P. McKenzie and Lesley Sharpe
AUSTRIAN STUDIES IX

THE AUSTRIAN COMIC TRADITION

Studies in Honour of W. E. Yates

Edited by John R. P. McKenzie and Lesley Sharpe

AUSTRIAN STUDIES IX

EDINBURGH UNIVERSITY PRESS

© Edinburgh University Press, 1998

Edinburgh University Press Ltd
22 George Square, Edinburgh

Typeset in Linotron Ehrhardt by
Koinonia Ltd, Bury, and
printed in Great Britain
by The University Press, Cambridge

A CIP record for this book is available
from the British Library

ISBN 0 7486 1086 3

Contents

Contents

Contents

W. E. Yates

This volume of *Austrian Studies* is dedicated to Professor W. E. Yates on his sixtieth birthday, and marks the gratitude of his colleagues in German and Austrian studies at home and abroad, not only for his pioneering scholarship, particularly in the field of Nestroy studies, but also for his wide-ranging activities as editor, adviser, supervisor, reviewer, encourager and friend. As a member of the editorial board of *Austrian Studies* and a frequent contributor to it, Gar Yates is closely associated with this yearbook, and we, the guest editors, are most grateful to Ritchie Robertson and Edward Timms for giving us the opportunity to compile the present volume in his honour.

Energy, scrupulous attention to detail, breadth of knowledge, critical acuteness and humane understanding – these are the qualities that character-ise Gar Yates's professional life and published work. He was closely associated with German studies from an early age. His father, Douglas Yates, was himself an eminent Austrian scholar and Head of the Department of German at Aberdeen University, and William Witte, Douglas Yates's successor and the first Professor of German at Aberdeen, was a close family friend. Educated at Fettes College in Edinburgh during the years between James Bond and Tony Blair, Gar Yates went up as a Scholar to Emmanuel College, Cambridge in 1958. In 1961 he moved on to write a doctoral dissertation under the supervision of F. J. Stopp on popular Viennese comedy from 1823 to 1923, completing it in three years, in spite of having been appointed to a lectureship at Durham in 1963, a post that required him to range from the sixteenth century to Hebbel and Hauptmann in the first two years. It is a tribute to his commitment to teaching as well as to research that students from his Durham days still keep in touch with him.

Appointed Professor of German at Exeter in 1972 as successor to H. B. Garland, Gar Yates had already made his mark as a scholar of Austrian literature with critical editions of Hofmannsthal's *Der Schwierige* and Grill-parzer's *Der Traum ein Leben*, as well as articles on Nestroy. His monographs on Nestroy and Grillparzer both appeared in the year he was appointed to the Exeter chair. The study of Nestroy, widely hailed as a trail-blazing publica-tion, provided a necessary focus for subsequent Nestroy research. This publication, together with a number of his articles, has defined critical approaches to vitally important research areas: for example, the genesis of Nestroy's texts and his adaptation of source material; indeed, the Yates expression 'creative adaptation' has become a recognised critical term in its own right. Gar Yates's very first publication on Nestroy, an article on stylistic elements, established the high standards that have characterised his work as a whole: it is perceptive, knowledgeable, methodical, and well written. Though we associate him first and foremost with studies of drama and the theatre, he published in the 1970s a number of articles on lyric poetry, culminating in 1981 with his volume *Tradition in the German Sonnet*.

Central to Gar Yates's work since the late 1970s has been the Nestroy critical edition. The need for a scholarly edition of Nestroy had been evident for many years when Jürgen Hein and Johann Hüttner launched *Sämtliche Werke. Historisch-kritische Ausgabe* (HKA) in 1977. Gar has been closely involved with the project since its early stages and, in 1992, he and Walter Obermaier joined the team of general editors, who oversee the work of thirteen editors of individual plays. One of the most prestigious critical editions currently being produced in the German-speaking world, the HKA aims to present Nestroy's texts in the most authentic version possible, supported by an extensive critical apparatus. The edition, which will run to over forty volumes, is scheduled for completion in 2001, the 200th anniversary of Nestroy's birth. The fact that publication is running to schedule is due to a considerable degree to Gar Yates's commitment and drive, and not least to his renowned chivvying skills. Many of the editors owe him a deep debt of gratitude for the untiring help he has offered them. He brings a rare combination of skills to the job of general editor: a gift for encouraging and motivating his colleagues, painstaking attention to editorial detail, encyclopaedic knowledge of Nestroy and his period, and, not least, an unrivalled ability to decipher Nestroy's notoriously crabbed handwriting (as a calligraphist he runs Nestroy a close second). Alongside his work as general editor, Gar Yates has also edited some ten plays and is working on the documentation volume that is due to appear in 2001 and completes the edition.

The early years of his association with the Nestroy edition coincide with his editorship of the Germanic section of the *Modern Language Review*, a role in which his formidable attention to detail and range of interests in the field of German studies were put to the service not only of the journal and its parent organisation, the Modern Humanities Research Association, but also of his fellow Germanists. One of Gar Yates's most admirable characteristics is his willingness to help and encourage colleagues, particularly younger ones, not only with advice but in practical and time-consuming ways, such as by reading their work with enthusiasm and engagement, giving them new opportunities, and taking genuine pleasure in their successes.

The expansion of Gar Yates's editorial activities coincided with the growth of his administrative responsibilities at the University of Exeter. He was Head of the Department of German for fourteen years, during which time, as the policies of the early Thatcher years caused severe cuts in the higher-education sector, he became a key figure in the University's policy-making team and chaired the Academic Development Committee. He then moved on to be a distinguished Deputy Vice-Chancellor. It is characteristic of Gar Yates's energy and range that, once freed from heavy administrative responsibilities, and alongside his work on the Nestroy edition and editorship of *Nestroyana*, he completed three important monographs, two outside the field of Nestroy studies: *Schnitzler, Hofmannsthal and the Austrian Theatre* (1992), which provided, among other things, the first detailed treatment of Schnitzler archive material housed in the Library of the University of Exeter; *Nestroy and the Critics* (1994), which earned him the accolade 'doyen of Nestroy studies'; and *Theatre in Vienna: A Critical History 1776–1995* (1996). He continues to serve his colleagues in the university and the wider community in Exeter with his characteristic wisdom and commitment to humane values. He also supports German studies at home and abroad not only through his published work but also as Vice-President of the Internationale Nestroy-Gesellschaft and by his membership of the Council of the English Goethe Society and of the Committee of the Modern Humanities Research Association. Equally at home in Vienna and in Exeter, and with as large a circle of friends in both cities, he is Vice-President of the Vienna Shakespeare Society, though whether he finds many outlets for his passion for cricket in Vienna must be doubtful. In 1995 he was made a Corresponding Fellow of the Austrian Academy of Sciences, an honour rarely bestowed on non-Austrian scholars. He continues also to combine his love of music with giving pleasure to opera-goers through his connections with the Welsh National Opera and the Royal Opera House, Covent Garden, producing lively and informative programme notes and giving occasional lectures to the Friends.

The present volume has a specific focus: the Austrian comic tradition. As editors we are aware that many more colleagues and friends would have liked to contribute to a volume in Gar Yates's honour and that only a small proportion of them work in this particular field. We are also aware that Gar's own interests are by no means circumscribed by this particular area. Yet we felt that he would be more honoured by a coherent collection of studies within a defined field. There are fourteen contributions. Louise Adey Huish poses the central question 'An Austrian Comic Tradition?', one to which her fellow contributors provide a variety of answers. A central group of six contributions concerns, fittingly, Nestroy. There are seven further contributions on writers in the Austrian comic tradition: Aloys Blumauer, Johanna von Weissenthurn, Friedrich Halm, Robert Scheu and Karl Kraus, Ödön von Horváth and Hugo von Hofmannsthal.

We should like to thank the contributors for their willingness to conform to the tight publication schedule we have had to impose and for the good humour with which they have responded to our editorial intrusions. Three contributions appear in English translation and we are indebted to Almut Dworak of the University of Exeter for the translations of Walter Obermaier's and Dagmar Zumbusch-Beisteiner's articles, and to Ritchie Robertson for translating Jürgen Hein's; we are also indebted to Peter Branscombe for his generous help in translating musical terminology. We should also like to recognise the patience and understanding of those contributors who have seen their contributions subjected to unavoidable linguistic surgery in translation. The Modern Humanities Research Association gave a generous gift to cover the cost of translation. Our Exeter colleague Sara Smart kindly assumed responsibility for compiling the list of Gar's publications. Finally, Ritchie Robertson deserves a special mention from us: he has read all the contributions, made many helpful suggestions, and, equally importantly, has provided us with a real sense of support throughout.

John McKenzie, Lesley Sharpe
Exeter, July 1997

Notes on Abbreviations

The following abbreviations are used in references to editions of Nestroy's works:

CG *Gesammelte Werke*, ed. Vincenz Chiavacci and Ludwig Ganghofer, 12 vols, Stuttgart, 1890-91.

GW *Gesammelte Werke*, ed. Otto Rommel, 6 vols, Vienna, 1948–49.

HKA *Sämtliche Werke. Historisch-kritische Ausgabe*, ed. Jürgen Hein and Johann Hüttner (from 1992: Jürgen Hein, Johann Hüttner, Walter Obermaier and W. Edgar Yates), Vienna, Munich, 1977–. Individual volumes are referred to by volume number, e.g. *Stücke 26/II*.

SW *Sämtliche Werke*, ed. Fritz Brukner and Otto Rommel, 15 vols, Vienna, 1924–30.

Titles and technical terms in German have been translated by individual contributors, at the first mention in each contribution. Although this means that some translations are repeated, we believe it to be helpful to the reader.

W. E. Yates: A Bibliography

1. (Ed. and intro.) Hofmannsthal, *Der Schwierige* (Cambridge: CUP, 1966).
2. 'Convention and antithesis in Nestroy's Possen', *Modern Language Review*, 61 (1966), 225–37.
3. 'Elizabethan comedy and the Alt-Wiener Volkstheater', *Forum for Modern Language Studies*, 3 (1967), 27–35.
4. (Ed. and intro.) Grillparzer, *Der Traum ein Leben* (Cambridge: CUP, 1968).
5. 'Nestroysche Stilelemente bei Anzengruber', *Maske und Kothurn*, 14 (1968), 287–96.
6. 'Anzengruber', 'Biedermeier', 'Nestroy', 'Raimund', 'Schönherr', in A. K. Thorlby (ed.), *The Penguin Companion to Literature* (Harmondsworth: Penguin, 1969), ii. 58, 113, 564–65, 640, 707.
7. *Grillparzer: A Critical Introduction* (Cambridge: CUP, 1972).
8. *Nestroy: Satire and Parody in Viennese Popular Comedy* (Cambridge: CUP, 1972).
9. 'Grillparzer-Forschungen in England', in H. Kindermann (ed.), *Das Grillparzer-Bild des 20. Jahrhunderts* (Vienna: Böhlau, 1972), pp. 109–21.
10. *Humanity in Weimar and Vienna: The Continuity of an Ideal* (Inaugural Lecture, University of Exeter, 1973).
11. 'Das Vorurteil als Thema im Wiener Volksstück', in Jürgen Hein (ed.), *Theater und Gesellschaft: Das Volksstück im 19. und 20. Jahrhundert* (Düsseldorf: Bertelsmann, 1973), pp. 69–79.
12. '"Die Jugendeindrücke wird man nicht los": Grillparzer's relation to the Viennese popular theatre', *Germanic Review*, 48 (1973), 132–49.
13. 'Josef Schreyvogel, critic and mentor: an enquiry into aspects of Schreyvogel's influence on Grillparzer', *Publications of the English Goethe Society*, 44 (1974), 83–108.
14. 'Architectonic form in Weinheber's lyric poetry: the sonnet "Blick vom oberen Belvedere"', *MLR*, 71 (1976), 73–81.
15. 'On sonnets on sonnets', *German Life and Letters*, 30 (1976–77), 187–98.
16. 'Cultural life in early nineteenth-century Vienna', *FMLS*, 13 (1977), 108–21.
17. 'Dramaturg and dramatist: on the relation of Schreyvogel to Grillparzer's mature dramas', *GLL*, 31 (1977–78), 106–14.

18. '*Der Schwierige:* the comedy of discretion', *Modern Austrian Literature*, 10 (1977), i. 1–17.
19. 'Mörike's conception of an artistic ideal', *MLR*, 73 (1978), 96–109.
20. 'An object of Nestroy's satire: Friedrich Kaiser and the "Lebensbild"', *Renaissance and Modern Studies*, 22 (1978), 45–62.
21. 'Prospects of progress: Nestroy re-edited', *Journal of European Studies*, 9 (1979), 196–205.
22. 'Nestroys Komödie der Freundschaft: *Der Zerrissene*', *Österreich in Geschichte und Literatur*, 23 (1979), i. 43–48.
23. 'Frances Trollope in Germany and Austria', *GLL*, 34 (1980–81), 155–66.
24. *Tradition in the German Sonnet*, British and Irish Studies in Germanic Languages and Literatures, 4 (Berne: Lang, 1981).
25. 'Zur Wirklichkeitsbezogenheit der Satire in Nestroys Posse *Eine Wohnung ist zu vermiethen*', *MuK*, 27 (1981), 147–54.
26. 'Mythopoeic allusion in Celan's poem "Die Krüge"', *Neophilologus*, 65 (1981), 594–99.
27. (Ed.) Johann Nestroy, *Stücke 13* (*Sämtliche Werke, hist.-krit. Ausgabe*) (Vienna: Jugend & Volk, 1981).
28. 'Hofmannsthal and Austrian comic tradition', *Colloquia Germanica*, 15 (1982), 73–83.
    *'Hofmannsthal und die österreichische Tradition der Komödie', *Hofmannsthal-Forschungen*, 7 (1983), 181–97.
29. 'Let's translate Nestroy', *FMLS*, 18 (1982), 247–57.
30. 'Nestroy im Studienprogramm an der Universität Exeter: ein kleiner Beitrag zur Rezeptionsgeschichte Nestroys im Ausland', *Nestroyana*, 4 (1982), 25–30.
31. (Ed.) Johann Nestroy, *Stücke 12* (*Sämtliche Werke, hist.-krit. Ausgabe*) (Vienna: Jugend & Volk, 1982).
32. (Ed.) Johann Nestroy, *Stücke 14* (*Sämtliche Werke, hist.-krit. Ausgabe*) (Vienna: Jugend & Volk, 1982).
33. 'Editing Nestroy', *GLL*, 36 (1982–83), 281–93.
34. 'Kriterien der Nestroyrezeption 1837–1838', *Nestroyana*, 5 (1983–84), 3–11.
35. 'Kann man Nestroy ins Englische übersetzen?', *Nestroyana*, 6 (1984–85), 24–29.
36. (Ed. with John R. P. McKenzie) *Viennese Popular Theatre: A Symposium – Das Wiener Volkstheater. Ein Symposion* (Exeter: Exeter University Press, 1985).
37. 'Das Werden eines Nestroystücks', ib., pp. 55–66.
38. 'Nestroy, Grillparzer, and the feminist cause', ib., pp. 93–107.
39. 'The idea of the Volksstück in Nestroy's Vienna', *GLL*, 38 (1984–85), 462–73.
40. 'Nachträge zu den Bänden *Stücke 12* und *Stücke 13* der neuen Nestroy-Ausgabe', *Nestroyana*, 6 (1984–85), 94–99.
41. 'Karl Kraus and the remembrance of things past', in Sigurd Paul Scheichl and Edward Timms (eds), *Karl Kraus in neuer Sicht* (Munich: text + kritik, 1986), pp. 76–89.

42. (Ed. with Robert Pichl, Alexander Stillmark, and Fred Wagner) *Grillparzer und die europäische Tradition: Londoner Symposium 1986* (Vienna: Hora, 1987).

43. 'Grillparzer and the fair sex', ib., pp. 71–83.

44. 'Nestroy und die Rezensenten', *Nestroyana*, 7 (1987), 28–40.

45. '"Die Sache hat bereits ein fröhliches Ende erreicht!" Nestroy und das Happy-End', in Jean-Marie Valentin (ed.), *Das österreichische Volkstheater im europäischen Zusammenhang 1830–1880* (Berne: Lang, 1988), pp. 71–86.

46. 'Nestroys Weg zur klassischen Posse', *Nestroyana*, 7 (1988), 93–109.

47. 'Erinnerung und Elegie in der Wiener Literatur 1890–1930', *Literatur und Kritik*, 223/224 (Apr./May 1988), 153–69.

48. '"Nicht des Verräthers braucht's": Zu einem Zitat im *Haus der Temperamente*', *Nestroyana*, 8 (1988), 48–49.

49. (Ed.) Johann Nestroy, *Stücke 34* (*Sämtliche Werke, hist.-krit. Ausgabe*) (Vienna: Jugend & Volk, 1989).

50. 'Franz Werfel and Austrian poetry of the First World War', in Lothar Huber (ed.), *Franz Werfel: An Austrian Writer Reassessed* (Oxford: Berg, 1989), pp. 15–36.

51. 'Franz Grillparzer', in Walther Killy (ed.), *Literaturlexikon: Autoren und Werke deutscher Sprache* (Munich: Bertelsmann, 1989), iv. 346–51.

52. 'A late Goethe letter rediscovered', *GLL*, 43 (1989–90), 18–22.

53. 'Harbingers of change in theatrical performance: Hofmannsthal's poems on Mitterwurzer and Kainz', in Dorothy James and Silvia Ranawake (eds), *Patterns of Change: German Drama and the European Tradition – Essays in Honour of Ronald Peacock* (Berne: Lang, 1990), pp. 193–206.

54. 'Changing perspectives: the "doppelte Sexualmoral" in 1841 and 1895. *Das Mädl aus der Vorstadt* and *Liebelei*', in Hanne Castein and Alexander Stillmark (eds), *Erbe und Umbruch in der neueren deutschsprachigen Komödie: Londoner Symposium 1987* (Stuttgart: Heinz, 1990), pp. 17–31.

55. 'The tendentious reception of *Professor Bernhardi*: documentation in Schnitzler's collection of press-cuttings', *Austrian Studies*, 1 (1990), 108–25.

56. (With J. M. Ritchie) 'Ein Handschriftenfund in London', *Nestroyana*, 10 (1990), 23–26.

57. 'Nachträge und Berichtigungen zum Band *Stücke 34* der historisch-kritischen Nestroy-Ausgabe (*"Nur keck!"*)', *Nestroyana*, 10 (1990), 79–80.

58. 'Friedrich Kaiser' and 'Johann Nestroy', in Walther Killy (ed.), *Literaturlexikon: Autoren und Werke deutscher Sprache* (Munich: Bertelsmann, 1990), vi. 189–90 and viii. 351–55.

59. 'Aus der Werkstatt eines "schreibelustigen" Genies. Zu Nestroys Bearbeitung englischer Vorlagen', in Gerald Stieg and Jean-Marie Valentin (eds), *Johann Nestroy 1801–1862: Vision du monde et écriture dramatique* (Paris: Institut d'Allemand d'Asnières, 1991), pp. 165–76.

60. '"In einem Branntweinhaus voll Betrunkener kann es nicht anders hergehen." Grillparzer und England', in Bernhard Denscher and Walter Obermaier (eds), *Grillparzer oder Die Wirklichkeit der Wirklichkeit* (Vienna: Historisches Museum der Stadt Wien, 1991), pp. 128–34.

61. 'Grillparzer als Theaterbesucher in Paris und London', *Anzeiger der phil.-hist. Klasse der Österreichischen Akademie der Wissenschaften*, 128 (1991), 75–95.
62. '"So schreiben Sie eine traurige Posse": Ein Zitat im *Talisman* als Scherz für Eingeweihte', *Nestroyana*, 11 (1991), 84–85.
63. (Ed.) Johann Nestroy, *Stücke 18/I* (*Sämtliche Werke, hist.-krit. Ausgabe*) (Vienna: Jugend & Volk, 1991).
64. *Schnitzler, Hofmannsthal, and the Austrian Theatre* (New Haven and London: Yale University Press, 1992).
65. 'Grillparzer und die Genialität', in Sieglinde Klettenhammer (ed.), *Zwischen Weimar und Wien: Grillparzer – Ein Innsbrucker Symposion* (Innsbruck: Inst. für Germanistik, 1992), pp. 157–72.
66. '*König Ottokars Glück und Ende* und *Der Traum ein Leben*: Realitätsbezug und Rezeptionsproblematik', *Études Germaniques*, 47 (1992), 201–14.
67. 'Nestroy im "Morgenblatt"', *Nestroyana*, 12 (1992), 81–86.
68. 'Hofmannsthal and the Renaissance; or: once more unto "Ein Brief"', *PEGS*, 61 (1992), 99–118.
69. '*The Difficult Man*', in Mark Hawkins-Dady (ed.), *The International Directory of the Theatre: Plays* (London and Chicago: St James Press, 1992), i. 185–86.
70. '"Des Dichters blendend, trauriges Geschick": zur Wiederentdeckung Grillparzers als Dichter der Enttäuschung', in Bernhard Denscher (ed.), *Grillparzer heute – wiederentdeckt oder vergessen?* (Vienna: Picus, 1993), pp. 27–40.
71. 'Recent Nestroy scholarship', *Austrian Studies*, 4 (1993), 158–70.
72. 'The Biedermeier Mozart', *London German Studies*, 5 (1993), 19–33.
73. 'Nestroy in 1847: *Der Schützling* and the decline of Viennese popular theatre', *MLR* 88 (1993), 110–25.
74. 'Verfluchtes Reisen: Reisen als Flucht', *Nestroyana*, 13 (1993), 110–20.
75. *Nestroy and the Critics* (Columbia, SC: Camden House, 1994).
76. (Ed.) *Vom schaffenden zum edierten Nestroy. Beiträge zum Nestroy-Symposium im Rahmen der Wiener Vorlesungen 28.–29. Oktober 1992*, Wiener Vorlesungen: Konversatorien und Studien, 3 (Vienna: Jugend & Volk, 1994).
77. 'Das Werden eines (edierten) Nestroy-Textes', ib., pp. 11–30.
78. 'Grillparzer und die Rezensenten', in Hilde Haider-Pregler and Evelyn Deutsch-Schreiner (eds), *Stichwort Grillparzer* (Vienna: Böhlau, 1994), pp. 17–28.
79. 'Nestroy and Bauernfeld', *Nestroyana*, 14 (1994), 11–22.
80. 'Grillparzer', 'Nestroy', and 'Hofmannsthal', in Mark Hawkins-Dady (ed.), *The International Directory of the Theatre: Playwrights* (Detroit, London, Washington, DC: St James Press, 1994), ii, 428–30, 481–85, 697–700.
81. 'Hidden depths in Hofmannsthal's *Der Unbestechliche*', *MLR* 90 (1995), 388–98.
82. 'Nestroys Kollektaneen', in Wolfram Malte Fues and Wolfram Mauser (eds), *"Verbergendes Enthüllen": Zu Theorie und Kunst dichterischen Verkleidens. Festschrift für Martin Stern* (Würzburg: Königshausen & Neumann, 1995), pp. 241–50.

83. *Theatre in Vienna: A Critical History 1776–1995* (Cambridge: CUP, 1996).
84. 'Nestroy zitiert Grillparzer. Zu Nestroys Anspielungskunst', in Ilona Slawinski and Joseph P. Strelka (eds), *Viribus Unitis. Österreichs Wissenschaft und Kultur im Ausland: Impulse und Wechselwirkungen. Festschrift für Bernhard Stillfried aus Anlaß seines 70. Geburtstags* (Berne: Lang, 1996), pp. 539–46.
85. 'Paul de Kock und Nestroy. Zu Nestroys Bearbeitung französischer Vorlagen', *Nestroyana*, 16 (1996), 26–39.
86. 'Grillparzer', in Walther Killy and Rudolf Vierhaus (eds), *Deutsche Biographische Enzyklopädie* (Munich: Saur, 1996), iv, 166–67.
87. (Ed.) Johann Nestroy, *Stücke 22* (*Sämtliche Werke, hist.-krit. Ausgabe*) (Vienna: Deuticke, 1996).
88. 'Sex in the suburbs: Nestroy's comedy of forbidden fruit', *MLR*, 92 (1997), 379–91.
89. '"Was ich abschreibe, das bleibt abgeschrieben." Zur Überlieferung von Nestroys Possen', in Georg Geldner (ed.), *Der Milde Knabe oder Die Natur eines Berufenen. Ein wissenschaftlicher Ausblick, Oskar Pausch zum Eintritt in den Ruhestand gewidmet*, Mimundus, 9 (Vienna: Böhlau, 1997), pp. 68–76.

Part One

An Austrian Comic Tradition?

Louise Adey Huish

The very notion of a specifically Austrian comic tradition is regarded with scepticism by many people.[1] Those who give the idea credence point to features that are derived mainly from the baroque tradition, and deduce from these a theatre of moral improvement, which uses allegorical characters and symbolic stage sets to promote a conservative, Providentialist *Weltanschauung*. The epitome of this kind of theatre is Raimund; later, more ambivalently, Anzengruber, and more self-consciously, Hofmannsthal. I aim to demonstrate that there is a second, equally characteristic Austrian comic tradition, one that functions by taking issue with the first, subverting and deconstructing a light-hearted, optimistic tradition of theatre. It can already be seen in Nestroy's work, and is to be found in Schnitzler, Kraus, Horváth, Soyfer, and Bernhard. It arises when belief in a coherent and benevolent world breaks down, and it uses the existing forms and conventions to create a very different kind of comedy: witty, bleak, satirical, even anarchic.

It would be misguided to suppose that such a scheme could account for every Austrian comedy; I believe a plausible case can be established, nevertheless, by examining the work of a dozen key dramatists across nearly two centuries. Some texts are undoubtedly more comic than others, but there are good grounds for including them all. The extent to which they may be regarded as 'comedies' is a question I shall return to at the end.

Because the notion of a 'baroque tradition' is central to my argument, I should begin by summarising certain key aspects. The tradition is defined, most importantly, by the existence of God. This conviction provides a transcendent framework, and guarantees a happy ending, because God is in control, and God is good. The presupposition of two worlds, earthly and divine, gives rise to a persistent theme of *Schein* and *Sein* (the material world is a transient world of delusion, while true values reside in the transcendent world). Two well-known plots, the *Jedermann* [Everyman] and the *Welttheater* [*theatrum mundi*], enable us to identify further characteristic themes:[2] *Jedermann* is the *locus classicus* of repentance in the face of the four last things, and provides a model for plays of moral improvement (*Besserungsstücke*), exemplifying the eternal conflict of spiritual and material values, of God and

3

Mammon. The *Welttheater* shows us that human life is played out for God's entertainment: God distributes our roles, and we have no choice but to accept them. It is a short step from the *theatrum mundi* to political quietism and the corporate state. After death, however, we are all equal in the eyes of God: Death the Leveller is frequently to be encountered (in Hofmannsthal's *Das Salzburger Große Welttheater*, Death is employed by God to remove the actors from the stage when their roles are played out). Within this ideological framework there belongs a figure whom we might describe as the 'pure fool', characterised by the cheerfulness of humility and understanding, who sees through the vanities of this world and is able to keep sight of lasting values.

Certain aspects of staging follow from the features outlined above: baroque theatre is allegorical, characters function as the embodiment of certain qualities and are named accordingly. Sets are also symbolic: a split-level stage is used, with God and the angels seated on scaffolding, earthly happenings played out below, and Hell represented by the area underneath the stage; locations and events are also allegorical or symbolic. The *Verwandlung* (transformation scene), an elaborate dramatic device which adds much to the spectacle and appeal of this type of drama, also points symbolically to the possibility of spiritual transformation, and to the constant presence of the wondrous behind the mundane. (Frequently to be found in Viennese plays of the late eighteenth and early nineteenth centuries, it is still used by Jura Soyfer in the 1930s.) Within this context, even the common comic device of the reversibility of events may also represent symbolically the possibility of redemption.

It is clear that not all these features are to be found in every play that conforms in general terms to the notion of a Viennese comic tradition. It is nevertheless a commonplace that many plays in the eighteenth-century and early nineteenth-century 'Volkstheater' tradition communicate a message of moral improvement, use symbolic situations and characters whose names are an indication of their qualities, and include a fool figure who may roughly approximate to what I have termed the pure fool; the metaphysical framework is frequently to be found, though usually reduced to a more functional, broadly benevolent *Zauberwelt*, or magical world (not least for reasons of censorship). With due allowance, then, for the fact that we are dealing with a trend, rather than with a rigidly defined convention, let us turn now to the plays themselves.

Most striking is the fact that, even in those plays that apparently constitute a canon of theocentric, benevolent comedy, there are consistently glimpses of a much bleaker vision. It would, of course, be inappropriate to overestimate these; but cumulatively they are telling, and they demonstrate how vulnerable the *Weltanschauung* could prove to be to hostile scrutiny. The disconcerting gaps opened up are quickly and emphatically closed again; but not before their depths have been shown to be abysmal.

My first example is provided by Schikaneder's libretto for Mozart's *Die Zauberflöte* (1791). Generally accepted as embodying Mozart's reconciliation with the father figure, by contrast with the terror of *Don Giovanni*, it portrays a benevolent world ruled over by the wise Sarastro, who imposes fearsome trials on the prince's son Tamino before he can marry his beloved Pamina and come into his inheritance. Yet Sarastro's kingdom of wisdom is predicated upon conformity, and the symbolic exclusion or subordination of the female (the Queen of the Night; Pamina) and the black man (Monostatos).[3] Both of these represent unredeemed humanity, that is, the physical, sexual, and irrational aspects of human existence. Papageno, too, forms part of unredeemed humanity, because his world view does not go far beyond the satisfaction of appetite. In one sense, he is the 'pure fool', not only for his irrepressible good humour, but also because he sees all human beings as simply human, and is unmoved by status:

TAMINO. Wer bist du?
PAPAGENO. Wer ich bin?
TAMINO. Ja!
PAPAGENO. Dumme Frage! Ein Mensch wie du. Und wer bist du?
TAMINO. Ich bin ein Prinz.
PAPAGENO. Prinz?
TAMINO. Mein Vater ist Fürst.
PAPAGENO. Fürst?
TAMINO. Er herrscht über viele Länder und Menschen.
PAPAGENO. Länder und Menschen? Ja gibt's denn außer diesen Bergen auch noch andere Länder und Menschen? (I, 2)

[TAMINO. Who are you?
PAPAGENO. Who am I?
TAMINO. Yes!
PAPAGENO. Silly question! A human being like you. And who are you?
TAMINO. I am a prince.
PAPAGENO. A prince?
TAMINO. My father is a sovereign.
PAPAGENO. A sovereign?
TAMINO. He rules over many lands and peoples.
PAPAGENO. Lands and peoples? So are there still more lands and peoples beyond these mountains then?]

Papageno stands for the possibility of redemption in all of us, because he is persuaded to go through the trials, not to achieve wisdom, but – recognising that he is lonely – in the hope of finding a mate. Thus, appetite can be transformed into something higher: the trials demonstrate Sarastro's requirement that human needs (food, communication, the absence of fear and pain) should be transcended. But even with the lure of a mate, Papageno is reluctant to go through this process – 'Ich bleibe ledig!' ['I'll stay single!'] – and Sarastro uses terror and violence to coerce him, just as he does with Monostatos and the Queen of the Night. Thunderclaps keep Papageno in line every step of the way; the exemplary removal of the Three Ladies through a trapdoor (II, 5) causes him to faint with terror; and, when he tries to stand his ground, lions are sent to scare him off: 'Der Stärkere bleibt da! Ich ging jetzt nicht fort, und wenn die Löwen des Herrn Sarastro mich holten. (*Die Löwen kommen heraus.*) Tamino, rette mich!' ['The stronger man stays where he is! I wouldn't go away now even if Mr Sarastro's lions came to fetch me. (*The lions appear.*) Tamino, save me!'] (II, 19).

Astragalus, the ruling spirit in Raimund's *Der Alpenkönig und der Menschenfeind* [The King of the Alps and the Misanthrope] (1828), is a similar figure to Sarastro, manipulating powerful forces in unsettling fashion for apparently benevolent ends. He is the divine *hunter*, significantly dressed in grey, and the opening scenes of the play present us with a bleak vision of barely controllable violence, both in the natural world and in the human sphere. True, the chamois that are hunted down by the spirits for the pleasure of the hunt are left for the benefit of the poor, and Astragalus's Temple of Knowledge offers a refuge from the moral chaos of the dark powers that dominate in the human world; but Raimund does not flinch from the fact that insight is achieved only through suffering: 'Denn wenn man sprödes Erz geschmeidig sucht zu biegen / So lasse man es in des Ofens Bauch erglühen' (I, 18) ['To make brittle ore pliant and supple, it must first burn in the heart of the fire']. Already in I, 5 Malchen sees that the bird, the freedom of which she envies, is robbed of that freedom by Astragalus's bullet; Rappelkopf, too, is coerced at gunpoint (I, 21) and terrorised by the elements he had defied (I, 21). His subsequent surrender already comically foreshadows that of Zwirn and Knieriem in Nestroy's *Der böse Geist Lumpacivagabundus*: 'Ich will mich bessern, ich sehs ein, weil mir das Wasser schon ins Maul 'nein lauft' (I, 21) ['I will mend my ways, that much is clear, as the waters are already pouring into my mouth']; while his final redemption is brought about only by a threatened duel with his double and a symbolic suicide, a leap into the abyss which is transformed into the Temple of Knowledge.

Der Alpenkönig und der Menschenfeind provides a further glimpse of bleakness in the scenes in the charcoal-burner's hut (I, 15–16), which demonstrate eloquently that poverty is not blessed: with a drunken and incapable husband (ironically named Christian), Salchen is left in wretched squalor to care for five children, including a baby, as well as the grandmother. When Rappelkopf offers money in return for their home, the desperate family allows itself to be evicted. The famous song of farewell, 'So leb denn wohl du stilles Haus' ['Farewell, then, you quiet house'] (I, 17), where even the household animals join in, covers the hunger and cursing with a veneer of sentimentality, but cannot entirely disguise the brutal realities of poverty.

Raimund takes up the theme of poverty again in *Der Bauer als Millionär* [The Millionaire Farmer] (1826), as well as in the later play *Der Verschwender* [The Spendthrift] (1834). The prevailing message is one of contentment with one's lot: Lakrimosa reverses the curse of penury and old age by admonishing the peasant Wurzel 'Sei, was du stets hättest bleiben sollen' (III, 7) ['Be what you should always have remained']; Wurzel's foster-daughter Lottchen finds a home with Contentment (again dressed in grey) in the Valley of Peace. The scene where Lottchen is evicted without a penny from Wurzel's town house (I, 13) nevertheless conveys her real panic and the indifference of others: the locksmith to whom she appeals for help replies '(*recht derb*): Ja, da muß man halt gut tun, mein Schatz, wenn man von ander Leut Gnaden lebt. Was soll denn unsereiner sagen, der sich vor Kummer nicht aus weiß? da heißts fleißig sein!' ['(*brusquely*) Well now, you'll have to be a good girl, sweetheart, if you live off other folk's kindness. What are the likes of us to say, who don't know which way to turn for worry – hard work, that's the thing!'] His self-righteousness is then ironically undercut by his exit to the tavern, after borrowing money from a friend, and Lottchen is saved by the intervention of magic powers. More shocking is the way in which Wurzel is brought to repentance by the sudden arrival of old age, which causes him to reject his fortune. The encounters with the allegorical figures of Youth and Old Age are highly effective in their directness, and even the haunting melody of the duet 'Brüderlein fein' ['My fine brother'] cannot disguise the chilling reduction of Wurzel to an *Aschenmann* [ash collector]. The figure of the *Aschenmann* contains allusions to death (our return to dust and ashes) and to poverty, because ash collecting was the work of the lowest of the low; the Alpenkönig is also popularly referred to as 'der Aschenmann' in *Der Alpenkönig und der Menschenfeind* (I, 18), presumably in acknowledgement of his power over life and death. Although the comic structure of the play allows the onset of old age to be reversed once Wurzel has repented, we nevertheless glimpse death as a ruthless leveller: Wurzel's song in I, 8 describes death as the black coffee that must inevitably conclude the richest 'Lebensschmaus' ['banquet of life'].

The two sides of poverty are shown to us in *Der Verschwender*: the riches-to-rags decline of the hero Flottwell, and, in Act III, the relentless everyday poverty of his former servants Valentin and Rosa. The audience's interest focuses on Flottwell, the more glamorous figure, and his redemption by the mysterious beggar, who has saved the charity once given to him, and now returns it to Flottwell in his hour of need. The supernatural origins of this redemption are clear, because the beggar is sent by the fairy Cheristane, and describes himself as 'ein Jahr / Aus deinem viel zu rasch verzehrten Leben' ['a year of the life you consumed too hastily'] (III, 10): the year that Flottwell once gave to Cheristane as a token of love. This glosses over the fact that Flottwell was annoyed by the beggar at the time, and gave to him most ungraciously; the same is true of his apparent generosity towards Valentin, which is arguably undertaken less out of kindness than for his own self-satisfaction. When Flottwell returns home destitute, Valentin insists on taking him in, regardless of his family's difficulty in making ends meet, and, while we feel warmly towards Valentin – an endearing example of the pure fool – we sympathise with Rosa's more practical attitude, and find ourselves shocked by Flottwell's denigration of her (III, 8). It is couched in terms that suggest that rank plays at least as significant a part as moral attitude, and shows Flottwell to be proud and self-righteous: 'Nein! Ich hab es nicht gehört! Es war ein Traum! So sprach sie nicht zu Julius von Flottwell, ihrem einst'gen Herrn' ['No! I did not hear this! It was a dream! She did not speak thus to Julius von

Flottwell, her former master']. Rosa is silenced first by Flottwell's vehemence, then by the children's disapproval, and finally by Valentin's threats to leave her, taking the children with him. Her prudent misgivings about money are played down, and her vanity is played up, so that the matter can eventually be resolved with good humour, and ultimately, of course, made irrelevant by the magic windfall. The episode nevertheless raises serious questions about whether Flottwell has learnt any genuine lesson in humility, as well as whether Providence can really encompass problems of human poverty.

Rustan, the would-be hero of Grillparzer's *Der Traum ein Leben (Dream-Life)* (1832), has a similarly bitter pill to swallow: in the course of a dream, he learns that his longing for adventure has no place in the divine scheme, and acquiesces in a hated life of obscurity. The dream, the colourfulness of which is signalled by the brightly dressed boy at Rustan's bedside lighting his torch from that held by the boy in brown (the process is reversed at the end), hurls Rustan from one calamity to the next. Like Tamino, he finds himself initially in a deadly encounter with a snake; but, whereas for Tamino this is a necessary preliminary to a benevolent process, for Rustan it is the first of many adventures that nurture his capacity for deceit, and leave him frightened and powerless. The dream culminates in parricide, chaos, and conflagration, and the wicked black man Zanga lives up to his name as the pair of tongs ready to fling Rustan into the flames. In fact, he flings him into the abyss, and, just as Rappelkopf awakens from his symbolic suicide in the Temple of Knowledge, Rustan awakens in his own house and renounces all further adventures:

> Eines nur ist Glück hienieden,
> Eins, des Innern stiller Frieden,
> Und die schuldbefreite Brust.
> Und die Größe ist gefährlich,
> Und der Ruhm ein leeres Spiel.
> Was er gibt sind nichtge Schatten,
> Was er nimmt, es ist so viel. (2650–56)

> [On this earth happiness lies in one thing, one alone: quiet inner peace and a heart free of guilt! And greatness is dangerous, and fame is hollow and vain. It creates worthless shadows and deprives us of so much.][4]

Potentially an acceptance of the established order, Rustan's words sound more like a lesson in capitulation. The symbolic logic of the play aligns him from the first with the man in brown, the 'Mann vom Felsen' ['the man from the rock'], who is identified by colour with the life of the everyday world, but by character with the Dervish, who renounces earthly existence altogether.

The Dervish is strongly reminiscent of Steinklopferhanns in Anzengruber's *Die Kreuzelschreiber (Making their Mark)* (1872), who sounds a dark note in an otherwise light-hearted comedy. Like the 'Mann vom Felsen', whom he also resembles in the identification with rock, Steinklopferhanns (the name implies one who breaks rocks) is able to sort out the muddle the other characters have got into, and ease violent confrontation into a happy ending. But his own life has been far from happy, as he tells Anton in III, 1: illegitimate and orphaned, he grew up penurious and unloved, and was finally set to work in the quarry, where he lived the life of a hermit. He became ill and was at the point of death when a revelation of the healing power of the natural world transformed his resentment into recovery and contentment. His experience of a *ne plus ultra* of the human condition frees him – but at what price – to become the pure fool whose company is so prized by others; once again we see a brutal encounter with poverty and death as the source of redemption.

Despite the fact that these two states, poverty and death, form the axis on which the plots of these comedies largely revolve, Anzengruber is able to close in a genuinely comic spirit of reconciliation. The predominant themes of *Der Meineidbauer* [The Perjured Farmer] (1871) and *Der G'wissenswurm* [The Worm of Conscience] (1874) are inheritance and bad conscience at one extreme, and illegitimacy and destitution at the other. But because we see that ungenerous wills and unhappy lives are usually caused by weakness and selfishness, while relationships out of wedlock arise out of genuine feeling, Anzengruber resolves such tangles without doing violence to credibility. He also celebrates the pure fool, in the characters of Vroni and Horlacher-Lies: both are poor and illegitimate, yet radiate cheerfulness, and embody the virtue born of courage and good sense. Admittedly, there are glimpses of bleakness that anticipate the gloomy realism of Naturalism, but Anzengruber acknowledges the strength of the comic tradition in which he is working by counterbalancing realism with symbolic locations, situations and names. Vroni's grandmother in *Der Meineidbauer* is an apparently godless character, who runs an isolated pub in the mountains, consorts with Jews, and turns a blind eye to black marketeers: she has rejected God because of the misfortunes that have befallen her family, but these are ultimately resolved, and the proximity of the border and the bridge over the abyss, as well as the activities of the 'Schwärzer', clearly fulfil a symbolic function in that resolution. In *Der G'wissenswurm* the grim poverty of the Kahle Lenten [Bare Heights] is echoed in the unforgiving landscape, and immorality is seen as an inevitable consequence of penury – a hard life has made Magdalen hard and foul tempered, and she is resigned to her sons' indiscipline and sexual misdemeanours – yet this is subordinated to an almost formulaic plot in which the weak-willed Grillhofer is released from the influence of Dusterer, hypocritical and puritanical, by the timely intervention of a heart attack (i.e. Death), and makes good his youthful seduction of Magdalen by leaving his wealth to their illegitimate daughter.

In *Jedermann* (1911) and *Das Salzburger Große Welttheater* (1922) Hofmannsthal bypasses the claims of Naturalism altogether to create two pieces of entirely symbolic, morally improving theatre; *Das Salzburger Große Welttheater* provides us with a final and telling example of the way in which a theocentric world order resolves questions of poverty and inequality. The Beggar is forced to ask the Countryman (Großbauer) for work to enable him to survive, and is offered a job overseeing his woods on condition that he evict others like himself who have taken refuge there; compromised and outraged, the Beggar raises his hand to strike his social superior. The moment of confrontation, which will unleash violence and revolution, is transfigured by a blinding moment of epiphany, after which he accepts his lot and lives as a hermit in the forest. How he survives, and what happens to the other beggars, is never explained; he becomes the pure fool, the only character whose redemption at the end of the play is never in doubt. In this way the play functions as a theodicy, so that events in the material world are significant only in so far as they affect man's immortal soul.

In his essay on the Everyman theme, 'Das alte Spiel von Jedermann', Hofmannsthal defines the essence of the Everyman narrative as moral rather than religious:

> Sein eigentlicher Kern offenbarte sich immer mehr als menschlich absolut, keiner bestimmten Zeit angehörig, nicht einmal mit dem christlichen Dogma unlöslich verbunden: nur daß dem Menschen ein unbedingtes Streben nach dem Höheren, Höchsten dann entscheidend zu Hilfe kommen muß, wenn sich alle irdischen Treu- und Besitzverhältnisse als scheinhaft und löslich erweisen [...] was gäbe es Näheres auch für uns?[5]

> [Increasingly, the core of the play revealed itself as absolute in human terms, not belonging to any specific time, not even indissolubly linked to Christian dogma; simply that an unconditional desire for higher things, for the highest, must come definitively to man's aid when all earthly relationships based on fidelity and possession prove illusory and unreliable: what could touch us more closely than this?]

It is, of course, necessary to recognise that Hofmannsthal had his own reasons for recreating the morality plays of what he defines elsewhere (in the essay 'Das Salzburger Große Welttheater') as an autochthonic Austrian and South German tradition: the Salzburg Festival, where both plays were ritually performed,[6] was intended to strengthen ethnic identity at a critical time, after the political changes brought about by defeat in 1918. This does nothing to undermine Hofmannsthal's observation that materialism is the great problem of the age, and it is arguable that *Jedermann* and the *Salzburger Große Welttheater* represent essentially the two sides of the problem of money – too much and too little, respectively – which are equally bars to contentment and 'redemption'. Money has blinded Everyman to the real things of life, so that compassion and commitment take second place to pleasure and the satisfaction of appetite. The confrontation with death leads to the recognition that nothing endures beyond the grave, incidentally opening up the matter of inheritance as well as the question of lasting values. The figure of the Beggar in the *Welttheater* epitomises the problems of poverty: the obsession with survival and material goods, venality and demoralisation, moral depravity, envy and violence.

This analysis provides us with a key to the work of other dramatists working within – but also against – the tradition, for, without the illumination of faith or the blinding flash of moral conversion, Mammon and his various evils are all that is left. Order, which is sacred because God-given, gives way to the sanctity of the *status quo* and the protection of property. Either meaning has to be imposed, or else the absence of meaning must be confronted.

The question of order is central to Nestroy's *Der böse Geist Lumpacivagabundus*: order in the fairy world is disrupted by Lumpacivagabundus, the evil spirit who leads the younger generation astray, just as order in the human world is challenged by shifting values. The name encapsulates the threats to the existing order: the evil spirit is a *Lump* (a ne'er-do-well), who flouts notions of hard work and prosperity, and a *Vagabund*, who stands outside society (like Soyfer's tramps in *Astoria*). The plot revolves around a trial devised by the magic figures to see whether three disaffected apprentices can be reformed more effectively by Amor or Fortuna; two of the three prove impervious to the lure of either, and their disillusion with bourgeois society is expressed succinctly by Zwirn in III, 9: 'Da thun s' nix als, arbeiten, essen, trincken, und schlafen, is das eine Ordnung?' ['They do nothing but work, eat, drink and sleep, is that Order?'] Their reform is brought about only by brute force on the part of Stellaris, the supreme spirit, who sends Furies to seize them: in a parodic version of a happy ending, we see them duly installed together with Leim in a three-storey house, extolling the virtues of hard work and contentment.[7] A variant ending expresses ambivalence towards the idea of order in an equally ironic close: the three apprentices are summoned to the magic world to share the joy of the spirits that Lumpacivagabundus has been overcome, and Amorosa promises to show them 'die wahre Liebe in ganz anderer Gestalt' ['true love in a very different form']: Leim appears with Peppi, while the other two are each shown kneeling at the feet of 'EIN WEIB *in altbürgerlicher Haustracht, welche eine Ruthe schwingt*' ['A WOMAN *in traditional domestic garb, brandishing a switch*'] – Furies indeed![8]

Profound disillusion with the notion of order is expressed most famously in Knieriem's (originally: Kneipp's) Couplet in III, 8, where disorder in the human world is seen as a reflection of cosmic disorder:

's Is ka Ordnung mehr jetzt in die Stern,
D' Kometen müßten sonst verbothen wer'n,
Ein Komet reist ohne Unterlaß
Um am Firmament und hat kein Paß;
Und jetzt richt ein so ein Vagabund
Uns die Welt bey Butz und Stingel z'Grund.
Aber laß ma das, wie's Oben steht,
Auch unt sieht man daß 's au'm Ruin losgeht.

[There's no order left in the stars
Otherwise comets would have to be forbidden
There's a comet on the loose in the firmament
Without papers, without official permission
And a vagabond like that is going to bring the whole world
        crashing down around our ears
But never mind what things look like above our heads
Down here you can see we're all headed for destruction too.]

It is well known that in performance Nestroy emphasised the definite article in the refrain ('*Die* Welt steht auf kein Fall mehr lang' ['*That* world won't last much longer']), specifically denouncing the corruption of the prevailing order.

The mutual necessity of earthly chaos and apocalypse is taken up again later by two admirers of Nestroy's work, Karl Kraus and Jura Soyfer. In his panoramic work *Die letzten Tage der Menschheit* [*The Last Days of Mankind*] (1922), Kraus offers a montage of human stupidity and corruption during the Great War, and closes with an apocalyptic vision of destruction. While in narrative terms the world is destroyed by forces from Mars, in real terms mankind destroys itself from within, with a poisonous cocktail of folly, brutality, and rhetoric, terrible in its absurdity. The prerogative of order has been usurped by the military hierarchy, which functions mechanically, and no longer attaches any meaning to the fact of death; an obsession with material goods among both soldiers and civilians leads to profiteering and breathtaking selfishness; truth is distorted out of all recognition by language; and underlying everything is the same indiscriminate, brutal belligerence so common in Nestroy and later in Horváth. God is lined up behind Austria in III, 32: 'Da winkte Gott – der Rächer kam, / Das Racheschwert zu zücken / Und, was dem Schwert entrann, im Schlamm / Der Sümpfe zu ersticken' ['A sign from God – the avenger came with his sword of vengeance; and any who escaped the sword choked to death in mud and filth']; but when the end comes in the Epilogue, and 'Zerstört ist Gottes Ebenbild' ['God's likeness is destroyed'], the voice of God is heard to say 'Ich habe es nicht gewollt' ['I did not want this'].[9]

Mankind's reaction to the impending Doomsday is also shown in Soyfer's *Der Weltuntergang* (*The End of the World*) (1936), subtitled (after Nestroy) *Die Welt steht auf kein' Fall mehr lang*, which once again takes up the idea of the comet that will destroy the Earth. Soyfer uses the conceit of a cosmic allegorical framework to show the Sun, Mars, and Venus engaged in a stately 'Planeten-Walzer' ['Waltz of the Planets'] which is disrupted by an 'ekelhafte Dissonanz' ['disgusting dissonance']: this turns out to be the Earth, which is 'aus dem Sphärentakt gefallen' ['out of tune with the harmony of the spheres'], and has to be brought to its senses by the destruction of mankind, viewed by the other heavenly bodies as an irritating minor infestation.[10] While there is a gentle, whimsical comedy in these opening scenes that demonstrates a certain affinity to Raimund and is characteristic of Soyfer's moral optimism, the body of the play uses bitter satire and cabaret *chansons* to anatomise human greed and stupidity. The media and the stock market have so much invested in the arrival of the comet that Professor Guck, the astronomer, can find no backing for his defence project (except in Austria, where lumbering bureaucracy will ensure that it will come far too late); superpower relationships are far too delicate for spontaneous reactions and 'quick fixes'; while the ordinary population is seduced by the frisson of death into terrifying frivolity:

> Gehn ma halt a bisserl unter,
> Mit tschin–tschin in Viererreihn,
> Immer lustig, fesch und munter,
> Gar so arg kann's ja net sein.
> Erstens kann uns eh nix g'schehen,
> Zweitens ist das Untergehen
> 's einzige, was der kleine Mann
> Heutzutag sich leisten kann.
> Drum gehn ma halt a bisserl unter,
> 's is riskant, aber fein! (Siebentes Bild)

> [Let's go dying just a little
> With crash boom bang and with hurray
> Always happy, dashing, snappy,
> It can't be as bad as people say.
> First, we've always been OK
> Secondly, to fade away
> Is about the only thing
> A poor guy can afford today.
> So let's go dying just a little!
> It's risky, but it's chic!]

In the end mankind is saved by an improbable happy ending: the comet falls in love with humanity and veers off course at the last minute. Such reversals, which are to be found in nearly all Soyfer's plays, are a secularised version of redemption, based on a profound belief in the potential of humankind (as realised in Marxism). In *Der Lechner-Edi schaut ins Paradies* (*Edi Lechner Goes to Heaven*) (1936), Edi – the main character – is prevented at the last minute from vetoing the creation of mankind precisely because human ambivalence is such a creative force: Edi and Fritzi's argument about whether human life is worth preserving gives the Heavenly Porter 'the key suggestion for man's construction' ('den entscheidenden Konstruktionsvorschlag' (Zehntes Bild)). The happy endings nevertheless sit uneasily on the material of the plays themselves,[11] and, without the invocation of a dream world, there would be nowhere to locate human happiness. This is pointedly demonstrated in *Astoria* (1937), where the tramp Hupka steps over an imaginary line that divides reality from fantasy and finds himself instrumental in the creation of a new state, Astoria. Astoria is a state without land but, because it has a judiciary, a military and a bureaucracy, and an existence on the stock market, it is deemed to exist. The Utopia envisaged by the dispossessed, who flock to apply for citizenship, is perverted into a machine of coercion and exploitation, and even Hupka is unable to dismantle it: when he attempts to tell people that it does not exist he is treated as a political dissident, and in the end he chooses to return to his comrades on the road. A brutal order has triumphed in Astoria; but what remains in the audience's mind is the dream of ease and contentment in the imaginary Astoria, expressed by the lovers Paul and Rosa in the fourth scene; and the haunting songs that express the solidarity of the destitute, such as 'Mein Bruder Vagabund' ['My brother vagabond'], which opens and closes the play.

Order, then, is repeatedly unmasked as an instrument of bourgeois manipulation. Nowhere is this more savagely demonstrated than in Horváth's *Geschichten aus dem Wiener Wald* [*Tales from the Vienna Woods*] (1931), which leaves the conventions of the Viennese popular theatre in tatters. Vestigial acknowledgement of the magic world is to be found in the figure of the Zauberkönig [Wizard King], Marianne's father, who is ostensibly given this name because he runs a toyshop, but actually because he embodies the rigidity, complacency and weakness of the prevailing order. He is ineffectual: he cannot even find his garters without Marianne to help him, and, once she leaves home, the toyshop falls into disrepair. He refuses to forgive her because she has entered into a relationship with a good-for-nothing gambler, Alfred, instead of marrying the respectable butcher Oskar, and is the mother of an illegitimate child. He is unmoved even when he comes across Marianne working in a strip-club after Alfred has abandoned her, and is thus indirectly responsible for her brief spell of imprisonment. Marianne is bewildered by what befalls her, having assumed that her middle-class upbringing was a guarantee of respectability ('Lieber Gott, ich bin im achten Bezirk geboren und hab die Bürgerschul besucht, ich bin kein schlechter Mensch – hörst du mich? – Was hast du mit mir vor, lieber Gott?' (II, 7) ['Dear Lord, I was born in the eighth district and went to the City School, I'm not a bad person – do you hear? – What do you want with me, dear Lord?']). A happy ending is brought about by the most brutal means: Marianne's child is effectively murdered by Alfred's mother and grandmother; Oskar agrees to marry Marianne, fulfilling his sadistic prediction that she would not escape him; and the busybody Valerie imposes reconciliation on all parties: 'Hier wird jetzt versöhnt!' (III, 3) ['Reconciliation, please!'] The play closes to the strains of a Strauss waltz, played by a 'heavenly string orchestra', pointing up the spuriousness of Viennese conviviality.

The concept of moral improvement is predicated upon a notion of divine order, and is closely linked with the acceptance of one's lot, an acknowledgement of the *theatrum mundi*. Its emptiness is repeatedly demonstrated by playwrights writing against the prevailing tradition: even for Soyfer *Besserung* is a matter of Marxist faith rather than of hard evidence, while Nestroy, Kraus and Horváth share a conviction that human stupidity is irredeemable. The motto to *Geschichten aus dem Wiener Wald*, 'Nichts gibt so sehr das Gefühl der Unendlichkeit als wie die Dummheit' ['Nothing conveys a sense of infinity half so well as stupidity'], echoes the title of Nestroy's play *Gegen Thorheit giebt es kein Mittel* [There's No Cure for Folly] (1838), where he quotes Schiller's tag, 'Gegen Dummheit kämpfen Götter selbst vergebens' ['The gods themselves battle in vain against stupidity']. *Gegen Thorheit* is indirectly based on *Der Verschwender* and shares its episodic, riches-to-rags structure.[12] Simplicius, the play's anti-hero, defies categorisation, however: he is not redeemed by his encounter with poverty, but at sixty years of age muddles along perfectly well as dogsbody to a travelling circus; despite his indifference to money and his ambiguously symbolic name, he is not a pure fool, as he has no sense of values at all, whether economic or moral. There is no magic world in this play to underwrite reform, and the only 'magic' interventions are the twice-repeated injections of cash provided by Simplicius's brother Richard, from their father's legacy. At the end of the play Simplicius intends to marry the seventeen-year-old daughter of his former retainer, who cannot stand the sight of him; in one version he does so, despite her threats of nagging him to death; in the other, she runs off with someone else, and he announces his intention of becoming a hermit on the remote island of Formentera. Yet even this does not betoken conversion, but is simply an ironic allusion to a play by Kotzebue, *Der Eremit auf Formentera* [The Hermit of Formentera].

It is impossible to deal with Nestroy's subversion of the *Besserungsstück* in any detail here;[13] a few key examples must suffice. In each case, money and moral improvement are ambiguously intertwined, so that the acquisition of wealth becomes synonymous with the possibility of redemption; the plays conclude with an ironic twist that appears to endorse the status quo but, in effect, undermines it. *Die beiden Nachtwandler* (*The Two Sleepwalkers*) (1836) is based on the fairytale of the fisherman and his wife: the poor rope-mender, Sebastian Faden, is rewarded for saving Lord Howart's fortune by the offer of as much money as he wants, provided he asks only for what is truly necessary. He sets up as a man of means and is about to marry a rich heiress when he objects in a fit of drunken obstinacy to Lord Wathfield's pigtail; Sebastian's insistence that it should be cut off is interpreted as superfluous, and all his wealth is taken away again. A happy ending is cobbled together when he proves repentant, and he is given just enough to enable him to pursue his profession and to marry Babette, the daughter of a herb-seller. The threat of political change constituted by the objection to the *Zopf* [pigtail], the symbol of absolutism pre-1848 (*Zopfensystem*), is thus safely contained, and Faden remains in the class to which he was born. The transformatory power of money is shown to be good only as long as it upholds the political status quo; the recognition of true values and Faden's acceptance of his role in life are made improbably synonymous.

The plot of *Der Talisman* [*The Talisman*] (1840) (which also contains an aggressive allusion to the *Zopfensystem*)[14] is also based on a fairy-tale structure: with the help of a wig, the talisman· of the title, to cover his red hair, the penniless Titus Feuerfuchs tries his fortune on the country estate of Frau von Cypressenburg, and wins the attention of the gardener's widow, the lady-in-waiting and the lady of the house in turn. At the peak of his success his intrigue is discovered, and he is thrown out of the house with nothing. Then it is revealed that he is the sole heir of a wealthy man, and all three ladies set their caps at him again; when the secret of his red hair comes out, he loses his inheritance, and the only one who will have him is Salome Pockerl the goose-girl, herself red-haired and penniless too. As in the case of Sebastian Faden, once Titus accepts his lot, it is modestly improved, provided he stays literally with his own kind. The moral lesson is undermined, however, by the triviality of the prejudice against Titus, and by his remarkable resourcefulness and powers of manipulation: one might readily infer that Titus is too much of a threat to the system *not* to be kept in his place.

Thus, in the case of *Die beiden Nachtwandler* and *Der Talisman*, potentially inflammatory material is controlled by the use of a strict form (the fairy-tale); this is also the case in *Zu ebener Erde und erster Stock* [Ground Floor – First Floor] (1835), where Nestroy uses the strict symmetry of a split stage to demonstrate the adage ''s Glück bleibt halt stets kugelrund' (III, 32) ['Luck always turns full circle']. In the course of the play, the poor but honest Schlucker family from the basement changes places with the speculator Goldfuchs and his family, who occupy the *bel étage*; the action on the two levels unfolds in parallel to show the Wheel of Fortune at work. This is enough in itself to contain the Schluckers' ambitions, because the Wheel turns unceasingly; the one character to profit disproportionately from the changes in fortune is the scheming servant Johann, and only the comic logic of the play ensures that he eventually gets his come-uppance. When Nestroy uses this motif again in his last play, *Frühere Verhältnisse* [The Way Things Were Before] (1862), where the master–servant relationship of Scheitermann and Muffl is reversed to great comic effect, the lesson is not drawn in the same way and we see a greater ironic acceptance of the ways of the world.

The economic order is the only one that really matters in Nestroy's world, and an unwavering recognition of the centrality of money to human existence pervades his works. Plots turn on fortunes gained and lost; the only misalliances are between rich and poor; the crucial importance of inheritance is acknowledged ironically in that famous remark about the number of uncles and aunts who have to die every year just so that things can turn out well (*Einen Jux will er sich machen* [High Jinks] III, 23). The self-satisfaction, gullibility and imperviousness of the well-to-do provide the constant butt of Nestroy's satire; cleverness is expressed through successful embezzlement and financial sleight-of-hand; while extreme poverty is portrayed over and over again, with compassion but without sentimentality. Titus Feuerfuchs apostrophises his hunger with ironic hyperbole: 'Nein Menschheit du sollst mich nicht verlieren, Apetit ist das zarte Band welches mich mit Dir verkettet welches mich alle Tag 3–4 mahl mahnt, daß ich mich der Gesellschaft nicht entreißen darf.' (I, 7) ['No, humanity, you shall not lose me, appetite is the delicate tie that binds me to you, that reminds me – three or four times a day – that I may not tear myself away from society.']

It is not until the 1930s that we find the same relentless focus on economic relations, in the works of Soyfer and Horváth. The preoccupation with unemployment which is apparent in *Der Lechner-Edi schaut ins Paradies* and *Astoria*, the recognition that people will do anything in order to eat, is even more brutally apparent in Horváth's plays because he lacks Soyfer's residual faith in the perfectibility of man, and because the structure of his plays will not permit anything but the most bitterly ironic of happy endings. *Kasimir und Karoline* (1932) echoes the structure of *Der Talisman*, as Karoline ditches her unemployed boyfriend in favour of the clerk Schürzinger and then his boss, Kommerzienrat Rauch; Rauch's attempted seduction of Karoline ends in a heart attack and a near-fatal accident, after which he dismisses her, and she fetches up with Schürzinger again, who is jubilant at the pay-off he has received from Rauch. Kasimir falls in with petty criminals and is clearly on the way down, while Karoline is on her way up – on her back. The spurious gaiety of the Oktoberfest barely disguises the underlying mood of aggression and resentment, and the evening degenerates in to a brawl triggered by class differences.

Elisabeth, the central figure in *Glaube Liebe Hoffnung* [*Faith, Hope and Charity*] (1932), also finds that survival is possible only if she regards herself as a saleable commodity: unable to sell her body at the mortuary (in advance), she is obliged effectively to sell it to stay alive, but still cannot escape the slow descent into criminality and suicide. Horváth wrote his play as a protest against the 'kleine Paragraphen' ['small print'] that governed employment regulations, but recognises in his preface that this is just a topical aspect of the eternal struggle between the individual and society. Both the title and the subtitle of his play *'Ein kleiner Totentanz'* [A Little Dance of Death] point to more enduring concerns: the action begins and ends with death, and Elisabeth can be seen merely as a fish on the line, struggling as she is played in. The little poem recited by the Accountant at Elisabeth's dead body ironically expresses the viewpoint of the pure fool, inaccessible to anyone in this joyless play: 'Ich lebe, ich weiß nicht wie lang,/ Ich sterbe, ich weiß nicht wann,/ Ich fahre, ich weiß nicht wohin,/ Mich wundert, daß ich so fröhlich bin.' (Fünftes Bild, Szene 18) ['I live, but how long I know not / I'll die, but when I know not / I am on my way, but whither I know not / How amazing that I am so happy.']

Zur schönen Aussicht [*Hotel Bellevue*] (1926) reverses the economic dependency seen in the other plays to show us men dependent on wealthy women: Ada von Stetten, 'ein aufgebügeltes, verdorrtes weibliches Wesen mit Torschlußpanik'[15] ['female mutton dressed as lamb, terrified of being over the hill'], has the entire personnel of the hotel, as well as her feckless brother Emanuel, in her pay, and exploits her financial control to behave as outrageously as she wants. Her domination is threatened, however, when Christine, the manager's former girlfriend, turns up with a baby: at first, all the men connive together to damage her reputation, thinking that she intends to claim maintenance from him, but then they discover that she has actually inherited a large sum of money – ten thousand marks – that she was planning to plough back into the hotel. Their attitude changes instantly, and each of them lays siege to her, hoping to get their hands on her money. It is inevitable that in this knife-edge comedy the device of reversibility no longer functions, and Christine leaves, alone, unable to forgive Strasser the public humiliation to which he has subjected her.

Christine's phrase 'Es hat der liebe Gott geholfen'[16] ['The dear Lord helped me'] runs as a leitmotif through the play, calling into question the notion of money as a transformatory force.[17] Until she comes into her inheritance, Christine is effectively in the same position as Horváth's other heroines: 'Not und Jammer stand nicht nur in den Briefen, und ich wäre ins Wasser gegangen, hätte sich nichts geändert.'[18] ['It wasn't just in the letters that there was wretchedness and misery, and I would have thrown myself in the river if nothing had changed.'] Ironic allusion is made to the ways in which money suddenly materialises in comedies: the hand of God manifests itself either through inheritance, or in the lottery. To the question, 'Was verstehst du unter "lieber Gott"?' ['What do you mean by the "dear Lord"?'], Christine replies simply 'Zehntausend Mark.'[19] ['Ten thousand marks.'] Although the device is treated with conscious irony, there is deadly seriousness underlying it. Christine is afraid of the hand of God, because she recognises that money will obscure every other aspect of her relationship with Strasser; Horváth demonstrates through his complex plot that money can replace, not only love, but also sexual power (Ada), rank (Emanuel), respectability (Müller) and legality (Max/Karl/Strasser). Divine intervention is seen as profoundly ambiguous:

> CHRISTINE: Es gibt einen lieben Gott, aber auf den ist kein Verlaß. Er
> hilft nur ab und zu, die meisten dürfen verrecken. Man müßte den
> lieben Gott besser organisieren. Man könnte ihn zwingen. Und dann
> auf ihn verzichten.
> KARL: Man soll nicht an ihn glauben.
> CHRISTINE: Man muß. (*Stille*.)[20]

> [CHRISTINE: There is a dear Lord, but you can't rely on him. He only
> helps now and again, he doesn't give a damn about most people.
> They ought to organise the dear Lord better. They could force him.
> And then do without him.
> KARL: They ought not to believe in him.
> CHRISTINE: They have to. (*Silence*.)]

Horváth's later plays bear witness to an increasing – though always ambivalent – preoccupation with the role of God in human affairs. At the same time, we see a shift, no doubt politically motivated, away from the realism of the *Volksstücke* towards symbolic plots, situations and staging.[21] *Der jüngste Tag* [Judgement Day] (1937), for example, can be seen as a complex morality play in which the truth about the railway accident is indeed brought to light, as the folksong 'Die Sonne bringt es an den Tag' predicts, but not in a way that anyone expects: dream-like sequences recreate the Fall of Man and the dead in Limbo, and one of the last lines of the play is a reference to the last trump: 'Waren das jetzt nicht Posaunen?' (Siebentes Bild) ['Weren't those trumpets just now?']. *Don Juan kommt aus dem Krieg* [Don Juan Comes Back from the War] (1936) deals with the repentance of a twentieth-century Don Juan in the face of death: like Hans Karl in Hofmannsthal's *Der Schwierige* [The Difficult Man] (1921), his experiences in the trenches force him to acknowledge what is truly important. Both men renounce their frivolous lifestyle but, whereas Hans Karl invokes a stable order based on commitment, Don Juan finds peace of mind only in death, and freezes to death as a human snowman. The two plays *Hin und Her* [Back and Forth] (1934) and *Himmelwärts* [Heaven-bound] (1935), couched in a more overtly comic idiom, make an entirely symbolic use of stage space: *Hin und Her* takes place on a bridge between two border posts, the only place where the stateless refugee Havlicek is allowed to exist; while *Himmelwärts* exploits the three-level division of the medieval moralities, into Heaven, Earth and Hell.

It would seem that in this tradition anti-naturalistic forms of staging consistently reflect the attempt to see human life in an existential context: even if it is not possible to engage with God, the confrontation with Death raises crucial questions about meaning and morality. This is certainly true of Soyfer: Edi Lechner and his girlfriend go back in their time-machine as far as the Garden of Eden in an attempt to make sense of human progress. *Vineta* (1937) recreates an occasion when the old sailor, Jonny, nearly drowned, and takes place in a kind of Limbo under the sea, where human life goes on as normal, except that time and memory have been ʾeradicated: the play can be read both as a plea for life and also as a satire on the moral abdication of the people of Vienna in the face of impending war.

It is in the context of symbolic staging that we can also examine the work of Schnitzler, who appears at first sight to defy categorisation into a Viennese tradition, except insofar as he undeniably writes in the mode of the *Lokalstück* and the *Konversationsstück*. The play *Reigen* [*La Ronde*] (1900) employs the conceit of a round-dance as the basis for a scandalous sequence of sexual encounters; beyond this the allusion is surely not to a carousel of love (Max Ophüls' interpretation in his 1950 film of the work), but rather to the Dance of Death.[22] Whereas for Nestroy, Soyfer and Horváth, human existence is ruled by Mammon, Schnitzler shows us a universe dominated by the world, the flesh and the devil. Long or short, roundabout or direct, each scene in *Reigen* focuses on the discreet dashes that stand for the sexual act; the social scale is played up and down to reveal corruption at every level. Medieval paintings of the Dance of Death show Death reaping indiscriminately, followed by everyone from Pope to prostitute;[23] Schnitzler's play – in which Eros and Thanatos go hand in hand – begins and ends with the prostitute, servicing first a soldier and finally a baron.

There is no framework: the repetition with variations speaks for itself, and the characters are condemned out of their own mouths for their hypocrisy and frivolity. Emptied of transcendental meaning, the concept of the *theatrum mundi* surfaces again here, with the Shakespearean emphasis on the poor player, strutting and fretting his hour upon the stage. Schnitzler's characters are permanently acting a part, mouthing platitudes or indulging in meaningless rhetoric; but there is no divine audience, and no plot. This can be seen too in the posturings of *Anatol* (1893), where fictions and narrative variations are rehearsed in every scene; and in far more complex and suggestive fashion in the 'grotesque', *Der grüne Kakadu* [The Green Cockatoo] (1899). Set in Paris on the eve of the French Revolution, it shows a fashionable bar run by a former theatre director, who uses actors to pose as revolutionaries and provide an unwholesome frisson for his aristocratic clientele. It becomes increasingly difficult to distinguish who is playing a part: the manager exploits the opportunity to abuse his clients to their faces; the newly employed actor Grain really is a criminal and murderer; the sounds of violent revolution outside are interpreted as 'noises off'. The aristocrats have a rigid sense of social hierarchy ('Auch zur Dirne muß man geboren sein – wie zum Eroberer oder zum Dichter'[24] ['You have to be born to the condition of prostitute – as you do to that of conqueror or poet']), which accounts for the gratification they derive from the violation of taboos. The explosive mixture of sexuality, violence and political chaos is neatly captured in one small incident, when Flipotte, posing [?] as a prostitute, starts to fondle Cadignan's dagger; and the play ends as Rollin's description of the bar – 'was ich hier so eigentümlich finde, ist, daß alle scheinbaren Unterschiede sozusagen aufgehoben sind. Wirklichkeit geht in Spiel über – Spiel in Wirklichkeit'[25] ['What I find so particularly effective here is the way in which all apparent differences are, so to speak, erased. Reality merges into fantasy – fantasy into reality'] – is about to be horrifically realised.

A similar preoccupation with acting is also to be discerned in the comedies of Thomas Bernhard much later in the century: the actor is 'Theatermacher, Fallensteller' (there are two levels of meaning here: he is both 'scene shifter, trap-door operator' and 'maker of scenes, setter of traps'), the truth may be contained in one of his parts, but which one is not clear. *Der Theatermacher* (1984) explicitly undermines the concept of the *theatrum mundi* through the play that the characters are to perform, *Das Rad der Geschichte* [The Wheel of History], an absurd montage of encounters between historical figures, which is described as a 'Menschheitskomödie'[26] ['human comedy'] and a 'Schöpfungs-komödie' (p. 19) ['creation comedy'], which must end in total darkness if it is not to be transformed into a tragedy. As it happens, the play is not performed at all, because a violent storm disrupts the proceedings and sets fire to the local vicarage: the parodistic use of thunderclaps invokes the *Zauberstück* tradition, while the conflagration at the vicarage (which makes total darkness impossible) raises ambiguous questions as to the existence of a moral framework. Bruscon's view of existence-as-theatre bears witness to a similar struggle with absurdity: 'Wer existiert / hat sich mit der Existenz abgefunden / wer lebt / hat sich mit dem Leben abgefunden / so lächerlich kann die Rolle gar nicht sein / die wir spielen' (p. 44–45.) ['Anyone who exists has come to terms with existence, anyone who lives has come to terms with life, the role we play cannot be as ludicrous as that']; and again,

Der Schreiber ist verlogen
die Darsteller sind verlogen
und die Zuschauer sind auch verlogen
und alles zusammen ist eine einzige Absurdität
ganz zu schweigen davon
daß es sich um eine Perversität handelt
die schon Jahrtausende alt ist
das Theater ist eine jahrtausendealte Perversität
in die die Menschheit vernarrt ist. (p. 38)

[The writer is a liar
The actors are liars
and the audience are liars too
and the whole thing is one single absurdity
to say nothing of the fact
that we are talking of a perversion
that is already thousands of years old
the theatre is a perversion which has lasted thousands of years
that humanity is crazy about.]

The hypochondriac Bruscon's blusterings in the face of mortality are echoed more subtly in *Einfach kompliziert* [Simply Complicated] (1986). The play focuses on an eighty-two-year-old actor called simply 'Er' ['He'] who lives alone in a decrepit flat (in the Hanssachsstraße!) without telephone or correspondence, waging a lonely war against mice, his only human contact a little girl who brings him milk. He identifies powerfully with Richard III, a role he claims to have played in his mother's womb, and which brought him great fame: for much of the time he wears the crown from the Duisburg production of the play. This initially appears appropriate because he has outlived his entire family; but the Machiavellian aspect of the role emerges at the end, when we find that everything we have witnessed has been play-acting, for his penultimate gesture is to turn on the tape-recorder which has been recording throughout, and will recapitulate the whole text *ad infinitum*.

In an earlier play, *Der Schein trügt* [Appearances are Deceptive] (1982), Bernhard focuses on the relationship between the performer Karl and his brother, Robert, an actor. Both have loved the same woman, Mathilde, who is now dead; the play inexorably teases out the truth about this three-sided relationship from the flat, repetitive, self-deceiving text, which takes the form of either monologue or monologue *à deux*. The confrontation with death, and also with legacy (Mathilde leaves her weekend cottage to Robert, and not to her partner Karl) forces Karl to reassess the nature of his feelings for Mathilde, the success or otherwise of his own life, and his rivalrous relationship with his brother. He complacently rates his own ability to perform juggling tricks far above Robert's career as a mediocre actor; but is shown – like Bernhard's other 'Theatermacher' – to lead a hollow, and desperately lonely, existence.

Bourgeois blindness and the shock of death; life as theatre. We appear to have come full circle, although the gulf between Raimund and Bernhard is a measure of how far an Austrian comic tradition has been modified and subverted in the process. In the hands of writers such as Nestroy, Schnitzler, Kraus, Soyfer, Horváth, and Bernhard, comedy may no longer reliably be defined by the existence of a 'happy ending', but derives only from the comic devices used within the plays themselves. These turn on comic discrepancy and irony, the unmasking of hypocrisy and stupidity, and the exposure of the mechanisms of comedy itself: chance, coincidence, plot reversal and the *deus ex machina*. Optimistic belief in resolution and redemption has splintered under the weight of reality: it is, of course, the essence of comedy to function on two levels, but it is, at the same time, desirable that those two levels should ultimately be reconciled. Comedy requires the eye of faith to give substance to the *trompe-l'œil*; otherwise one admires the graceful trickery, but declines to be deceived. Comedy then no longer reinforces any sense of benevolent order, but underlines the absence of order, all the more painful because once glimpsed. In the words of Samuel Beckett, 'The only true Paradise is the Paradise that has been lost.'[27]

Notes

1. The authoritative account is given by Otto Rommel, *Die Alt-Wiener Volkskomödie: Ihre Geschichte vom barocken Welt-Theater bis zum Tode Nestroys* (Vienna, 1952). The assertion of an autochthonic tradition inevitably gives rise to suspicions of ideological bias, however, and recent research has preferred to emphasise the links between Viennese theatre and commercial theatre in the rest of Europe: see W. E. Yates, *Theatre in Vienna: A Critical History 1776–1995* (Cambridge, 1996). The playwrights whom I consider in this essay are nevertheless regularly examined in the light of an 'Austrian' tradition, and I acknowledge a debt to the following studies: Dorothy Prohaska, *Raimund and Vienna: A Critical Study of Raimund's Plays in their Viennese Setting* (Cambridge, 1970); Bruno Hannemann, *Johann Nestroy. Nihilistisches Welttheater und verflixter Kerl. Zum Ende der Wiener Komödie*, Abhandlungen zur Kunst-, Musik- und Literaturwissenschaft, Bd. 215 (Bonn, 1977); W. E. Yates, *Grillparzer: A Critical Introduction* (Cambridge, 1972); W. E. Yates, '"Die Jugendeindrücke wird man nicht los...": Grillparzer's relation to the Viennese popular theatre', *Germanic Review*, 48 (1973), 132–49; Edward McInnes, 'Ludwig Anzengruber and the popular dramatic tradition', *Maske und Kothurn*, 21 (1975), 135–52; Patricia Howe, 'End of a Line: Anzengruber and the Viennese Stage' in *Viennese Popular Theatre: A Symposium*, ed. W. E. Yates and John R. P. McKenzie (Exeter, 1985), pp. 139–52; W. E. Yates, *Schnitzler, Hofmannsthal and the Austrian Theatre* (New Haven and London, 1992); W. E. Yates, 'Hofmannsthal and Austrian Comic Tradition', *Colloquia Germanica*, 15 (1982), 73–83; Edward Timms, *Karl Kraus, Apocalyptic Satirist: Culture and Catastrophe in Habsburg Vienna* (New Haven and London, 1986); Christopher B. Balme, *The Reformation of Comedy: Genre Critique in the the Comedies of Ödön von Horváth*, Otago German Studies 3 (Dunedin, 1985); Horst Jarka (ed.), *Jura Soyfer, Das Gesamtwerk* (3 vols, Vienna, Munich and Zurich, 1984), vol. 3: *Szenen und Stücke*; Thomas Schmitz, *Das Volksstück*, Sammlung Metzler Bd. 257 (Stuttgart, 1990); Sigurd Paul Scheichl, 'Nestroy den Österreichern! Oder: Darf Jürgen Hein Nestroyedieren?' *Nestroyana*, 17 (1977), 13–23.

2. 'Schließlich ist es ja gewiß kein Zufall, daß die Erneuerung des „Jedermann" und des „Großen Welttheaters" von Wien aus für die Welt gelang' (Rommel, p. 852).
3. For an outspoken critique of *Die Zauberflöte*, see John Milfull, 'The Sexual Politics of Mozart's *Magic Flute* and the Genesis of Viennese "Charm"', in Ritchie Robertson and Edward Timms (eds), *Theatre and Performance in Austria: From Mozart to Jelinek*, Austrian Studies 4 (Edinburgh, 1993), pp. 20–26.
4. Translation: Yates, *Grillparzer*, p.129.
5. Hugo von Hofmannsthal, 'Das alte Spiel von Jedermann', in *Gesammelte Werke*, (ed.) Bernd Schoeller with Rudolf Hirsch, 10 vols (Frankfurt, 1979–80), vol. III, 89–102 (p. 90).
6. Michael P. Steinberg, *The Meaning of the Salzburg Festival: Austria as Theater and Ideology, 1890–1938* (Ithaca and London, 1990), pp. 233–35.
7. Cf. W. E. Yates, 'Die Sache hat bereits ein fröhliches Ende erreicht! Nestroy und das Happy-End', in Jean-Marie Valentin (ed.), *Das österreichische Volkstheater im europäischen Zusammenhang 1830–1880* (Berne, 1988), pp. 71–86; Jürgen Hein, 'Biedermeiers Glück und Ende. Johann Nestroys *Der böse Geist Lumpazivagabundus*', in Winfried Freund (ed.), *Deutsche Komödien. Vom Barock zur Gegenwart* (Munich, 1988), pp. 97–109; Ken Mills, 'Alcoholism and the Apocalypse? Reflections on a norm in nineteenth-century literature', in Brian Keith-Smith (ed.) *Bristol Austrian Studies* (Bristol, 1990), pp. 117–37.
8. Johann Nestroy, HKA, *Stücke 5*, ed. Friedrich Walla, p. 132.
9. Cf. Timms p. 380: 'It is in short a play not for a static *theatrum mundi* but for a dynamic revolving stage'.
10. All translations follow Horst Jarka (ed.), *'It's Up to Us!' Collected Works of Jura Soyfer* (Riverside, 1996).
11. See Jarka, *Szenen und Stücke*, p. 11; Calvin N. Jones, 'The Dialectics of Despair and Hope: the Modernist *Volksstück* of Jura Soyfer', *Maske und Kothurn*, 32 (1986), 33–40 (p. 39).
12. Louise Adey Huish, 'A Source for Nestroy's *Gegen Thorheit giebt es kein Mittel*', *Modern Language Review*, 87 (1992), 616–25.
13. See Hannemann, pp. 29–33; Walter Dietze, 'Tradition und Ursprünglichkeit in den "Besserungsstücken" des Wiener Volkstheaters', *Weimarer Beiträge*, 12 (1966), 566–72.
14. See Nestroy, HKA, *Stücke 17/1*, ed. Jürgen Hein and Peter Haida, p. 358 (note 80/40).
15. Ödön von Horváth, *Gesammelte Werke*, 4 vols, ed. Traugott Krischke and Dieter Hildebrandt, 2nd edn (Frankfurt, 1972), vol. I, p. 15.
16. Ibid., p. 27 and thereafter.
17. For a detailed treatment of the phrase 'der liebe Gott', see Ian Huish, *Horváth: A Study* (London, 1980), pp. 18–22.
18. Horváth, *Gesammelte Werke*, vol. I, p. 54.
19. Ibid., p. 55.
20. Ibid., p. 73.
21. Horst Jarka, 'Everyday Life and Politics in the the Literature of the Thirties: Horváth, Kramer and Soyfer', in Kenneth Segar and John Warren (eds), *Austria in the Thirties: Culture and Politics* (Riverside, CA, 1991), pp. 151–77 (p. 154).
22. Yates, *Schnitzler, Hofmannsthal and the Austrian Theatre*, p.134.
23. I am indebted to my colleague Dr Almut Suerbaum (Oxford) for this information.
24. Arthur Schnitzler, *Die dramatischen Werke*, vol. I (Frankfurt, 1962), p. 536.
25. Ibid., p. 541.
26. Thomas Bernhard, *Der Theatermacher* (Frankfurt, 1984), p. 14.
27. Samuel Beckett, 'Proust', in *Proust; and three Dialogues with Georges Duthuit* (London, 1965), p. 26.

Heroes in their Underclothes:
Aloys Blumauer's Travesty of
Virgil's *Aeneid*
Ritchie Robertson

Aloys Blumauer (1755–98) was well known in his day as a poet and journalist of the Austrian Enlightenment and, above all, as the author of *Virgils Aeneis travestirt*. The earliest part, a parody of Book I of the *Aeneid*, appeared in Vienna in 1782. Having thus whetted the public's appetite, Blumauer published his travesty of Books I to IV in 1784, and further instalments in 1785 and 1788.[1] After his death it was completed by one Schaber, an opportunistic ne'er-do-well who wrote revolutionary poems and anti-Jacobin satires, but his continuation lacks the anticlerical animus and the vigorous wit that made Blumauer's travesty popular.

Blumauer's *Aeneis* helped to establish travesty and parody as central to the Austrian comic tradition. The two terms are often used interchangeably and, though attempts have been made, especially by August Wilhelm Schlegel, to distinguish the comic imitation of style from that of subject matter, in practice the two concepts constantly overlap.[2] Blumauer's poem was dramatised by K. L. Gieseke as *Der travestirte Aeneas. Eine Farce mit Arien und Machinerie in 3 Akten*, and performed on 13 August 1799 at the Wiedener Theater.[3] As W. E. Yates has described, Blumauer's example helped to unleash a flood of travesties. Gluck's famous opera was mocked in Josef Richter's *Die travestirte Alceste* (1800), Shakespeare in Ferdinand Kringsteiner's *Othello, der Mohr in Wien* (1806), Schiller in J. A. Gleich's *Fiesko der Salamikrämer* (1813), and Grillparzer in Karl Meisl's *Die Frau Ahndel* (1817), while Nestroy continued this tradition by travestying not only Hebbel's *Judith* (as *Judith und Holofernes*, 1849) but also Wagner's *Tannhäuser* and *Lohengrin*.[4]

Travesty and parody may mock their original for its literary faults, pomposity, or false ideals. Or they may simply offer some light relief from the occasionally burdensome deference owed to a classic. The latter is the main aim of the best-known travesty of the *Aeneid* before Blumauer, *Vergile travesti* (1648–51) by Paul Scarron (1610–60), but this poem is leisurely and expansive where Blumauer's is brisk, and teasingly humorous where Blumauer engages in satirical aggression.[5] Blumauer himself was inspired by Wieland, who travestied classical models, such as Lucian and Ovid, in his *Komische Erzählungen* (1765). As Charlotte Craig points out, however, Wieland's satirical

24

verse narratives, culminating in *Oberon* (1780), move towards the special blend of "sweet travesty", a rendering which aesthetically enhances his model rather than seeking to depreciate its niveau by pejorative means'.[6] At least as important for Blumauer was Voltaire's *La Pucelle* (1755–62), a mock epic modelled, like Wieland's narrative poems, on Ariosto, and in which the ostensible subject, Joan of Arc's mission, is used as the occasion for anticlerical satire and interlaced with a series of erotic adventures. Blumauer shares with Voltaire an aggressive mockery of those aspects of Catholicism that the Enlightenment considered worthless or superstitious: monastic orders, saints, relics and miracles.

Near-contemporary comment on Blumauer's *Aeneis* dwells on whether travesty is justified. Wieland wrote Blumauer a flattering letter, praising his talents enthusiastically, and commending him for using travesty to promote the reforming aims of Joseph II.[7] The young Grillparzer went even further, paying tribute to Blumauer's *Aeneis* in his poem 'Mein Traum' (*c*.1806), and, in an essay on the nature of parody (1808), maintaining: 'dieses Mannes Werk ist vielleicht das Beste was je in dem Gebiete der Parodie emporgeblüht ist' ['this man's work may well be the best thing that has ever flowered in the realm of parody'].[8] Kant cites Blumauer, along with Fielding's *Jonathan Wild*, to show the salutary effects of parody in exposing contradictions in a text and thus restoring the purity of our feelings.[9] Hegel, who shares the usual German tendency to disparage Virgil and to exalt Homer's 'primary epic' far above the 'secondary epic' of Virgil or Milton, argues that Blumauer's travesty is justified in exposing the artificiality of the gods in the *Aeneid*.[10] Schiller, however, in *Über naive und sentimentalische Dichtung* (1795), condemns 'die herzlose Satire und die geistlose Laune' ['heartless satire and mindless humour'] represented by the 'schmutzigen Witz des Herrn Blumauer' ['Blumauer's filthy wit'].[11] Similarly, in his poem 'Das Mädchen von Orleans', with Voltaire's *Pucelle* in mind, Schiller condemned wit in general for its hostility to beauty and its desire 'das Erhabne in den Staub zu ziehn' ['to drag sublimity down to the dust'].[12] Here Schiller typifies the high-minded severity that pervades classical German literature and, as Richard Sheppard has shown, tends to exclude from it such themes as carnival and folly along with the genres of satire and parody.[13] Earlier, in his *Allgemeine Theorie der schönen Künste* [General Theory of the Fine Arts, 1771–74], Johann Georg Sulzer had recounted seeing a tragedy about Orestes and Pylades parodied in a French theatre, and added: 'Man muß es weit im Leichtsinn gebracht haben, um an solchen Parodien Gefallen zu finden; und ich kenne nicht leicht einen größeren Frevel als den, der würklich ernsthafte, sogar erhabene Dinge, lächerlich macht' ['One must be far gone in frivolity to enjoy such parodies; and I know scarcely any greater offence than that which turns truly serious, even sublime things to ridicule'].[14]

Before we examine Blumauer's *Aeneis* to see whether it deserves such criticisms, we must recall Blumauer himself from the near-oblivion into which he has fallen. He was born in Steyr, in Upper Austria, attended the Jesuit grammar school there, and joined the Society of Jesus in Vienna in 1772.

25

The order was suspended the following year. For the rest of the decade Blumauer's life is obscure. He was encouraged by the Enlightened statesman Joseph von Sonnenfels to write a play, *Erwine von Steinheim*, which was performed successfully at the Burgtheater in 1780, and in 1782 he was admitted to the Masonic lodge 'Zur wahren Eintracht' [True Harmony] which, under the presidency of Ignaz von Born, included many leading figures of the Austrian Enlightenment, such as Alxinger, Ratschky, Sonnenfels, Retzer, Leon and Sonnenfels himself.[15] In 1782 he was appointed official censor of books, operating the censorship legislation that had been relaxed by Joseph II the year before. He was active in journalism, co-editing with Ratschky the *Wienerischer Musenalmanach* from 1781 to 1792, and single-handed in 1793–94; from 1782 to 1784 he also edited the *Wiener Realzeitung*, a major organ of liberalism where, in 1782, he published his essay 'Beobachtungen über Österreichs Aufklärung und Literatur' ['Observations on Austria's Enlightenment and Literature'];[16] and from 1784 to 1787 he edited the *Journal für Freymaurer* issued by the lodge 'Zur wahren Eintracht', to which he was secretary. He and his associates left the lodge in 1786 after a decree by Joseph II restricted Masonic activity. His poems and his travesty made him a prominent writer. He is described as solitary and morose; in one of his verse epistles to Johann Pezzl he calls himself a 'Grämler' and 'Grübler' ['a melancholy brooder', B II 165, 169].[17] In 1787 he became a bookseller, and published a catalogue of his rare books which has bibliographical value, but his business did not prosper, and he left large debts when he died of tuberculosis on 16 March 1798. A month later, on 24 April, his *Aeneis* was banned by a court decree as 'contrary to good morals and religion'.[18] Blumauer's life was summed up in an alphabetical obituary:

> Aloys Blumauer
> Censor, Dichter
> Epikuräer, Freigeist, Genie, Hagestolz, Jesuit
> Kenner Latiums
> Maurer
> Naso Österreichs
> Pfaffenfeind
> Quälte Rom
> Spöttelte
> Travestirte
> Unsterblich Virgils Werk
> Xenophthalmisch, Ybischartig
> Zollte der Natur den Tribut.[19]

[Aloys Blumauer: censor, poet; Epicurean, free-thinker, genius, confirmed bachelor, Jesuit; expert on Latium; Mason; Austria's Ovid; priest hater; tormented Rome; mocked, travestied immortally Virgil's work; xenophthalmic, poplar-like; paid his dues to Nature.]

Blumauer was devoted to the reform programme executed by the Emperor Joseph II, whom he celebrates in the poem 'Joseph der Zweite' (B II 36–9). Although he sought to destroy the political power of the Catholic Church as an obstacle to his mercantilist programme of maximising the productive power of his citizenry, the reforms that Joseph undertook, first as joint ruler with his mother Maria Theresia and then, from 1780 to 1790, as sole ruler, were not anti-Catholic. Instead, they expressed the aspirations of the Catholic reform movement which had developed in the Habsburg territories by the mid-eighteenth century.[20] Reform Catholicism was opposed to the 'baroque piety' instituted by the Counter-Reformation, with its ostentatious Mariolatry, saints' cults and ceremonial observances.[21] The reformers sought to raise educational standards and to promote practical Christian charity. They wanted the Catholic faith to be taught on the basis of rational conviction and a historical understanding of the Scriptures, while advocating tolerance towards non-Catholics. In 1781, Joseph issued the Edict of Toleration, allowing his Protestant and Orthodox subjects to conduct private worship. In 1782, he began to suppress the contemplative monastic orders and, in the next five years, he seized 738 of the 2047 abbeys in his domains, compelling some 27,000 monks and nuns either to retire or to take up productive work.[22] He also asserted his control over the Church hierarchy, requiring all bishops to give an oath of allegiance to the crown, and improving the education and pay of parish priests. Joseph alienated some supporters through the desire for absolute control that led him, in 1785, to limit severely the activities of Freemasons and, in 1789, to strengthen the powers of the secret police to counteract supposed subversion. His devotion to his subjects' welfare was almost superhuman, and many of his reforms were necessary, salutary, and popular; but he adopted the utilitarianism of Enlightened reformers with a doctrinaire zeal that prevented him from appreciating other viewpoints. Thus, while the notorious self-indulgence at some monasteries did indeed need curbing, Joseph showed his narrowness by dismissing the contemplative orders wholesale as 'completely and utterly useless'.[23]

In keeping with his Josephinism, Blumauer makes his Aeneas the founder, not only of Imperial Rome but, still more, of the Vatican, its degenerate heir. Hence, while Virgil's Aeneas is 'pius', that is, devoted to his father (whom he rescues from burning Troy) and to the will of the gods, Blumauer deliberately mistranslates 'pius' as 'fromm' (e.g. B I 8).[24] Aeneas' piety is naïve and linked with superstition. 'Der fromme Ritter glaubte noch / An Hexen und dergleichen' ['The pious knight still believed in witches and the like'], we are told (B I 17), so he is obedient when he encounters his mother Venus in the guise, not of a huntress, but of a gypsy woman who asks him to cross her palm with silver. Passing Circe's island, where men are transformed into beasts, Aeneas feels in danger of being turned into a sheep (B I 175). Similarly, in his verse-epistle to Pezzl from Gastein, Blumauer contemptuously describes the country folk as pious sheep who allow their spiritual pastors to fleece them:

27

Das Volk ist gut und fromm, so wie es Schafen ziemt,
Die unter einem Hirtenstabe weiden,
Der geistlich ist, und küßt darum mit Freuden
Die Hand, die ihm die Wolle nimmt. (B III 69)

[The people are good and pious, as is proper for sheep grazing beneath
a clerical shepherd's crook, and hence they joyfully kiss the hand that
takes away their wool.]

Familiar forms of intolerance and fanaticism are also attacked. Mount Etna
makes two appearances, once spewing out such clerical paraphernalia as
amulets, rosaries, cowls, chains and instruments of torture, and later as the
den where the Cyclops forge such weapons of fanaticism as interdicts,
censures and absolutions that interfere with secular law (B I 212). Delos,
Virgil's sacred island, is now 'ein Nest voll Pfaffen' ['a nest of priests'], the
priest-king of which sends the Trojans on their journey after they have kissed
his foot and received some of his corns as holy relics (B I 53–4). The Harpies,
who spoil the Trojans' dinner, resemble monks: they are brown, with shaven
heads and a rope round their bellies, and sing 'Miserere' in chorus (B I 57).

Blumauer includes much satire on Baroque piety. His characters continually invoke saints. St Florian, an Austrian saint who suffered martyrdom by
drowning in the River Enns in 304, and who is supposed to offer protection
against fire, is particularly popular. When the Trojan ships are burnt – not, as
in Virgil, by Trojan mothers unwilling to travel further, but by old maids
desperate for husbands and afraid that Aeneas will compel them to be nuns at
Rome – St Florian promptly appears in person and douses the flames with a
bucket of water (B I 120). In return Aeneas builds the saint a monastery; this
alludes to the abbey of St Florian, built over the saint's tomb outside Linz,
which Blumauer knew well. Having received a cynical lesson in priestcraft
from Helenus, Aeneas promises to sacrifice at Mariazéll (B I 60), the Styrian
shrine where the Virgin Mary has been revered since the twelfth century as
Magna Mater Austriae; Joseph II expressly forbade pilgrimages to it in 1783.
Later in the poem, Mariazell is compared to the magnificent temple occupied
by the Sibyl (B I 128), which contains images of saints performing what
Blumauer considers absurd actions: St Aloysius Gonzaga, a Jesuit famous for
his chastity, flees from a woman's mere silhouette; St Macarius, one of the
Desert Fathers, sleeps in a nest of horse-flies; and the Franciscan St Anthony
of Padua preaches to the fishes (a familiar image, modelled on St Francis
preaching to the birds). 'Popular' devotion, stigmatised by the Enlighteners as
intellectually contemptible, is pilloried also in the person of 'Pater Kochem'
(Martin von Kochem, 1630–1712), a much-read writer on such subjects as the
life of Christ, forms of prayer and asceticism, and the reception of the
sacraments; he makes several appearances, most spectacularly (with a pun on
'Koch', cook) as head chef in hell's kitchen (B I 122, 132, 150).

Superstition is seen at its most disastrous when it misleads the Trojans into
surrendering their city. The hermit from Argos, who corresponds to Virgil's
treacherous Greek Sinon, tells them that the horse was built in fulfilment of a

vow to the mounted knight St George; he attests its genuineness by declaring that anyone who refuses to believe in its sanctity will be excommunicated. Finally convinced by two bats, the appearance of which they consider miraculous, the Trojans adopt the horse as their 'Schutzpatron' ['patron saint'] and take it into their city in a solemn procession. A mass is sung in the horse's honour, and, because Blumauer's satire is ecumenical, the sermon is delivered by 'Herr Pastor Götz' (Hauptpastor Goeze of Hamburg, who had recently conducted a controversy with Lessing about the biblical criticism of H. A. Reimarus). Three hours later all the Trojans are dead drunk, an allusion to the disorder that was supposed to accompany religious processions.

With his Jesuit education in mind, Blumauer harshly satirises the Jesuits' alleged abuse of casuistry. Instead of her sister, as in Virgil, Dido consults her spiritual adviser, a Jesuit who immorally advises her to remarry because he hopes to profit from Aeneas' piety. He argues that of two evils she should choose the lesser, whereupon she gives thanks to 'dem heiligen / Patron Probabilismus' ['the holy patron probabilism', B I 74]. Probabilism is a principle in moral theology advanced by the Jesuits in the sixteenth and seventeenth centuries. It provides guidance when authorities differ about whether a proposed action is licit or illicit. Provided at least one substantial authority supports the action, one can do it, even if the authorities on the other side are more numerous. Pascal delivered a famous attack on probabilism in the sixth of his *Lettres provinciales* (1656–57) on the grounds that it licensed moral laxity by enabling one to choose whichever option one preferred. When Aeneas descends to the underworld, he finds that the dead are judged by three Jesuits, Escobar, Busenbaum and Sanchez. Antonio de Escobar (1589–1669) and Tomás Sanchez (1550–1610), as moral theologians, were leading exponents of probabilism and appear among Pascal's targets. Blumauer illustrates their supposed laxity by showing how they issue absolutions according to a tariff, and give an incestuous murderess a light penalty because she made a pious death ('weil sie fromm gestorben war', B I 145).

Blumauer's major target, however, is the Papacy's claim to temporal power. Aeneas is 'Urpapa' [B I 14; 'grand-daddy'] of the Curia, i.e. the Papal Court, and the datary, the branch of the Apostolic Chancery at Rome organised in the thirteenth century for the purpose of dating Papal bulls and other documents. His spiritual descendants will be the Popes whose misdeeds are described, first when Aeneas encounters some of them in hell, then in a prophecy by his father Anchises, and finally in a vision inspired by the sign of the inn 'zu'n röm'schen Päpsten' (B I 220).[25] In hell Aeneas meets, along with Pachomius, the originator of monasticism, and Berthold Schwarz, the Franciscan monk said to have invented gunpowder, the great pope Gregory VII (reigned 1073–85; here called 'Herr Höllenbrand', B I 155, after his baptismal name Hildebrand), who enforced the rule of clerical celibacy and thus, as Blumauer says, forbade love to the preachers of love ('Und selbst der Liebe Predigern / Das Lieben untersagte'). Anchises foretells the reign of Boniface VIII (reigned 1294–1303), whose bull 'Unam sanctam' of 1302 asserted papal supremacy over all temporal princes and declared that it was necessary for salvation that every creature should be subject to the Pope (B I 166). The line of future popes closes, however, with the broad-minded Benedict XIV (ruled 1740–58) and the reformer Clement XIV (ruled 1769–74), who is given full credit for reducing the number of feast days and, especially, for suspending the Jesuit order (B I 168). Later, the inn sign reveals to Aeneas such papal exploits as the conflict with Sicily, which was initiated in 1282, during the short reign of Martin IV (1281–85), by the 'Sicilian Vespers' in which the Sicilians massacred their foreign rulers, and which included the excommunication of the entire Sicilian people in 1286 by Honorius IV. It also shows him how an 'ungezogner Schlossersohn' [B I 218: 'a locksmith's unmannerly son'], Gregory VII, imposes papal authority on the German Emperor Heinrich IV at Canossa in 1077, and how a cobbler's son, John XXII (ruled 1316–34), seeks the German Imperial throne – a hostile interpretation of John's action, when the rival candidates for the Imperial throne could not resolve their dispute, in declaring the throne vacant and returning the administration of the Empire to the Holy See. For Blumauer, however, the high point of papal aggrandisement is the division of the unexplored globe by Alexander VI (ruled 1492–1503) who, in 1493, drew a line on the map 370 leagues west of the Cape Verde Islands, assigning the western zone to Spain and the eastern to Portugal. Much is made also of the False Decretals (B I 220), a collection of documents wrongly attributed to St Isidore of Seville, and intended to justify papal supremacy, which were accepted as genuine until 1558. Blumauer also alludes several times to the Donation of Constantine, a document forged in the eighth or ninth century to support the claims of the Papacy to primacy over other sees and temporal dominion over Italy; this again was accepted as genuine until it was success-fully challenged by early Renaissance humanists. Aeneas appeals to the Donation when taking possession of Latium:

> Nun landet an dem nahen Strand
> > Die ganze Karavane;
> Aeneas stieg sogleich ans Land
> > Mit einer weißen Fahne:
> "Kraft Constantins Donation,"
> Rief er, "nehm' ich für meinen Sohn
> > Besitz von diesem Lande." (B I 176)

[Now the entire caravan lands on the nearby beach; Aeneas promptly stepped ashore with a white flag: 'By virtue of Constantine's donation,' he cried, 'I take possession of this land for my son.']

The other side of the inn sign, however, shows a pope submissively visiting a German monarch: this is Pope Pius VI (ruled 1775–99) who, alarmed by the Josephine reforms, visited Vienna in 1782 and was received by Joseph II, celebrated here as the 'römisch-deutschen Kaiser'. Blumauer objects to all ecclesiastical claims to intervene in temporal affairs. Hence he shows his infernal Jesuits giving absolution to the Dominican monk Jacques Clément, who assassinated Henri III of France in 1589.[26] One of these judges, Hermann Busenbaum (1600–68), was indeed the author of a much-used manual of casuistry, *Medulla theologiae moralis* (1645), which was condemned by the Parliament of Paris in 1757 for containing the proposition that it is permissible to kill a prince in defence of one's own life. Hence Evander warns Aeneas that his subjects believe in tyrannicide:

> "Sie sagten: einen Volkstyrann
>   Den dürfe man verjagen,
> Und so was läßt der Pöbel dann
>   Sich nicht gern zweimal sagen,
> Seit Busenbaum und Compagnie
>   Die fromme Monarchomachie
>   Die Unterthanen lehrte." (B I 214)

['They said that it is permissible to drive away a tyrant, and the mob has not needed to be told such a thing twice, ever since Busenbaum and company taught subjects to wage pious warfare against monarchs.']

As a counterpart to his polemic against ecclesiastical claims to power, Blumauer shows how Aeneas finds opponents of clerical tyranny – Luther, Huss, Rousseau – leading a pleasant existence in the underworld, corresponding to that of Virgil's warlike heroes (*Aeneid* VI 477–78). They include 'Febronius' who, we are told, can now call himself by his real name (B I 148). Febronius was the pseudonym adopted by Nikolaus von Hontheim (1701–90), suffragan bishop of Trier, for his book *De statu ecclesiae et legitima potestate Romani pontificis* (*On the State of the Church and the Legitimate Power of the Bishop of Rome*, 1763), which argued that secular rulers had a duty to promote the reform of the Church.[27]

Blumauer's treatment of the papacy aligns him with Reform Catholicism. He has no blanket hostility to the Catholic Church, but objects to its overweening claims to intellectual authority and political dominion. He admires moderate popes like Benedict XIV and Clement XIV. Admittedly, if we look at Blumauer's shorter poems on religious questions, we find a more complicated picture. In 'An meinen lieben P*', he tells Pezzl that the philosophical search for truth is futile, and is rewarded only with black bile and dyspepsia (B II 164–69). His long poem 'Glaubensbekenntniß eines nach Wahrheit Ringenden' ['Confession of Faith by a Seeker after Truth'] explores the irreconcilable discrepancy between the emotional convictions of the Christian and the rational certainties of the Enlightener, and raises the vertiginous possibility that neither faith nor reason may bring one any closer to truth:

> Und ach! in diesen dichten Finsternissen,
>   Worin mein Geist stets mit sich selber ringt,
> Wer sagt mir, ob mein Glauben oder Wissen
>   Hienieden mich der Wahrheit näher bringt? (B II 12)

31

[And alas! in this thick darkness where my mind perpetually struggles with itself, who can tell me whether it is my faith or my knowledge that will bring me closer to truth here below?]

Seen in this light, Blumauer's anticlericalism looks less like an attempt to promote a reformed Catholicism, and more like a frantic effort to distract himself, by satirical aggression, from the abyss of religious doubt exposed by philosophical reflection.

We need, however, to consider not just Blumauer's ideas but his satirical techniques. For, while there is certainly a tension, there is no necessary opposition between satire and Christianity.[28] The satires of Erasmus and Rabelais express a desire for the reform of the Church together with a profoundly Christian vision of life.[29] Does Blumauer belong in this tradition?

The most immediately obvious of Blumauer's techniques is his continual use of anachronism.[30] Thus, the building of Carthage is described as though it were Vienna, with prominence given to the Church and to instruments of punishment:

> Die Einen gruben Brunnen aus,
>   Die Andern bauten Ställe;
> Hier baute man ein Opernhaus,
>   Dort eine Hofkapelle:
> Da wurden Brücken aufgeführt,
> Und Nepomuke drauf postiert;
>   Dort sah man einen Pranger. (B I 19)

[Some were digging wells, others were building stables; here an opera-house was under construction, and there a court chapel: bridges were being erected and statues of St Nepomuk placed on them; over there a pillory could be seen.]

On arriving in Carthage, Aeneas goes to a coffee-house and reads about his escape from Troy in a newspaper; in Virgil, he sees his adventures depicted in the temple (*Aeneid* I 453–58). Dido is a society lady who suffers from vapours and keeps a pet pug dog (B I 71). She entertains her Trojan visitors with a performance of *Othello*. Aeneas quotes Wieland; Dido reads *Werthers Leiden*; and the love-sick Lavinia consoles herself with *Siegwart*. When a rainstorm comes on, the pilot Palinurus proposes that they should land and buy umbrellas ('Parapluis', B I 98).

Blumauer employs anachronism particularly in his detailed evocations of food and drink. A nineteenth-century commentator remarks: 'Echt österreichisch, speciell wienerisch erscheint das sichtliche Behagen an der Schilderung von Tafelfreuden' ['His visible enjoyment in describing the pleasures of the table is authentically Austrian, and particularly Viennese'].[31] The dinner that Dido gives for Aeneas is described with great relish. The dishes are imported from all over the world: sauces from Paris, beef from Hungary, fowls from America, ice-cream from Lapland:

32

Meerspinnen, Karpfen aus der Theiß,
　　Forellen kaum zu messen,
Granelli, von der Pfanne heiß,
　　Aeneens liebstes Fressen.
Ein ganzer Ochs war's Tafelstück,
Der Spargel, wie mein Arm so dick,
　　Und Austern groß – wie Teller.

Auch Kirschen, Ananas sogar,
　　Und Erdbeer' im Burgunder:
Und dann die Torte! – ja die war
　　Der Kochkunst größtes Wunder!
Sie präsentirte Trojens Brand,
Und oben auf den Flammen stand
　　Aeneas – ganz von Butter. (B I 24)

[Spider-crabs, carp from the Tisza (a river in Hungary), trout almost too big to measure, sweetbreads hot from the pan – Aeneas' favourite grub. The joint of beef was a whole ox; the asparagus was as thick as my arm, and the oysters as big as plates.

Cherries too, even pineapple, and strawberries in Burgundy; and then the cake! – that was the greatest miracle of cookery! It presented the burning of Troy, and atop the flames stood Aeneas, all in butter.]

Can mock-epic deflation go any further than presenting an image of the hero in butter? Blumauer continues with a mouth-watering description of the wines, culminating in champagne which excites him so much that he inserts himself among the drinkers by using the pronoun 'wir' (B I 24). Plenty of drinking goes on throughout the poem. On landing in Libya, the Trojans drink punch (B I 13). Those who survive the sack of Troy assemble at an ale-house (B I 44, no doubt suggested by Ceres' mound, *Aeneid* II 742), where they drink all night, apparently untroubled by the fall of their city. The helmsman Palinurus drowns after drinking too much rum (B I 123) though, in Virgil, he is tipped overboard by the god of sleep (*Aeneid* V 857–60). Aeneas' father, Anchises, is a great drinker and, in Elysium, he is found in the inn that serves draughts of the best Lethe (B I 163).

The counterpart to Dido's dinner is the description of hell's kitchen during Aeneas' descent to the underworld. Here the culinary punishment fits the crime. Usurers' souls are boiled till they are soft; cowards are roasted like hares; cardinals (in their red robes) are boiled like red crabs; and geniuses are made into broth ('Kraftsuppen', a punning reference to the 1770s' cult of the powerful and original 'Genie' or 'Kraftkerl').

As for heaven, when Aeneas visits Elysium, he finds it to be a perpetual dinner, modelled on the traditional Utopia of the Land of Cockaigne or 'Schlaraffenland' (B I 149). Beneath a firmament of sky-blue silk, the blessed idle away eternity in a paradise of food which Blumauer describes with irresistible buoyancy and gusto:

Das Wasser war hier Milchkaffee,
    Das Erdreich Chokolade,
Gefrornes aller Art der Schnee,
    Die Seen Limonade,
Der Rasen lauter Thymian,
    Die Berge Zuckerhüt' und dran
    Die Felsen Zuckerkandel.

Champagner, Sekt und Meth sah man
    An den Kaskaden schäumen,
Es wuchsen Torten, Marzipan
    Und Karpfen auf den Bäumen:
Die Flüsse führten Wein und Bier,
Und Maulwurfshügel waren hier
    Die köstlichsten Pasteten. (B I 159–60)

[The water here was *café au lait*, the soil was chocolate, the snow was ice-cream of every kind, the lakes were lemonade, the lawns consisted only of thyme, the mountains were sugar-loaves and the crags on them were icing.

Champagne, Sekt and mead were seen foaming in the waterfalls; cakes, marzipan and carp grew on the trees; the rivers flowed with wine and beer, and mole-hills here were delicious pies.]

In his descriptions of food and drink, Blumauer is of course appealing to the hedonism for which the Viennese have been so much censured by visitors. 'The Viennese', wrote Charles Sealsfield in 1828, 'were always reputed a sensual thoughtless sort of beings, content if they could enjoy a drive in their Zeiselwagen into the Prater, with their wine and roast-meat.'[32] But he is also joining a long satirical tradition by celebrating the life of the senses.[33] His Elysium is a perpetual carnival. And hence these parts of his satire accomplish two things: they redeem the senses from official disapproval; but they also gently deflate pretensions to heroism by reminding us that heroes, too, are only human.

Deflation is also achieved by the constant disrespect with which Blumauer treats gods and heroes. Juno is called 'Jupiters Xantippe' and 'Frau Wunderlich' (B I 7). Mercury is Jupiter's 'Hofcourier' ['court courier', B I 83] who carries despatches by harnessing a zephyr and buckling wings on its feet. Aeneas himself is not only naïvely pious but 'ein Hasenfuß' ['a coward', B I 13], an 'Eisenfresser' ['braggart', B I 19], and, in the opinion of his mother Venus, 'ein dummer Hans' who cannot attract Dido without her aid (B I 22). Other satirical techniques favoured by Blumauer include diminution, specificity and punning. His similes often diminish his characters by comparing them to small creatures: thus the Trojans run from the Greeks like fleas (B I 36), and the souls in the underworld crowd round Charon like herrings in the nets of Dutch fishermen (B I 139). The leafy boughs used for masts in the *Aeneid* (IV 399) are here specified as 'ein Ast / Voll Kirschen' ['a bough covered in cherries', B I 87]; and Acestes in his bearskin is described in detail as 'In eine Bärenhaut genäht, / Mit Pfeilen ganz den Rücken, / Gleich einem Stachelschwein, besä't' ['sewn into a bearskin, with his back full of arrows, like a porcupine', B I 98; cf. *Aeneid* V 37]. As for puns, these are occasionally witty, as when Tartarus becomes Tartary and Lucifer the Tartar Khan (B I 149), but usually silly: Lavinia is always called 'Miß Lavendel' [Miss Lavender], Pergama is turned into 'Bergam' and hence into the Austrian-sounding 'Amberg' (B I 54), and Aeneas, recounting his adventures to Dido, addresses her as 'Infantin' (B I 31), a merely verbal pun on 'Infandum, regina, iubes renovare dolorem'.[34]

Blumauer especially likes deflating his characters by showing them in their underclothes. He shares this taste with Voltaire who, in *La Pucelle,* has Jeanne steal the velvet breeches of an English knight; later she herself is robbed of her clothes, and is stark naked for several cantos.[35] Blumauer's Trojans, on arriving in Libya, take their shirts off and hang them up to dry (B I 12). The presents Aeneas brings Dido include Helen of Troy's petticoat (B I 22). When the Greeks attack Troy, Aeneas runs out without putting on his trousers (B I 37). Breaking into Priam's palace, Pyrrhus catches the king in his dressing-gown and slippers (B I 39). Out hunting, Aeneas takes refuge from the rain in a cave where Dido is drying her underwear:

> So mußt' Aeneas unverhofft
> In eine Höhle kommen,
> Wo eben, bis auf's Hemdchen naß,
> Die so verliebte Dido saß,
> Ihr Unterröckchen trocknend. (B I 79)

[Thus Aeneas was obliged unexpectedly to enter a cave where, just at that moment, soaked to the skin, the love-sick Dido was sitting and drying her petticoat.]

Showing heroes in their underclothes is an age-old humorous device. Besides reminding us that no man is a hero to his valet, the humorist mocks our pretensions by recalling the bare forked animal that is decently but precariously concealed beneath a thin layer of fabric. But while comedy thus celebrates our common humanity, the satirist, more darkly, reduces our impulses to their physical bases. In doing so, Blumauer expresses a more negative view of the senses than when rhapsodising about food and drink. Although he is coy about what Aeneas and Dido did in the cave, he makes it clear that their love is brutally sensual. At the dinner given on his arrival, Dido sits on Aeneas' lap. She admires the strength of his chest and loins (B I 72), and her desire for him is a physical itch:

> Beständig fuhr dem armen Weib
> Ein Jücken durch die Glieder,
> Bald kam's ihr in den Unterleib,
> Bald in die Kehle wieder.

Sie lief herum ohn' Unterlaß,
Wie ein geplagtes Füllen, das
   Die bösen Bremsen stechen. (B I 75)

[The poor woman had a constant itching through all her members, now
in the stomach, now in the throat. She ran about incessantly like a foal
tormented by the stinging of nasty gadflies.]

When ordered by Mercury to leave Dido and return to his mission, Aeneas
has satisfied his first 'Liebeshunger' but is not yet satiated and still has a good
appetite (B I 84). Abandoned, Dido takes from her bosom the ribbon
('Zopfband') with which Aeneas secured his pigtail, apostrophises it in
pathetic language, and uses it to hang herself. Because she has just been
reading *Werther*, her sentimental language seems inspired by the book, and
the 'Zopfband' presumably parodies Lotte's pink ribbon which Werther keeps
and which is to be buried with him. Dido's sentimentalism shows up the
discrepancy between her shallow emotions and her physical lust; indeed, she
kills herself only because Virgil, to Blumauer's regret, insists on it, and
Blumauer ends Book Four with a punning reflection on the conduct of other
jilted women:

Sie hegen gleichen Appetit,
Und hängen sich, wenn Einer flieht,
   Sogleich – an einen Andern. (B I 93)

[They have the same appetite and, when one man runs away, they hang
themselves – on to another.]

Appropriately, Blumauer's Elysium is an asexual paradise. The only women
are virgins, who dance to the music of the spheres, and St Cecilia, the
patroness of music, who is busy playing a Haydn concerto. Otherwise its
inhabitants seem all to be bachelors like Blumauer, engaged in enlightened
discussion over their beer and pipes:

Hier schmauchen Solon, Wilhelm Penn,
   Confuz und Zoroaster,
Und Montesquieu beim himmlischen
   Bierkrug ihr Pfeifchen Knaster [...]. (B I 161)

[Here Solon, William Penn, Confucius, Zoroaster and Montesquieu
smoke their tobacco-pipes in the heavenly inn.]

The lower bodily functions also feature in Blumauer, as in much satire. In
Troy, Aeneas and his companions, disguised as Greeks, have chamber-pots
emptied over their heads (B I 37). But it is especially the gods who are
associated with defecation. Zeus is always in a good mood, and disposed to
make people happy, when sitting on his 'Leibstuhl', the 'chaise-percée' or seat
concealing a chamber-pot (B I 13). It is hinted that his excrement forms the

River Styx, which is a sewer, as smelly as the River Spree at Berlin (B I 139);
the gods swear by it, according to the Cumaean Sibyl,

> Denn wahre Götter schwören nur
> Bei ihren Excrementen. (B I 140)

[For true gods swear only by their excrement.]

Thus, although Blumauer's satire celebrates the senses, it expresses a reductive
and negative view of sexuality and an ambivalent fascination with scatology.
The impulses behind his satire are too complicated, and his relation to
Christianity too sceptical, for us to align Blumauer with Rabelais as a
Christian celebrator of the flesh.

There remains the question whether his travesty is justified. Does it, as
Schiller charged, drag sublimity down to the dust? One near-contemporary,
Caroline Pichler, complained that, having read Blumauer's travesty first and
Virgil only later, she could never take to Virgil's Aeneas, always associating
him with his effigy in butter at Dido's dinner.[36] But Blumauer's travesty is
not really directed at Virgil and cannot spoil a thoughtful reader's apprecia-
tion of Virgil's heroic ideal, any more than Voltaire's rollicking *Pucelle* can
diminish one's admiration for the historical Joan of Arc. Blumauer appropri-
ates the *Aeneid* for his anticlerical polemic which, however obsessive it
sometimes seems, does target a number of real abuses and pillories them in a
fast-moving, entertaining and inventive way. The same passage came into
Georg Forster's mind in 1790 as he contemplated the statue of the Emperor
Charles V in Ghent:

> Der Kaiser steht wirklich sehr unsicher auf dieser gefährlichen Höhe;
> das Zepter und der Reichsapfel von ungeheurer Größe scheinen ihn
> völlig aus dem Gleichgewichte zu bringen; seine Kniee sind gebogen,
> und bald möchte ich fürchten, er sei im Begriff herabzugleiten. Im
> Glanz der Abendsonne, welche diesen vergoldeten Koloß bestralte,
> konnte ich mich einer Reminiszenz aus *Blumauers* travestirter Äneis
> nicht erwehren; ich dachte an jenes Backwerk, wo der fromme Held
> zuoberst 'ganz von Butter' stand.[37]

> [The Emperor, indeed, stands very insecurely on this dangerous eleva-
> tion; the huge sceptre and orb seem to wreck his balance entirely; his
> knees are bent, and I almost feared that he was about to slip and fall. As
> the evening sunlight illuminated this gilded colossus, I could not help
> remembering a passage in Blumauer's travesty of the *Aeneid*: I thought
> of the cake atop which stood the pious hero, 'all in butter'.]

Here Forster anticipates Heine's prose by adding an allegorical dimension to a
tourist description: the statue comes to typify the instability of monarchs in an
age of revolution, and the final quotation from Blumauer deflates the Emperor
and also implies a context of ecclesiastical as well as Imperial power.

Outside Nestroy's work, it would indeed be hard to find a better parody in the German language than Blumauer's *Aeneis*, and it is significant that it is the work of an Austrian, as is the defence of parody by Blumauer's admirer Grillparzer. Despite their criticisms of the Church, both bear the mark of Vienna's sensuous and expansive Catholic culture. Vienna, as J. P. Stern says, 'never knew the dour Protestant philistinism of the German Sunday parlours' occupied by 'those unbending figures which chill the air of many a play and novel from Hebbel to Hauptmann'.[38] Instead, like Nestroy with his satire on the megalomaniac Holofernes, Blumauer treats claims to heroism with a healthy scepticism. It is salutary to remember that heroes, too, wear underclothes.

Notes

1. For publication details, see Edith Rosenstrauch-Königsberg, *Freimaurerei im josephinischen Wien. Aloys Blumauers Weg vom Jesuiten zum Jakobiner* (Vienna and Stuttgart, 1975), p. 116. This study supersedes and often corrects the older studies by P. v. Hofmann-Wellenhof, *Alois Blumauer. Literarhistorische Skizze aus dem Zeitalter der Aufklärung* (Vienna, 1885); Gustav Gugitz, 'Alois Blumauer', *Jahrbuch der Grillparzer-Gesellschaft*, 18 (1908), 27–135; and Bärbel Becker-Cantarino, *Aloys Blumauer and the Literature of Austrian Enlightenment* (Frankfurt, 1973).
2. See A. W. Schlegel, 'Das scherzhafte Heldengedicht', in his *Vorlesungen über Ästhetik I [1798–1803]*, ed. Ernst Behler (Paderborn, 1989), pp. 643–49; further Wido Hempel, 'Parodie, Travestie und Pastiche. Zur Geschichte von Wort und Sache', *Germanisch-Romanische Monatschrift*, 15 (1965), 150–76; Jürgen von Stackelberg, 'Vergil, Lalli, Scarron. Ein Ausschnitt aus der Geschichte der Parodie', *Arcadia*, 17 (1982), 225–44.
3. See Rosenstrauch-Königsberg, *Freimaurerei*, pp. 171–79.
4. See W. E. Yates, *Nestroy: Satire and Parody in Viennese Popular Comedy* (Cambridge, 1972), chs 2 and 5; also Otto Rommel, *Die Alt-Wiener Volkskomödie* (Vienna, 1952), esp. pp. 530–41.
5. See Scarron, *Le Vergile travesti*, (ed.) Jean Serroy (Paris, 1988).
6. Charlotte Craig, *Christoph Martin Wieland as the Originator of the Modern Travesty in German Literature* (Chapel Hill, NC, 1970), p. 46.
7. Letter of 25 September 1783, in *Wielands Briefwechsel*, vol. 8/i, (ed.) Annerose Schneider (Berlin, 1992), p. 128.
8. Franz Grillparzer, *Sämtliche Werke*, ed. Peter Frank and Karl Pörnbacher, 4 vols (Munich, 1960–65), vol. 1, pp. 12–18; vol. 3, p. 298.
9. Immanuel Kant, *Werke*, ed. Wilhelm Weischedel, 6 vols (Frankfurt, 1964), vol. 6, pp. 458–59.
10. G. W. F. Hegel, *Ästhetik*, ed. Friedrich Bassenge (Berlin, 1955), pp. 966–67. On the German reception of Virgil, see Theodore Ziolkowski, *Virgil and the Moderns* (Princeton, 1993), and on 'primary' and 'secondary' epic, C. S. Lewis, *A Preface to 'Paradise Lost'* (London, 1942).
11. Friedrich Schiller, *Sämtliche Werke*, ed. Gerhard Fricke and Herbert G. Göpfert, 5 vols (Munich, 1958), vol. 5, p. 739. See Norbert Christian Wolf, '"Der schmutzige Witz des Herrn Blaumauer". Schiller und die Marginalisierung populärer Komik aus dem josephinischen Wien', in Wendelin Schmidt-Dengler, Johann Sonnleitner and Klaus Zeyringer (eds), *Komik in der österreichischen Literatur* (Berlin, 1996), pp. 56–87.
12. Ibid., vol. 1, p. 460.
13. Richard Sheppard, 'Upstairs-Downstairs – Some Reflections on German Literature

in the Light of Bakhtin's Theory of Carnival', in Sheppard (ed.), *New Ways in Germanistik* (New York, Oxford, Munich, 1990), pp. 278–315 (esp. p. 298).

14. Quoted in Hempel, 'Parodie, Travestie und Pastiche', p. 156.

15. See 'Austrian Writers of the Enlightenment and Biedermeier: A Biographical Directory' in *Austrian Studies*, 2 (1991), 161–67.

16. Reprinted in *Literatur der Aufklärung 1765–1800*, Österreichische Bibliothek 8, ed. Edith Rosenstrauch-Königsberg (Vienna, Cologne, Graz, 1988), pp. 162–94.

17. The edition quoted is *Aloys Blumauer's gesammelte Schriften*, 3 parts (Stuttgart, 1871), by part and page number. *Virgils Aeneis, travestirt* occupies the whole of the first part.

18. Quoted in *Literatur der Aufklärung*, p. 326.

19. Constant von Wurzbach, *Biographisches Lexikon des Kaiserthums Österreich* (Vienna, 1856–91), vol. 2, p. 439. He explains that 'xenophthalmisch' refers to Blumauer's eye trouble, while 'ybischartig', meaning 'like a tall yellowish poplar', alludes to his yellow complexion and tall thin build.

20. See Eduard Winter, *Der Josefinismus und seine Geschichte. Beiträge zur Geistesgeschichte Österreichs 1740–1848* (Prague, 1943); and for the European context, Owen Chadwick, *The Popes and European Revolution* (Oxford, 1981), ch. 6.

21. See Ludwig Andreas Veit and Ludwig Lenhart, *Kirche und Volksfrömmigkeit im Zeitalter des Barock* (Freiburg, 1956); Anna Coreth, *Pietas Austriaca. Ursprung und Entwicklung barocker Frömmigkeit in Österreich* (Munich, 1959); for Enlighteners' disapproval of what they classified as 'popular religion', Christof Dippel, 'Volksreligiosität und Obrigkeit im 18. Jahrhundert', in Wolfgang Schieder (ed.), *Volksreligiosität in der modernen Sozialgeschichte* (Göttingen, 1986), pp. 73–96; and for Blumauer's place in Austrian anticlerical writing, Peter Horwath, *Der Kampf gegen die religiöse Tradition. Die Kulturkampfliteratur Österreichs, 1780–1918* (Berne, 1978).

22. Figures from Charles Ingrao, *The Habsburg Monarchy 1618–1815* (Cambridge, 1994), p. 199.

23. Quoted in T. C. W. Blanning, *Joseph II* (London, 1994), p. 96.

24. On the semantic range of 'pius', see Colin Burrow, *Epic Romance: Homer to Milton* (Oxford, 1993), pp. 39–40. That Aeneas was too good to be true was a well-known criticism, quoted and questioned by Voltaire in his *Essai sur la poésie épique*: 'Saint-Evremond dit qu'Enée est plus propre à être le fondateur d'un ordre de moines que d'un empire' (Voltaire, *Oeuvres complètes* (Paris, 1868), vol. 2, p. 362).

25. Blumauer's allusions can mostly be identified from such standard sources as Eric John (ed.), *The Popes: A Concise Biographical History* (London, 1964), and J. N. D. Kelly, *The Oxford Dictionary of Popes* (Oxford, 1986).

26. As Blumauer doubtless knew, Voltaire execrates Clément as an example of fanaticism in Canto 5 of his *Henriade*: see *Oeuvres complètes*, vol. 2, p. 307.

27. See Chadwick, *The Popes*, pp. 408–11.

28. See Edward Timms, 'The Christian satirist: a contradiction in terms?', *Forum for Modern Language Studies*, 31 (1995), 101–16.

29. See M. A. Screech, *Rabelais* (London, 1979), esp. pp. 41–56.

30. On anachronism in Blumauer, Scarron and elsewhere, see the brief comparison in Stackelberg, 'Vergil, Lalli, Scarron', p. 235.

31. Hofmann-Wellenhof, *Blumauer*, p. 65.

32. Charles Sealsfield – Karl Postl, *Austria as it is: or Sketches of continental courts, by an eye-witness. London 1828. Österreich, wie es ist, oder Skizzen von Fürstenhöfen des Kontinents. Wien 1919*, ed. Primus-Heinz Kucher (Vienna, Cologne, Weimar, 1994), p. 95. Sealsfield explains a 'Zeiselwagen' as 'a strange species of locomotion, loaded with no less strange occupants, and hams, wine-flaggons, and everything necessary to the Viennese' (p. 88). With Dido's dinner, cf. Sealsfield's description of a four-course dinner, with five wines, in a noble household (p. 87).

33. See Mikhail Bakhtin, *Rabelais and his World*, tr. Helene Iswolsky (Cambridge, MA, 1968).
34. 'Beyond all words, O queen, is the grief thou bidst me revive', *Aeneid* II 3. The text and translation are those of H. Rushton Fairclough in the Loeb Classical Library (2 vols, London, 1935).
35. See Voltaire, *Oeuvres complètes*, vol. 2, pp. 391, 456.
36. Caroline Pichler, *Denkwürdigkeiten aus meinem Leben*, ed. Emil Karl Blümml, 2 vols (Munich, 1914), vol. I, p. 134.
37. Georg Forster, *Ansichten vom Niederrhein*, ed. Gerhard Steiner (Berlin, 1958), p. 247.
38. J. P. Stern, *Re-interpretations: Seven Studies in Nineteenth-Century German Literature* (London, 1964), p. 60.

The Comedies of Johanna von Weissenthurn

Ian F. Roe

It would be an understatement of the first order to admit that Johanna von Weissenthurn (also known as Johanna Franul von Weissenthurn from her husband's full surname) has not exactly established herself as a major figure in Austrian literary history. The actress and dramatist, born as Johanna Grünberg in Koblenz on the Rhine in 1772,[1] but resident in Vienna from 1789 until her death in 1847, merits a brief entry in a number of biographies and literary encyclopaedias, especially of the nineteenth century, including ten pages in Goedeke.[2] Even the increasing interest in women writers in recent decades has failed to discover her, however: among the editors of modern reference works in that field, only Elisabeth Friedrichs considers her worthy of mention, although two that fail to include her (Gisela Brinker-Gabler, et al. (1986) and Elke Frederiksen (1989)) both include scarcely better-known writers of the century, such as Sophie von Knorring, Johanna Kinkel and Malwida von Meysenbug.[3] The recent survey of Austrian theatrical history by the scholar to whom this volume is dedicated does at least accord her five lines,[4] but a collection of essays on the women of Vienna mentions her in neither of the essays on actresses and writers.[5] In combining a brief survey of her career as a whole with a more detailed introduction to her comedies, I can attempt, if only in a very small way, to redress this imbalance and to consider whether the total neglect of her work is justified.

Whatever the literary qualities, or lack of them, in her work that might have merited such a deafening silence, her career as a writer was certainly not without success during her lifetime, not to mention her many major roles on the stage of the Burgtheater after brief engagements at the court theatre in Munich and in Baden near Vienna. Her acting career in Vienna became firmly established in 1800 with the role of Leonore in Schiller's *Fiesko*, and, especially after the death of Betty Roose in 1808, she took on many other Schillerian roles: Agnes Sorel in *Die Jungfrau von Orleans* [*The Maid of Orleans*] (initially the equivalent role in Escherich's version of 1802), Isabella in *Die Braut von Messina* [*The Bride of Messina*], Elisabeth in *Maria Stuart*, and Gräfin Terzky in the one-play version of *Wallenstein* by Hans Wehner that was premièred in April 1814 as the first production of Schreyvogel's

41

regime. From 1808 and 1810 respectively she took the parts of Lady Macbeth and Phaedra in Schiller's versions of the plays by Shakespeare and Racine. In the latter role and in that of Isabella in *Die Braut von Messina* she was replaced in 1815 by Sophie Schröder but, in many of the others listed, she continued well into the 1820s, during which decade she also played the Kurfürstin in Kleist's *Prinz Friedrich von Homburg* (under the title 'Die Schlacht bei Fehrbellin' [The Battle of Fehrbellin]) and Gertraude [*sic*] in the same dramatist's *Die Familie Schroffenstein* [The Schroffenstein Family], in addition to performing in many of her own plays.

Contemporary reports indicate that she was a competent actress of feeling and not inconsiderable versatility, able to take on roles that were quite the opposite of her own character. In 1820, Costenoble referred to her performing 'mit unverkennbarem Verstande, mit Fleiß und regem Gefühle' ['with obvious understanding, with energy and considerable feeling'], but nevertheless repeatedly criticised her for her sing-song style of declamation ('singende Manier').[6] In part as a result, he found her performance as Elisabeth so dreadful that one was glad when she left the stage (I, 127). In contrast, Costenoble praised her interpretation of the Kurfürstin in *Prinz Friedrich von Homburg*, and it was in playing older women that she received most acclaim as she increasingly found herself having to relinquish younger roles to Sophie Schröder. In 1829, on the fortieth anniversary of the start of her Burgtheater career, she received the 'Civilverdienstmedaille' from the Emperor Franz; the fiftieth anniversary in 1839 brought her the gold medal for art and science from the Prussian King Frederick William III. By the 1830s she was inevitably playing grandmothers and other old women's roles, and Costenoble reports more than one scheme to have her and other older members of the company pensioned off.[7] Her last major role was at the end of 1841 as Belmont in Schiller's version of Picard's *Der Parasit* [The Parasite]. By this time a number of last-minute corrections to the theatre bills were indicating the ageing actress's unavailability through illness – probably gout, according to one obituary[8] – and she left the Burgtheater in March of the following year, soon after her seventieth birthday, and died in 1847, aged seventy-five.

Weissenthurn's first play for the stage was a one-act comedy *Das Nachspiel* [The Epilogue], based on a play by the French dramatist, Alexandre Vincent Pineux-Duval. The comedy was premièred on 12 May 1800, without the author's name on the theatre bill, and was favourably reviewed in the journal *Wiener Theater-Kritik*, which praised the well-drawn characters, the pleasing plot and the natural unravelling of the intrigue.[9] It achieved the rather modest total of eighteen performances during the following two years. Even less successful was a three-act drama, *Liebe und Entsagung* [Love and Renunciation], which was performed only four times between February and May 1801. The actress's first major success as an author came on 3 March of that year with the première of the 'Originallustspiel' *Beschämte Eifersucht* [Jealousy Shamed], which was to be performed a total of sixty-two times between then and 1844. Similarly successful was a further adaptation of a play by Pineux-Duval; the one-act comedy *Ein Haus zu verkaufen* [A House for Sale] was first staged on

28 September 1801 and enjoyed sixty-nine performances in all. Success was far from assured, however. Ventures into more serious forms of theatre met with little acclaim and merited few performances; in particular, her first attempt at historical drama, *Totila, König der Gothen* [Totila, King of the Goths], based on an Italian play by Federici, was performed only four more times after its première in October 1804. Comedies or domestic dramas remained a more reliable source of success (*Versöhnung* [Reconciliation] (1806), *Es spukt* [Haunted] (1810), *Welche ist die Braut?* [Which is the Bride?] (1813)), together with the occasional 'romantisches Schauspiel': one of these, *Der Wald bei Hermannstadt* [The Forest of Hermannstadt] was her greatest success, at least in terms of the number of performances. Premièred on 14 July 1807, it was performed a total of 117 times, a number equalled or bettered at the Burgtheater by very few plays.[10]

Her plays were also often performed on other stages. For *Welche ist die Braut?* Goedeke lists performances in eighteen cities in addition to Vienna,[11] and one review of that play provides an interesting indication of the popularity of her work and also of contemporary taste: the day after Weissenthurn's play had been put on for a full and appreciative audience in Graz, *Emilia Galotti* was performed to a virtually empty auditorium.[12] The conclusions that might have been drawn from such a comparison were not always heeded, however. The failure of *Totila* in 1804 was matched by *Hermann,* a further unsuccessful attempt at historical drama in November 1813; and, from that year onwards, the failures – plays for which the performances failed to reach double figures or even half-a-dozen – rather detracted from relative successes such as *Welcher ist der Bräutigam?* [Which is the Bridegroom?] (1816, 28 performances), the title of which indicates the attempt to cash in on the popularity of an earlier success, *Das letzte Mittel* [The Last Resort] (1820, 59 performances), *Pauline* (1826, 35), *Das Manuskript* [The Manuscript] (1826, 32), *Die Fremde* [The Stranger] (1838, 44).

The majority of her plays were published during her lifetime, with approximately one-quarter of them as individual volumes. A first collection of *Schauspiele* [Plays] appeared as early as 1804, a two-volume edition published by Degen; four more volumes followed in 1809, and the complete set of six appeared in the following year. In 1817 a two-volume collection of plays was published by the firm Kaulfuss und Armbruster under the title *Neue Schauspiele* [Recent Plays], followed between 1821 and 1836 by six volumes of *Neueste Schauspiele* [Most Recent Plays]. The volumes were also numbered in the overall sequence, so that what was, in effect, the fifteenth volume of plays appeared posthumously in 1848, published by Wallishauser. Two further posthumous volumes were planned but never published, so that five plays have survived only in manuscript form.[13]

Weissenthurn's plays fall into a number of categories: historical tragedies; romantic historical plays; domestic dramas; society comedies, many of them in one act. Least successful were the historical plays, lacking in tragic inevitability and depth of character, and often of monotonous versifying. *Totila*, in particular, is an unconvincing exercise in early PR strategies, seeking to present the king of the Goths as a humane and enlightened ruler and leader who is revered as 'König und Mensch' ['king and human being'] (III, 134)[14] and whose armies maraud and pillage only because they fail to heed the message and example of their noble king. Why Weissenthurn kept turning to serious drama must remain a matter for speculation because there are no statements by the dramatist that might provide clues. The reasons may be not dissimilar to those that, twenty years later, constantly drove Raimund to abandon comedy in his quest to emulate what he saw as the 'many beautiful words' of Schillerian and Grillparzerian tragedy.[15] Not unlike Raimund, Weissenthurn had greater success with conventional forms of comedy, and I shall concentrate here on her comedies and also on the domestic dramas, which contain a considerable comic element either in the treatment of the plot or in the use of comic characters. These plays employ a number of typical comic elements of the time: mistaken identities; letters that finish up in the wrong hands; love intrigues of various kinds; people enamoured of inappropriate would-be partners, especially ones who are much younger or older; exaggerated and unfounded jealousy and misconceived plans to cure such people; excessive aversion to love and marriage; and, last but by no means least, characters confused as to who is in love with whom, convinced erroneously that someone is in love with them or that the person they are in love with has formed an attachment for someone else. Typical of the more trivial treatment of such themes is the two-act comedy *Es spukt*, first performed in March 1810. A young man, Jacob, is convinced that his father's fiancée, Gertraud, is in fact meant for him, when he wants to marry Hannchen. As Gertraud tries to introduce herself to her future stepson, he rejects what he sees as the overtures of an elderly bride, and, as his father tries to get him to retract his professed dislike of Gertraud, he again misunderstands all references to 'bride' and 'marriage':

> JACOB. Ich hab's ja schon gesagt: sie ist zu alt, sie sollte an keine Heirath mehr denken.
> PÄCHT[ERINN GERTRAUD]. Nun ziehe ich meine Hand von ihm; nun, Herr Gevatter, lass' er seine Strenge walten. Sperr' er ihn ein, geb' er ihm nichts zu essen, vielleicht bringt ihn der Hunger zur Vernunft.
> JACOB. Und wenn ich auch verhungern sollte, ich ändere meinen Sinn doch nicht mehr.
> KRUMM (*im höchsten Zorn*). Bube, ich erwürge dich. (Act I, Scene 10)

> [JACOB. I've told you already, she's too old, she shouldn't be thinking of marriage any more.
> GERTRAUD. That's enough, I've tried to be nice to him; now you must be strict with him. Lock him in his room, don't give him anything to eat, perhaps he'll come to his senses if he's hungry.
> JACOB. Even if I were to starve to death, I wouldn't change my mind.
> KRUMM (*in a rage*). I'll throttle you, boy.]

The second act then takes place in adjoining cellars in which Hannchen and Jacob are kept imprisoned or are hiding and which are also rumoured to be haunted, and all ends happily with the message that 'Die Jugend *ehrt* das Alter, doch sie *liebt* es nicht' ['Youth respects old age but doesn't fall in love with it'] (VII, 163) and a final refrain typical of the endings of so many Viennese comedies,[16] if not particularly common in Weissenthurn's plays:

> Soll denn der Mensch nicht fröhlich seyn?
> Ihm blüht das Korn, ihm wächst der Wein!
> *(Alle wiederhohlen)*
> Drum soll er sich bey Lieb' und Wein,
> Gott dankend, seines Lebens freun.
> *(Alle wiederhohlen und gehen ab)*.

> [Should man not be happy? For him the corn ripens and the wine grows. *(all repeat)*
> And so, whether it be love or wine, let him thank the Lord and take pleasure in life. *(all repeat and exit)*.]

The whole situation seems terribly contrived, with Jacob's assumption that he is to marry Gertraud resulting from the most implausible of misunderstandings. Nevertheless, the play was performed forty-two times in all and was obviously well liked, with the scenes in which characters creep around in dimly lit and supposedly haunted cellars and accuse each other in exaggerated terms of trespass no doubt effective on stage.

Es spukt is a very slight piece, containing nothing of depth or subtlety, but designed solely to be effective on stage and to entertain in a somewhat superficial way. Other plays appear more fully to reflect the author's ideas and serious intentions, and undoubtedly have more to commend them. In the preface to the first published edition of her plays, Weissenthurn wrote of her 'Gefühl des Schicklichen und Wahren' ['feeling for what is true and seemly'], and stressed that her plays owed much to her knowledge of human nature ('Menschenkenntniß': I, vi). The theme of social intercourse, of dealing with one's fellow human beings ('der Umgang mit Menschen'), is one that recurs in her plays (VI, 130; XIII, 30), and associated with it is the idea of overcoming antisocial attributes and excesses. Jealousy is seen as a particularly dangerous emotion in *Beschämte Eifersucht* while in *Die Radikalkur* it is Wolken's jealous and suspicious nature that needs the drastic remedy of the title. Avarice and too great a concern with wealth are criticised in *Kindliche Liebe* [Children's Love], in which Wunder is told he has too much money for his own good, and the message is spelled out that poverty is not something inherently negative: 'Armuth drückt nicht, wenn ein unbescholtenes Gewissen und die Liebe guter Kinder sie uns tragen hilft' ['poverty is not a burden if an untroubled conscience and the love of good children help us to bear it'] (I, 26).

Rejection of excesses also applies to one of the most common motifs in the comedies, namely love and marriage. If *Welche ist die Braut?* castigates obsession with the importance of marriage, *Die Ehescheuen* [Reluctant to Marry] criticises excessive aversion to marriage. In the programmatically entitled *Liebe und Entsagung*, Julie has to overcome her desire for Wilhelm, who is already secretly married to Amalie but, in the end, decides she can reciprocate the love of Fritz, the man who has sought her from the start and has shown himself to be the most altruistic of the characters and the most capable of the renunciation referred to in the title. One aspect of love and marriage that is frequently ridiculed is the idea of marrying for money. In *Welche ist die Braut?*, the bankrupt baroness is determined that none of her daughters shall marry Waldberg, who does not even have a 'von' to his name, and insists that it is the financial consideration that must be uppermost in any bride's mind; only common folk are interested in actually seeing their potential partner, while 'Vornehme berechnen erst alle Vortheile, dann lieben sie sich' ['respectable people first weigh up all the advantages, then they fall in love'] (VIII, 144). The interests of the daughters are looked after rather better by Wolf, the friend of the baroness's late husband, and his honesty and integrity are in turn contrasted with the baroness's adviser, the scrounging and fawning Blümlein, who is hoping to inherit money from the various ageing ladies of the nobility that he courts. In *Kindliche Liebe*, Wunder wants his son Fritz to marry the Mayor's daughter, who is hunchbacked, hard of hearing, much older than his son, but very rich. Not entirely coincidentally, but equally reprehensibly, Wunder himself would like to marry Amalie, the girl in love with his son. Similarly, the miserly bookkeeper, Gehrmann, in *Das Manuskript* wants to marry off his idealistic nephew, August, to a rich bride of somewhat limited intellect. August, however, is increasingly attracted to the blind but proud Albertine who has been left to a life of poverty and disability after being abandoned by her fiancé when her father's business collapsed. The character of Gehrmann is also a vehicle for a sharp satire on those men who think that the only place for women is in the home. He sees it as his mission to prevent any more women deserting the kitchen and their sewing (XIII, 34). Women, he thinks, should not know anything, and he is particularly scathing on the subject of women of letters: 'Ich gebe dem Manne die Feder, und dem Weibe die Nadel in die Hand. Eine Frau, die mehr Tinte braucht, als ihr Mann Wein trinkt, kommt nicht in mein Haus' ['To the man I hand a pen, to the woman a needle. A woman who needs more ink than her husband drinks wine is not coming into my house'] (XIII, 125).

The words of Gehrmann undoubtedly reflect the author's own concerns, as the criticism to which women writers were exposed was something of which she was very conscious. In the preface to Volume 1 of her works, Weissenthurn speaks of the dangers facing women who venture into an essentially male domain that should normally be avoided by 'sanfte Weiblichkeit' ['gentle femininity']. The danger is that of being isolated: 'ein solches Weib steht allein zwischen beyden Geschlechtern – ihr Eigenes verachtet sie selbst, die Männer verachten sie; man bewundert, was sie weiß, aber man liebt und schätzt es nicht' ['such a woman stands alone between the two sexes – her own she herself despises, and men despise her; people admire what she knows but do not love or value it'] (I, v–vi). She is prepared to take the risk, for, as she admits ironically, she hates knitting and also feels assured that, if she is badly treated, she can in future remain in the confines of a woman's role (I, viii). Three years later she took up similar themes in a letter to Schreyvogel's *Sonntagsblatt*: the path she has followed has been a difficult one without the support or protection of any man.[17] Admitting that her plays may be no more than 'sehr mäßige Hausmannskost' ['very moderate plain fare'], she insists that they have enjoyed some success; nevertheless they have been heavily criticised when plays of much worse quality written by men have been treated very lightly (p. 361). She also suggests, with some justification, that her plays have been more successful when they have appeared anonymously.

Contemporary reviews appear to bear out some of her complaints, although the major attacks were on her more serious works rather than on her comedies. On the one hand the production of *Ruprecht, Graf zu Horneck* [Ruprecht, Count of Horneck] in 1820 prompted the reviewer in the *Modenzeitung* to suggest that she was incapable of writing tragedies, which were in fact way beyond the abilities of any woman ('weit außer dem Kreise weiblicher Kräfte'). Indeed, the reviewer considers that, if there were ever a female Shakespeare, it would be a sign of a dangerous new age that no man should want to experience.[18] Similar views are expressed in *Der Sammler*, on *Ruprecht* (the eponymous hero of which, it is thought, completely lacks the inner qualities of a tragic hero) and, seven years earlier, in a review of *Hermann*: 'Frau von Weissenthurn scheint der Aufgabe nicht gewachsen, die höchste Manneskraft mit voller männlicher Energie auszusprechen' ['Frau von Weissenthurn is apparently not equal to the task of expressing the supreme strength of men with full manly energy'].[19] In a review of 1816, Wilhelm Hebenstreit in the *Modenzeitung* detected a lack of depth in the characters in *Welcher ist der Bräutigam*, with the male roles in particular 'flach und seicht' ['shallow and superficial'], while illogicalities in the plot are excused condescendingly as being typical of female forgetfulness.[20] At the same time as being attacked in this way for lacking the supposed strengths of a male writer, she is also criticised for features that are thought unseemly for a female writer, the 'Unebenheiten und rauhe Verknüpfungen' ['unevenness and rough joins'] in the plot of *Das letzte Mittel*,[21] for example, and it is with not a little condescension that the reviewer of *Welche ist die Braut?* in *Der Sammler* feels it worthy of admiration 'wie aus der Feder in zarten Frauenhänden eine so männlich derbe Satyre habe fließen können' ['how such a coarse masculine satire could have flowed from a pen held in a woman's delicate hands'].[22]

Das Manuskript is one of a number of Weissenthurn's plays that reflect her concern with the role and position of women. In the early play, *Kindliche Liebe*, Frau Hartmann delivers a sharp rebuke to men, such as Wunder, who treat women as chattels (I, 23) and, on the whole, it is the male characters who are subject to prejudices, to exaggerated behaviour, to excessive and un-founded jealousy, who fail to recognise the merits and qualities of others. Typical is Wolken in *Die Radikalkur*, jealous, convinced that Friederike has at least three lovers and suspicious of any man that comes near her, and listing catalogues of supposedly female faults: 'Neugierde, Eitelkeit, Koquetterie, zu was können die sie nicht verleiten' ['curiosity, vanity, coquettishness, what can't they tempt a woman to do'] (IV, 134). In contrast to the plays of Iffland, however, in which the female characters are often either empty-headed or the source of dangerous or vain ideas,[23] the women in Weissenthurn's plays are frequently models of common sense and solid virtue. Julie, in the early comedy *Die Erben* [The Heirs], is determined to forge her own destiny and to adhere to her principles of honour and virtue (III, 31,35). Marie, the ill-treated daughter of the baroness in *Welche ist die Braut?*, has stoically accepted her harsh fate but has remained an example to all of 'hohe Sanftmuth und stille Größe' ['noble gentleness and quiet greatness'] (VIII, 216). A similar harsh fate has been experienced by Albertine in *Das Manuskript*, who is considered as blessed with every feminine virtue: 'Anmuth! Duldung! Würde! kindliche Hingebung! geläuterten Verstand! anspruchslose Bescheidenheit! Frohsinn! Frömmigkeit' ['grace, patience, dignity, child-like devotion, purity of mind, unassuming modesty, cheerfulness, piety'] (XIII, 123–24). The plays contain several other independent female characters, such as the flirtatious but ultimately virtuous and victorious Marie and Julie in *Beschämte Eifersucht*, or Räthin Sommer in *Welche ist die Braut?*, who stands aloof from the world of gossip and fashion, even if such characters are restricted in part by their limited circumstances, by the laws that men impose upon them, as Julie laments in *Beschämte Eifersucht*, or even by disability as in the case of Albertine.

Two women who have no such limitations are Gräfin Buchberg in *Die erste Liebe* and Baronin Waldhüll in *Das letzte Mittel*. The former rules her domain with kindness and humanity, much to the disgust of her brother, who clings to more traditional ideas of class and prejudice, and to the discomfort of the inspector, who deals in deceit and bribery. To her son she insists on the importance of worldly wisdom learnt 'in dem freyen Umgang mit Menschen' ['in associating freely with one's fellow men'] (VI, 130), on recognising people with all their faults (144). It might be regretted that the countess is at times a peripheral figure and that her noble sentiments are buried in a conventional tale of love and renunciation. As Karl is forced to accept that Röschen is still in love with Philipp, the play might be seen to be reinforcing the idea that to marry beneath one's status is something to be avoided. It is at his mother's behest, however, that he joins the hands of the two lovers, and the influence of the countess is once more underlined in the final scene as she involves Karl in the rebuilding of the village whose livelihood has been destroyed by an epidemic among the animals: 'du legst dort den Grundstein zu zwei friedlichen Hütten. Dieß Denkmahl erbaue dem heutigen Tage, Friede wohne in jenen Hütten, und in deinem Herzen' ['you will be laying the foundation for two peaceful cottages. Let them be a reminder of this day: may peace dwell in those cottages and in your heart'] (VI, 199). Baronin Waldhüll is an independent woman of a different kind, determined to try everything, even the last desperate means of the title, to get the man she loves, the rather moody, distrustful and, one might even suggest, undeserving Graf Sonnstett. She is particularly concerned to follow her own interests and feelings on occasions, such as going to dance at a ball, rather than being subject to a man's whims, even if it is a man she loves.

Female characters such as Buchberg and Waldhüll do not conform to the contemporary understanding of women as second-class citizens, which was codified in the laws of the land and idealised in uplifting literary visions of circumscribed but idyllic domesticity and moral purity as, for example, in Schiller's 'Macht des Weibes' [The Power of Woman] or 'Das Lied von der Glocke' [The Song of the Bell]. The ideal woman was 'a pretty, girlish creature, affectionate and impulsive, but submissive, practical and hard-working',[24] the obedient and naïve young girl who became wife, mother and housekeeper and remained throughout an essentially asexual, de-eroticised creature.[25] The romantic vision of emotional, if not necessarily social, equality and liberation was short-lived, and, for the women of the Biedermeier period in Austria, the world was one of 'enge Grenzen' ['narrow confines'];[26] those who sought to overcome such restrictions, by attempting to become the dominant partner in a relationship, by seeking independence, or by pursuing a life of education and learning, were the objects of scorn, criticism or ostracisation. In the conventional image of the day, learning in a woman was dangerous,[27] but, in Weissenthurn's plays, such women (Gräfin Buchberg, Albertine) are not in any way satirised as dangerous blue-stockings but are seen as positive figures. By way of contrast, Emerike in *Das Manuskript* may be good, pious and a sensible housekeeper, but she is also innocent and naïve to the point of stupidity, sheltered to the extent that she appears gauche, and in desperate need of social intercourse and of the 'Weibererziehung' ['education for women'] that the countess's brother in *Die erste Liebe* [First Love] finds so abhorrent. Similarly, the character of Ida in *Das letzte Mittel*, who is a conventional ideal of beauty, innocence and devotion, is overshadowed by the very unconventional Baronin Waldhüll and remains largely in the background. In other plays, Weissenthurn appears especially critical of women who conform to negative stereotypes of female behaviour, in particular the tendency to gossip, as with Frau von Silben in *Das letzte Mittel* or the obnoxious group of snobbish gossipers who gather for the soirée in Act III of *Welche ist die Braut?*, but also the excessively fashion-conscious and consequently insolvent baroness in that same play. The *Modenzeitung* wondered whether *Das letzte Mittel* could really have been written by a woman[28] but, on the contrary, the way in which conventional pictures of women are seen at times in a critical light and compared to women of independence and intelligence might indicate an, admittedly very cautiously, critical female perspective.

However cautiously it may be expressed, the questioning of the traditional female role is arguably the most obvious of the otherwise very few manifestations of social criticism. In *Welche ist die Braut?*, the young and stupid Baron Dürrer has paid for his promotion over the heads of those more qualified; plays such as *Welche ist die Braut?* and *Die erste Liebe* tentatively offer understanding for the situation of the peasant farmers. In the latter, Gruber stands up to the snobbish baron and insists on honesty as the peasant's sign of nobility, and the play is the most unequivocal in its attack on class snobbery in the negative portrayal of the baron (the countess's brother) who is horrified that his nephew is in love with a peasant's daughter. Nevertheless, Karl's reading of books with titles such as 'Das geadelte Bauernmädchen' ['The ennobled peasant-girl'] might indicate the limits of his classless ideals[29] and, as already seen, the independent and enlightened characters in the plays are often members of the aristocracy. Any criticism is directed at individuals, not at institutions or at whole social groups, and there is no trace of the contrast between a morally upright bourgeoisie and a corrupt and dishonest aristocracy that is a recurring theme of Iffland's work. Instead, the specific 'message' of the plays is often a traditional one of virtue victorious (*Welche ist die Braut?*, VIII, 246), simplicity and morality (*Kindliche Liebe*, I, 115), or happiness arising from making others happy (*Das Mißverständniß* [The Misunderstanding], III, 268). Karl in *Die erste Liebe* must learn to 'aus Verstand und Grundsätzen entsagen, nicht aus Gehorsam' ['renounce through common sense and principles, not out of obedience'] (VI, 183), and *Liebe und Entsagung* ends with the message that 'der Mensch sollte aus Eigennutz tugendhaft sein, weil er nur durch Tugenden sich und Andere glücklich machen kann' ['people should be virtuous out of self-interest, because it is only through virtues that they can make themselves and others happy'] (II, 87).

The dramatist's basic moral intentions are also reflected in an essay written in 1829, in which she criticises recent dramas for neglecting the real aim of the theatre as 'eine Schule des Schicklichen, des Schönen, des Großen, und Würdigen' ['a school for teaching what is seemly, beautiful, great and worthy'], and calls on dramatists: 'schildert mehr die Menschen, wie sie sein sollen, nicht wie sie sind' ['depict people as they should be, not as they are'].[30] Inevitably, however, comedy does involve the presentation of characters 'wie sie *nicht* sein sollen', although the comedy of character in Weissenthurn's plays is largely confined to certain stock roles, such as the occasional comic servants with their set phrases reminiscent of the many similar characters of the suburban theatres: the all-knowing, slightly cheeky Paul in *Liebe und Entsagung*; the drunken Christian in *Beschämte Eifersucht*. Similar in conception, if not exactly servants, are: Guthmann, the friend of the family in *Die Erben*, with his standard phrase 'Ein guter Kerl bin ich, aber ...' ['I'm a good chap, but...']; the timid sister Martha and cousin Gürge in *Es spukt*; or the verbose inspector in *Die Ehescheuen*. The use of such characters is, however, confined to the earliest plays (before 1810).

In general, presentation of characters was not Weissenthurn's strong point, and there is some justification for Hebenstreit's criticism in the *Modenzeitung* (9 May 1816) that there is a lack of depth in the character portrayal. Instead, the principal type of comedy in the plays is that of situation, at times somewhat contrived, as in the example of *Es spukt* referred to earlier, or in the mock court martial to which Wolken is subjected in *Die Radikalkur*. In Act III of *Welche ist die Braut?* the potentially, and in part genuinely, witty presentation of the maliciously gossiping women at the soirée degenerates into farce and slapstick as the noble Räthin Sommer is barged off the sofa.[31] More successful is the situation that develops in *Das letzte Mittel* as Graf Sonnstett, in his annoyance at what he considers Baronin Waldhüll's independent and unacceptable behaviour, decides to marry Ida; but his failure to look at her as he praises her qualities belies his words, and the eagerness with which he approves of her lack of ability at dancing and languages underlines the stupidity of his rejection of the more accomplished Baronin Waldhüll:

> GRAF. So tanzt sie wohl auch nicht?
> DÜTHELM. Nie, um sich dadurch einige Auszeichnung zu erwerben.
> GRAF. Vortrefflich!
> DÜTHELM. Sie spricht wohl einige Sprachen –
> GRAF. Ich verlange nur eine, die Sprache des *Herzens*.
> DÜTHELM. Aber sie sucht darin keinen Ruhm, die fremde Sprache besser, als ihre eigene zu sprechen.
> GRAF. Mein Ideal! Mein Ideal! Herrlich, vortrefflich, alle meine Wünsche sind erfüllt!
> DÜTHELM. Die Einfachheit meiner Tochter –
> GRAF. Ist das, was ich suche, sie macht mein Glück. In der großen Welt ist das nicht mehr zu finden. (Act II, Scene 4)

> [COUNT. So she doesn't dance either?
> DÜTHELM. Never in order to acquire some mark of distinction.
> COUNT. Excellent!
> DÜTHELM. She does speak some languages –
> COUNT. I demand only one, the language of the *heart*.
> DÜTHELM. But she does not seek praise for speaking the foreign language better than her own.
> COUNT. My ideal! My ideal! Wonderful, excellent, all my wishes are fulfilled!
> DÜTHELM. My daughter's simplicity –
> COUNT. Is what I am looking for, it will guarantee my happiness. It is something one can no longer find in the world outside.]

The baroness, meanwhile, pretends she is to marry Gluthen to make Sonnstett jealous, but her scheme has the opposite effect, as Sonnstett resolves even more firmly to marry Ida. Gluthen, who wants to marry Ida, finds himself having to go along with Waldhüll's scheme and, while desperately hoping that the charade can be brought to an end, he in fact plays his part so well that the baroness mistakenly suspects that he may be in love with her.

In *Beschämte Eifersucht*, Marie's and Julie's long-lost brother, Werthen, has returned home incognito and tries various ploys to cure Marie's husband and Julie's fiancé of their extreme jealousy; for example, declaring his love for Marie when he knows that the two men are hiding in another part of the garden house. In turn, Solm and Walling are convinced that Werthen is involved with their respective partners, but their desire for satisfaction is frustrated by Werthen having returned from the war with his wounded arm in a sling, while their insistence on their confidence in their partners' honour is undermined by the fact that their over-suspicious natures have caused them to spy on Marie and Julie. In *Liebe und Entsagung*, the fathers of Fritz and Julie are convinced that the two are in love and are so concerned with their desire to seal the engagement that they fail to notice that Julie has fainted at the mention of a wedding because she is in love with someone else:

> STEIN. ¯ ... Ja, Fräulein, Hochzeit mit meinem Friz!
> JUL[IE]. (*erschrickt*).
> STEIN. Nun, was hast du denn da zu erschrecken?... – Ich weiß nicht, wo ich vor Freude bin. (*Er nimmt sie in die Arme, sie bleibt mit dem Gesicht auf seiner Schulter liegen*). So eine Schwiegertochter in meinen alten Tagen. Habe ich dir nicht gesagt, mit so fröhlichen Dingen müsse man nicht zaudern? – siehst du, daß sie sich freut? (*will ihr den Kopf aufrichten und sieht, daß sie ohnmächtig ist*). Alle Teufel! was ist das? (Act I, Scene 12)

> [STEIN. Yes, young lady, marriage to my Fritz!
> JULIE. (*startled*).
> STEIN. Now what have you got to be frightened about? ... I'm so happy, I hardly know what I'm doing. (*He takes her in his arms, she remains with her face on his shoulder*) A daughter-in-law like this at my time of life. Didn't I tell you one mustn't hesitate in such happy matters? – can you tell how happy she is? (*tries to lift her head and sees that she has fainted*) The devil! What's happened?]

Particularly ingenious is the comedy of the one-act play *Das Frühstück*, in which two friends, Giesbach and Wilhelm, find themselves each trying to entertain guests in their own room while acting as butler for the friend next door. The play is not original, however, being derived from an unnamed and unidentifiable French source, and the same applies to a number of Weissenthurn's plays, the earliest ones in particular.[32]

Not surprisingly in plays written with performance as the overriding consideration, there is a certain amount of ironic reference to theatrical matters. In *Das Nachspiel*, Baron Berg complains that actors cannot capture the conversational tone of his plays, but either shout or lisp (II, 165); a similar point is intended by the rejection of natural styles of acting by the guests at the soirée in *Welche ist die Braut?* who demand an exaggerated style of declamation that is demonstrated to comic effect by the performance of Frau Impfen. The same play satirises people, such as Blümlein, who have to wait for the reviews to appear before deciding whether a play is good. In *Ein Mann hilft dem anderen* [One Man Helps Another], another character called Berg, this time a doctor,[33] suggests that Grillparzer's *Sappho* is so popular because it is about an ungrateful man (XV, 215). The second act of *Das Manuskript*, set at the office of a book publisher, provides ample scope for satire on the way the system encourages bad writing; the firm could not survive on the works of good writers alone. The scenes introduce various cameo roles, such as the would-be poet and admirer of Schiller who cannot get his ideas together to produce anything, or the newly ennobled Herr Giebel who wants to buy a library by the yard. The effect was obviously a positive one on stage, and the play had very favourable reviews, the second act being singled out for praise by the critic in *Der Sammler*.[34] The impression today, however, must be that the act is extremely episodic and has little to do with the main plot, a criticism that could also be levelled elsewhere, such as at the third act of *Welche ist die Braut?*, which, although an effective theatrical spectacle, is only loosely connected with the development of the plot.

In *Beschämte Eifersucht*, the drunken servant Christian is asked whether he has come alone, and replies that only the capon and the bottle of wine have accompanied him (II, 125); in *Das letzte Mittel* the baroness says of the glum looking Baron Gluthen, 'so sieht man wohl aus dem Ehestand heraus, aber nicht in den Ehestand hinein' ['that's the way you look when you are in a marriage, not the way of looking forward to one'] (XI, 19). Somewhat forced jokes of this kind are indicative of the generally uninspiring verbal humour in the comedies, as are the puns on 'einnehmend' and 'jemanden einnehmen' (*Die Erben*, III, 58), on 'verbitten' and 'verbieten' (*Beschämte Eifersucht*, II, 92), on 'Buchhalter' and 'jemandem die Bücher halten' (*Das Manuskript*, XIII, 27), and others along similar lines.[35] There are some passages of comic dialogue, as when Wunder in *Kindliche Liebe* cannot understand what he lacks as a suitor for Amalie:

> WUND[ER]. Welcher Vater wird mir und meinem Gelde seine Tochter abschlagen?
> MUTTER. Ihnen Jeder – Ihrem Gelde Wenige.
> WUND. Warum? was fehlt mir?
> MUTTER. Fehlen? Nichts! Im Gegentheil, Sie haben an Geld und Jahren zu viel. (I, 23)

> [WUNDER. What father can deny his daughter me and my money?
> MOTHER. You: any one – your money: very few.
> WUNDER. Why? What do I lack?
> MOTHER. Lack? Nothing! On the contrary, you have too much, both money and age.]

In *Das letzte Mittel*, the loquacious gossip, Frau von Silben, is reduced to the monosyllabic 'Wie, der? Sie? Du?' by the apparent news that the baroness and the baron are to marry (XI, 41). Despite the lack of comic verbal fireworks, however, the dialogue and construction of amusing situations are well handled, even if the sometimes rather implausible confusions and misunderstandings are maintained longer than necessary. Equally, with the occasional exception, such as Albertine in *Das Manuskript*, the sentimental language of the more serious plays and the tear-drenched pathos of Kotzebue's plays, such as *Menschenhaß und Reue* [Misanthropy and Regret] or *Die Jäger* [The Hunters], are mercifully avoided in Weissenthurn's comedies.

Despite the author's comments in her letter of 1807 to the *Sonntagsblatt*, her work received some considerable praise on occasions. Even before her comments, the *Allgemeines Theaterjournal* in 1806 had considered *Die Versöhnung* to be a masterpiece, apart from a few minor faults, and looked forward with enthusiasm to her next play.[36] In March 1826 the *Modenzeitung* wrote of her considerable contributions to the theatre, particularly in the realm of comedy (though in reviewing a play (*Burg Gölding*) that it considered not one of her best), and in November of that year the same journal was fulsome in its praise of *Das Manuskript*, not least for its well-chosen theme, its 'geregelter Gang, lebenvolle Situation, [...] gesunde Moral' ['regular construction, lively situation, healthy message'], and rejected all suggestions that women should not become writers, claiming that their depth of feeling made them ideally suited for certain types of writing, especially comedy, an area in which German literature was virtually barren.[37] The impressive construction of the plot and intrigue was underlined in other reviews of *Das Manuskript* (*Theaterzeitung*, 16 November 1826), and also of *Das letzte Mittel* (*Modenzeitung*, 3 October 1820). Reviewers frequently commented on the theatrical effectiveness of her works and on the way that the audience's attention was retained,[38] though also indicating that, at times, the action and characters were tailored too much to fit particular actors and actresses.[39] Not surprisingly, perhaps, the journals were full of praise as the dramatist took her leave of the stage in 1842: according to Emanuel Straube, writing in the *Modenzeitung* of 7 March 1842, 'als Schauspielerinn und Dichterinn hat Johanna Weißenthurn einen vollen Kranz verdient' ['as actress and as dramatist Johanna Weissenthurn has deserved the highest praise']. Over the years, a degree of consensus was reached on which were her best plays: comedies such as *Beschämte Eifersucht*, *Welche ist die Braut?*, *Das letzte Mittel* and *Das Manuskript* received generally favourable reviews and continued to be singled out for commendation,[40] together with plays not considered here, such as *Pauline* and *Der Wald bei Hermannstadt*.

For a number of years after her retirement, her work continued to be performed. In 1847, the year of her death and the year before the turmoil of the March revolution, the *Theaterzeitung* reported (22–24 May 1847) that many of her plays were still in the repertoire of numerous German theatres. In that year five of her plays were staged at the Burgtheater, including *Des Malers Meisterstück* [The Painter's Masterpiece] and *Pauline*, which continued in the repertoire until 1851 and 1853 respectively. *Das letzte Mittel* continued until 1865, appropriately perhaps in as much as it is one of her liveliest and more unusual comedies with a number of effective scenes. To claim too much more for Johanna von Weissenthurn could be seen as an exaggeration. As the *Theaterzeitung* and *Der Sammler*, in 1813, and the *Modenzeitung*, in 1816, all commented,[41] her plays were very much in keeping with the literary taste and fashions of the time, but the reviewers had doubts as to whether their appeal would be lasting. With their frequent failure to question traditional social structures, their generally positive picture of life, and their overall use of comedy as a pleasant means of escape from life's problems, rather than as a vehicle for confronting them, the plays certainly reflect the first decades of the century, the years in which the dramatist enjoyed her major successes; indeed, it is surprising that her plays survived as long as they did when competing with the more critical and satirical styles of Nestroy and Bauernfeld. As documents of the time, however, her plays are not without interest. The reviewer in the *Theaterzeitung* of 1826 suggested that, in various aspects, her plays were superior to those of Iffland and Kotzebue;[42] and while to the modern theatre-goer or critic that might seem an example of damning with faint praise, one may at the very least argue that she does not deserve to have been condemned to a greater degree of literary oblivion than those writers. With her instinct for creating comic and dramatically effective situations and scenes, with her sound grasp of realistic dialogue that avoids the sentimental excesses of contemporaries such as Kotzebue, but also with her presentation in a number of her plays of independent female characters of intellect and good sense, who challenge the prevailing image of woman and who in turn draw on her own experiences as a female writer defending her right to participate in a field which she no doubt justifiably saw as male-dominated, her plays and career deserve more attention than they have hitherto received.

Notes

1. Some early sources give two different days in 1773 as her date of birth.
2. Karl Goedeke, *Grundriß zur Geschichte der deutschen Dichtung*, Vol XI, 2 (Düsseldorf, ²1953), pp. 90–99. See also Joseph Kürschner, *Allgemeine Deutsche Biographie*, Vol. 7 (Leipzig, 1878), pp. 276–77; *Deutsches Literatur-Lexikon*, founded by W. Kosch, Vol. 5 (Bern, 1978), columns 481–82. The 1935 edition of Brockhaus still accords her an entry, the 1957 edition does not.
3. Elisabeth Friedrichs, *Die deutschsprachigen Schriftstellerinnen des 18. und 19. Jahrhunderts* (Stuttgart, 1981), p. 86; Gisela Brinker-Gabler, Karola Ludwig, Angela Wöffen, *Lexikon deutschsprachiger Schriftstellerinnen 1800–1945* (Munich, 1986); Elke Frederiksen, *Women Writers of Germany, Austria and Switzerland* (New York, 1989).
4. W. E. Yates, *Theatre in Vienna. A Critical History, 1776–1995* (Cambridge, 1996), p. 54.
5. Eva Geber, Sonja Rotter, Marietta Schneider (eds), *Die Frauen Wiens* (Vienna, 1992). See especially the sections on actresses by Elisabeth Mattes (pp. 64–77) and on women writers by Eva Mattes (pp. 215–24); the latter specifically emphasises (p. 215) that she will not restrict herself to women actually born in Vienna.
6. Carl Ludwig Costenoble, *Aus dem Burgtheater 1818–1837*, 2 vols (Vienna, 1889), I, 103 (6 November 1820); I, 284–85 (13 January 1824).
7. Costenoble, II, 232 (8 June 1835), II, 336 (2 June 1837).
8. F[ranz] C[arl] Weidmann in *Theaterzeitung*, 22–24 May 1847 (no. 122/123), pp. 488–89.
9. *Wiener Theater-Kritik*, 2, 1800 (no. 6), pp. 16–21.
10. Schreyvogel's *Donna Diana*, an adaptation of Moreto's *El desdén, con el desdén*, achieved exactly the same number of performances, and his adaptation of

Schlegel's translation of *Romeo and Juliet* 111. Kotzebue's *Die deutschen Kleinstädter* had 130 performances between 1802 and 1855, the same dramatist's *Das Intermezzo* 134 between 1808 and 1847 but, for most other productions at the Burgtheater, fifty to seventy performances were a sign of considerable success. During the first quarter of the century, productions of·*Macbeth, Egmont, Tasso* and *Fiesco* fell considerably short of such numbers.

11. A dozen venues are listed for a number of other plays.
12. *Der Sammler*, 27 May 1813 (no. 84), p. 336.
13. Most of the plays are in the manuscript collection of the Austrian National Library. The manuscript collection in the 'Stadt- und Landesbibliothek' in Vienna holds a hand-written version of just one play, *Johann Herzog von Friedland*, together with a number of her letters to and from fellow actors, such as Julie and Ludwig Löwe.
14. References to Weissenthurn's plays are to volume and page in the overall sequence (details of the editions are given in the previous paragraph); act and scene numbers are given for longer quotations.
15. Richard Smekal, *Ferdinand Raimunds Lebensdokumente* (Vienna, 1920), p. 49.
16. For an examination of the endings of Viennese comedies of the period, see my article 'Raimunds Dramenschlüsse und die Tradition des Wiener Volkstheaters', *Nestroyana*, 10 (1990), pp. 4–22.
17. *Das Sonntagsblatt*, 28 June 1807 (no. 20), pp. 358–64 (p. 359).
18. *Wiener Zeitschrift für Kunst, Literatur, Theater und Mode* (henceforth referred to as *Modenzeitung*), 15 February 1820 (no. 20), pp. 158–60.
19. *Der Sammler*, 12 February 1820 (no. 19), p. 75; 7 December 1813 (no. 195), p. 780.
20. *Modenzeitung*, 9 May 1816 (no. 19), pp. 176–79.
21. *Modenzeitung*, 3 October 1820 (no. 119), p. 1011.
22. *Der Sammler*, 31 January 1813 (no. 18), p. 72.
23. Anton's mother in *Die Jäger*, for example, or Frau Ruhberg in *Verbrechen aus Ehrsucht*. See also Karl Heinz Klingenberg, *Iffland und Kotzebue als Dramatiker* (Weimar, 1962), p. 69.
24. Eda Sagarra, *A Social History of Germany* (London, 1977), p. 413.
25. See Ute Frevert, *Women in German History* (Oxford, 1989), esp. pp. 11–21, 31–37, 63–72; Helga Kraft, Elke Liebs (eds), *Mütter — Töchter — Frauen. Weiblichkeitsbilder in der Literatur* (Stuttgart, 1993), esp. pp. 59, 73.
26. Willi Geismeier, *Biedermeier* (Leipzig, n.d.), p. 49.
27. Frevert, op. cit, pp. 17f., 34.
28. *Modenzeitung*, 3 October 1820 (no. 119), p. 1011.
29. A variation on this motif, which is found in the historical plays and 'Schauspiele' (e.g. *Pauline*), is the man attracted by the simple girl who conveniently turns out to be of noble or royal stock.
30. Paul Alfred Merbach, 'Zwei Aufsätze von Johanna Franul von Weissenthurn', *Jahrbuch der Grillparzer-Gesellschaft*, 24 (1913), pp. 211–24 (p. 224).
31. The reviewer in *Der Sammler* (31 January 1813 (no. 18), p. 72) found the scene 'abscheulich ... abstoßend' and not appropriate for the court theatre.
32. To examine the various sources and inspirations for the comedies, some of which are acknowledged, would not be feasible within the scope of this article; obvious German influences are Iffland and Kotzebue, while contemporary French sources which are acknowledged are Alexandre Vincent Pineux-Duval and Benoît Pelletier-Volméranges, to whom could be added dramatists from the previous century, such as Dancourt and Marivaux.
33. Like many other dramatists of the time, Weissenthurn was not particularly inventive with the names of characters: there is more than one Berg, Fritz, Albertine, and a considerable number of Julies, Amalies, Maries.

34. *Der Sammler*, 16 November 1826 (no. 137), p. 548.
35. Puns, by their very nature, cannot be translated, and I have not attempted to do so.
36. *Allgemeines Theaterjournal*, 1806 (no. 2), p. 130.
37. *Modenzeitung*, 2 March 1826 (no. 26), pp. 199–200; 18 November 1826 (no. 138), pp. 1110–11.
38. *Modenzeitung*, 3 October 1820 (no. 119), p. 1011–12; 2 March 1826 (no. 26), p. 200.
39. *Der Sammler*, 31 January 1813 (no. 18), p. 72; *Modenzeitung*, 9 May 1816 (no. 19), p. 178.
40. See *Theaterzeitung*, 28 January 1813, 16 November 1826, 22–24 May 1847; *Modenzeitung*, 3 October 1820, 18 November 1826; *Der Sammler*, 31 January 1813, 7 October 1820, 16 November 1826, 5 March 1842; Costenoble, I, 98, 284–85.
41. *Theaterzeitung*, 28 January 1813; *Der Sammler*, 30 January 1813; *Modenzeitung*, 9 May 1816.
42. *Theaterzeitung*, 16 May 1826 (no. 58), p. 234.

Nestroy and Schiller

Peter Branscombe[1]

The art of quotation for satirical and parodistic purposes is almost as old as literature itself. Not all deliberate quotation is satirical; it can, of course, also convey respect, or it can seek to support a point with the weight of received authority. As I shall hope to show, there is something of all three of these attitudes behind Nestroy's use of quotations taken from the works of Friedrich Schiller, though the satiric and parodistic elements dominate, and even the apparently most respectful have an ironic edge. Although this article examines Nestroy's use of quotations from the plays and poems of Schiller, it should be pointed out that the latter was by no means the only target for Nestroy's shafts, even if he was the principal one almost throughout Nestroy's career. On occasion he also turned his satirical and parodistic attention to the popular minor dramatists of his day, opera composers great and small, and the major contemporary German-language dramatists Hebbel (in *Judith und Holofernes* (1849)) and Grillparzer (in *Theaterg'schichten durch Liebe, Intrigue, Geld und Dummheit* (1854) [Theatre Tales of Love, Intrigue, Money and Stupidity]); even Goethe was not entirely safe from Nestroy's mild mockery.[2]

Schiller had already suffered parodistic treatment at the hands of Viennese dramatists before Nestroy's time, though, in contradistinction to the latter's concentration in his comedies on salient speeches or stage action taken from Schiller, Nestroy's predecessors had attempted to mock entire plays. Often the comedy extended little further than a trivialising title – Gleich's *Fiesko der Salamikrämer* [Fiesco the Salami Dealer], aimed at the 'republican tragedy' *Die Verschwörung des Fiesco zu Genua* [The Conspiracy of Fiesco at Genoa]; Bäuerle's *Maria Stuttgartin* (mocking Schiller's *Maria Stuart*) – or the localisation to a Viennese setting, as with Herzenskron's *Die Jungfrau von Wien* [The Maid of Vienna], and Told's *Johanna Dalk, oder Die Jungfrau von Oberlans* [Johanna the Fathead, or the Maid of Oberlans] aimed at Schiller's *Die Jungfrau von Orleans* [The Maid of Orleans]. Of the ten or twelve identifiable Viennese parodistic versions of Schiller plays in the first half of the nineteenth century, only one achieved any measure of popularity, Adolf Bäuerle's *Kabale und Liebe* [Cabal and Love], keeping Schiller's title, which, with music by Joseph Drechsler, was performed thirty-five times in the principal comic

58

theatre, that in the Leopoldstadt suburb, between 1827 and 1838. This was the only Schiller parody in which Nestroy acted; he played the hero, Ferdinand, 'Kadett bei der Stadtguardi' ['Cadet in the Town Militia'] on two occasions in Graz in 1829 and 1830.

In Nestroy's day, the works of Schiller were widely performed and read, and were generally available; any young person of good education was almost bound from an early age to have been made more or less familiar with several of the plays and poems. We know little about Nestroy's exposure to literature at school or at home, but it is reasonable to assume that his later and frequent resort to phrases taken from Schiller, sometimes with departures from the text that suggest faulty memory rather than the deliberate distortion that he often allowed himself for comic effect, had its basis in knowledge acquired during his boyhood. There are just two references to Schiller in the Nestroy letters that survive, neither of much relevance in the present context. The letter (to Moriz Bermann) of 16 January 1858 merely lists Schiller's *Maria Stuart* as one of the plays to be performed in the Carltheater by a visiting Italian company.[3] And, in the letter written to his friend Ernst Stainhauser from Paris on 19 June 1858, Nestroy inverts King Philipp's observation to Posa in III, 10 of Schiller's *Don Carlos*, 'Ihr habt / Auf meinem Thron mich ausgefunden, Marquis. / Nicht auch in meinem Hause?' ['You have discovered me on my throne, Marquis. Not also in my house?'] (lines 3301–3) in a manner (use of the familiar 'du' for the more formal 'Ihr') that implies reliance on memory rather than on a checking of the text: 'Nun spreche ich zu Dir, als umgekehrter König Philipp, den Satz den dieser zu Marquis Posa spricht in umgekehrter Folge, "Du hast in meinem Hause mich ausgefunden, nicht auch auf meinem Throne"' (HKA, Briefe, p. 170); ['I shall say to you now, as inverted King Philipp, the sentence that he speaks in inverted order to Marquis Posa, "You have discovered me in my house, not also on my throne"'].

A problem that will be familiar to anyone who has read much Nestroy, or who has experienced his work in the theatre, is the feeling that a phrase, or a piece of stage business, is more familiar than the context in which it currently occurs; for anyone attempting to analyse Nestroy's plays in detail, let alone edit them, that problem is magnified. The critical apparatus in the old standard Nestroy edition (SW) was almost inevitably inconsistent in the thoroughness with which individual plays were treated; some volumes contain a considerable quantity of valuable information about variant readings, reception, and especially explanatory notes covering references and quotations; other volumes show every sign of having been hastily edited, and with restrictions imposed by the publisher limiting the number of pages, with consequent reduction in notes and other editorial material. The new complete edition (HKA) is exemplary in the thoroughness of its editorial principles and techniques. Even here, though, it happens from time to time that the editor of a particular play has not succeeded in identifying every literary or intellectual borrowing such as would probably have been spotted by a well-informed Viennese contemporary of Nestroy.

Specifically with Nestroy's quodlibets – musical numbers comprising usually brief quotations from works then in vogue (popular songs as well as operas, singspiels and farces) – the problem of identification can be daunting. Adolph Müller, the composer who supplied the music for most of Nestroy's plays, has been frequently blessed by modern-day commentators for his habit of identifying the source by a word or two entered in the score at the start of each new snippet; where this labelling is absent, the problems become serious – the words sung can be subtly, or drastically, different from their original, and, where an opera was familiar to Nestroy's audiences through German translation (often free adaptation) of the original French or Italian text, the problem for the late twentieth-century academic can prove insurmountable.

With a literary figure of the stature and continued familiarity of Schiller, the problems are – at least in theory – far less daunting. All that is required is an excellent knowledge of Schiller's *œuvre*, specifically of the dramas and poems; mercifully for the scholar, Nestroy seems almost entirely to have ignored Schiller's historical and philosophical writings.[4]

Nestroy's early years as an actor, before he began to specialise in comic roles, saw him take a range of mainly minor parts in Schiller's plays. It is worth listing them, because his later quotations come most frequently from plays of which he had direct experience (by no means all such quotations are taken from the speeches of the characters he played; anyone with experience of amateur dramatics will be familiar with the ease with which lines, even whole speeches, of other characters become part of one's own stock-in-trade of quotations).

Nestroy's first recorded performance in a Schiller role was as Gessler in *Wilhelm Tell* at Brünn on 28 December 1825; his last was with two tiny roles in *Wilhelm Tell* on 6 January 1836. Table 1 (overleaf) lists his performances in his various Schiller parts.[5]

This amounts to ten roles in six plays by Schiller (in the case of *Turandot* and *Macbeth*, by Schiller as adapter); the total number of Nestroy's performances in these roles is a modest thirty, and, because he played three of these roles just once, it is easy to imagine that learning the parts was a waste of his time. But that is to misunderstand the circumstances of the age when, particularly in theatres in small towns, the audience expected a different play most nights, and plays that did not draw were swiftly removed from the company's repertory. A further point that needs to be made is that a minor role, such as 'eine Magistratsperson' (altered by the censor from Schiller's original *Pater*, or priest) in *Die Räuber*, was treated by directors such as Karl Carl, and actors, such as Nestroy and Wenzel Scholz, as a comic role.

The actor, Franz Wallner, tells in his memoirs[6] of a performance of *Wilhelm Tell* that must have caused Schiller to turn in his grave:

> In der bekannten dritten Szene des dritten Aktes erschien Nestroy als
> Frießhart mit einem riesigen Barte, Scholz als Leuthold mit glattem
> Gesicht, knallroten Backen und über den Augen zwei schwarzen,
> kurzen, dicken, aufrechtstehenden Wülsten, welche die Brauen

60

vorstellen sollten. Mit steinernem Ernste, der umso drastischer wirken mußte, nahmen die Söldlinge Tell – von Wilhelm Kunst dargestellt – gefangen, "weil er dem Hut nicht Reverenz erwiesen".[7]

[In the familiar third scene of Act III Nestroy appeared as Friesshart[8] with a huge beard, and Scholz as Leuthold with close-shaven face, bright red cheeks and, above his eyes, two black, short, thick, upward-pointing bulges to represent his eyebrows. With stony faces, which only emphasised the exaggerated seriousness of their actions, the mercenaries arrested Tell – played by Wilhelm Kunst – 'for failing to show respect to the [governor's] hat'.]

By constantly repeating their lines about Tell's lack of respect for the hat, and thereby breaking the flow of the scene and causing gales of laughter in the audience, Scholz and Nestroy wished to persuade the theatre director to

Table 1

Play	Role	Place	Dates
Wilhelm Tell	Gessler	Brünn	1825: 28, 30 Nov., 21 Dec.
	Fürst	Graz	1828: 2 March, 16 April, 9 May
	Leuthold, ein Söldner	ThadW[a]	1833: 24 June, 21 Aug.
			1835: 17 June, 2 Aug., 16 Nov.
			1836: 6 Jan.
	Frießhardt, ein Söldner		1834: 3 Nov.
			1835: 17 June, 16 Nov.
			1836: 6 Jan.
Maria Stuart	Burleigh	Brünn	1826: 21 Feb.
	Paulet	Graz	1829: 28 May
Die Räuber	Magistratsperson	Graz	1827: 6 Jan., 29 June
			1828: 23 April
			1829: 30 Dec.
		Pressburg	1830: 27 April
		ThadW[a]	1832: 29 June
			1833: 28 Jan., 11 March, 14 Aug.
Turandot[b]	Pantalon	Graz	1827: 21 Nov.
Die Jungfrau von Orleans	Lionel	Graz	1828: 20 April
Macbeth[b]	Rosse [Ross]	Pressburg	1831: 5 Feb.

[a] ThadW = Theater an der Wien
[b] as revised by Schiller

relieve them of the task of playing such roles in serious dramas; they were punished by the director, but thereafter were not employed in roles of this kind. We should beware of taking this report as the literal truth – Friedrich Kaiser[9] and Heinrich Börnstein[10] tell differing versions of it – but it is reasonable to assume that, by the time he had established himself as the principal comic actor (and dramatist) in Carl's company in the early 1830s, Nestroy regarded himself as above playing minor roles in serious plays; as the above table shows, he ceased to perform in plays by Schiller after January 1836.

At this inevitably imperfect stage in the documentation of Schiller quotations in Nestroy's plays, one can suggest only a limited concordance between the appearance of such quotations and Nestroy's knowledge of them derived from his own performances in Schiller plays. The quotations from Schiller's poetry, of course, indicate Nestroy's reading knowledge of the verse, or his recall of quotations acquired from early exposure to it. Here, too, his reliance on memory, rather than on direct reference to an edition of Schiller's texts, is sometimes suggested by small departures from the authentic wording, though deliberate distortion for satirical and parodistic reasons cannot be excluded; and, in the case of Nestroy's memorising based on his theatrical experience, the variant versions then in vogue in Vienna may be responsible for departures from Schiller.

Nestroy the dramatist began very early in his career to make use of quotations from, and references to, Schiller. If we accept the likely dating of 1827 for *Prinz Friedrich* (HKA, *Stücke 1*, 357) and consider it before *Der Zettelträger Papp* [Bill-sticker Papp], following the order chosen by Friedrich Walla for the new *Historisch-kritische Ausgabe* of Nestroy's works, we find two possible allusions to Schiller plays: in I, 3 Wachtendonck quotes verbatim an axiom of Hippocrates that served Schiller as motto to *Die Räuber*: 'Quae medicamenta non sanant, ferrum sanat, quae ferrum non sanat, ignis sanat' ['What medicines do not cure, is cured by iron, what iron does not cure, is cured by fire']; and in III, 10 Theodor seems to be recalling Wallenstein's 'Schnell fertig ist die Jugend mit dem Wort, / Das schwer sich handhabt, wie des Messers Schneide' ['Youth is quick with the word, which is as hard to handle as the knife's blade'][11] in his rather lame assertion: 'Die Jugend urteilt schnell, und mit geläuf'ger Zunge verdammt sie' ['Youth is quick to judge, and with rapid tongue to condemn'].

Inconclusive as these identifications may be, there is no doubt about the Schillerian references in the little dramatic prelude about the bill-sticker, which was first given on 15 December of the same year – even though this is even less of a strictly original product of Nestroy than usual. Subtitled on the playbill of the première 'Neue dramatische Kleinigkeit, verbunden mit einem beliebten Quodlibet, als scherzhafte Einleitung zu dieser Vorstellung [...]' ['New dramatic trifle, combined with a well-loved Quodlibet, as playful prelude to this performance'], Nestroy's adaptation of Hermann Herzenskron's *Die Heirat durch die Pferdekomödie* [Marriage by Horse-comedy], which was available to Nestroy through manuscripts of Ferdinand Raimund's adaptation,[12] contains numerous comic allusions to Schiller. Nestroy declined to take over

Papp's misattribution of 'die "Glocken" von Göthen' [' "The Bells" by Goethe'), the ' "Jungfrau von Orleans" von Schickmirsbier' [i.e. 'Shakespeare'], the mention of the ' "Braut von Messing" von Lessing' ["'The Bride of Brass" by Lessing'],[13] and the reference to 'der Schillerer, von dem die "Kabbala und Lieb" ist' ['The Dazzler, author of "Kabbala and Love" ']; indeed, though there are still numerous traces of the older comedy of insufficiency, such as malapropisms and puns, there are also signs of the subtler satirical comedy that we associate with the mature Nestroy. As Friedrich Walla makes clear in his edition of *Papp*, there are two versions of Nestroy's text extant, plus part of a third, which were intended to introduce different main plays in the evening's programme. As far as the Schiller references are concerned, they offer interesting variants.

The first Nestroy version ('Fassung A' in HKA, *Stücke 1*) introduced Louis Angely's *Zwölf Mädchen in Uniform* [Twelve Girls in Uniform] – the number of girls frequently varied – which provided Nestroy with a new role, that of the invalided old soldier, Sansquartier, that he played longer than any other in his career. When, in the second scene of *Der Zettelträger Papp*, the major-domo conveys to the touring company's bill-sticker that his gracious lady favours plays in which a woman of their own day appears in a heroic role, Papp says that, if only he had known sooner, he would have adapted *Die Jungfrau von Orleans* to her taste: 'Man läßt den Dunois im Frak spielen, der Talbot stirbt im Schlafrok, und Phillip dem Guten zieht man einen monotonen Spenzer an, dann kann sich kein Mensch darüber aufhalten, wenn die Johanna d'Arc in der Grenadier-Mützen kommt.' ['You let Dunois wear a frock coat, Talbot dies in his night-shirt, and you dress Phillip the Good in a monotone spencer, then no one can complain when Joan of Arc comes in wearing a grenadier's cap'] (HKA, *Stücke 1*, 98/19–23).[14] The major-domo interjects that it is unforgivable to alter Schiller, but Papp refuses to be silenced:

> Die Schillerischen Stück haben alle durch die Bank einen schlechten Schluß. Z.B. nehmen wir den "Don Carlos". "Ich habe das meinige gethan, thun Sie das Ihrige." Ist das ein Ausgang für ein honettes Stück? Nach meiner Bearbeitung heirathet der Don Carlos die Prinzessin Eboli; Herzog Alba macht den Brautführer, und die Marquisin von Montican, die sie im 2. Act nach Frankreich fortschummeln, die kommt als Kranzeljungfer zurück. Das ganze schließt mit einem fröhlichen Auto-Kaffée. (p. 98)

> [All Schiller's plays have an unhappy ending. Take *Don Carlos* for example: 'I have done my duty, now do yours.' Is that a fitting conclusion for an honest play? In my arrangement Don Carlos marries Princess Eboli; Duke Alba gives away the bride, and the Marchioness of Montican,[15] whom they send packing to France in Act II, comes back as bridesmaid. The whole ends with a jolly auto-café [i.e. *auto-da-fé*].]

Papp hasn't finished with Schiller yet: in place of Wallenstein's curtain-line, 'Ich denke einen langen Schlaf zu tun' ['I intend to have a long sleep'], which Papp is sure will encourage the audience to nod off, he plans something much more exciting: 'Bei mir reitet der Wallenstein am Schluß in Wien als Courier ein, und bringt 's Extra-blattl, daß die Schweden geschlagen sind. Das ist doch ganz ein anderer Ausgang?' ['In my version Wallenstein rides into Vienna as a courier at the end of the play and distributes the stop-press news that the Swedes have been defeated. That's a quite different conclusion, isn't it?']. *Die Verschwörung des Fiesco* is not spared either: no conspiracy there for Papp, 'das Stück schließt mit der Privat-Komedie, die der Fiesko gibt, wobei sich die Familien Doria und Lavagna ungeheuer blamieren. – So wird doch der Schluß komisch; da müssen die Stück einen Effect machen.' ['the play ends with home dramatics put on by Fiesco, in which the Doria and Lavagna families disgrace themselves on a grand scale. – In that way the ending becomes comic; the plays are bound to be effective.']

The second Nestroy version of *Papp* ('Fassung B') was intended to introduce a performance by a company of acrobats ('indianisch-equilibristische Kunstvorstellungen' – 'Performances by Indian balancing artists'). Papp proudly informs the major-domo that he has arranged a few Schiller plays for the Indians:

> Zum Beyspiel, im "Wallenstein", da wird aufgezogen, da sieht man, wie der Wallenstein, auf einem schmalen Brett [...] zwischen Recht und Unrecht hin und her balanciert. Endlich macht er einen Salto mortale von der Unterthans-Pflicht, bis zur Verrätherey hinüber, weil er aber statt einer ordentlichen Balancierstange, nur ein dalkets astrologisches Zauberstaberl in der Hand hat, so fällt er grad bey der böhmischen Gränz auf die Nasen. (HKA, *Stücke 1*, 99/28–37)

> [For example, in *Wallenstein* the curtain rises to reveal Wallenstein standing on a narrow plank and balancing right and wrong this way and that. Finally he makes a somersault from submissive duty to treachery but, because instead of a proper balancing-pole he has only a stupid little magician's wand in his hand, he takes a tumble on his nose, right by the Bohemian frontier.]

Similar indignities are wished on *Don Carlos*, with King Philip wobbling on the swaying tightrope of his own mistrust. Some of Papp's notions here will strike a modern reader as far-fetched and not very funny, but the playbill-sticker should be granted the last word: 'Wissen Sie ich hab das Ganze mystisch behandelt [...]' ['D'you know, I've treated the whole thing mystically'].

In I, 4 of *Dreyßig Jahre aus dem Leben eines Lumpen* [Thirty Years from the Life of a Scoundrel],[16] the principal character, Longinus, wittily distorts *Don Carlos*, at the same time steering clear of the censor's possible objection to the reference to God: 'O Vater, das Leben ist doch schön' ['O father, life is indeed beautiful'] (cf. *Don Carlos*, where Posa ends IV, 21 with the line: 'O Gott! das Leben ist doch schön'). In II, 5 the same character refers specifically to Schiller when quoting the familiar last line from the prologue to *Wallensteins Lager*: 'der Schiller hat ganz recht: "Ernst ist das Leben, heiter ist die Kunst."'

['Schiller is quite right: "Life is serious, Art is joyous"'].

A distinct category is Nestroy's occasional quotation from Schiller poems; here, of course, there can be no dramatic parallel situation, though the use of a serious axiom in an inappropriate or directly comic context can achieve a similar effect. An early example occurs in *Der Tod am Hochzeitstag* [Death at the Wedding] (1829), where Dappschädel's monologue after his entry-song (I, 10) opens with the lines:

> Auch ich war in Arkadien gebohren, aber im Land des Glücks habn s' mir den Laufpaß gegeben, und jetzt fahr ich ohne dem Kompaß des Trostes auf'm schwarzen Meer des Kummers herum. Des Lebens May blüht einmal und nie wieder; mir hat er abgeblüht. (HKA, *Stücke 1*, 263/35–264/2)

> [I too was born in Arcady, but they've given me my marching orders from the land of happiness, and now I'm drifting around the black sea of grief without the compass of consolation. Life's May blooms once, and never again; for me its bloom is over.]

These lines are bound to remind the well-informed listener or reader of the opening of Schiller's Phantasy, 'Resignation': 'Auch ich war in Arkadien geboren, / Doch Tränen gab der kurze Lenz mir nur. // Des Lebens Mai blüht einmal und nicht wieder, / Mir hat er abgeblüht.' ['I too was born in Arcady, but tears were all that the brief spring gave me'].[17] The question of the extent to which Nestroy could rely on the powers of recognition of enough of his theatre audience to appreciate the comic point, and laugh, must remain unanswered; much the same is true of the quodlibets, though there the chances are that tunes would have been recognised as familiar, even where the precise point of the verbal and musical parody was not perceived; it was probably enough if the majority of the spectators responded on a more or less well-informed basis to the allusion that was being made; in other words, the text cited worked in differing ways for diffent sections of the audience.

We turn now to further examples of Schillerian verse occurring in a Nestroy play, this time from very late in his career, *Umsonst* (1857) [In Vain]. Nestroy wrote for himself the part of Pitzl, an ageing and third-rate actor, and gave Carl Treumann the role of the *jeune premier* that, in earlier years, he would have played. The first of the verse borrowings from Schiller is a familiar theatrical tag that need not necessarily have been associated by Nestroy directly with the Schiller source: in I,6 the brilliant young actor, Arthur, defends his hopes of marriage as no betrayal of the acting profession, which his colleagues had surmised it to be, but on the contrary as a potential enrichment of the stage:

> Im Gegenteil, wenn ich heirate, wird sich die mir angetraute talentvolle Dilettantin in eine wirkliche Priesterin Thaliens verwandeln, ich bereichere daher die Bühne um ein Mitglied, ungerechnet der möglichen künftigen Mitglieder, die aus dieser Künstlerehe den Brettern erblühen dürfen, die die Welt bedeuten. (HKA, *Stücke 35*, 14/21–26)

[On the contrary, when I marry, the talented dilettante betrothed to me will be transformed into a true priestess of Thalia, thus I shall enrich the stage by one member, not counting the possible future members who may spring from this artistic marriage to blossom on the boards that betoken the world.]

The reference here is to. Schiller's poem 'An die Freunde' [To the Friends], the final strophe of which contains the lines: 'Sehn wir doch das Große *aller* Zeiten / Auf den Brettern, die die Welt bedeuten, / Sinnvoll, still an uns vorübergehn' ['For we see the great deeds of all periods pass by in front of us on the boards that betoken the world'].

When Pitzl remarks that he would like to accompany his young friend and the latter's wife-to-be, Emma, into their uncertain future, he phrases it in a way that recalls the ballad 'Die Bürgschaft' [The surety]: 'du gehst mit deiner Geliebten in die Welt, und da möcht ich halt im Bunde der Dritte sein' ['you go off into the world with your beloved, and I should like to be the third in the alliance']; the echo here is to the final lines of the Schiller poem, where the tyrant is so impressed by the willingness to sacrifice himself of the young man who risks everything to redeem the friend who has stood surety for him, that he wishes to be admitted as their companion: 'So nehmet auch mich zum Genossen an, / Ich sei, gewährt mir die Bitte, / In eurem Bunde der Dritte' ['So take me as your companion, I should like to be, if you grant my request, the third in your alliance'].

The third quotation is remarkable for being immediately set off by a bathetic, emphatically non-Schillerian, rhyme. The Schiller poem is not especially familiar nowadays, and was perhaps equally unfamiliar in 1857, as Nestroy implies by his naming of the author – against his normal practice with borrowings. In I, 18 Arthur says to Emma, who has just agreed to elope with and marry him in spite of her guardian: 'Baue auf mich und auf Schiller, welcher sagt: "Uns führt ein kühner Schritt zum Traualtar, / Der Vormund fahrt sich selber in die Haar"' ['Put your trust in me and in Schiller, who says: "A bold step leads us to the bridal altar, your guardian will tear his hair out"']. The Schiller reference is to the long, satirical poem 'Die berühmte Frau' [The famous Woman], subtitled 'Epistel eines Ehemanns an einen andern' [Epistle of one married man to another], where the henpecked husband observes that things were different before their marriage: 'Das süße Wort: Ich liebe dich! / Sprach aus dem holden Augenpaare. / So führt ich sie zum Traualtare, / O wer war glücklicher als ich!' ['The sweet word: I love you! spoke from those precious eyes. So I led her to the bridal altar, oh who could be more fortunate than I!'] (lines 119–22).

The final quotation from Schiller's poetry in Act I comes at the beginning of the penultimate scene, where Pitzl observes: 'Man sagt nicht umsonst: "O, daß sie ewig grünen bliebe, / die gar so schöne Zeit der jungen Liebe"' ['One does not say in vain: "O, that it might for ever continue to flourish, the indeed so beautiful time of young love"']. This is a misquotation (due, it might at first be thought, to a faulty memory rather than to deliberate alteration) from 'Das Lied von der Glocke', where the lines read: 'O! daß sie ewig grünen bliebe, / Die schöne Zeit der jungen Liebe!' (lines 78–79).[18]

There is no obvious reason to account for the frequency of quotations in Act I of *Umsonst*. It may be that Nestroy, at this stage of his career, was more than usually dependent on the work of other authors so as to give substance to his own; a definitive answer to this question will have to wait until more evidence from Nestroy's middle years has been accumulated and evaluated. The large number of citations from drama, Schiller's in particular (not one of them is identified in either of the Rommel editions), may well be due to the theatrical context of this first Act, in which Pitzl is trying to salvage his career by learning his lines for a crucial forthcoming appearance in *Die Räuber*. This is the only role from Nestroy's long involvement with Schiller, other than the wash drawing of him in a tiny part in *Wilhelm Tell*,[19] of which a pictorial record is extant: a photograph by Hermann Klee from 1861 shows Nestroy immersing himself in his part as the hero's villainous brother, Franz Moor.[20]

I turn now to the quotations in Act I of *Umsonst* from Schiller's dramatic *œuvre*. To put these references in context, it must be pointed out that they are set alongside quotations from, or allusions to, several other dramatic works: Louis Angely's *Von sieben die Häßlichste* [The Ugliest of Seven], Pius Alexander Wolf's *Preziosa* (with music by Weber, one number of which is played and sung by the two women with dramatic relevance), Seybold's Hugo-based *Der Tyrann von Padua* [The Tyrant of Padua], Donizetti's opera *Belisario*, and Müllner's *Die Schuld* [Guilt]. There are a few other·as-yet unidentified quotations but they are almost certainly not from Schiller. The principal source from which Nestroy draws is *Die Räuber*, though earlier Schiller references are to the old actor Pitzl's execrable performance as Wurm in *Kabale und Liebe* on the previous evening, and to Arthur's 'Don Carlos Blicke' (the passionate glances that Arthur had cast towards Emma in her seat in the stalls during one of the troupe's earlier performances).

In Nestroy's own drafts for *Umsonst* (the only material for the play that survives in his hand), Pitzl is striving to learn his role for a forthcoming performance of *Richard III*; by the time of the final version, the play in question has been altered to Schiller's first drama. With increasingly brilliant appropriateness, Nestroy has Pitzl (who is rehearsing alone in Arthur's room in the left-hand half of the divided stage) speak phrases from the Schiller play that match the situation in the room on the right-hand side of the stage, where Arthur is trying to exchange loving glances and words with Emma, while attempting to conceal his intentions from Fräulein Anastasia Mispl, Emma's elderly foster-mother (who erroneously believes that Arthur is in love with her). Pitzl quotes from Franz Moor's speeches, thumbing back and forth through the play (thus ensuring the relevance of the quotations). By the time that Anastasia starts to take offence at Arthur's tone and grow angry with him, Pitzl has already uttered five exclamations of the evil Moor, including one that neatly unites his own two principal concerns, filling his stomach – there is a link here with the traditional gluttony of the popular comic character – and learning his next role: '"Mich deucht, ich hätte ein königliches Mahl gehalten" – Wenn <u>der</u> Traum ausginge, das wär mir das liebste vom ganzen Franz Moor.' (I, 15; cf. *Die Räuber*, V, 1). He then finds ideally appropriate lines from his part to project from the next room: 'Mich ergötzt der Grimm eines Weibes' (I, 15; cf. *Die Räuber*, III, 1) ['Woman's anger delights me'] and 'Du allein bist verworfen' (*Die Räuber*, V, 1) ['You alone are rejected']; these snippets are followed a minute later by two taken from the first scene of Schiller's Act V.

When, in I, 17, Arthur's uncle and guardian interviews Pitzl, who pretends to be Emma's beloved, the old actor continues to rely on Franz Moor's lines in his attempts to intimidate his visitor ('Ha, Schreck! Nichts widersteht dieses Giganten eiskalter Umarmung' ['Ha, terror! Nothing can resist this giant's ice-cold embrace'].[21] Much of the comedy of this scene arises from the contrast between genuine Schiller, heightened language such as an actor may affect ('Herr, noch einmal, was beaugapfeln Sie mich so penetrant?' ['Sir, once more, why do you stare at me so penetratingly?'], and down-to-earth emphasis on Pitzl's everyday concerns, principally his need for money. At the very end of the Act, Pitzl again quotes – seems to be quoting – from a Schiller play when he cries, refusing to be restrained by Finster from his pretence of trying to steal a kiss from Emma, 'Und kettete die Hölle sich an meine Fersen' ['And if hell itself were chained to my heels'].[22]

Schiller references and quotations also figure in the last play that Nestroy wrote, *Frühere Verhältnisse* (1861) [Earlier Circumstances];[23] as in *Umsonst* – and, of course, in *Theaterg'schichten durch Liebe, Intrige, Geld und Dummheit* – here, too, there is a link with the theatre, owing to the presence of the former actress, Peppi Amsel. *Die Jungfrau von Orleans*, *Die Räuber* and *Kabale und Liebe* (twice) are all quoted or referred to.[24]

Considerations of space dictate only the briefest of summaries of the Schiller quotations from the rest of Nestroy's *œuvre*. It must be borne in mind that, for plays currently available only in SW, identification of quotations in the notes is something of a hit-and-miss affair. Statistics, as far as they can be assembled, imply a gap in Nestroy's conscious employment of quotations from Schiller between *Der Tod am Hochzeitstage* (1829) and *Tritschtratsch* (1833); thereafter, there are a number of plays in which borrowings from Schiller have not been noted, but only for three or four years of Nestroy's career as a dramatist do quotations from Schiller seem to be absent. The total number of these borrowings may conservatively be estimated at around 125.

What conclusions can one draw from Nestroy's prolific use of quotations from Schiller, and from the plays in particular? It is highly likely that Schiller outnumbers all the other sources of references and quotations that occur in Nestroy's entire *œuvre*. Why should this be? There is no incontrovertible documentary evidence and so one can only speculate that Nestroy was drawn to Schiller by a combination of factors, positive and negative. Negative is what one might call Nestroy's exasperated admiration for a classical dramatist to whom he had been exposed in youth, and then in his apprentice years as an actor, when he had to learn and perform ten roles in six Schiller plays, a task that was alien to his burgeoning comic genius. Positive from Nestroy's point of view is the fact that it was easy to mock the high-flown aspirations of the typical Schiller hero and heroine, and the bombast of the villain, knowing as he did that Schiller was more familiar to the theatre-going public, and also more vulnerable, than the other great Weimar dramatist, to whom he alludes comparatively seldom. The individual, whether as member of a theatre audience or as reader, responds instinctively to the challenge of trying to identify a Schillerian high-flown phrase set in a mundane context; even if success is only partial, one feels gratified to have glimpsed the implication, if not the exact details, of Nestroy's elusive allusions. The direct borrowings, and more subtly the gentle nudges, take on a life of their own within the context of Nestroy's many-faceted language.

Notes

1. I wish to express my gratitude for the help and advice I have received in preparing this contribution from the editors of the volume, from my wife – and (though he could not have known the purpose of my questions) from the recipient of this volume.
2. A very valuable and wide-ranging study of Nestroy's attitude to the established canon of German and Austrian literature is the article by Jürgen Hein, 'Nestroy als Klassiker? – Sein Verhältnis zu den "Klassikern"', *Nestroyana*, 7 (1987), 3/4, pp. 77–92.
3. *Johann Nestroy. Briefe*, ed. W. Obermaier (Vienna and Munich, 1977), p. 161. References to this edition are identified in the text as, e.g., HKA, *Briefe*, p. 161.
4. W. E. Yates draws attention to a similarity between Nestroy's contrasting of *Wirklichkeit* (reality) and *Phantasie* in Schlankel's *Lied* in *Das Haus der Temperamente*, II, 15, and Schiller's discussion of *Wirklichkeit* and *Ideal* in the essay *Über naive und sentimentalische Dichtung* [*On naive and sentimental poetry*]; HKA, *Stücke 13*, 281 (note to 156/22f.).
5. Compiled from Otto Rommel's listing of all the roles played by Nestroy, SW XV, 428–516.
6. *Bilderschau in meinem Zimmer. Erinnerungsblätter, Gartenlaube*, (1866), here pp. 173–75.
7. Cited after Rommel, SW XV, 577.
8. A pencil and wash drawing of Nestroy in this role is reproduced as no. 188 in the iconographical volume of the HKA: Heinrich Schwarz, *Johann Nestroy im Bild. Eine Ikonographie*, bearbeitet und herausgegeben von Johann Hüttner und Otto G. Schindler (Vienna, 1977), p. 104.
9. *Unter fünfzehn Theater-Direktoren. Bunte Bilder aus der Wiener Bühnenwelt* (Vienna, 1870), p. 30, cited by Rommel, SW XV, p. 578.
10. *Fünfundsiebzig Jahre in der Alten und Neuen Welt* (Leipzig, 1881), pp. 157–58, cited by Rommel, SW XV, 578.
11. *Wallensteins Tod*, II, 2, lines 779–80.
12. A convenient modern edition is in *Ferdinand Raimund's Nachlaß, Ferdinand Raimunds Werke*, ed. F. Brukner and E. Castle, III (Vienna, 1932), 49–61.
13. Cf. Nestroy's parody of Hérold's best-known opera *Zampa, ou La Fiancée de marbre* which, as *Zampa der Tagdieb oder Die Braut von Gips* [The Bride of Plaster], was first performed in 1832.
14. Tempting as it may be to see here a precursor of the love of late twentieth-century directors to stage historical works in the dress of their own day, or at least of a

period closer to it, this practice is attested for Vienna in the late eighteenth century; the diary of Count Karl Zinzendorf occasionally indicates that actors appeared on stage dressed in their own, informal clothes.

15. 'Marquisin von Mondekar' in Schiller's play.
16. 1829; also contained in HKA, *Stücke 1*.
17. The same poem is quoted again in *Müller, Kohlenbrenner und Sesseltrager* (HKA, *Stücke 7/II*) [Miller, Charcoal-burner and Sedan-chair Carrier] (1834), I, 30, when Rübezahl says: 'Des Lebens May blüht Einmahl und nicht wieder, Ihnen hat er abgeblüht'; Stegreif quotes the same lines in *"Nur keck!"* (1855; HKA, *Stücke 34*), I, 7.
18. Is Nestroy/Pitzl here attempting to 'improve' Schiller by pandering to the reader's uncertainty about the metre? – In the present context it might be thought entirely appropriate that Pitzl has added the intensifier *Gar* in turning Schiller's iambic tetrameter into a pentameter. That Nestroy was quite capable of getting the quotation right, or almost right, is shown in *Müller, Kohlenbrenner und Sesseltrager*, II, 4, where Sigwart says: '[...] O, daß sie ewig grünend bliebe, die schöne Zeit der jungen Liebe!'
19. See footnote 8.
20. In this context it is worth pointing out that Nestroy played (part of) the role of Karl Moor in his quodlibet *Der unzusammenhängende Zusammenhang* at Pressburg between 28 January and 13 June 1830; see SW XV, 462–63.
21. Cf. *Die Räuber*, II, 1: 'Was kann der Schreck nicht? – Was kann Vernunft, Religion wider dieses Giganten eiskalte Umarmung?' ['What cannot terror accomplish? What can reason, religion do against this giant's ice-cold embrace?'].
22. Certainly a quotation, but perhaps not an accurate one? – cf. *Die Räuber*, IV, 2, Franz Moor's first monologue: '[...] als schlich immer ein Spion der <u>Hölle</u> meinen <u>Fersen</u> nach'; and from his second monologue in this scene: '[...] unsere kühnste Entschlossenheit sperren, unsere erwachende Vernunft an <u>Ketten</u> abergläubischer Finsternis legen – <u>Mord!</u> wie eine ganze <u>Hölle</u> von Furien um das Wort flattert – [...]'. J. Hüttner suggests as an alternative Schiller source an amalgam of lines from *Die Jungfrau von Orleans*, III, 9: JOHANNA: 'Warum verfolgst du mich und heftest dich / So wutentbrannt <u>an meine Fersen</u>?' (lines 2407f.), and 'Und käm <u>die Hölle</u> selber in die Schranken, / Mir soll der Mut nicht weichen und nicht wanken!' (lines 2452f.).
23. Translating Nestroy is a thankless, if not an impossible, task; here *Verhältnisse* also implies 'relationships'.
24. Cf. HKA, *Stücke 38*, pp. 123–25, and notes (*Anmerkungen*) to pp. 10/10f., 11/32f., 18/23f., 22/14f. and 29/9ff.

Music in Nestroy's Plays

Dagmar Zumbusch-Beisteiner

Following the historical tradition of musical entertainment theatre in Vienna, Nestroy observed developments in the world of music beyond his own sphere of activity and, as a responsible playwright and dramatist, he sought to incorporate them in his own works. He succeeded in capturing the musical trends of his age by making musicians appear, even act, on stage, and by including musical quotations in his plays. For example, in the third act of *Weder Lorbeerbaum noch Bettelstab* [Neither Laurel Wreath nor Beggar's Staff], his parody of Holtei, he alludes to the new generation of harpists who enter the stage, accompanied by a group of actors and musicians; he mocks the contemporary practice of amateur music-making in a song in his farce *Der Färber und sein Zwillingsbruder* [The Dyer and his Twin Brother (1840)]; and three years later, in *Eisenbahnheirathen oder Wien, Neustadt, Brünn* [Railway-Weddings or Vienna, Neustadt, and Brünn], he shows on stage a Viennese maker of lutes and violins as well as a wind-instrument-maker from Krems.[1] Furthermore, Nestroy asked the various composers who provided musical numbers for the extensive quodlibets and several kinds of songs in his plays to include quotations from the contemporary world of opera and concerts. His sensitivity to the musical trends of his age is also evident in the amount of musical activity in the Carl-Theater in the late 1850s when, assisted by two colleagues, the actor Karl Treumann and the kapellmeister Carl Binder, Nestroy introduced adaptations of Offenbach's one-act plays and parodies of Wagner's operas. He was able to address the Wagner phenomenon with parodistic versions of *Tannhäuser* and *Lohengrin* because Wagner's revolutionary operatic scores and political views had provoked heated debates long before a complete version of any of his operas had been given in Vienna.[2]

Music appears on two levels within Nestroy's *œuvre*. First, music is performed: it is present in the theatre acoustically (and sometimes also visually if musicians appear on stage in, for example, a ball-room orchestra). Secondly, verbal references to music often occur in the text, on a non-musical level, as it were.

Stylistic Characteristics of the Music in Nestroy's Plays

All Nestroy's plays contain different kinds and varying amounts of vocal and instrumental music,[3] from the *Zauberspiele* (plays with supernatural elements) and the first opera parodies of the early 1830s, to his favourite dramatic form, the *Posse mit Gesang* [farce with songs], and, finally, in the two Wagner parodies in 1857 and 1859 and his last work, the Offenbach operetta of 1862. By today's standards, this music comes in a curious mixture of different musical styles: elements of the *opera buffa*, the *vaudeville* and the *opéra comique* are combined with component parts of *Volksmusik* [popular music] and passages culled from the Viennese waltzes of Joseph Lanner and Johann Strauss the Elder. The stylised form of the waltz provides the basis for most of the musical entr'actes and parts of the overtures, and its rhythm also characterises almost all the songs to be found in Viennese popular theatre.[4] Despite this, it is evident that audiences in the early 1840s disliked the inclusion of dances in the popular music played in Viennese suburban theatres – a report in the *Allgemeine Wiener Musik-Zeitung* of 18 May 1841 (no. 59, p. 248) reads: 'Wahrhaft unleidlich wird jetzt schon das Absingen und Herunterjohlen eines Walzers am Schlusse jeder Strophe und der deutlich ausgesprochene Widerwillen des Publicums hiegegen möge den Componisten für die Zukunft als Warnung dienen' ['The raucous rendition of waltzes at the end of every strophe is truly disagreeable and the public's obvious aversion to this practice should function as a warning to composers in the future']. A year later the same journal complained of the predominance of dance music in the adaptation of a French *vaudeville*:

> Kaum fällt der Vorhang, und man will sich von diesem ewigen Geklingel [der Tanzmusik] erholen, als plötzlich eine unendlich lange Introduction uns wieder 'Walzer' bringt, die Hr. Capellmeister Müller jeden viermal vorführte. Ich glaube, es ist doch kein Mangel an Compositionen, die geeignet wären, in Zwischenacten aufgeführt zu werden, warum den ohnehin für das Bessere in der Musik gesunkenen Geschmack des Publicums durch solche Wirtshaustänze noch mehr herabstimmen.[5]

> [When the curtain has been lowered and everyone is looking forward to a respite from the endless clattering [of the dance music], another endless musical introduction brings us yet more 'waltzes', each of which the kapellmeister, Herr Müller, repeats at least four times. I do not believe that there is a shortage of compositions that could suitably be played between acts, so why should the public's taste in music, which has already sunk so low, be debased even more by the playing of such tavern music.]

It is surprising that as early as 1832 – at a time when popular comedy still retained its traditional *Singspiel* character – the *Theaterzeitung* reported that 'Die Lieder nach den Melodien von Straußischen Walzern [...] in der letzten Zeit zu häufig dagewesen [seien, um] derselben nicht schon überdrüssig [zu sein]'[6] ['Songs based on the melodies of Strauss waltzes have been heard so often lately that one cannot help but tire of them'].

Within the great diversity of lyrics and music created by Nestroy and his composers (of whom Adolf Müller the Elder is the most important for the period up to 1847), the following two examples are among the most distinctive adaptations of popular dance tunes: the waltz duet in the farce *Die verhängnißvolle Faschings-Nacht* [The Fateful Carnival Night (1839)] and the extensive dance aria in *Die Familien Zwirn, Knieriem und Leim oder Der Welt-Untergangs-Tag* [The Families Zwirn, Knieriem and Leim or The End of the World (1834)], the sequel to *Der böse Geist Lumpacivagabundus* [The Evil Spirit Lumpacivagabundus].[7] The songs in the hugely successful farce of 1842, *Einen Jux will er sich machen* [High Jinks], provide representative examples of vocal numbers that adapt and incorporate compositional elements of contemporary dances, in particular waltzes, in their own melody and rhythm.[8] Two of the three songs delivered by the main character Weinberl favour ¾ time and ⅞ time, and their rhythm is accentuated by the instrumental accompaniment (for example, the dotted rhythm of the introductory ritornello in the song in II, 8, and the characteristic pounding rhythm with which the strings accompany the voice). Broken triads, played normally by second violins and violas (and in the case of Weinberl's first song (I, 10) also by a clarinet solo), appear alongside the melodic line played by the bass instruments, which use predominantly fifths and octave intervals, played sequentially (for example, in the middle section of the song in III, 16). The broken triads and the fifths/octave sequences are characteristic accompanying phrases borrowed from Austrian dance music and *Volksmusik*.[9]

While Nestroy and his kapellmeister, Adolf Müller, dispensed with the usual incorporation of *Singspiel* elements in *Einen Jux will er sich machen*, thus breaking with a long musical tradition in Viennese popular comedy (see note 3 above), the instrumentation of the three songs in this work still closely resembles the scores of older colleagues. From this point in time instrumentation developed only gradually, moving away from the principle of providing varied accompaniment to each strophe – where the vocal line is enveloped in a melodically developed form – to a simpler, more restrained orchestration in which the instruments carrying the melody (usually first violins and high woodwind) are reduced to supplying little more than literal accompaniment.

The music in Nestroy's early works directly imitates the Viennese *Singspiel*, which had been nurtured in particular in the popular *Zauberoper* and *Zauberpossen* [opera and farce with supernatural elements] produced in the Theater in der Leopoldstadt from the end of the eighteenth century. The characteristic stylistic features of the various genres mentioned above – in particular the *parlando* of the Italian *opera buffa*, and the characteristic melodic and rhythmic features typical of Austrian popular song and dance (favourite 'yodler intervals', for example) – had already been blended in Wenzel Müller's scores and those of many of his colleagues.[10] In a variety of ways they succeeded in achieving 'the harmonious combination of text and music, of song and dance, and of chorus and pantomime, without allowing any particular form to dominate'.[11]

This combination of different elements characterises the compositions written for Nestroy's *Zauberspiele*, parodies and farces of the early 1830s and also allowed for the assimilation of elements taken from the repertoire of the musical theatre (a repertoire made known primarily by performances of contemporary Italian and French opera and *vaudeville* productions in the Kärnterthortheater, the Court Opera). It was against this background that musical elements by Nestroy and his composers[12] developed and gradually broke free from the traditional components of the *Singspiel,* and then establish their own, highly individual and characteristic forms and means of expression. This is apparent above all in the *Couplets,* satirical songs that are normally delivered by the main character in Nestroy's plays.

Vocal Music

Apart from overtures and entr'actes (or intermezzi), which exist outside the action of the play – music, played when the curtain is down, that often serves only the purpose of bridging the gap between scenes – the surviving musical material for Nestroy's plays consists mainly of musical numbers that form part of the dramatic action and fulfil a particular function within it. The following fall into this category of text-related music:[13] choruses, quodlibets, and complete songs.

1 Choruses

Choruses often mark the beginnings and ends of acts and scenes; they introduce the action and provide commentaries on it. The *Zauberspiele,* which Nestroy wrote at the beginning of his career as a playwright, but also later works, such as the 'dramatisches Gemälde' [dramatic portrait] *Der Treulose* [The Unfaithful Husband] (1836), contain choruses that are presented in combination with one or more soloists in the form of extensive *Singstücke* (vocal ensembles); these often follow on directly from the preceding dialogue. In *Die Familien Zwirn, Knieriem und Leim* (1834), for example, there are two such song-scenes (I, 27–28; II, 22) – the music for Knieriem's 'Tratschlied' [gossip song] with female chorus in the first act has unfortunately been lost, but the text of the number survives (see *Stücke 8/I,* 37/20–38/37). In both cases Nestroy, playing the role of the cobbler Knieriem, would sing the extensive solo passage himself. The song in the first Act shapes the dialogue in an entertaining way and could conceivably be performed outside the context of the action, while the vocal part of the second act reflects a specific situation at the very climax of the action (the anticipation of the expected comet) and finally deflates the dramatic suspense with an acoustic effect:

> (*Nach einer Pause angstvoller Erwartung hört man unter der Musik in abgemessenen Schlägen zehn Uhr schlagen. Mit dem ersten Schlage machen* ALLE *einen ängstlichen Schrei und verstecken sich unter die Tische, bis auf* KNIERIEM, *welcher sitzenbleibt.*) Ach! – (*Stücke 8/I,* 86/21–5)

[*After a period of anxious anticipation, the bell sounds ten o'clock in slow strokes to the music. At the first stroke,* ALL *cry out in anxiety and hide under the table, except* KNIERIEM, *who remains sitting.*] Ach! – [14]

The quicker pace of the action in the subsequent fight scene had to be reflected by the music, which Nestroy wanted composed '*in verändertem, sehr lebhaftem Tempo*' ['in a different, very lively tempo'].

After 1836, Nestroy's plays no longer contain such extensive vocal ensembles (*Singstücke*). In cases such as the brief vocal scene at the end of the first act of *Das Mädl aus der Vorstadt* [The Girl from the Suburbs] (1841), the song replaces the usual instrumental finale and serves purely to enhance the motivation of the plot, in that it comments on the action, a similar function to that of the chorus at the beginning or end of a scene.

2 Quodlibets and songs for one or more vocal parts
These are among the most popular musical elements in Nestroy's plays: if the performance of such elements was to the public's taste (this did not necessarily apply to the whole work), resourceful publishers were quick to use the Viennese press to announce the publication of the music – in the form of printed piano scores so that the songs could be performed at home. For the most part they appeared separately in the series *Komische Theatergesänge* [Comic Theatre Songs], issued by Anton Diabelli, or in *Theatralisches Panorama* [Theatrical Panorama], issued by Tobias Haslinger, series that specialised in popular theatre songs. In a letter to the composer Adolf Müller, written in November 1842, Nestroy refers to the danger arising from an absence of copyright regulations: he feared that 'die Provinzbühnen [seine *Couplets*] gleich als Einlage benützen' ['the provincial theatres might copy the *Couplets*'] once the songs had been published and were available for sale commercially. So, while the publication of the songs points to the extent of their contemporary popularity, it is unlikely that these publications were sanctioned either by the author of the text or by the composer (significantly, the wording in Müller's original scores still appears practically unchanged in the printed versions).[15]

The insertion of quodlibets is one of the oldest traditions of providing musical entertainment in Viennese popular drama.[16] A medley of the best-known quotations from opera, from popular theatre tunes, and from folk-dances and folk-songs, quodlibets provided the interpreter with the opportunity to parody and caricature serious operatic works in the repertoire of the court opera in the Kärntnerthortheater. The quality of the performance in such parodies should not be underestimated; indeed, the actors were usually professional singers. Public expectations were high in the early nineteenth century: weaknesses in intonation were not tolerated even in the suburban theatres of Vienna, and the press criticised any vocal indisposition, particularly in performances by well-known actors, for whom composers often had to write especially demanding musical passages. In the *Wiener Musik-Zeitung* of 31 December 1842 (no. 157, p. 630), one critic comments explicitly on the performance of one of the most popular singers in Vienna, Ida Brüning[-Wohlbrück], during a *vaudeville* production in the Theater an der Wien:

> Die Musik Hrn. Ad. Müller's ist unstreitig eine der bessern, die er seit langer Zeit geschrieben, sie ist aber auch für Mad. Brünning berechnet, welche zur Zeit noch die Mittel besitzt, durch Stimme und Vortrags-künste *musikalischen* Effect hervorbringen zu können. Leider dürfte dieß bei der Stellung, welche die geschätzte Künstlerinn jetzt einnimmt, nicht von zu langer Dauer seyn, indem sie von jetzt an nur ihr Augenmerk darauf richten muß, *komischen* Effect zu erzielen, wobei natürlich die Cultur und daher auch die Schönheit ihrer Stimmittel leiden müssen. Schon dießmal war ein Schwanken der Intonation, welche aber durchgehends zu tief war, und ein übermäßiges Forciren der höheren Töne zu bemerken, welche Sünde gegen ihr Stimmorgan nicht lange ohne merkbare Folgen seyn wird.

> [Ad. Müller's music is undoubtedly among the best he has written for some time, but it is intended to suit Madame Brünning who, at the moment, is still capable of producing *musical* effect through her singing and acting. Sad to say, this will probably not be the case for much longer, for the esteemed artist has now taken on a part in which she must concentrate on achieving *comic* effect, and therefore the culture and beauty of her voice will suffer. In this performance her intonation was already unstable and altogether pitched too low, and the higher notes were unnecessarily forced – a sin against her voice, and one that will soon take its toll.]

It is evident from the manuscripts[17] that Nestroy, formerly a professional opera singer with considerable practical experience,[18] did not leave the choice of quotations for his quodlibets solely to the composers. What is more, he also worked on the scores, often providing most of the text for the vocal parts of the quodlibet and including detailed musical instructions. His professional expertise and his precise expectations of musical interpretation are demon-strated, for example, in his notes in the scores for *Das Gewürzkrämer-Kleeblatt* [The Trio of Grocers] (HKA, *Stücke 22*, edited by W. E. Yates, pp. 539–40) and for *Der Treulose* ('Melodram für Pianoforte', I, 48) (HKA, *Stücke 10*, edited by Johann Hüttner, p. 131).

In as much as Nestroy and his composers consciously reacted to contempo-rary musical trends, the quodlibets give us an accurate reflection of the variety in musical genre and repertoire of Nestroy's time. Without the references to their sources given in the scores,[19] it would now be extremely difficult, or even impossible, to unravel the origins of many quotations, for whereas many popular dramas and the latest Italian operas, including numerous works by Rossini, Bellini and Donizetti, remained enormously popular in Vienna until the 1840s, some works disappeared quickly from the repertoire.[20]

When creating the quodlibets for his plays, Nestroy clearly took great pains with his own role and with that of Marie Weiler, his partner on stage and in private life. In the quodlibet quartet of his 'comic tragedy' *Gegen Thorheit giebt es kein Mittel* [There is no Cure for Folly (1838)], Nestroy and Weiler appeared together on stage twice, as well as taking part in the ensemble scenes. In the quartet they performed passages taken from Donizetti's operas (20 bars from *L'Elisir d'amore* and 49 bars from *Gemma di Vergy*). Weiler had a further 33-bar solo from Donizetti's *Belisar*, while Nestroy sang the lead part in a duet in which 42 bars of Rossini's *Il turco in Italia* are quoted, and sang an extract from Rossini's *L'asserio di Corinto*. The contemporary repertoire of the Kärntnertortheater is reflected in other quotations (for ensembles): no fewer than six passages taken from Donizetti's operas; the quodlibet contains four passages borrowed from Mozart (three of them from *The Magic Flute*),[21] two from Rossini, as well as quotations from Isouard and from folksongs; there is also a self-quotation by Adolf Müller. One year after *Gegen Thorheit giebt es kein Mittel*, Nestroy created the famous 'waltz duet' for *Die verhängnißvolle Faschings-Nacht*, in which he took the lion's share for himself as Lorenz (with Weiler in the part of Nanny), and in 1841 he wrote the extensive and demanding quodlibet in *Das Mädl aus der Vorstadt*, which gave both actors the opportunity to perform what can only be described as a true masterpiece of musical self-presentation. In both cases musical form and textual content correspond perfectly – though to a far greater extent in the quodlibet of *Das Mädl aus der Vorstadt* than in the 'waltz duet'. The effect of musical parody results here from the juxtaposition of contrasting passages taken from German and Italian operas, and is further enhanced by the text passages. This was so skilfully put together that an autonomous piece was created, one that is capable of existing outside the farce. The quodlibet, two separate publications of which appeared shortly after its first performance in *Das Mädl aus der Vorstadt* (see Hilmar 1972, pp. 80–1), was reportedly performed by Nestroy and Weiler also in the context of a 'musikalisch-deklamatorische Akademie', a kind of entertainment in which music and speech were presented.[22]

While the function and use of the Viennese theatrical song in general, and in Nestroy's plays in particular, have been the subjects of a considerable amount of literary and theatre criticism,[23] musicology has so far not devoted much time to the analysis of this kind of everyday poetry.[24] One reason for this may be that the established methods of musical analysis would either prove unable to describe the various types of songs to be found in Nestroy's plays, or would merely provide an inadequate superficial summary. The texts and music of Nestroy's songs can be forced into a framework of traditional formal terms, but these terms fail to capture the diversity of Nestroy's and his composers' experiments with musical modes of expression. They also fail to pay sufficient regard to the conditions under which commercially run music-entertainment theatres had to operate. When working for one of the three great suburban theatres in Vienna – Theater an der Wien, Theater in der Josefstadt, Theater in der Leopoldstadt – the kapellmeister not only had to hold regular daily rehearsals, he was also under great pressure to produce new music; this meant taking full account of the current taste of the audience. His decisions were also dependent on the wishes of the playwright and the director – this was clearly the case with Adolf Müller when he was working with Nestroy and the director Karl Carl.[25] In addition to Nestroy's detailed notes on musical articulation mentioned above, the composer was given lists of plans detailing musical aspects of the theatrical production as a whole[26] as well as the sources of quotations (see below) and indications of the metric stress (Nestroy usually underlined stressed syllables in the texts of his songs). The composers were expected to accommodate the musical abilities of individual actors, whether to give them an opportunity to show their skills or to ensure that they were not overtaxed vocally. The critic Wittmann makes this very point in an article published on 30 November 1843 in the *Allgemeine Wiener Musik-Zeitung* (no. 143, p. 604). '[Kein Wunder, wenn] die Gesangspiecen der Mad. Brüning […] nicht recht ansprechen [wollten]' – 'kein Wunder, wenn Hr. Capellmeister Müller, der in Einem fort für diese Sängerinn Lieder und Arien einrichten und zurichten muß, auch einmal monoton würde' ['It is not surprising that the songs written for Madame Brüning were not well received, or that the kapellmeister, Herr Müller, should write something monotonous once in a while, given that he constantly has to adapt and arrange songs and arias to cater for this particular singer'].

3 Complete songs
The vocal numbers for one voice in the scores for Nestroy's plays are written in a variety of through-composed and strophic forms (the duets belong to this second category). These include the following: extensive and demanding arias, such as Fatime's *Stimmungsarie*, or *Sehnsuchtsarie* (an aria conveying atmosphere or longing) in *Der Zauberer Sulphurelectrimagneticophosphoratus* [*The Magician Sulphurelectrimagneticophosphoratus*] (1834) (II, 10);[27] songs in which strophes end in long yodelling passages – they are listed in the scores as 'Arietten' or cavatinas;[28] and finally, the most important musical component, the *Couplets* sung by Nestroy's main characters, which, with their characteristic two-part musical structure, also fall into the category of strophic song with refrain. A further important category is the *Einlagelied* [literally: 'inserted song'], a song that follows on directly from the previous dialogue but which is so conceived that it is capable of existing independently of the action.[29] Typical *Einlagelieder* can be found in *Weder Lorbeerbaum noch Bettelstab*, the 'Punschlied' [drinking song] in I, 11 and the 'ballad' in III, 10 are modelled directly on Holtei, in contrast to the 'song without accompaniment' (I, 8).[30] The *songs with parodistic effect* are especially important; the parody[31] is achieved either by quoting directly from the opera (i.e. text and music) or by adding a new text to the original music, and also, of course, by the degree of their comic presentation. *Müller, Kohlenbrenner und Sesseltrager* [Miller, Charcoal-burner and Sedan-chair Carrier] contains the following examples: the chambermaid Nanette's *Ariette* with a quotation from Mozart's *Magic Flute* (I, 21)[32] and the Italian opera singer Nero's *song with chorus* (III, 5).[33] The function of these songs is no different from that of the quodlibets: in Nero's song, in which the parody of Italian opera is reinforced by Nestroy's text, the recognition of well-

known melodies and the comic effect combine to produce highly successful parody and caricature.

Nestroy exploits every opportunity to make comic interpretations by employing caricature. Many comments in the contemporary press document his ability to perform parodying songs and to speak and sing very fast – this must have been especially effective in passages of *buffo*-style parlando. The *Theaterzeitung* admired:

> [die] kaum glaubliche [...] Schnelligkeit, mit welcher er [im *Tritschtratsch*] sprach und sang. Im Vortrage komischer Gesänge und Quodlibets ist Hr. Nestroy schwer zu erreichen, und zwar nicht blos wegen seiner klangvollen und geschulten Stimme, sondern noch mehr wegen der launigen und originellen Behandlung des Textes und der Note[34]

> [the incredible speed with which he spoke and sang [in *Tritschtratsch*]. Herr Nestroy would be hard to match in the performance of comic songs and quodlibets, not only because of his full and well-trained voice, but even more because of the amusing and imaginative way in which he interprets text and music].

As a playwright, Nestroy also employed the 'unfailingly comic device'[35] of having Wenzel Scholz appear silent on stage (it was Scholz who sang Nero's song). Scholz, one of the most popular actors of his time, was an accomplished performer; physically, he was remarkably squat, in contrast to Nestroy's lanky figure, a contrast that provided its own comic effect. The following example illustrates the way in which Nestroy made use of Scholz's physical appearance. One of Scholz's most striking exits was the one following his first song in the role of the porter Plumpsack in the oriental setting of *Der Zauberer Sulphur...* (I, 6); Plumpsack, forced out of his original job, has now become a 'Lauffer' [runner]:

> LISETT. Das kann ich mir gar nicht dencken, wie du laufst.
> PLUMPSACK. Das wirst gleich sehen. (*Leise, sehr schnelle Musik fällt ein,* PLUMPSACK *macht in zierlichen Laufferschritten eine Tour um die Bühne, und entfernt sich so zur Mittelthüre.*) (*Stücke 6*, 15/36–40)

> [LISETT. I can't imagine how you'd run.
> PLUMPSACK. I'll show you. (*Soft, quick music;* PLUMPSACK *does a lap around the stage in a delicate run, and runs off through the centre door.*]

A similar comic element may be found in *Die Familien Zwirn, Knieriem und Leim*, in which Scholz appeared as Zwirn; Zwirn's first appearance on stage is accompanied by an introductory ritornello containing a few bars from Schubert's song *Der Wanderer* [The Wayfarer] D 489, 'Ich komme vom Gebirge her', during which he remains silent for a relatively long period (see HKA, *Stücke 8/I*, 379 and 385). A further example occurs in this play in the quodlibet when Nestroy made his colleague stop singing abruptly: '*er will weiter singen, aber die Stimme versagt ihm, und er macht blos die Miene des*

Gesanges ['*he tries to continue singing, but his voice fails and he just mimes the song*'] (HKA, *Stücke 8/I*, 53/24–25 and 389).

Instrumental Music

Although Nestroy often gave detailed instructions about how his texts should be set to music, he usually gave only a generalised description of the scenic *instrumental music*, that is, pieces required by the dramatic situation, such as *melodramas* and *finales* at the end of an act, which are followed by entr'actes or intermezzi ('attacca' or 'nach kurzer Pause') ['*attacca*' or 'after a short pause']. Thus the stage directions often read as follows: '*The music starts*', '*very joyful music begins*', '*loud music starts*', '*the music takes on a mystical note*' or '*the curtain falls, accompanied by appropriate music*'. ['*Musik fällt ein*'; '*eine äußerst lustige Musik beginnt*'; '*die Musik fällt rauschend ein*'; '*die Musik nimmt einen mystischen Charakter an*'; '*unter passender Musik fällt der Vorhang*'].[36]

The *melodramatic music* in Nestroy's early *Zauberspiele* is still modelled on the Romantic *Zauberopern* and *Singspiele* with their ghostly or chilling elements. But, during the 1840s, when Nestroy produced a number of adaptations, many of his farces were influenced primarily by French *mélodrames*, in which a complicated plot of innocently suffering protagonists and criminal conspirators is framed by visual and acoustic stage effects.[37] The terms used to describe instrumental pieces, which are directly connected with text and action, are as imprecise as those used for the songs. In most cases, Nestroy provides a stage direction (such as *characteristic music begins*) whereas the composer either inserts a numeric indicator in his score or uses the term *Melodram* (melodramatic music) itself.[38] Occasionally, more specific terms appear: in a *Zauberspiel* in 1832, *Der konfuse Zauberer oder Treue und Flatterhaftigkeit* [The Confused Magician or Faithfulness and Fickleness], Nestroy uses the terms 'Harmoniemusik' ['music for wind instruments'], 'Galoppmusik' ['gallop music'], and 'Trauermusik' ['funeral music'].

Normally, the dramatic function of melodramatic music in Nestroy's plays is either to accompany the action or to emphasise and enhance it, or both. Employing simple methods of musical intensification,[39] melodramatic music marks decisive scenes: in the *Zauberspiel* celestial characters are lowered from the flies to pronounce their verdict 'tutta la forza'; they then disappear again up into the sky scenery, accompanied by a few bars of music ('einigen Takten Musik'). Spectacular transformation scenes take place while the strings play tremolos or the wind instruments sound *sforzato* chords. In some scenes, which are enacted in silence against a scenic background of a ghostly landscape setting (for example, II, 23 in *Die Familien Zwirn, Knieriem und Leim*) or which create suspense in other ways, the music from the orchestra pit is reinforced with stage thunder and lightning, to emphasise acoustically the uncanny atmosphere and the dramatic effect. In such scenes the music is sometimes referred to as 'Gewittermusik' (thunderstorm music), as, for example, in *Der böse Geist Lumpacivagabundus*, III, 12. Where it serves the purpose of *Verwandlungsmusik* – music played before a transformation scene –

the melodramatic music can scarcely be differentiated from finales. In essence, they are short pieces of instrumental music needed to cover the noise of scene shifters between scenes or between acts.

Whenever the music was meant to characterise and to illustrate, to offer more than purely picturesque effects, the composers resorted to different methods of achieving their desired effect. This is true of the descriptions in *Der konfuse Zauberer* mentioned above, and is also the case in, for example, the knights' marching on stage in *Die Zauberreise in die Ritterzeit oder Gegenwart und Vergangenheit* [Magic Journey to the Age of Chivalry or Past and Present] (1832; I, 18), or in the melodramatic music that accompanies Wendelin and his father Pfrim on their voluntary pilgrimage to Rome in *Höllenangst* [Fear of Hell] (1849; III, 17): Nestroy's stage direction calls for 'im Kirchenstyl[40] gehaltene Musick' – indeed, Nestroy may have intended this to recall the pilgrims' chorus in Wagner's *Tannhäuser*.[41]

Pieces of instrumental music were normally used in more than one work – not, as was the case with the songs or quodlibets, because of their popularity, but to minimise the enormous workload. Working with ready-made musical pieces meant a considerable reduction of pressure and so one finds that overtures and entr'actes were freely interchanged, not only within one composer's works but also between works by different composers. The knights' march in *Die Zauberreise in die Ritterzeit*, for example, was also used for part of the overture, and, in *Die Familien Zwirn*, the final theme of the overture is identical to a dance variation in Mathilde's aria in the same play (HKA, *Stücke 8/I*, pp. 380–81).

When first sketching, and later preparing, the final drafts of his plays, Nestroy did not confine his interest to the purely musical features of musical compositions; again and again, his instinct for current trends in the world of concert music and opera is reflected by the text – it extends beyond the acoustic experience of the music performed. In the early nineteenth century the press provided an interested public with a regular diet of musical topics – these have long since become part of music history. They attracted Nestroy's attention, for his broad education had given him a life-long interest in such matters, and keeping abreast of current trends was a requirement for his job. At a time when musical culture in the middle classes, a culture in which he had grown up, was at the height of its development, he could not have failed to notice that amateur performances in concerts were increasingly considered unacceptable or that the performances of German-speaking or Italian star singers at the Viennese Court Opera were followed with great interest.[42] The leading daily and weekly newspapers of his era contain pages and pages of reports about the court opera in the Kärntnerthortheater; they also could not resist occasionally playing off the special features of the Italian manner of singing against the characteristically German style.[43] This is how the controversy surrounding Richard Wagner's music began in the mid-1840s: in 1843, August Schmidt, the editor of the *Wiener Allgemeine Musik-Zeitung*, wrote a damning review of the opera *Rienzi*, provoking the young Wagner into openly declaring his enmity.[44] When Nestroy wrote the following *Couplet* lines for his

Gewürzkrämer-Kleeblatt (*Stücke 22*, pp. 397 and 402) in 1845 (they were not used in the final version), we do not know whether he was thinking of Wagner, whose music at that time was said by hostile critics to be without melody and impossible to sing ('unmelodiös' and 'unsingbar'); it is tempting to think that this was Nestroy's intention, because he refers to a 'kapellmeister full of musical knowledge [who] says, I'm going to write an opera as it should be, I won't have any trace of melody in the song passages, because true music lies only in the counterpoint':

> ein Kapellmeister von Musikkenntniß ganz voll,
> sagt ich werd jetzt a Oper schreibn wie sie sein soll,
> keine Spur Melodie leid ich in die Gsangstück,
> denn im Contrapunkt nur b'steht die wahre Musik.

Notes

1. In the play's French source the characters are a lute-maker and a violin-maker: see HKA, *Stücke 20*, ed. Jürgen Hein, pp. 250–63.
2. See Andrea Harrandt, 'Wagner und seine Werke in Wien (1857–1883). Ein Beitrag zur Wagner-Rezeption im 19. Jahrhundert', unpublished doctoral thesis, University of Vienna 1985; D. Zumbusch, 'Richard Wagners *Tannhäuser* im Vorfeld der Wiener Erstaufführung und frühe parodistische Wirksamkeit', in Petr Macek (ed.), *Richard Wagner – Nationalkulturen – Zeitgeschichte*. Musikwissenschaftliche Kolloquien der Internationalen Musikfestspiele in Brno, 30 (Brno, 1996).
3. Peter Branscombe comments on the drastic reduction of musical elements in Nestroy's works after 1842 (beginning with the farce *Einen Jux will er sich machen*): 'Music in the Viennese Popular Theatre of the Eighteenth and Nineteenth Centuries', *Proceedings of the Royal Musical Association*, 98 (1971–72), 132–48.
4. See Otto Brusatti, 'Vorläufer und Wurzeln für die Wiener Operette im 19. Jahrhundert', in Jean-Marie Valentin (ed.), *Das österreichische Volkstheater im europäischen Zusammenhang* (Berne, Frankfurt, New York, Paris, 1988), pp. 155–70 (p. 159): 'The Viennese dance music developed in the first half of the 19th century not only became a new genre, but because of its melody, metre and musical structure this music was also fit to form the basis for songs, be it individual songs or a whole ensemble' (translation).
5. *Allgemeine Wiener Musik-Zeitung*, 30 November 1843 (no. 143), pp. 603–04.
6. *Wiener Theaterzeitung*, 22 October 1832 (no. 211), p. 843; the comment appears in a report about the first performance of Nestroy's *Zauberreise in die Ritterzeit oder Die Übermütigen*, with music by Adolf Müller.
7. For a discussion of the waltz duet, see HKA, *Stücke 15*, ed. Louise Adey Huish, pp. 457–72, which includes a facsimile print of the piano score that was published only a month after the first performance; for the dance aria, see HKA, *Stücke 8/1*, ed. Friedrich Walla, pp. 401–03, which reproduces the text and music of Adolf Müller's autograph score.
8. See the facsimile prints of contemporary piano scores in HKA, *Stücke 18/1*, ed. W. E. Yates, pp. 279–85.
9. See Diether de la Motte, *Melodie. Ein Lese-und Arbeitsbuch* (Munich, Kassel, 1993), pp. 88–92.
10. For contemporary theatrical composers see Peter Tomek, 'Die Musik an den Wiener Vorstadttheatern 1776–1825. Theatermusik und Zeitgeist. Eine Bestandsaufnahme', 2 vols, unpublished dissertation, Vienna, 1989; see also Peter Branscombe's articles

on Wenzel Müller, Ignaz Schuster and Joseph Drechsler in *The New Grove Dictionary of Music and Musicians* (London, 1980), vol. 12, pp. 772–73, vol. 16, pp. 875–76, and vol. 5, pp. 611–12.

11. Translated from Rossana Dalmonte, 'Die Zauberharfe in der Zauberwelt', in Werner Aderhold, Walther Dürr and Walburga Litschauer (eds), *Franz Schubert, Jahre der Krise 1818–1823, Arnold Feil zum 60. Geburtstag* (Kassel, Basle, London, 1985), p. 77.

12. Nestroy's composers and the music they wrote for his plays have hardly been discussed. See the bibliographical references in Jürgen Hein, *Johann Nestroy* (Stuttgart, 1990), pp. 121–22; see also D. Zumbusch, 'Ansätze zu einer Typologie des Wiener Theaterlieds, dargelegt insbesondere an den Stücken Nestroys', unpublished master's dissertation, University of Bonn, 1992, and, by the same author, the section 'Musik' in the volumes of the HKA published since 1995.

13. For different aspects of the function of vocal music, see Jürgen Hein, 'Zur Funktion der "musikalischen Einlagen" in den Stücken des Wiener Volkstheaters', in Valentin (ed.), *Das österreichische Volkstheater*, pp. 103–26.

14. 'The retarding effect of the ten strokes of the bell reminds us of Kasperl's uncanny encounter in Friedrich Hensler's *Teufelsmühle am Wienerberg* (The Devil's Mill on the Wienerberg), with music by Wenzel Müller, although the parodistic effect is more dominant in Nestroy's play' (translated from D. Zumbusch's introduction to the music in *Die Familien Zwirn, Knieriem und Leim oder Der Welt-Untergangs-Tag* in HKA, *Stücke 8/1*, 377–81 (p. 381)).

15. Interestingly, Müller's wording in the original score still appears practically unchanged in the printed versions; see Ernst Hilmar, 'Die Nestroy-Vertonungen in den Wiener Sammlungen', *Maske und Kothurn*, 18 (1972), pp. 39–40, which quotes from Nestroy's letter; see also HKA, *Briefe*, ed. Walter Obermaier (Vienna, 1977), p. 62.

16. See P. Branscombe, 'Music in the Viennese Popular Theatre of the Eighteenth and Nineteenth Centuries', *Proceedings of the Royal Musical Association*, 98 (1971–72), pp. 132–48, and P. Branscombe, 'The Connexions between Drama and Music in the Viennese Popular Theatre from the Opening of the Leopoldstädter Theater (1781) to Nestroy's Opera Parodies (ca. 1855), with Special Reference to the Forms of Parody', unpublished doctoral dissertation, University of London, 1976; see also W. E. Yates, *Theatre in Vienna. A Critical History 1776–1995* (Cambridge, 1996), esp. pp. 138–49.

17. See Nestroy, HKA, *Stücke 15*, 317–18 and the quodlibet drafts for *Sie sollen ihn nicht haben oder Der holländische Bauer*, HKA, *Stücke 28/1*, ed. Walter Obermaier, pp. 390–93 and 424–32.

18. See especially Alfred Orel, 'Opernsänger Johann Nestroy', in *Jahrbuch des Vereins für Geschichte der Stadt Wien*, 14 (1958), pp. 94–113.

19. Adolf Müller meticulously lists the pieces from which he quotes: was this simply because he was given the details by Nestroy, or did he wish to be 'correct' in his work – especially in a realm where it was part of a composer's job to borrow elements from other works, be they his own or those of other composers – by distinguishing between quotations and his own compositions?

20. See Franz Hadamowsky, *Die Wiener Hoftheater (Staatstheater). Ein Verzeichnis der aufgeführten und eingereichten Stücke mit Bestandsnachweisen und Aufführungsdaten.* Part 2: *Die Wiener Hofoper (Staatsoper) 1811–1974* (Vienna, 1975).

21. *The Magic Flute*, in which the young Nestroy in the role of Sarastro made his debut in Vienna's court opera, is one of the operatic scores most frequently quoted in the quodlibets.

22. See Nestroy, SW XI, 537.

23. See Herbert Zeman, 'Das Theaterlied zur Zeit Joseph Haydns, seine theatralische

Gestaltung und seine gattungsgeschichtliche Entwicklung', in H. Zeman (ed.), *Haydn und die Literatur seiner Zeit* (Eisenstadt, 1979), pp. 35–59; Jürgen Hein, 'Zur Funktion der "musikalischen Einlagen" in den Stücken des Wiener Volkstheaters', in Valentin (ed.) *Das österreichische Volkstheater*, pp. 103–26.

24. See D. Zumbusch, 'Ansätze zu einer Typologie des Wiener Theaterlieds', p. 6.

25. See D. Zumbusch, 'Komponist oder Notensetzer? Ein musikalisches Intermezzo mit Instrumentalmusik Adolf Müllers sen.', *Nestroyana*, 15, 1–2 (1995), 49–67 (esp. 53–54).

26. See, for example, Karl Carl's plans as described by P. Branscombe, 'The Connexions between Drama and Music in the Viennese Popular Theatre', pp. 142–48.

27. See HKA, *Stücke 6*, ed. F. Walla, 40/24–41/13 and 379–80.

28. See, for example, the songs in the theatre version of *Die Gleichheit der Jahre* (Equality in Years) (1834), in HKA, *Stücke 7/I*, ed. F. Walla, pp. 144–45, 281–82, and 286.

29. The tradition of such songs is described by Martin Ruhnke, 'Das Einlage-Lied in der Oper der Zeit von 1800–1840', in Heinz Becker (ed.), *Die 'Couleur locale' in der Oper des 19. Jahrhunderts* (Regensburg, 1976), pp. 75–97.

30. See HKA, *Stücke 8/II*, ed. F. Walla, in preparation.

31. See J. Hein, 'Themen und Formen der Parodie in Nestroys Theaterliedern', *Nestroyana*, 5 (1983–84), 62–65.

32. It is worth mentioning in this context that (according to his autobiography) the young Grillparzer first came into contact with the libretto of *The Magic Flute* through his mother's chambermaid.

33. See HKA, *Stücke 7/II*, 71/5–33, 113/5–114/10; see also p. 405 and pp. 417–20.

34. See *Allgemeine [Wiener] Theaterzeitung*, 13 July 1840 (no. 167), p. 706.

35. See *Sonntagsblätter*, 8 May 1842 (no. 19), p. 333.

36. D. Zumbusch, 'Komponist oder Notensetzer? pp. 54–55.

37. See, for example, *Die Papiere des Teufels* (1842), end of I, 12; *Höllenangst* (1849), I, 9–10, and III, 19–21.

38. For an exact definition of the term (distinguishing between on the one hand the genre of 'Melodrama' in literature and music, a term used in contemporary encyclopedias, and on the other hand the formal technical term 'Melodram') see, for example, *The New Grove Dictionary of Music and Musicians* (London, 1980).

39. See the chapter 'Musik' in HKA, *Stücke 27/II*, 341–43.

40. For the conventional distinctions between 'Kirchen-, Cammer- oder Concert-, und Theater- oder Opernstyl' (church style, chamber or concert style, and theatre or opera style), see *Encyclopädie der gesammten musikalischen Wissenschaften, oder Universal-Lexikon der Tonkunst*, ed. Gustav Schilling, 6 vols (Stuttgart, 1835–38), vol. 6, article 'Styl', pp. 531–33.

41. Ruprecht Wimmer proposed this hypothesis in 1986: 'Lange bevor diese Oper 1857 zum erstenmal vollständig in Wien aufgeführt werden konnte, waren bereits Teile aus ihr, die Ouvertüre und der Pilgerchor, aus Aufführungen von Johann Strauß' Volksgartenkonzerten bekannt' [Long before this opera received its first complete production in Vienna in 1857 sections of it – the overture and the Pilgrims' Chorus – had become familiar from performances by Johann Strauss in his concerts in the Volksgarten]. See HKA, *Stücke 27/II*, (ed.) Jürgen Hein, pp. 262 and 341–42.

42. For a discussion of Nestroy's familiarity with the contemporary media, see W. E. Yates, 'Nestroy und die Rezensenten', *Nestroyana*, 7, 1–2 (1987), 28–40; Walter Obermaier, 'Nestroy und die Presse', in Gerald Stieg and J.-M. Valentin (eds), *Johann Nestroy 1801–1862. Vision du monde et écriture dramatique* (Asnières, 1991), pp. 109–18; F. Walla, 'Zeitungslesen als Inspiration. Ein kleiner Beitrag zur Vorlagenforschung bei Nestroy', *Nestroyana*, 15, 3–4 (1995), 104–13.

43. A detailed review by 'Carlo' published in the *Wiener Zeitschrift für Kunst, Literatur, Theater und Mode* of 29 February 1840 (no. 34, pp. 269–71) commences thus: 'As this institution [the Kärtnertortheater] caters more for the Italian than for the German taste and takes more and more southern operas into the German repertoire, it is not surprising that the opera-lover should demand that the performing singers employ Italian ways of singing despite their underlying German characteristics' (translation).
44. See A. Harrandt, *Wagner und seine Werke in Wien* (Vienna, 1985), pp. 15–16.

Nestroy's 'Epic' Theatre

Jürgen Hein

Auch in der Posse ist noch der Hauptgegenstand eine dramatische Handlung (Adolf Bäuerle)[1]

Ich bin der Kolumbus einer neuen Methode (Johann Nestroy)[2]

Among the reviews of the première of Nestroy's *Das Mädl aus der Vorstadt* [The Girl from the Suburb], that in *Der Sammler* [The Collector] claimed that the play demonstrated the impossibility of turning a narrative into a 'durable work for the stage', for 'the main requirement of a stage play' was the 'action':

> Überall guckt aus der Posse die Erzählung hervor. Die Hauptsachen werden erzählt und die Nebensachen gespielt und eine natürliche Folge davon sind empfindliche Longueurs und widrige Stagnation des Restchens der Handlung, die sich mit Aufgebot alles möglichen Witzes nicht verkleistern und verdecken lassen.
> Herr Nestroy hätte die Posse füglich in zwei Akte zusammendrängen können!
> Abgesehen von der Handlung, scheinen uns auch die Charaktere mangelhaft und es beweisen auch sie, daß sie einer Erzählung entnommen sind. In einer solchen läßt sich vieles verreden, was die Fehlerhaftigkeit in Anlage und Durchführung eines Charakters bezeugen könnte, nicht so aber in einer Posse. Hier entscheidet das Wort nicht, sondern die Handlung.[3]

[Wherever you look in this farce, the narrative peeps out. The main events are narrated and the subsidiary events enacted, and this naturally produces considerable *longueurs* and a repellent stagnation in what little remains of the action, which no amount of wit can paper over or conceal. Herr Nestroy could perfectly well have compressed the farce into two acts!
Apart from the action, we also find the characters deficient, and they prove, too, that they are taken from a narrative. In such a work, the

faulty conception and execution of a character can largely be concealed by verbiage, but that is not the case in a farce. Here it is not the words but the action that counts.]

Apart from the fact that, in this instance, Nestroy was not adapting a narrative, and that some novels were adapted to make successful farces, the critic highlights important aspects of the contemporary discussion concerning a 'good' farce, which is heavily indebted to a poetics governed by 'classical' standards.[4]

Over a century later, despite acknowledging the law of dramatic motivation, Bruno Hannemann was to articulate a contrary position, asserting that Nestroy never feels:

> den Drang, seine Figuren zum Erzählen, zu einer Selbstdarstellung kommen zu lassen. Er hindert sie, einen Faden zu spinnen, läßt sie, wenngleich auf schmalem Raum, nicht erklären, wie es zu ihrer jetzigen, miserablen Lage gekommen ist, dabei wäre das höchst interessant. Es geht hierin nicht um die Schwierigkeit bei der Unterbringung epischer Strukturen im dramatischen Handlungszusammenhang. Nestroy verfügt über seine Figuren recht willkürlich; er läßt sie oft seitenlang sprechen, überall dort, wo es sich um philosophische Exkurse handelt. Dieser draufgängerische Parodist läßt seine Figuren nicht zum Ansatz des Erzählens kommen, weil er nicht geschichtlich denkt. [...] Weil er die Motive verwischt, anstatt sie zu erklären, verurteilt Nestroy seine Figuren zur Geschichtslosigkeit und daher auch zur Statik.[5]

> [the urge to allow his characters to tell a story, to give an account of themselves. He prevents them from spinning a yarn and does not let them explain, however concisely, how they arrived at their present miserable situation, highly interesting though that would be. This is not due to the difficulty of accommodating epic structures within dramatic action. Nestroy deals with his characters just as he pleases, often letting them hold forth for pages, especially in philosophical digressions. The reason why this reckless parodist does not let his characters get started on a story is that he does not think historically. [...] By effacing motives instead of explaining them, Nestroy condemns his characters to an ahistorical and hence static existence.]

What is dramatic and what is epic in the action of a farce that oscillates between life and art, fictionality and referentiality? Is there a contradiction between epic, which points to reality and employs a distancing mode of representation, and drama with its immediacy, that is, the 'absence of a mediating narrative function'?[6] The two quotations indicate some fundamental problems of the poetics of farce in the context of drama governed by 'rules'. It seems to be a hallmark of popular theatre that, to assert itself as theatre in its own right, it must constantly confront the charge of breaking the rules. Here Nestroy steers his own course between tradition and modernity.

Manfred Pfister emphasises that the discussion of the validity of norms and the justifiability of transgressing them – stimulated, above all, by Bertolt Brecht's development of an anti-Aristotelian, 'epic' theatre – has sharpened our awareness of epic tendencies in dramatic texts.[7] At any rate, epic forms of theatre have always been frequent in comedy. They originate in part from mime.

Mimetic representation by 'showing' instead of 'telling', acting by mime and gesture, and the dethronement of literariness by an emphasis on playfulness and dialogue with the public, all combine to make comedy a decidedly non-classical form of drama, without any illusion of reality. Of course, comedy too is 'imitation', right down to the 'imitation of a literary imitation' or parody.

Despite efforts to subject farces to rules and to dignify them as dramatic art, it was recognised early on (for example, by Adolf Bäuerle, Søren Kierkegaard, Gottfried Keller) that the farce is characterised by 'epic' distance, constitutes its own reality, and has a distinct effect on its audience.[8] Bäuerle emphasises 'double laughter' and various degrees of illusion and verisimilitude [Wahrscheinlichkeit] in the action (pp. 138–39), and sees in the farce a 'caricatural image of life' ['karikirtes Bild des Lebens', p. 148], though it, too, must conform to the universal laws of dramatic action. It has been excluded from the realm of dramatic art because of its proximity to parody, its marked affinity to real, local circumstances, and its fondness for physical, material and 'low' subject matter. The farce oscillates between drama and 'relaxed' ('locker') entertainment.

In the light of Aristotle's *Poetics*, the representation of 'low' subjects and specific individuals and actions brings comedy close to epic narrative.[9] Brecht says in his 'Anmerkungen zum *Dreigroschenoper*' ['Notes on *The Threepenny Opera*']:

> Überall aber, wo es Materialismus gibt, entstehen epische Formen in der Dramatik, im Komischen, das immer materialistischer, 'niedriger' eingestellt ist, am meisten und öftesten.[10]

> [But wherever materialism exists, epic forms develop in drama, especially and most often in comedy, which is always more materialist and 'lower' in its outlook.]

In this context we should not forget dialect, which always breaks the dramatic illusion. It is incongruous in elevated drama because it is too close to reality. Although this scarcely applies to the farce, here, too, the ambivalence between dialect as 'natural' everyday language and as a stylistic device for comic realism, along with its distancing effects, deserves closer investigation. Nestroy's contemporary, Heinrich Theodor Rötscher, at any rate, considered dialect and local comedy as incompatible with the 'essence of dramatic art'.[11]

Even a casual glance at the history of drama and theatre shows that the shattering of illusion, 'open form', modern drama and 'epic theatre' must not be lumped together. For comic theatre is always constituted on two levels: as dramatic action and epic commentary, as enactment and satire. Drawing on Harald Weinrich's distinction between 'talking' and 'telling' about the world ('besprochene Welt' and 'erzählte Welt'), one could also distinguish between the portrayal of the world in epic commentary and in dramatic scenes. Here one must refer also to the link between epic and satire.[12] The satirist functions as a kind of narrator; the referential character of satire, as an art of 'showing', demands a break with fictional illusion.

Herbert Herzmann maintains that 'Viennese popular comedy marks an important bridge between the theatre of the Baroque and the epic theatre of the twentieth century'. This is to overlook both the international quality of comedy and the general connections, stretching back to antiquity, between comedy, alienation, and epic elements in drama.[13]

Pfister undertakes to define the 'three most important tendencies that have been linked with the modification of drama by epic' ('Episierung'). These are: 'the abolition of teleology', so that the separate parts of the drama become self-sufficient; 'the abolition of concentration', so that reality can be portrayed in leisurely detail; and 'the abolition of absoluteness', so that an anti-illusionary level of play and story-telling comes into being.[14] He draws up a scheme of epic structures of communication, linguistic and non-linguistic, with some dependent on dramatic characters and some independent of them, and thus provides a clear and systematic account of how various levels of the dramatic text can be modified by epic, including the 'authorial accompanying text', 'the "personal union" between the dramatic character and the mediating story-teller', 'narrative responses, reflection and commentary', the 'gesture of pointing' and the 'laying-bare of the theatrical apparatus'.[15]

The modification of drama by epic implies interrupting the sequence of scenes by undramatic, anti-dramatic, and lyrical elements, changes of perspective, distance from the material and the action, and the involvement of the audience, combined with a style of representation that seeks to demonstrate how things *might* have happened and to provide explanatory comment on them. Epic structures in Nestroy – not only the break with fictional illusion – have been pointed out by scholars in diverse forms. Thus, Ulrich Fülleborn shows how his dramatic form involves the public and thus approaches epic;[16] I have myself pointed out the epic effect of incorporating comic songs within farce;[17] Volker Klotz has remarked on Nestroy's delight in dramatic experiments and his anti-classical, anti-rhetorical 'Radikaldramatik' ['radical drama'];[18] and many people have noted parallels with Brecht's epic theatre and with Ödön von Horváth's renewal of the 'Volksstück' (a popular dramatic form in Germany and Austria in the nineteenth and twentieth centuries, normally writtin in dialect).[19] 'Epic' is not synonymous with 'modern'.[20] Nor does it refer only to the ways of breaking the fictional illusion and introducing alienation on which Nestroy scholarship has repeatedly commented: it refers also to the traditional elements (chorus, songs, role-play, play-within-the-play, stories, commentaries, letters), hence to various forms of distancing the audience from the farcical action by emphasising its artificiality, for example, the discrepancy between character and role, the linguistic mask, rhetorical devices, the intensification of comedy and conscious theatricality.[21] Nestroy's proximity to 'authorial theatre' has been pointed out by Günther Mahal, especially in the comic songs, where the relation between author, actor, character and role in the central, 'mediating' figures requires a more differentiated investigation:

> Auktoriales Theater – das ist ein Theater, das dem Zuschauer zwei Ebenen auf einmal anbietet, die des Spiels und die des Urteils, die des Schauens und die des Bewertens, die der Bühnenhandlung und die der Stellungnahme – einer Stellungnahme, die vom Autor über Mittlerfiguren vorgegeben wird zum Zwecke der Zustimmung.[22]

> [Authorial theatre is a theatre that offers the spectator two levels at once: play and judgement, gazing and evaluation, stage action and reflective response – a response supplied by the author through mediating figures with the aim of securing agreement.]

There have been many studies of interactions and interrelations between comedy and alienation, comedy and epic theatre, and here 'alienation' can apply to the author, the staging and the acting.[23] When material is given comic treatment, attention must also be paid to the distinction between 'alienation *in* comedy and alienation *of* comedy' and between 'acting as disclosure and acting as self-disclosure' ['zwischen zeigendem und sich zeigendem Spiel'].[24]

Taking Lessing's *Minna von Barnhelm* as his example, Helmut Arntzen has shown that almost all criteria of epic theatre can be applied to it, and that the realisation of the 'generic intention' is significantly determined by the interrelations between comedy and alienation. Among others, he mentions delays in the action and the comic effects of 'running on the spot' and repetition.[25] For farce, one may add genre scenes, interpolated episodes, and the non-development of character. An essential relationship between comedy and alienation in Nestroy has been asserted by Reinhold Grimm, who maintains that, in *Der gefühlvolle Kerkermeister* [The Sentimental Jailer], comedy has primacy over alienation while, in *Zu ebener Erde und erster Stock* [Downstairs, Upstairs], alienation threatens to crowd out comedy.[26] Arntzen points out affinities between parody and alienation in the happy ending of *Einen Jux will er sich machen* [High Jinks].[27]

Nestroy does not offer Brecht's stark alternatives of 'theatre of entertainment' versus 'theatre of instruction'. His theatre is not reduced to two modes of reception, empathy or critical detachment; it offers ample scope for 'critical' pleasure that can distinguish between stage reality and real reality, without aiming at any transformation of reality, which would mean seeing the farce through Brechtian spectacles or as part of a programmatic, didactic theatre. Nor, however, does it resemble Romantic comedy in using alienation devices simply as means of representation without further insight.[28] Thanks to its epic features, Nestroy's farce offers critical entertainment which is also an end in itself.

Employing a wide-ranging concept of parody, Gerda Baumbach asserts that Nestroy's texts could be read like episodes of a novel, and that, just as a sequence of plays featuring Harlequin is called a harlequinade ('Harlekinade'), one could speak, not of a dramatic work, but of a 'Nestroyade'.[29] Here we may disregard the question whether distancing, parodistic technique tends to dissolve a work or to reconstitute it, possibly in the sense of deconstruction. At all events, the epic quality seems once again to be significant.

And this epic quality can be seen from yet another angle, if we follow Horst Turk in understanding the dramatic text as the 'translation' of social conventions into theatrical equivalents. Turk maintains that, by playing with theatrical conventions, society can be presented through a repertory of theatrical devices. If the strands of the action are linked, not through what Brecht called a 'Gestus', a vivid incident (a typically epic device, one might add), but rather through words, then, in Turk's view, a paradigm shift brings into being the new 'Volksstück'. He illustrates this paradigm shift by comparing Nestroy's *Das Mädl aus der Vorstadt* with Horváth's *Geschichten aus dem Wiener Wald* [*Tales from the Vienna Woods*]:

> The figures in the old 'Volksstück' excelled in a certain oratorical and manipulative facility, but this was only imitative, inasmuch as they were playing members of society. The new 'Volksstück' ceases to be a popular comedy as soon as the active involvement of ordinary people, their emancipation as speakers and decision-makers, is not simply a matter of acting and presentation but is realised in the action.[30]

This sheds light on the part played by Nestroy in contemporary discussion of the 'Volksstück'.[31] The charges levelled by critics, and the conflicts between the farcical model and the references to social reality which, in some plays, are unmistakable, are also linked with epic and dramatic problems of representation.[32]

We still need a study of the poetics of theatrical space in farce to provide us with a deeper understanding of Nestroy's dramaturgical employment of images and 'silent rhetoric', which also involves epic features.[33] The functional value of topographical references in his plays needs to be explored: places and spaces, including settings with realist and social significance and local colour, indicating 'indoors/outdoors' or 'upstairs/downstairs' and giving theatrical life to changes of place and movement from one setting to another. A tendency towards direct representation has been noted. Nestroy avoids almost entirely having action reported by messengers or happenings off-stage described by spectators ('teichoscopia'); he wants everything to be shown.[34] He sketches visual settings to describe a milieu, to bring out character or to provide contrasts. Stage sets serve to satisfy the audience's enjoyment of spectacle. Increasingly he favours a space defined by movable stage properties, perhaps at the expense of 'local reality'. While satisfying the demands of theatrical practice, Nestroy uses stage properties to make his setting dynamic and visual in the manner of tableaux vivants, and to include aspects of up-to-date reality, which means giving epic form to the events portrayed.[36] Nestroy works with all the theatrical signs, mingling baroque, neo-classical, romantic and Biedermeier sets, right down to stage settings at the beginning of the Industrial Revolution. One might also point out the link between the language of the stage and the staging of language, language as a commentary on the action, and the interplay between linguistic and visual action.

'Epic' stage directions can be found, for example, in *Der Tod am Hochzeitstag* [Death on the Wedding-Day], (I, 21; HKA, *Stücke 1*, 285–87) and in *Der Treulose* [The Disloyal Man], (I, 53; HKA, *Stücke 10*, 60–61) with the contrast between action and language; in addition, non-verbal behaviour in general has an illustrative and epic function. Regula Rüegg investigates 'Kinegramme', taking *Der Talisman* [The Talisman] as her example.[37] These 'kinegrams' also include tableau and pantomime. There are also noteworthy temporal discontinuities, as in *Dreyßig Jahre aus dem Leben eines Lumpen* [Thirty Years in the Life of a Scoundrel], *Weder Lorbeerbaum noch Bettelstab* [Neither Laurel Wreath nor Beggar's Staff], *Der Treulose*, and *Der alte Mann mit der jungen Frau* [The Old Man with the Young Wife], contradicting the prevailing view, held by Grillparzer among others, that comedy required the unity of time.

The presentation of events running parallel in different settings (for example, *Zu ebener Erde*, *Das Haus der Temperamente* [The House of Temperaments] and *Umsonst!* [In Vain!], I, 9–21) not only shows how ingenious and innovatory Nestroy was, as Pfister says, but also represents much more than a movement towards epic by means of stage technique.[38] The sets are used to narrate complex stories which otherwise, as a mere sequence, would remain colourless and unmemorable. The interplay of simultaneity and succession in *Der Tod am Hochzeitstag* drew comments from Friedrich Dürrenmatt.[39] As for Nestroy's magical plays (*Zauberspiele*), they are in general more epic than dramatic in their structure.

Many dialogues and comic songs in Nestroy's farces explicitly discuss literature and the theatre and compare 'life' with 'art'. Examples include *Der Tod am Hochzeitstag* (II, 14; HKA, *Stücke 1*, 310–12), the ballad of the theatre in *Weder Lorbeerbaum noch Bettelstab* (III, 9; SW III, 402–4), Weinberl's allusion to the novel in *Einen Jux will er sich machen* (II, 1; HKA, *Stücke 18/I*, 36–37), and the theatrical intensification through parodistic play-acting in *Die Papiere des Teufels* [The Devil's Documents] (II, 5–6; SW XI, 307–17).[40]

In *Die Verbannung aus dem Zauberreiche* [Exile from the Realm of Magic] Longinus defends the 'Ritterstück' (pseudo-medieval drama) as the triumph of art against 'das Ifflandische Thränenwasser' [Iffland's floods of tears]:

> Der Ritter kommt zurück, aus blutiger Fehde, und findet seine Geliebte treulos, das ist interessant – er geräth in Wuth, das ist heroisch – er flucht der Falschen, verläßt sie auf immer, das ist Edelmuth – er zieht ins gelobte Land, kommt aber gleich wieder zurück, das ist Consequenz – er zecht mit seinen Kampfgenossen, bis die Geisterstunde schlägt, und herein schwankt der Schatten des Gemordeten mit der bleichen Silberlocke in der geballten Faust, das ist dramatische Gerechtigkeit. Aber beim Iffland, o je, da lamentiren die Familien aktweis daher, daß

man's Teufels werden möcht, – und um was handelt sich die ganze
Verzweiflung? Um 200 fl. Schein, wenn s' den Bettel im Parterre
zusammen schießeten und hinaufschicketen, so hätt ein jede solche
Comödie im 1. Act schon ein End. (HKA, *Stücke 1*, 210).

[The knight returns from bloody warfare and finds his sweetheart
unfaithful, that's interesting – he flies into a rage, that's heroic – he
curses the false-hearted woman and abandons her forever, that's nobility
– he sets off for the Holy Land, but comes back right away, that's
consistency – he tipples with his fellow warriors till the witching hour
strikes, and in totters the shade of the murdered man with a faded lock
of silver hair in its clenched fist, that's poetic justice. But in Iffland,
dear oh dear, families spend whole acts lamenting away, it's enough to
drive you to distraction, – and what's all their despair about in the end?
A bank-note for 200 florins. If someone passed the hat round the stalls
and handed the proceeds up to the stage, none of these comedies would
get beyond the first act.]

Narrative summaries and commentaries can also be interpreted as programmatic statements by the author, putting the case for conscious theatricality
with epic elements against kinds of drama, such as bourgeois sentimental
plays that claimed to depict everyday life and to offer realistic conversation.

Nestroy lets his characters tell stories; his comic songs provide epic
integration; letters read out on stage form another epic element. *Pace* Hannemann, epic situations, 'life-stories' told by the main character or characters,
and narrative expositions can be found in many plays, including *Der Feenball*
[The Fairy Ball], where a character declares: 'Meine Lebensg'schicht müßts
hören' ['You must hear the story of my life'] (I, 7; HKA, *Stücke 5*, 19). In
Judith und Holofernes Judith describes her relationship with Manasses (scene
24; HKA, *Stücke 26/II*, 107–09; 136–37). And in *Der Schützling* [The
Protégé] Gottlieb Herb not only tells the story of his life and love but reflects
on the act of story-telling and cites Siegwart, Abelard and Werther as
unfortunate lovers analogous to himself. He begins self-consciously:

Es war an einem schönen Sommermorgen – nichts da! Zu was bei einer
gediegen-tragischen Sache mit einem romantischen Gewand kokettieren
– also glattweg: vor acht Jahren [...].[41]

[It was on a fine summer morning – hold it! What's the point of
dressing up a solid, tragic story in a romantic costume? All right, here
goes. Eight years ago ...]

Further instances of epic structures of communication, for example, anachronistic allusions to the contemporary context, have been noted by Pfister in
Judith und Holofernes (scenes 7 and 9, HKA, *Stücke 26/II*, 90, 91–92, 122,
123–24). The same applies to comic songs in travesties.[42]

Another type is represented by interpolated stories. These have diverse
functions and, in some cases, their comedy becomes independent of the play

as a whole. Examples include Staberl's story from 'Gumpendorf an der Loire' in *Der Kobold* [The Brownie] (I, 3; HKA, *Stücke 14*, 101–02); the 'Pintsch-Pantsch' story in *Zampa* (I, 15; SW, III, 195); and the beginning of the monologue in *Der Schützling*, which functions as a means of epic integration:

> 'Es war einmal ein Bauer und eine Bäurin, die hab'n ein' Bub'n gehabt, und der Bub is mit der Zeit ein Bauer worden und hat eine Bäurin g'nommen, und wie er lang genug mit der Bäurin g'lebt hat g'habt, nachher is er g'storben.' – Diese interessante Schilderung [...] (I, 2; SW VII, 114)

> ['Once upon a time there were a farmer and his wife; they had a little boy, and by and by the boy became a farmer and married a wife, and after living with her for a good long while, he went and died.' – This interesting account ...]

Or the fable in *Mein Freund*:

> Es war einmal ein Pintsch, der zehn Jahr' an der Kette hing, und nicht verlassen hat das treue Tier das Haus. Vor kurzem riß der Pintsch sich los und rannte in die Welt, doch alsogleich fängt ihn ein Wäscher, der ihn bei der Nacht zum Wachen zwingt und ihn bei Tage einspannt in seinen Wäsche-Schubkarren. 'Ach wär' ich doch in meiner alten Hütte!' – so winselte der Pintsch – [...] Die Fabel is schon aus. (III, 6; SW VII, 357)

> [Once upon a time there was a dog that was kept on a chain for ten years, and the faithful beast never left the house. Not long ago the dog broke free and rushed into the world, but he was at once caught by a laundryman, who made him keep guard at night and pull the laundry-cart during the day. 'Oh, if only I were back in my kennel!' whined the dog – ... That's the end of the fable.]

Not to mention the drastic summary of Grillparzer's *Sappho* in *Heimliches Geld, heimliche Liebe* [Secret Wealth, Secret Love]:

> Ich und eine reiche Wittwe, das wär g'rad' so, als wie die poetische Gutsbesitzerin, von der s' a Stück aufführen, – Sapho hat s' g'heißen – die sich aus dem damahligen Circus gymnasticus einen griechischen Tagdieb nach Haus bracht hat. Selbstmord war der weltbekannte Ausgang dieser Histori, – sie hat sich in's Wasser g'stürzt, und er hat sich in's Stub'nmadl verbrennt. (I, 24; HKA, *Stücke 32*, 33–4)

> [Me and a rich widow, that would be just like the poetic lady with the estate in the play – her name was Sappho – who brought home a Greek layabout from the 'Circus gymnasticus' they had in those days. All the world knows that the story ended in suicide, – she jumped into the water, and he fell for the parlour-maid.]

This category also includes the ballad-like narratives in *Robert der Teuxel* (I, 4; HKA, *Stücke 6*, 82–83) and *Weder Lorbeerbaum noch Bettelstab* (III, 10; SW

III, 402–04). In addition, the examination of Willibald in scene 10 of *Die schlimmen Buben in der Schule* [The Naughty Schoolboys] (SW XIII, 222–28), where the action comes to a stop, can be described as epic. The stage letters with their various functions (for example, in *Der Tod am Hochzeitstag, Der böse Geist Lumpacivagabundus, Der Affe und der Bräutigam, Das Mädl aus der Vorstadt, Heimliches Geld, heimliche Liebe*), deserve a study in their own right.[43]

When adapting his sources, Nestroy used to sketch the action of a farce by retelling the story in his own words, summarising the content, drawing up plans, and making prose drafts.[44] Even in the scenarios that were conceived dramatically, resembling the scenarios of travelling companies in their ambivalence between defining the action and leaving it open, epic elements are to be found. Epic drafts and dramatic production (an idea and its development) are not mutually exclusive.

Finally, Nestroy's technique of adaptation, which is also characterised by epic modification, will be illustrated by two extracts from sketches for *Theaterg'schichten durch Liebe, Intrigue, Geld und Dummheit* [Theatrical Tales of Love, Intrigue, Money and Stupidity]. The drafts and sketches document how Nestroy took Alexandre Dumas' novel, *Olympe de Clèves*, and changed its emphasis. They let us discern the hand of the dramatist, tautening his material by stripping away everything inessential, but also introducing epic features in inventing new incidents and characters. In general, they provide qualified substantiation of Yates's observation that Nestroy 'is unwilling to take over comic material that is already in the original'.[45] He transfers the material from the courtly and monastic world to the middle-class commercial setting of the pharmacist's shop, from the court theatre of the Comédie-Française to the middle-class urban theatre. Because censorship would, in any case, have prohibited the scenes in the monastery, the police station, and the court-room, the only settings left were the theatrical milieu and the lunatic asylum, and Nestroy was obliged to invent the third setting – the pharmacist's shop – along with new incidents and plot elements. The restructured plot is filled out with stock motifs from the source and from elsewhere. This is done partly through epic modification, as in Conrad's story at the end of the farce (II, 33; HKA, *Stücke 33*, 79). The qualities that generally characterise Nestroy's adaptation of narrative sources – concentration and tautening, simplification of the atmosphere, of the plot strands and of the groups of characters – can also be demonstrated here, but epic features are apparent as well.

In *Höllenangst* [Fear of Hell], for example, there are more scenes than in the French original, but their number, rather than heightening the dramatic qualities, brings the action closer to epic, a tendency enhanced by theatrical effects. This is supported by the idea of ending the play by sending the father Pfrim and the son Wendelin off on a journey of penitence and atonement (see HKA, *Stücke 27/II*, 118).

In transforming his sources, Nestroy always introduces domestic life, reduces powerful emotions, gives events a comic turn, and tones down theatrical effects. He transfers the action from the monastery and the court to the world of the middle-class family with its social life (Stössl is head of a family and also a councillor with responsibility for theatrical privileges), which demands the invention of new characters and action.

The open-air performance of Grillparzer's *Sappho* in *Theaterg'schichten*, and the parodistic medley of tunes known as a 'Quodlibet', express a heightened tendency to make material more fictional, comic and theatrical. Theatrical themes are given a worldly colouring: the 'sin' of devotion to comedy is turned into a misguided middle-class mania for the theatre. Nestroy reduces theatrical discourse to commonplaces of middle-class theatre-mania while developing the playful and satirical dimension with his scenes set in the open-air theatre ('Arena') and the asylum. He exploits all the motifs and groupings of the novel that are suitable for the transformation of the material into the world of farce, which is simultaneously close to everyday life and at a playful remove from it.

The first extract reveals the dramatic sequence of events proceeding along basically epic lines (the characters still bear the names of the actors or their parts: Treuman[n], Rön[nekamp], Sch[ol]z, N[e]st[ro]y, Gr[ois]; ARth [Alter Rath], Theatermeister). The short sketch of dialogue already indicates the dissolution of epic features mentioned earlier in II, 33. Epic features give rise to drama insofar as the dramatist thinks in terms of parts and roles, imagining himself both as designing roles and as an actor (seen in his use of the first person):

Trman's Schspielverhältniß folgendermaßen:
Treuman aus Kunstliebe durchgegangen dem Vater ARth und engagiert worden, und hat an einem Theater eine Schauspielrn kennen gelernt Rön und geheurathet. später nach unglücklicher Ehe, hat er die Flucht ergriffen das Theater ebenfalls satt gekriegt, hat sein Malergeschäft hervor gesucht, seinen wahren Nahmen angenommen, und um alle Verbindungen mit dem Theater, hauptsächlich aber die mit seiner Frau abzubrechen einen Brief bey seiner Flucht hinterlassen, wo er seiner Frau schrieb er hat sich in's Wasser gestürzt. Dieses ist vor einem Jahre geschehen. Wenige Tage vor Anfang des Stückes ist Trmn zurückgekommen in's väterliche Haus, nachdem er sich als Maler einen Nahmen gemacht, denn er wollte nicht directe, als verlorener Sohn zurückkehren. Am Tage wo das Stück beginnt heißt es daß die erste Vorstellung einer Gesellschaft ist die Arena erbaute. Ein Director ist da, den Trm nicht persönlich kennt, nur Nahmen. Bey diesem Dirctor ist eine Schauspielrn, die als die Tochter des Drctor gilt, und folglich auch den Nahmen dieses Drctrs führt.

[rechte Spalte:]   Gr Du bist ihr Mörder
                        Tr Nein ich bin nur ihr Mann.
Theatermeister hilft dem Trm in seiner Intrigue gegen Nsty um zu hintertreiben daß ich dem Theaterdirector Schz auf die Beine helfe durch mein Vermögen welches ich, laut Testament bekomme wenn ich heurathe. Der Theatermeister speculiert nehmlich auf die Direction des Schoz, ist ein practischer gescheidter Mann, und will so Schz aus dem

Jürgen Hein

Sattel heben. (HKA, *Stücke 33*, 230–31)

[Treumann's relation to the theatre as follows:
Treumann's love of art made him run away from his father, the Old
Councillor, and become an actor. At a theatre he met and married an
actress, Rönnekamp. Later, after an unhappy marriage, he took flight
and was also sick of the theatre, he resumed his profession as a painter
under his real name and, to break off all links with the theatre and,
above all, with his wife, he left behind a letter telling his wife he had
drowned himself. This happened a year ago. A few days before the play
begins, Treumann has returned to his paternal home after making a
reputation as a painter, not wanting to return merely as a prodigal son.
On the day the play begins, there is said to be the first performance by
a company that set up the open-air theatre. There is a director whom
Treumann does not know personally, only by name. With this director
is an actress who passes as his daughter and therefore also bears his
name.
[*right-hand column*:]   Gr You're her murderer
                            Tr No, only her husband.
The theatre manager helps Treumann in his intrigue against Nestroy to
prevent me from helping the director Scholz with the fortune which,
according to the will, I am to receive on marrying. For the theatre
manager, a clever, practical man, wants Scholz to be director so that he
can unseat him.]

Further insight into the epic and dramatic shaping of the material is provided
by the prose sketch of the dramatic 'quodlibet' in II, 22–5:

22ᵗᵉ Scene
(DAMISCH, WÄRTER; DIE VORIGEN.)
*(DAMISCH wird unter großem Lärmen von (x den x) mehreren WÄRTERN zur
Mittelthüre gewaltsam hereingebracht. Ein WÄRTER sagt dem DOCTOR, daß
dieser Mensch (DAMISCH) von der Wache gebracht worden sey, und
überreicht dem DOCTOR eine Schrift; dieser liest: 'Wollte mit Gewalt ohne
Geld das Entrée im Theater erzwingen, und, infolge seines Benehmens, als
ein Wahnsinniger arretiert'. DAMISCH in Extase erzählt, daß die Angebethete
ihn verlassen habe, und aufgetreten sey, er müsse zu ihr; er will sich mit
Gewalt losreissen. Der DOCTOR erklärt ihn für einen Rasenden.)*

23ᵗᵉ Scene
(MAXNER; LISI, MALI, mehrere Neugierige beyderley Geschlechts; DIE VORIGEN.)
*(Die Benannten drängen sich zur Mittelthüre herein. MAXNER will gutstehn
für DAMISCH, und sagt, daß er ihn kenne, und daß DAMISCH bey ihm wohne,
er sey wohl dumm, aber nicht närrisch.)*

24ᵗᵉ Scene
(STÖSSL, CONRAD; DIE VORIGEN.)
(STÖSSL kommt um die Loslassung des DAMISCH, ist jedoch sehr ergrimmt

97

über dessen Streiche, CONRAD *hält* STÖSSL's *Wuth in Schrancken, und sagt er wolle zu* DAMISCH's *Herzen sprechen; richtet gegen* DAMISCH *eine höchst gefühlvolle Stelle, in welche* DAMISCH *einfällt, in dieses Duo fällt* STÖSSL *ebenfalls mit Rührung ein. Als das Zureden vergebens bleibt, wird* STÖSSL *rabiat, und tritt dictatorisch gegen* DAMISCH *auf. Dieser, hierüber aufgebracht, erklärt, daß* STÖSSL *ihm sein Vermögen auszahlen müße, wenn er heurathe, und nun werde er heurathen, und zwar keine Andere als die, trotz ihres Verrathes, noch immer heiß angebethete Rosaura. Alle rufen staunend aus: Welche Verblendung!)*

*25*ᵗᵉ *Scene*
(SCHOFEL; DIE VORIGEN*)*
(SCHOFEL *ist, wie* DAMISCH *seinen Entschluß ausgesprochen, aus der Seitenthüre rechts getreten, ein* WÄRTER *begleitet ihn.* SCHOFEL *stürzt vor, und sagt, daß er seinen Verstand wiedererwachen fühle; er umarmt* DAMISCH *als künftigen reichen Schwiegersohn.* MAXNER *sagt zu* SCHOFEL, *daß es Unrecht sey, die Dummheit eines jungen Menschen solchergestalt auszubeuten, da es aber nun einmahl so geschehn, so werde er (*MAXNER*) nun auch seine Forderungen geltend machen.* SCHOFEL *sagt, er fühle abermahls einen Anfall von Irrsinn, welcher sich jedesmahl einstellt, so oft ihn Jemand mit einer Geldforderung anspricht.* DAMISCH *sagt in freudiger Extase: Alles was sein ist, gehört auch dem Onkl meiner Rosaura?* STÖSSL *ist ergrimmt, er,* MAXNER, LISI, *und* MALI *rufen: Nicht möglich! das darf nicht seyn! Der* DOCTOR *sagt, es seyen wohl Alle beynahe Halbverrückte, jedoch noch nicht ganz reif, um in der Anstalt verbleiben zu können.* STÖSSL *sagt im Tone des Vorwurf's zu* CONRAD: *'Du hast sauber Dein Versprechen gehalten.'* CONRAD *erwiedert mit Zuversicht: 'Er heurathet sie doch nicht, ich schwöre es Ihnen.' Hier beginnt die Schluß-Stretta des Quodlibets, nach derselben Alle ab. Die Musick endet.)*
VERWANDLUNG.   (HKA, *Stücke 33,* 287–88)

[Scene 22. Damisch, warders; previous cast. – Damisch is forcibly brought in through the middle door by several warders with much noise. A warder tells the Doctor that this person (Damisch) was brought in by the watchmen, and hands the doctor a note. The latter reads: 'Wanted to force his way violently into the theatre without paying, and in view of his behaviour was arrested as a madman'. Damisch recounts in ecstasy that the woman he adores has left him and gone on the stage; he has to join her; he tries to tear himself away by force. The Doctor declares him a maniac.

Scene 23. Maxner; Lisi, Mali, several inquisitive onlookers of both sexes; the previous cast. – Those named crowd in through the middle door. Maxner, willing to vouch for Damisch, says he knows him and that Damisch lives with him and is certainly stupid, but not mad.

Scene 24. Stössl, Conrad; the previous cast. – Stössl has come to procure

Damisch's release, but is very annoyed at his antics; Conrad moderates Stössl's fury and says he will appeal to Damisch's heart; he sings a very tender song to him, in which Damisch joins; Stössl likewise joins emotionally in this duet. When persuasion proves vain, Stössl flies into a rage and addresses Damisch dictatorially. The latter indignantly declares that Stössl is obliged to hand over his fortune to him when he marries, and he is now going to marry none other than Rosaura, whom he still adores despite her treachery. All exclaim in astonishment: 'What blindness!'

Scene 25. Schofel; the previous cast. – As Damisch uttered his decision, Schofel entered by the right-hand door, accompanied by a warder. Schofel rushes forward and says that he feels his reason reawaking; he embraces Damisch as his future rich son-in-law. Maxner tells Schofel that it is wrong to take advantage of a young person's stupidity in this way, but, now that it has happened, he (Maxner) will also put forward his demands. Schofel says he feels another attack of madness coming on; this happens whenever anyone asks him for money. Damisch says in a joyous ecstasy: 'Does all his property belong also to the uncle of my Rosaura?' Stössl is angry; he, Maxner, Lisi and Mali cry: 'Impossible! That musn't happen!' The Doctor says they all seem to be half crazy, but not ripe enough to stay in the asylum. Stössl says to Conrad in a reproachful tone: 'That's a fine way you kept your promise.' Conrad answers confidently: 'He won't marry her, I swear.' Here begins the closing *stretta* of the 'Quodlibet', whereupon *exeunt omnes*. The music ends. The scene changes.]

The transposition of this epic plan into dramatic scenes (see HKA, *Stücke 33*, 67–73) shows how epic material is transcended and preserved in being transformed into drama and adjusted to the demands of the theatre. The 'cited' situation and the dramatic effect are interdependent. Nestroy's eye for the theatre and his technique of staging reflect the conventions of theatrical practice and put their devices to artistic use. Being interested in creating a theatre for spectators rather than in producing a 'work', he preserves in his adaptation the dialectical relation between the openness of the framework and the need for a definite text. The words of the cake-baker, Krapfl, in *Sie sollen ihn nicht haben oder Der holländische Bauer* [They Shan't Have him, or: The Dutch Farmer], can be applied to Nestroy the dramatist and his craft of farce: 'I treat my craft as a science and through my craft I elevate myself to a loftier viewpoint' (HKA, *Stücke 28/I*, 13).

Notes

1. 'Even in farce the main subject is a dramatic action': Bäuerle, 'Über die Posse', *Allgemeine Theaterzeitung*, 1 (1806), 136–40, 147–51 (p. 147).
2. 'I am the Columbus of a new method': Nestroy, 'Reserve', no. 169.
3. SW XI, 522–23; cf. HKA, *Stücke 17/II*, ed. W. E. Yates (1998).

4. See W. E. Yates, *Nestroy and the Critics* (Columbia, SC, 1994).
5. Hannemann, *Johann Nestroy: Nihilistisches Welttheater und verflixter Kerl. Zum Ende der Wiener Komödie* (Bonn, 1977), pp. 134–35.
6. Manfred Pfister, *Das Drama. Theorie und Analyse* (Munich, 1977), p. 103.
7. Pfister, *Das Drama*, p. 104.
8. See Jürgen Hein, '"Eine Posse sehen, heißt für den Gebildeten gleichsam Lotterie spielen." Produktions- und Wirkungsbedingungen der Wiener Posse im internationalen Kontext', in Wolfgang Jansen (ed.), *Unterhaltungstheater in Deutschland. Geschichte – Ästhetik – Ökonomie* (Berlin, 1995), pp. 29–53.
9. See Helmut Arntzen, 'Komödie und episches Theater', in Reinhold Grimm and Klaus L. Berghahn (eds), *Wesen und Formen des Komischen im Drama* (Darmstadt, 1975), pp. 441–55 (p. 442).
10. Brecht, *Gesammelte Werke*, 20 vols (Frankfurt, 1967), vol. 17, p. 999.
11. Rötscher, *Die Kunst der dramatischen Darstellung*, mit einem Geleitwort von Oskar Walzel (Berlin, 1919), p. 40.
12. See Kurt Wölfel, 'Epische und satirische Welt. Zur Technik des satirischen Erzählens', *Wirkendes Wort*, 10 (1960), 85–98.
13. Herzmann, 'Das epische Theater und das Volksstück', *MAL*, 28 (1995), i. 95–111 (p. 96). Since I completed this contribution, my attention has been drawn to Herzmann's recently published monograph *Tradition und Subversion. Das Volksstück und das epische Theater* (Tübingen, 1997). Herzmann comes to the conclusion that Viennese popular comedy anticipated Brecht's epic theatre and, in examining the concept 'epic', he concentrates on the way in which Brecht made coarse theatre literarily acceptable, on his use of local colour, on his dramatisation of fate and also on the different forms of laughter.
14. Pfister, *Das Drama*, pp. 104–05.
15. Ibid., p. 123.
16. Fülleborn, 'Offenes Geschehen in geschlossener Form: Grillparzers Dramenkonzept. Mit einem Ausblick auf Raimund und Nestroy', in Reinhold Grimm (ed.), *Deutsche Dramentheorien*, vol. 2 (Frankfurt, 1971), pp. 293–322.
17. Jürgen Hein, *Spiel und Satire in der Komödie Johann Nestroys* (Bad Homburg, Berlin, Zürich, 1970); '"Gesungene Philosophie". Aspekte des Nestroyschen Coupletwerks', in Gerald Stieg and Jean-Marie Valentin (eds), *Johann Nestroy (1801–1862): Vision du monde et écriture dramatique* (Asnières, 1991), pp. 61–74.
18. Klotz, *Radikaldramatik. Szenische Vor-Avantgarde von Holberg zu Nestroy, von Kleist zu Grabbe* (Bielefeld, 1996), pp. 185–214.
19. E.g. Siegfried Brill, *Die Komödie der Sprache. Untersuchungen zum Werke Johann Nestroys* (Nuremberg, 1967); Roger Alan Crockett, *Nestroy and Brecht: Aspects of Modern German Folk Comedy*, diss. (University of Illinois at Urbana-Champaign, 1979); Hannemann, *Nestroy*; Hein, *Spiel und Satire*; Ansgar Hillach, *Die Dramatisierung des komischen Dialogs. Figur und Rolle bei Nestroy* (Munich, 1967); G. S. Slobodkin, 'Nestroy und die Tradition des Volkstheaters im Schaffen Brechts', *Weimarer Beiträge*, 24 (1978), ix. 99–117.
20. See Franz H. Mautner, 'Nestroys Kunst und unsere Zeit', *Jahrbuch der deutschen Schillergesellschaft*, 7 (1963), 383–415; Hein, 'Johann Nestroy und das moderne Drama des 20. Jahrhunderts', *Neue Zürcher Zeitung*, 10 March 1974, 51–52.
21. On discrepancies, see Hillach, *Dramatisierung*; on linguistic masks, Brill, *Komödie der Sprache*; on rhetoric, Wolfgang Neuber, *Nestroys Rhetorik. Wirkungspoetik und Altwiener Volkskomödie im 19. Jahrhundert* (Bonn, 1987).
22. Günther Mahal, *Auktoriales Theater – die Bühne als Kanzel. Auktoritätsakzeptierung des Zuschauers als Folge dramatischer Persuasionsstrategie* (Tübingen, 1982), p. 155. On comic songs, see ibid., pp. 117–19.
23. See Arntzen, 'Komödie und episches Theater', p. 257.

Jürgen Hein

24. See Horst Turk, 'Von der Volkskomödie zum sozialen Drama. Ein Problem der Übersetzung', in Ursula Hassel and Herbert Herzmann (eds), *Das zeitgenössische deutschsprachige Volksstück* (Tübingen, 1992), pp. 35–64 (pp. 37, 51).
25. Arntzen, 'Komödie und episches Theater', pp. 451–53.
26. Grimm, 'Verfremdung. Beiträge zu Wesen und Ursprung eines Begriffs', *Revue de Littérature Comparée*, 35 (1961), 207–36.
27. Arntzen, 'Komödie und episches Theater', pp. 448–49.
28. Cf. Arntzen, ibid., pp. 450–51.
29. Baumbach, *Seiltänzer und Betrüger? Parodie und kein Ende. Ein Beitrag zu Geschichte und Theorie von Theater* (Tübingen and Basle, 1995), p. 33.
30. (Trans. from) Turk, 'Von der Volkskomödie zum sozialen Drama', pp. 52–53.
31. See W. E. Yates, 'The idea of the "Volksstück" in Nestroy's Vienna', *German Life and Letters*, 38 (1985), 462–73.
32. See Klotz, *Radikaldramatik*, discussing *Heimliches Geld, heimliche Liebe*.
33. See Neuber, 'Stumme Rhetorik: sprachlose Wirkungsstrategien in Nestroys Possen *Der Talisman* und *Einen Jux will er sich machen*', in Stieg and Valentin (eds), *Nestroy*, pp. 101–08.
34. See Friedrich Walla, *Untersuchungen zur dramatischen Technik Johann Nestroys*, diss. (Vienna, 1969).
36. On the up-to-date staging of *Eisenbahnheiraten*, see Johann Hüttner, 'Nestroys Räume im Text und die realen Bühnenräume', lecture delivered at the 21st International 'Nestroy-Gespräche', Schwechat, 1995.
37. Rüegg, *'Im Abgehen ein Schnippchen schlagend': Zur Funktion von Kinegrammen in Volksstücken des 19. und 20. Jahrhunderts* (Berne, 1991), pp. 170–82.
38. See Pfister, *Das Drama*, p. 364; Grimm, 'Verfremdung', pp. 264–65.
39. Dürrenmatt, *Theaterprobleme* (Zürich, 1955), p. 24; cf. Pfister, *Das Drama*, p. 363.
40. For further examples, see Jürgen Hein, 'Bild und Rolle des Theaters in Nestroys Werk', *Nestroyana*, 4 (1982), 98–103.
41. III, 7; SW VII, 187–88 (cf. 114–17). For further examples, see *Kampl*, I, 9 (HKA, *Stücke 31*, 12); *Der Talisman*, III, 18 (HKA, *Stücke 17/I*, 79–80); *Die Papiere des Teufels*, Prologue, 1 (SW XI, 240); and the stories of Kathi and Gluthammer in *Der Zerrissene*, I, 3 (HKA, *Stücke 21*, 30–32).
42. Pfister, *Das Drama*, p. 361; Hein, *Spiel und Satire*, pp. 114–18.
43. See Klotz, *Bühnen-Briefe: Kritiken und Essays zum Theater. Davor eine Abhandlung über Briefszenen im Schauspiel und Oper* (Frankfurt, 1972), pp. 25–27, 46–48.
44. See W. E. Yates (ed.), *Vom schaffenden zum edierten Nestroy* (Vienna, 1994).
45. See W. E. Yates, *Nestroy: Satire and Parody in Viennese Popular Comedy* (Cambridge, 1972), p. 103.

Nestroy and Slavery

Walter Obermaier

Nestroy did not leave us any writings or documents that reveal his views on slavery. In this article, therefore, I will focus primarily on Nestroy's acting career as far as it concerns plays that are set in the mysterious Orient and in which slaves appear on stage. My starting point is Nestroy's play *Der Zauberer Sulphur* [Sulphur the Magician], followed by a discussion of the contemporary Viennese theatre-goer's potential knowledge of slavery. I then turn to the theme of slavery in Nestroy's own plays, above all in *Genius, Schuster und Marqueur* [Genie, Cobbler and Marqueur], *Der Zauberer Sulphur* and *Moppels Abentheuer* [Moppel's Adventures]. Finally, I reflect on the idea of the 'slavery' of everyday life at the time, in particular with regard to Nestroy's own life.

Even Nestroy's early plays, which still feature numerous traditional figures from the *Zauberkomödie* [comedy with supernatural elements] as well as from the hugely popular Viennese blend of *Volkstheater* and the fantastic, hardly ever contain slaves, despite an abundance of fairies, genies, magicians, nymphs, exotic extras and dazzling stage effects. There is only one *Zauberposse* [farce with supernatural elements] of Nestroy's that expressly puts slavery on the stage, even if it is not the central theme of the play, and that is *Der Zauberer Sulphurelectrimagneticophosphoratus und die Fee Walpurgiblocksbergiseptemtrionalis oder Des ungerathenen Herrn Sohns Leben Thaten und Meinungen, wie auch seine Bestrafung in der Sclaverey und was sich alldort ferneres mit ihm begab* [Sulphurelectrimagneticophosphoratus the Magician and Walpurgiblocksbergiseptemtrionalis the Fairy or The life, deeds and opinions of the wayward son, as well as his punishment in slavery and all the other things that happened to him during it] (1834).

It is strange that none of the play's reviewers, not even Franz Wiest, who made persistent fun of it in *Der Sammler*, was struck by the parodistic character of the title. Nestroy exaggerates with his title the use, common in popular theatre and popular novels of the time, of a subtitle introduced by 'or' and followed by the corresponding baroque models. In my view, he meant to emphasise from the outset that the new play was a parody, because the audience itself could hardly be expected to recognise the object of the parody in Ernst Raupach's original, *Robert der Teufel* [Robert the Devil].[1]

The theme of slavery was not considered worthy of note by contemporary critics nor has it been commented on in the secondary literature.[2] This is no doubt justifiable because it formed part of the familiar trappings of an oriental setting. Nestroy himself had sung and acted in a whole series of plays with oriental elements. The Orient as an exotic setting, and in particular the native of Vienna who suddenly finds himself there, was a frequent feature of the *Volkskomödie* and other genres. Transport to this setting was brought about by the miraculous interventions of fairies and spirits or by purely earthly, though nonetheless improbable events, such as pirates, who sold Europeans as slaves in an Orient of the imagination, composed chiefly of Turkish, North African and Indian set pieces. The romance of the harem might complete the backdrop. Although slaves and slavery do not have entries in contemporary dictionaries of the theatre, Turkish and oriental costumes are discussed in detail.

As is well known, Nestroy made his debut on stage with the Vienna Court Opera in the role of Sarastro in Mozart's *Magic Flute*. There are slaves at Sarastro's court who are kept in subjection by the Moor Monostatos, their guard and a kind of superior slave himself. In him we encounter that type of slave who, having acquired a modest degree of power, exhibits the worst kind of tyranny. Admittedly, a problematic factor here is the equation of black with evil. Grillparzer's black slave, Zanga, in *Der Traum ein Leben* [Life is a Dream] (1834) also belongs to that tradition.

In Amsterdam in 1824–25, Nestroy played Bassa Selim in Mozart's *Die Entführung aus dem Serail* which, in its thematic combination of Orient, slavery, harem, happy ending and return home provides a classic example of its kind. In Amsterdam he also appeared for the first time in the light but popular farce after Eugène Scribe *Der Bär und der Bassa* [Bear and Bassa]. He appeared successfully in the role of Ali Hatschi for years after in the Theater an der Wien and, above all, in the Theater in der Leopoldstadt (later renamed the Carltheater). The play is set in the Turkey of fairy-tale. Female slaves are in abundance, and Bassa is an essentially good-hearted character even if he does have a fatal weakness for decapitations. The ending, with its mistaken identities and bear disguises, could almost have served as the inspiration for *Häuptling Abendwind* [Chief Evening Wind].

In the following years, Nestroy appeared on stage in Brünn and Graz in Boïeldieu's *The Caliph of Bagdad*, in Rossini's *The Italian Girl in Algiers* and *The Turk in Italy*, and in Meyerbeer's *Der Kreuzritter in Ägypten* [The Crusader in Egypt]. Furthermore, he frequently played the leading role in *Peter Stieglitz*, a didactic play by Joseph Alois Gleich, which is similarly set in a fictive Orient. He also played in Adolf Bäuerle's didactic *Zauberstück* entitled *Wien, Paris, London und Constantinopel*. In this play the audience is presented, in the middle of London itself, with a sort of slave market, namely a market for wives, where husbands offer their wives for sale. Clearly this is an allusion to the slave market in the Haymarket in London's West End. This had been a well-known area for prostitution since the eighteenth century.[3] As late as 1849 it was mentioned in a dramatic portrait by Louis Flex entitled *Der*

103

Weiberverkauf in London [Wives for Sale in London], which was performed with moderate success at the Carltheater.

For Nestroy, his public, and his reviewers a fantasy Orient was therefore nothing new, and slavery on the stage nothing unusual. The men who end up in the Orient in plays such as *Die Entführung aus dem Serail*, *Der Bär und der Bassa*, or *Wien, Paris, London und Constantinopel* are, in fact – even though they indeed become slaves – simply protagonists in an escape story in which slavery plays only a folkloristic role. In Nestroy's *Zauberer Sulphur*, slavery is an essential part of the stage reality, and Robert, the play's main character, has to endure it before liberation beckons.

Even fictitious dramatic situations are received by the audience in a specific context of the general knowledge that an author can expect from the spectators. Therefore, we might legitimately wonder what the average contemporary of Nestroy knew about slavery as a real social and ethnic phenomenon. Of course, slavery was not a problem that affected the citizens of Vienna directly. The abolition of slavery, however, for decades a topic of debate, had been a negotiating point at the Congress of Vienna, where Spain and Portugal had agreed in 1814 to terminate all slave trade north of the Equator.

The Viennese theatre-goer would hardly have been thinking of that. The Orient of the stage with its abundance of slaves – even if, as in the case of *Der Zauberer Sulphur*, the location is 'East India' – was above all associated with a kind of imaginary Turkey. Drawing on the image of Turkey created by the wars with Turkey and the Turkish siege of Vienna, this was for the normal citizen the nearest thing to experience of the Orient.[4] The Ottoman Empire was still considered great and powerful even if its zenith was passed, and if it began, so to speak, on one's own doorstep, it then stretched into the far distance via the already slightly fairy-tale Constantinople to the realms of Africa and the Near East, in short to the mysterious Orient with its completely different cultures and mentality. The political reality was in fact quite different and, even before the catch-phrase 'der kranke Mann am Bosporus' ['the sick man of the Bosporus'] was in general circulation,[5] Grillparzer's verdict on the occasion of his journey to Greece in 1843 had captured the situation: 'Dieses Reich ist verloren. Der Untergang steht nicht bevor, er ist schon da. [...] Es ist aus, da hilft kein Gott'[6] ['This Empire is finished. The end is not imminent, it has already come [...] It is over and nothing can save it']. Over twenty years previously, Austria, together with the whole of Europe, had watched with engagement and sympathy the Greek War of Independence. Even though the governments of Europe followed events with suspicion, the bulk of Europe's youth took the side of those who had risen up under Prince Ypsilanti in 1821. The decaying Ottoman Empire remained intact only as a land of literary fairy-tale.

In 1845, the inquisitive reader could find the following dictionary description of slavery:

> a condition of absolute servitude, that is one connected with loss of all personal freedom, in which the servant is regarded and treated not as a

person but as an object, such that the master may make use of him or his property as he wishes, sell him, exchange him, give him away, treat him according to his whim and perhaps even kill him. Slavery developed in the Orient, the cradle of all despotism, but it also moved to the Occident [...] No-one is a slave by law of nature, even though among the Ancients Aristotle asserted this seriously and counted as slaves all barbarians, that is all non-Greeks, and in the modern world this sophistical justification for slavery has been taken up again.

The dictionary goes on to explain that slavery and the slave trade had been or were being abolished everywhere except in North Africa and North America. Here in particular, it says, there was no question of emancipating the Negroes from slavery:

the likelihood of this was even less because one did not wish to intervene too violently in the existing property arrangements. Also two factors militated against the emancipation of the slaves: no other workers would be suitable for the plantations, as the climate was dangerous for white workers, and in a free state Negroes are naturally sluggish and dull-witted and would be capable neither of caring for themselves nor of being civilized.[7]

Though it seems strange today, this estimation was shared by many a prominent contemporary. Charles Sealsfield, who was such a penetrating and unsparing critic of the conditions in Austria in the Metternich era and who found the situation in his native country unbearable precisely because of the lack of freedom – albeit primarily a lack of intellectual freedom – defends the slave-owning mentality of the southern states, at the same time as holding up America as a free country in contrast to the enslavement that prevailed generally in Europe. Friedrich Sengle sums up this aspect of Sealsfield's work thus:

To advocate an immediate and unconditional freeing of the negro slaves, without whom the southern plantations cannot be worked, seemed to him plainly ridiculous. In this respect, he more or less takes up the economic argument of the southern states, to which he had material and party-political ties [...] Wherever Negroes are discussed in his novels either a paradisiacal or idyllic picture is painted of the love the slaves have for their masters, or he shows with pedagogic irony how incapable these 'children' are of self-determination. They must be well provided for but kept in strict order if they are to fulfil their natural purpose.[8]

The average contemporary, however, showed a rather romantic interest in oriental slavery in particular. The entry on Constantinople in a geographical and statistical encyclopedia contains the laconic sentence: 'Für Konstantinopel wichtig ist der Sklavenmarkt, nach den Geschlechtern in 2 Abtheilungen'[9] ['An important part of Constantinople is the slave market, divided into two sections according to sex.']. This slave market was situated in the vicinity of the Beyazid mosque, near to the site of the ancient slave market. Especially the market for female slaves, imbued with the erotic connotations of the harem, aroused the interest of the contemporary traveller. Travel writing on the Orient was popular and contributed to the popular image of the Orient at that time. The slave market in Constantinople was described thus in 1800:

> Under no circumstances does a female slave appear completely naked before a buyer, because that would offend the strict propriety of Ottoman customs. But he can send a matron to the bazaar and have the requisite inspection done by her, particularly to establish that she is still a virgin. The Turks too can inspect several parts of them without offending propriety. They lift their veils, open their mouths, examine their hands and seem to inspect them just as one would do with animals, horses in particular.
>
> The female slaves wear ordinary clothing made of rough white or blue linen. The Negro women are often seen quite naked in the bazaar except for a small loin cloth, secured by a simple belt. Expensive and beautiful slaves are dressed in the most attractive manner. As a rule, slaves in the bazaar seem anything but miserable. They are often seen laughing and joking. Forgetting the past, they think only of the present. Since most are the daughters of poor parents their situation has improved. They flatter themselves that a happy future awaits them, for in passing into the care of strangers they can hope it will be in their owners' interests to treat them well.[10]

A generation later, on 9 February 1836, Helmuth von Moltke, at that time Prussian military adviser in Constantinople, noted:

> When the subject of slavery in the Orient arises, people almost always overlook the fact that there is a considerable difference between a Turkish slave and a Negro slave in the West Indies. Even the name slave, in the sense we normally attach to the word, is wrong. 'Abd' does not mean slave but rather servant [...] A Turkish servant who has been bought is infinitely better off than a hired one. Because he is the property of his master, and an expensive bit of property at that, the master treats him with consideration; he looks after him when he is ill and takes care not to wear him out with overwork. There is no question of his working like the slaves on the sugar plantations. [...] A slave's life is still much easier than the life of the serf-farmer. [...] On the other hand, the altogether justified objection one can raise to oriental slavery is that it is the direct cause of the cruelty with which a Circassian father, in exchange for a sum of money, parts for ever from his child, that it is the cause of the pursuit of human prey instigated every year in Sennar by the great merchant of the Nile (Mehmed Aly), and of other such atrocities.
>
> While walking recently on the Asiatic coast I chanced to meet a group of black slave women, who came, I think, from Upper Egypt. They

pressed round me and shouted incomprehensible words with great animation and in guttural voices. An old Turk in charge of them indicated to me that they were asking if I wanted to buy one of them. They cost on average 150 guilders, in other words somewhat less than a mule. At the slave market in Constantinople I was not allowed to see the female white slaves, though a great many black ones were sitting in the marketplace. They fell hungrily on the pastries we handed out among them and all of them wanted us to buy them.[11]

The Mehmet Ali mentioned by Moltke, who, amongst other things, sold Ethiopian slaves in Cairo, had been Turkish Pasha (Viceroy) in Egypt since 1806 and acted on the whole independently of his overlords. In 1833, despite opposition from Turkey, he took control of Syria in addition to Egypt and the Sudan, though finally he had to restrict himself to the African territories. One of his sons even fought against the Greeks in 1827. Mehmet Ali was known throughout Europe. Nestroy alludes to him through the very sound of the name Alib-Memeck in the play *Zauberer Sulphur*.

The contemporary theatre-goer was therefore familiar with much that was described in travel accounts of the Orient. Already in Nestroy's early work we find occasional allusions to the Orient and to slavery. *Prinz Friedrich*, with its North African elements, its gypsies and a plot centring on robbers, could conceivably have included these themes, but slaves do not appear, and also *Der konfuse Zauberer* [The Confused Magician] (1832) manages, in spite of its pirates, to get by without slaves. The odd female slave is found among the broad range of characters in some dramatic quodlibets. In *Humoristische Eilwagen-Reise durch die Theaterwelt* [Humorous Whistle-stop Tour of the Theatre World], Sappho is accompanied by slaves male and female, and in *Magische Eilwagenreise durch die Comödienwelt* [Magical Whistle-stop Tour of the World of Comedy] (1830) there appears, in addition to an Indian fairy queen and a Chinese postilion named 'Tratatadidadadi, diehtradatata', Adelma, 'eine liebe tartarische Sclavinn' ['a sweet Tartar slave']. And later there is, of course, Zelima, a slave of Turandot, in *Das Quodlibet verschiedener Jahrhunderte* [The Quodlibet of Various Centuries] (1843), though she has only one line. Pointing to Turandot, who is being wooed by Don Carlos, she says, 'Das ist die Herrscherin' ['That is the mistress']. But this very mistress bemoans her lot as a slave. With solemn feeling she contradicts her father, who would like finally to find her a husband and thus encourages her to set easier riddles:

Ich bin nicht grausam, frei nur will ich leben,
Ich sehe durch ganz Asien das Weib
Erniedrigt und zum Sklavenjoch verdammt,
Und rächen will ich mein beleidigtes Geschlecht.[12]

[I am not cruel. I want only to live as a free woman. Throughout all Asia I see woman degraded and condemned to the yoke of slavery and I want to avenge my offended sex.]

Slaves are, however, more in evidence in three particular plays. There is an interesting treatment of slavery in *Genius, Schuster und Marqueur* (SW I, 419–527) but it remained inaccessible to the contemporary general public. Written in 1832, the play was not performed, although significant parts of it were incorporated into other plays, among them *Zauberer Sulphur*. When the daughters of the fairy Kaffeluzia are expecting a declaration of love from the sons of Sonnenglanz king of the spirits (who, of course, has slaves at his court) they drive away the nymphs from their entourage with the words: 'Fort, Gschlavinnen, das ist ein Schauspiel für Götter, da braucht man euch nicht dabei' (I, 1; p. 424) ['Be gone slaves, this is a performance for gods, your presence is not needed']. The arrogant tone is its own punishment: the 'Gschlavinnen' (a Viennese dialect expression for slaves ('Sklavinnen')) would only have witnessed the two sisters being rebuffed.

On the intervention of the fairy, Pantoffeline, two young unmarried men from Sonnenglanz's empire must now be delivered up every year to enforced marriages with the Amazons. The Amazons consider man to be 'ein wertlos Ding. Drum ist der beste und der schlechteste uns gleich' (I, 23; p. 459) ['a worthless thing. Thus the best and the worst are all the same to us']:

SULPHUR: Was geschieht denn dann diesen Jünglingen?
SONNENGLANZ: Sie werden von Amazonen geheiratet und hernach schmählich von ihren Weibern malträtiert.
SULPHUR: Glückliches Land, wo dies alle Jahre nur zwei Jünglingen geschieht! (I, 8; p. 431)

[SULPHUR: What happens to these youths then? SONNENGLANZ: They are married by Amazons and after that despicably maltreated by their wives. SULPHUR: Happy the land where that happens to only two youths each year!]

Pechberger and Kipfl, two foolhardy earthlings, are ready to volunteer themselves to the Amazons. With the words 'Nun, fort mit den Sklaven in unser Gebiet!' ['Off to our territory with these slaves!'] (I, 24; p. 460), Bellona the Amazon has them led away captive. The men must now serve the Amazons as slaves, do women's work and are constantly humiliated, while the Amazons still consider themselves to be kind to them. The black slave woman Milibu plays a role in the plot's confusions of black, white and red – the number of skin colours that peoples the stage – only as a 'Tintenfleck der Natur' ['an ink stain of nature'] (III,1; p. 500) as Pechberger puts it. To her the foolish spirit, Lulu, uses the same words that we hear from Plumpsack regarding the Negro slave, Nelli, in *Zauberer Sulphur*: 'Wenn's nicht so schwarz wär', man kennet gar nicht, daß sie eine Mohrin is' ['If she weren't so black you'd never know she was a Moor'] (III, 6; p. 509).

A similar undertone to that of the 'ink stain of nature', a phrase that sounds racist today, not least because of the bitter experiences of the twentieth century, can be found in Nestroy's work in 1846. The old painter, Kranz, replies to the question why he fled after he had rescued the millionaire, Wandling, from a panther in the forests of Boston:

> KRANZ: Weil mein' Flinten abg'schossen war, und hinter Ihnen hat sich ein großmächtiger Orangutan gezeigt.
> WANDLING: Irrtum! Das war mein Neger!
> KRANZ: Da haben wir die Folgen der Sklaverei! Werden es denn die Engländer nie dahin bringen, daß man die Mohren unter die Weißen zählt?[13]

> [KRANZ: Because my shotgun was empty and a huge orang-utan had appeared behind you. WANDLING: Wrong! That was my Negro! KRANZ: That's where slavery gets you! Will the English never get to the stage of counting the Moors among the whites?]

The real slavery is that of the men under the yoke of the Amazons, and Nestroy leaves us in no doubt that, in this case, it is self-inflicted slavery – he must have been well aware of what he was writing. In addition to employing the reliable theatrical device of the reversal of the normal world, as witnessed by the act set among the warlike Amazons, whose husbands spin and rock cradles, the behaviour of the Amazons to Pechberger and Kipfl is a parody of the men's behaviour in the inn towards their own wives. These in turn, in spite of everything, will not pass up the chance of freeing their husbands and receive them back chastened from the realm of the fairies. Doubts may be raised about how convincing the ending to this farce is.

Nestroy's most pronounced 'slave play' is *Der Zauberer Sulphur* (HKA, *Stücke* 6). Written in 1833 as a parody of Ernst Raupach's *Robert der Teufel*, which had been performed in March of the same year, the play was, for various reasons, not performed on stage until 1834 and lacked any direct connection with the original, where slavery plays only a very superficial role. The dramatis personae of the first printed version[14] does list a slave trader, but this character does not actually appear in the play itself. As voluntary penance for his misdeeds, Robert lives as a mumbling servant at the court of the Italian king, Astolf, and fetches and carries for everyone, even for Scapa, the evil genie of Prince Osorio of Capua. To draw him away from the path of penitence, he is shown a deceptive mirror on the future in which he sees himself as 'nackter Sklav im Heidenlande – Anstatt des Stieres an den Pflug gespannt' ['a naked slave among the heathens – made to plough like an ox'] (p. 147). Towards the end of the play, Scapa considers sending Robert 'als Sklaven nach Afrika [...]. Ich [...] bin schon mit einem Sklavenhändler eins: er zahlt mir 20 Unzen und der Narr ist sein.' (p. 157). ['sending Robert as a slave to Africa. [...] I [...] have already struck a bargain with the slave trader: he pays me 20 ounces and the fool is his']. Everything turns out well in the end. Cinthia, whom Robert worships, ponders on the body that keeps the soul in thrall:

Was macht ein menschliches Geschöpf zum Weibe,
Das heißt zur Sklavin, die auf höchster Höhe,
Wo doch die Luft der Dienstbarkeit nicht weht,
Auf einem Throne selbst noch Sklavin bleibt?
Es ist der Leib. (p. 153)

[What makes a human creature a woman, that means a slave, who even
in the most exalted sphere, where there is no trace of servitude, even on
the throne itself, remains a slave? It is the body.]

Robert's slavery in *Der Zauberer Sulphur* is of another kind. It begins when his
parents hand their failure of a son over unconditionally to the fairy, who
pronounces his fate: 'Als Herr warst du die Geißel anderer auf Erden,/ Zur
Strafe sollst du ein verworffner Sclave werden' ['As master you were the
scourge of your fellow creatures; as a punishment you are to become an
outcast slave'] (I, 18; p. 30). For Robert, the son of rich parents who were
helpless to check him, accustomed to untrammelled freedom, which he used
simply to insult and oppress others, there could be no worse punishment.
Thus he fetches up on Indigo's cotton plantations (the East Indies' cotton was
world-famous). Here Robert lands in the slave market, where the slaves,
bemoaning their imminent sale, make clear to him his fate: 'Der erste Beste
kauft uns dann/Und maltraitiert uns was er kann' ['Somebody or other buys
us and then does his best to maltreat us'] (II, 1; p. 32). Now he is himself
confronted with a fate worse than any he had imposed on others as a spoilt
son of the landed gentry. Even Emma, Indigo's daughter, whom Robert loves and
by whom he is loved in return, warns the dreamer, 'Bedenckt – daß ihr Sclave
seyd –' ['Remember you are a slave –'] (II, 13; p. 43) and is surprised at how
love can overturn social realities: 'er ist ja nur ein Sclave – warum herrscht er
aber in meinem Herzen, wenn er ein Sclave ist, warum –? ['but he's only a
slave – why does he rule my heart, if he is a slave – why?'] (II, 17; p. 47).
     Nestroy does not, as Walla points out, portray an 'orientalisches Märchenreich,
wie man das vom Volkstheater vielleicht hätte erwarten können. Die europäischen
Zustände sind nur dünn verschleiert. Auf dem Sklavenmarkt herrschen die
Sitten des Wiener Naschmarktes' ['a world of oriental magic, as one might
have expected from the *Volkstheater*. The European setting is only thinly
veiled. In the slave market we find the customs of the Vienna food market']
(HKA, *Stücke 6*, 182). Robert turns out to be a slave in a number of respects.
In fact, even as a free man, he had been the slave of his own lack of restraint
and of his desire to be the untrammelled leader of his band of admiring
followers. He had never been aware, however, of his dependency on his own
moods and momentary impulses. Later, he is at the mercy of the whims of the
fairy Walpurgiblocksbergiseptemtrionalis, whose very name conjures up the
terrors of the witches' dance which, according to legend, takes place every St
Walburga's Eve (Walpurgis Night, 30 April/1 May) on the fabled Blocksberg.
Finally, he is sold as a slave, only to serve then his own servant, Plumpsack,
who fetched a better price on the market than his master. Furthermore, Robert
becomes the slave of his love for Emma.

110

Many situations that occur in the first act recur in reversal in the second
and third, and Robert experiences personally the results of his own misdeeds.
His helpless father, who has a 'Schwäche im Kopf' [who is a little 'weak in the
head'] (I, 3), in Act I hands out guilders to peasants injured by his son either
by the killing of their cattle or by arson, rather as in Act II the hardly more
intelligent Pasha Alib-Memeck promises every real or supposed criminal '100
mit'n Bambusröhrl' ['100 lashes of the cane']. In their passivity and besotted-
ness, the parents, like their guests, are Robert's slaves, a point particularly
emphasised when Robert subordinates the grand young ladies at the ball to
the servants at his command. It is a scene of role reversals that grows out of
Robert's relationship to his footman and servant, Plumpsack. Robert forces on
him the role of 'Lauffer' [runner]. The master–servant relationship is, of
course, another kind of slavery, and the real slavery to which Robert is
subjected in the second and third acts and which compels him to be a servant
to his servant, is therefore again a simple reversal of the existing circumstances.

Nestroy's last 'slave play' is the farce *Moppels Abentheuer im Viertel unter
Wiener Wald in Neu-Seeland und Marokko* [Moppel's Adventures in the
Vienna Woods, in New Zealand and Morocco] (1837), which is 'eine leichte
Gelegenheitsarbeit, die zunächst als Rahmen für die Künste zweier englischer
Gymnastiker dienen sollte' ['a lightweight, occasional work designed in the
first instance for the talents of two English gymnasts'] (Yates, HKA, *Stücke,
12*, 83). The travelling aristocrat, Lord Steolequeastle, is not afflicted with
spleen, unlike many Englishmen in Nestroy's plays, but he does show
'caprice'. For him, his servant Moppel is like a slave, the 'bortirter
Privatvollstrecker seiner jeweiligen Befehle' ['the uniformed private executor
of whatever commands he might issue'] (I, 7). It must be said that the slavery
in this case is more verbal: Lord Steolequeastle is constantly making Moppel
buy bullwhips for a punishment that is planned but never meted out, causing
Moppel to remark: 'Das ist noch das einzige Trinkgeld, was ich hab, daß er
mir alle Tag ein Zwanziger auf ein Ochsenzemt gibt, und den andern Tag
weiß er nix davon' ['That's the only tip I ever get. Every day he gives me
money for a bullwhip and the next day he can't remember'] (I, 8).

On his travels, Moppel loses his master in a shipwreck, then escapes the
New Zealand natives, finally falling into the hands of the governor Ramram as
a slave in the Moroccan empire. Slaves kneeling and female slaves playing
harps provide the setting for their master. Along with two mute slaves,
Ramram sets Moppel apart from the others. On pain of death, every day he
has to come up with a jest that makes Ramram laugh; otherwise he will be
beheaded (II,2). Moppel's ironical comment is 'Hier Hofkomiker zu sein, das
ist ein Genuß' ['It's a real pleasure being the court jester here']. It may well be
that Nestroy is alluding here to the 'slave aspects' of his own life, to which we
shall return. The necessity of coming up constantly with new and funny plays
and his dependency on their favourable reception by director, public and press
may have been very present in his mind after the scandalous flop a few months
previously of his play *Eine Wohnung ist zu vermiethen* [Apartment to Let].

When Moppel reminds Ramram that a year has passed since 'ich und die zwei Stummen so frei sind, Ihre Sklaven zu sein' ['the two mutes and I took the liberty of being your slaves'] and that Ramram had promised to set them free, the latter answers that he could take his word back, it is *his* word, he is master of it, 'oder glaubt ihr, ich werde euretwegen der Sklave meines Wortes sein?' ['or do you think that for your sakes I shall be slave to my own word?'] (II, 2). In this case, the promised liberation from slavery becomes an empty, rhetorical shell masking boundless caprice. Instead Ramram wants to give Moppel the European slave Hermine (a name as deliberately unsuitable and out of place as Emma in *Zauberer Sulphur*) as a wife. Both feel they are 'elende Spielwerke seiner marokkanischen Launen' ['wretched playthings of his Moroccan whims'] (II, 5). After an exciting escape, Moppel, who had once distributed theatre bills, returns home, where he is hailed as the theatre superintendent from Morocco.

Slavery of sorts – even when not expressly so named – occurs in quite a number of other Nestroy plays. For example, there is the way Berengar, 'famoser Tyrann und renommierter Verfolger der Witwen und Waisen' ['splendid tyrant and renowned persecutor of widows and orphans'], as the playbill calls him, behaves towards Adelheid in *Der gefühlvolle Kerkermeister* [The Sentimental Jailer] (1832); or *Nagerl und Handschuh* [Button-hole and Glove] (1832), in which, thanks to her father and sisters, Rosa acquires her characterisation as a 'miserabel gehaltene Tochter und enorm malträtierte Schwester' ['daughter kept in want and a grossly mistreated sister']. In *Judith und Holofernes* (1849), all those dependent on Holofernes are slaves, even if none bears that title in the cast list and slaves appear only as silent servants in Holofernes's camp. His vanity and predilection for executions as well as his confident, self-adoring and lordly manner make Holofernes a cousin of Ramram and Alib-Memeck. Finally, there is the dependency evident in abundance in every Nestroy play on such things as people, circumstances, moods, desires – the forms of slavery of everyday life.

But what importance should we attach to slavery in Nestroy's work? Is it a disguised caricature of actual conditions, of social conditions in particular, just as the words of Chiefs Evening Wind and Biberhahn conceal a political element? It is in general the case that any mythicisation is in part an unconscious process, that of 'der Sublimierung einer konkreten Gesellschaft in eine malerische, sichere und geordnete Märchenwelt'[15] ['of the sublimation of a concrete society in a picturesque, secure and ordered make-believe world'], which, in Nestroy's case, however, is not only already showing the cracks but is positively turned on its head. His 'zeitloses Wien' ['timeless Vienna'] (Magris, p. 32) no longer tallies with the popular refrain 'Ja nur ein Kaiserstadt, ja nur ein Wien'[16] ['There's only one imperial city, there's only one Vienna']. Rather the fairy-tale happenings, fairies and magicians point to the reality of contemporary Vienna; behind theatre convention and tradition there is often hidden satire on everyday existence.

Even if I cannot subscribe fully to the theory that *Zauberer Sulphur* has a strong element of social criticism[17] (in this case awareness of the later plays of

Nestroy may have led to exaggerated interpretations of this kind), such an element is discernible in particular in Act 1. Above all, Nestroy wants to use the image of the slave, as he does many other images, to show by means of contrast and in defamiliarised form the Vienna of his own day with its various characteristic types, who are (admittedly only tentatively) subjects of parody or verbal comedy. Nestroy's main concern seems to have been comic entertainment, not yet didactic intent. His main aim is not to confront or hurt the spectator with a negative reflection of contemporary circumstances, but to entertain the audience and make people laugh. The attentive spectator was able to detect elements of criticism under the surface of easy entertainment, however, even though the criticism was limited by censorship. If this criticism gave food for thought, so much the better. But the play was certainly not meant to be a new form of didactic play (*Besserungsstück*); rather it was designed to expose the ineffectiveness of the traditional genre and to ridicule it, as Nestroy does in *Der Talisman* with the 'portrait of life' (*Lebensbild*) genre as written by Friedrich Kaiser.[18]

Where slaves appear in Nestroy's early plays, they are aware of their state of dependence and attempt to escape from it, yet they are unable to achieve this by themselves. Whatever higher power caused them to fall into slavery also rescues them from it later; the slaves do not undergo a process of reformation. But, beyond the slaves that appear as such on stage, Nestroy's plays also reflect a form of 'slavery' as a real element of life during the Biedermeier period (in a political sense as well as in everyday life) – slavery is even somehow inherent in life. We encounter helplessness and dependency on others, on circumstances, on fate and not least on one's own ego and obsessions.

We could apply to Nestroy and his time the sentence 'Die Welt scheint sehr glatt [...] aber fürchterlich rauh ist die Welt' ['The world seems to be very smooth, but it is terribly rough'] (*Die beiden Herrn Söhne*, HKA, *Stücke 22*, 46–47). It sounds like the sentence from the final scene of Goethe's *Götz von Berlichingen* (1773): 'Die Welt ist ein Gefängnis' ['The world is a prison.']. It is a world that will not remain intact for much longer. There are many forms of slavery, and we encounter several in Nestroy's characters. In *Einen Jux will er sich machen*, Weinberl, for example, is a slave to his professional life, and suffers because 'er von Jugend auf ans Gwölb gefesselt war wie ein Blaßl an die Hutten. [...] Der Diener ist der Sclav des Herrn, der Herr Sclav des Geschäfts. Erhaben ist die zweyte Sclaverey aber so biglem mit Genuß begabt als wie die erste.' ['since his youth he has been tied to the shop like a watchdog tethered to its kennel [...]. The servant is a slave to his master, the master is a slave to his business. Yet the higher form of slavery is no more fun than the other one.'] (I, 13; HKA, *Stücke 18/I*, 27). Knieriem is a slave to alcohol, Lips is a slave to boredom, Titus a slave to his wig (and consequently a slave to appearances and prejudice) and most of them are slaves to money. And not only in the play *Frühere Verhältnisse* [Former Circumstances] are many characters slaves to their former circumstances. Nestroy hints at the fact that job routine, too, can be seen as a form of slavery; the term 'Localitäts-Sclav' ['slave to the pub'] applied to a waiter expresses this (*Der holländische Bauer*,

III, 31; HKA, *Stücke 28/I*, 86) [The Dutch Farmer].

Nor is Nestroy himself free of dependency – consciously or unconsciously. He is above all a slave to the theatre which is, of course, a voluntary slavery (as are many): he is a slave to being up to date, to choosing the right cast, and to public opinion as it is expressed by the audience and the critics. Not even occasional outbursts of rage, such as the one he is supposed to have had after the failure of *Zauberer Sulphur* in Vienna, could save him from this: 'Kanonen, Kanonen! Zusammenkartätschen diese Kanaillien dort unten'[19] ['Cannons, cannons! To shoot all that rabble down there!']. There was no faraway country of slavery, from which the audience could return reformed as Nestroy would have wished. Nestroy himself had experienced what he has his character Titus Feuerfuchs say:

> Wer in der Früh aufsteht, in die Kanzley geht, nacher Essen geht, nacher präferanzeln geht, und nacher schlafen geht, der vegetiert, wer in der Fruh in's G'wölb geht, und nacher auf'd Mauth geht, und nacher essen geht, und nacher wieder in's G'wölb geht, der vegetiert, wer in der Fruh aufsteht, a Roll durchgeht, nacher in die Prob geht, nacher essen geht, nacher in's Kaffehaus geht, nacher Comödiespielen geht, und wenn das alle Tag so fortgeht, der vegetiert. (*Der Talisman*, I, 17; HKA, *Stücke 17/I*, 24–25)

> [If you get up in the morning, go into the office, go to lunch, then go and play cards, then go to bed, you just vegetate; if you get up in the morning, go to the shop, go to the customs house, go to lunch, then go back to the shop, you just vegetate; if you get up in the morning, study a part, go to the rehearsal, go to lunch, go to a café, go and play in a comedy, if that goes on day after day, you vegetate.]

Nestroy spent 'keinen Abend ohne Theaterbesuch'[20] ['not one single evening without going to the theatre'], even when he was not appearing on stage himself or when retired in Graz. He tried hard to escape from the slavery of censorship, but what liberty he had in this respect was always like walking the tightrope. Nestroy was, of course, a slave not only to the theatre. He was also a slave to card games, and he knew it. He complained to his friend Ernst Stainhauser (HKA, *Briefe*, p. 234): 'Abermahls Malheur, abermahls hat mich der Teufel geritten' ['I've been unlucky again, again I had the devil in me'], when he had lost at 'Höllen-Piket' ['damned piquet'], and he had to borrow money repeatedly; even in the pensionopolis of Graz, he spends the days of his retirement playing cards (HKA, *Briefe*, p. 215).

Nestroy thought he lived another form of 'slavery': he felt a slave of marriage, called himself 'Ehekrüppel' ['crippled by marriage'] (HKA, *Briefe*, p. 115), and puts in the mouth of Herr von Falsch's friend in *Der Treulose* [The Unfaithful Husband] the words: 'Scheidung heißt das kleine und doch so große Wort, das dir mehr als Millionen, das dir deine Freyheit wiedergibt' ['Divorce is the small and yet great word, which will give you more than millions, it will give you freedom'] (II, 39; HKA, *Stücke 10*, 88). In reality, however, he was not a slave to marriage but to his inclination to 'Mädlerie' [womanising], which he might have thought to be freedom. His dependency on Marie Weiler, however, was the dependency of a relationship lasting several decades, but probably also the dependency of someone who knows that he needs guidance in many things. The fact that he admitted the former and denied the latter proves that this was true. Nestroy wrote to Stainhauser in 1858: 'Sie ist jedenfalls, was unser häusliches Zerwürffnis anbelangt, mehr im Recht als ich. [...] Sie sollte und dürfte Vieles, sehr Vieles nicht wissen; daß sie es aber weiß, ist [...] nicht Mangel an Delikatesse meinerseits [...], sondern [...] an die spanische Inquisition mahnendes Spionieren ihrerseits.' ['As far as our domestic disagreements are concerned, she is more in the right than me. There are many things that she should not know about. The fact that she does know about them is not due to lack of delicacy on my part, but because she spies on me like the Spanish Inquisition.'] (HKA, *Briefe*, p. 169–71) He claims not to waste money, for which Weiler reproaches him, but admits: 'Ich habe in mancher Beziehung vielleicht mehr ausgegeben als ich klugerweise hätte sollen'. ['In some respects, I may have spent more than I sensibly should have done.'] And finally:

> Ich werde Alles (das heißt das Möglichste) thuen, Sie zu versöhnen, ohne meine Rechte über einen gewissen Grad hinaus [...] zu beeinträchtigen. Zu diesem Entschluße treibt mich wahrlich nicht ihr Geld, ich werde es nie bedürfen, ebensowenig ihr Directionstalent, das habe ich selbst, obschon es mir Mancher vielleicht nicht zutraut, weil es nicht meine Sache ist, damit zu prunken – daß ich Alles thuen werde sie zu versöhnen, geschieht aus wahrer auf Dreyßigjähriges Zusammenseyn gegründeter Anhänglichkeit des Herzens, aus der innersten Überzeugung daß man ein frohes Alter nur an der Seite des Wesens hoffen kann, mit welchem man das Leben in allen seinen Wechselfällen durchgemacht. (p. 170)

> [I will do anything (that is, whatever I can) to make up with her, without giving up my rights beyond a certain degree. It is not her money that brings me to this decision, I will never need that, nor is it her gift for directing, I have it myself, even though many people might not think so, because I am not one to boast about it – I want to do anything to make up with her because of true, heart-felt devotion based on having been together for thirty years, because of the inner conviction that I can hope for a happy old age only at the side of the being with whom I have spent my life with all its ups and downs.]

But back to *Zauberer Sulphur* in the Vienna of the early 1830s. The first performance, the text of which was mutilated, would hardly have made the audience think of slavery as a real problem. Most inhabitants of Vienna were more familiar with one particular 'slave woman' than with the social conditions within and outside of the Habsburg monarchy or the slaves male and female who occasionally appeared on stage in the provincial theatres and even in the Hoftheater. 'Zur schönen Sklavin' ['The beautiful slave woman'] was the name of a well-known inn in Erdbergerstrasse, which has even been commemorated in literature.[21] Franz Xaver Gewey places the inn with poetic licence on the spot where Richard the Lionheart was recognised after the Third Crusade in 1192 and taken prisoner by his Babenberg opponent, Duke Leopold V of Austria. Gewey emphasises that the roast meat served in the 'Schöne Sklavin' was cooked 'Wie sie kein König besser kocht' ['better than by any king']. It cannot be denied that many citizens of Vienna during the Biedermeier period were also slaves to their appetite: 'Wenn das Volk nur fressen kann! Wie s' den Speisenduft wittern, da erwacht die Eßlust, und wie die erwacht, legen sich alle ihre Leidenschaften schlafen; sie haben keinen Zorn, keine Rührung, keine Wut, keinen Gram, keine Lieb', keinen Haß, nicht einmal eine Seel' haben s'. Nix haben s' als ein' Appetit.'[22] ['As long as people can gorge themselves! When they smell food, their appetite awakens, and then all passionate feelings disappear; they no longer feel rage, or pity, or anger, or sorrow, or love, or hatred, they don't even have a soul then. They don't have anything but appetite.']

Notes

1. See *Stücke 6*, ed. by Friedrich Walla, p.168 ff.
2. This can be seen from the literature specified in note 1.
3. William Acton, *Prostitution [...] in London* (London, 1870), esp. p. 21. See also the comments made by Otto Rommel, *Barocktradition im österreichisch-bayrischen Volkstheater*, 6 vols (Leipzig, 1935–39), vol. 4, p. 324.
4. Walter Obermaier, 'Das Türkenthema in der österreichischen Dichtung', in *Die Türken vor Wien. 1683*, ed. by Robert Waissenberger (Salzburg and Vienna, 1982), p. 324–31.
5. Georg Büchmann, *Geflügelte Worte: Der Zitatenschatz des deutschen Volkes*, ed. by Walter Heichen (Berlin, 1915), p. 494 f.
6. Franz Grillparzer, *Tagebuch auf der Reise nach Konstantinopel*, in: *Sämtliche Werke*, ed. by August Sauer, II/11 (Vienna, 1924), p. 32.
7. *Universal-Lexikon der Gegenwart und Vergangenheit*, ed. by H. A. Pierer, vol. 29, (2nd edn Altenburg, 1845), pp. 3 and 16.
8. Friedrich Sengle, *Biedermeierzeit: Deutsche Literatur im Spannungsfeld zwischen Restauration und Revolution 1815-1848*, 3 vols (Stuttgart, 1971–80), vol. 3 (1980), p. 760.
9. *Ritter's geographisch-statistisches Lexikon* (6th edn Leipzig, 1874), p. 799.
10. *Istanbul*, ed. by Esther Gallwitz (Frankfurt a. M., 1981), p. 128 f.
11. Helmuth von Moltke, *Unter dem Halbmond: Erlebnisse in der alten Türkei 1835–1839*, ed. by Hermut Arndt (Tübingen and Basel, 1979), p. 78 ff.
12. Nestroy, SW IX (Vienna, 1927), p. 476.
13. Nestroy, *Zwei ewige Juden für einen*, in SW XIII, 110. I am grateful to Dr John R. P. McKenzie for bringing this reference to my attention.
14. Ernst Raupach, *Robert der Teufel: Romantisches Schauspiel in fünf Aufzügen* (Hamburg, 1834). The following page references refer to this work.
15. Claudio Magris, *Der habsburgische Mythos in der österreichischen Literatur* (Salzburg, 1966), p. 9.
16. Adolf Bäuerle, 'Aline oder Wien in einem anderen Weltteile (1822)', in: Otto Rommel, *Barocktradition*, vol. 3, p. 114 f.

17. Siegfried Diehl, *Zauberei und Satire im Frühwerk Nestroys. Mit neuen Handschriften zum Konfusen Zauberer und zum Zauberer Sulphur*, Frankfurter Beiträge zur Germanistik, 9 (Bad Homburg, Berlin, Zürich, 1969).
18. See W. E. Yates, 'An Object of Nestroy's Satire: Friedrich Kaiser and the "Lebensbild"', *Renaissance and Modern Studies*, 22 (1978), 45–62.
19. Helmut Ahrens, *Bis zum Lorbeer versteig' ich mich nicht: Johann Nestroy – sein Leben* (Frankfurt, 1982), p. 143.
20. Letter to Karoline Köfer, 12. 3. 1855, in: Johann Nestroy, *Briefe*, ed. by Walter Obermaier (Vienna, Munich, 1977), pp. 114–17. See also the letter to Karl Remmark, 28. 9. 1861, in: *Nestroyana*, 6 (1984–86), 3/4, p. 100.
21. Franz Xaver Gewey, *Komische Gedichte über die Vorstädte Wiens*, 4th issue, Vienna 1813. The poems were so popular that Karl Meisl added two more issues in 1824/25 and published a new edition.
22. Nestroy, *Weder Lorbeerbaum noch Bettelstab*, SW III, 387.

'Crying out loud in silence':
Social Inequality in Nestroy's
Die Gleichheit der Jahre

Friedrich Walla

Nestroy's early work *Die Gleichheit der Jahre* [Equality in Years] long remained inaccessible – Rommel omitted it from GW, his convenient six-volume edition of 1948–49 – and Nestroy scholarship took little note of the play. When it was discussed, critics tended to repeat the judgement Rommel made in 1924 (in SW) that the work marks Nestroy's rejection of the outdated genre of *Zauberspiel*[1] in favour of the more realistic genre of *Posse* [farce]. In fact, *Die Gleichheit der Jahre* is a reworking of an earlier version, *Das Verlobungsfest im Feenreiche oder Die Gleichheit der Jahre*; for the revised version, Nestroy discarded the main title of the first play [Engagement Party in the Spirit Realm] and used only the subtitle.[2] The new title seemed to express the theme and message of the play clearly, and it aroused little curiosity among Nestroy commentators. In this respect one may usefully compare *Die Gleichheit der Jahre* with Nestroy's later work *Der Zerrissene* [A Man Torn Apart]. While there is no lack of critical discussions of *Der Zerrissene*, they miss the essence of the play, as W. E. Yates points out in his ground-breaking interpretation: 'der Titel [sei] keineswegs als programmatisch aufzufassen'[3] ['the title should not be interpreted as a statement of intent']: the title has to be seen in the light of the play, rather than the play in the light of the title.

Lack of scholarly interest in the play may well be due in part to the fact that Rommel's text (in SW) suffered from his inability to keep the two versions apart (sections of the second version having been written as corrections in the manuscript of the first); this did not help the cohesiveness of the play; in particular, it spoilt the clear characterisation of the juvenile hero. In the new critical edition, which makes the play available once more, it was possible to improve considerably upon Rommel's text and furthermore to identify and to reproduce Nestroy's source, *Die Schloßmamsell* [The Manor House Demoiselle], a story by K. G. Prätzel.[4] Significantly, the question of equality of years plays no part in it. It is a crime story, and this may have attracted Nestroy, especially the cold-bloodedness with which an ageing spinster commits the crime to further her desires.

This neglected work provides a good opportunity to consider the point of social inequality. The generally accepted view of Nestroy's attitude to social

118

questions has recently been challenged. W. E. Yates summarises the prevailing critical opinion in his 1972 monograph: '[...] his plays betray from the early 1830s an oppressive dissatisfaction with existing society that is indicative of the winds of change gathering in Metternich's Austria.'⁵ Generally, critics located Nestroy's social attitudes (or, rather, those depicted in his works) somewhere between the radical, the liberal or the revolutionary.⁶ Developing a new direction evident in studies by Rio Preisner and Friedrich Sengle,⁷ Eva Reichmann detects a conservative message in Nestroy's plays.⁸ In her recent book she accuses previous researchers of having based their findings on single statements of individual figures taken out of the context of the plays. But Reichmann's method of examining certain motives in his complete *œuvre* is also open to criticism, especially when a lack of familiarity with individual plays leads her to make sweeping statements and to draw conclusions that cannot be sustained. Certain details in her summaries of some of the plays are simply wrong,⁹ and some of her generalisations do violence to other plays. *Die Gleichheit der Jahre* is a case in point. For her the play exemplifies Nestroy's conservative philosophy. '[...] in diesem Stück zeigt uns Nestroy einen patriarchalischen Haushalt in ländlicher Gegend nur von der positiven Seite' ['in this play Nestroy depicts a patriarchal household in a rural setting as wholly positive'] (p. 166). Even if this assertion were correct, it fails to take note of the fact that the play depicts three distinct social spheres, all of which are patriarchal: first, the dynastic aristocratic society of the framework setting; secondly, the world of the customs collector; and finally, the estate of the count (the one singled out by Reichmann). All three are interconnected, and only when they are considered together can we form a full picture of the patriarchal society presented in this play.

Because the work is so little known, my discussion of the social aspect follows in part the delineation of the plot. Nestroy took the plot of the central scenes from his source, but he surrounded these with the framework of what at first sight appears to be a typical *Zauberspiel*. The framework looks at the same problem from a slightly different angle: Regina, an elderly fairy, and a would-be philandering servant spirit called Schladriwuxerl must be led to choose suitable marriage partners. From this it would appear that we are dealing here with an example of a *Besserungsstück*, hundreds of which were performed in popular Viennese theatres at the end of the eighteenth and beginning of the nineteenth centuries. They depict the correction of human foibles, usually through the intervention on stage of supernatural powers. A closer look at Nestroy's play reveals a different picture, however: financial gain is the reason why Tranquillus, cousin of the spirit king, desires the hand of Regina:

SUPERNATURALIS. Du [...] erhältst in Reginen eine Fee die unermeßliche Reichthümer besitzt.
TRANQUILLUS. Solch eine Frau habe ich vonnöthen. (p. 12)

[SUPERNATURALIS. In the fairy Regina you will receive a wife of immeasurable wealth.
TRANQUILLUS. Such a woman is what I need.]

Tranquillus wants to enter into marriage to settle his financial affairs, and Regina agrees to oblige the wishes of the sovereign. Even a woman of 'immeasurable wealth' (her name, Regina, reflects her position – in the source she is called Jeannette) is prepared to accept a marriage of convenience for social reasons. She does not follow her inclinations and there is no talk of feelings when she states: 'Du hast mich [...] für deinen Vetter [...] bestimmt. Dein Winck war uns Befehl' ['You have destined me for your cousin. Your hint is my duty'] (p 13). Warned about Regina's temper, Tranquillus dismisses the idea that problems may arise: '[...] wird [meine Frau] halsstärrig, so bin ich auch ruhig, nur [...] daß ich dann alle zweckmäßigen Zwangsmittel der Reihe nach versuche und in größter Ruhe appliciere' ['If my wife becomes obstinate, I stay tranquil but I will apply one after the other all necessary forceful means'] (p. 12). The term 'Zwangsmittel' – means by which others can be made to conform to a person's wishes – assumes the status of a keyword in the play. They soon prove to be necessary. Repeated allusions to Regina's being a spinster of a more than certain age awaken her spirit of opposition. She expresses her desire for a young and handsome marriage partner, and this leads to her being exiled from the spirit kingdom to Earth. Schladriwuxerl is similarly punished.[10] Their banishment is intended to cure them of their wrongful behaviour: after their experiences on Earth they should be ready to obey the wishes of the ruler.

Rommel maintained it was possible to detach the *Posse* 'mit dem Rotstift' ['with red ink'] from the *Zauberspiel*. This, however, is not wholly true of the middle part, and is certainly not the case with the beginning. Nestroy does not simply discard the supernatural action framing the main play, for he is reluctant to do without the doubling of motifs made possible by it. The mechanism of the *Zauberspiel* is replaced with more earthly machinations.[11] Instead of the spirit king, we find Hirschwald, the Chief Forester (literally: 'Stagwood'), who, in his neck of the woods, seems to be endowed with powers similar to those of Supranaturalis (as Chief Forester he is above all living creatures of the animal kingdom) and the play now opens in his manor house.[12] Thus, the fairy kingdom of the *Zauberspiel* is a mirror of the dynastic imperial and aristocratic society: Supranaturalis is the Emperor Francis in the guise of Oberon.

Hirschwald covets the hand (or more precisely the riches) of Regina: 'Die alte Mamsell Regin mit ihre Capitalien, ist und bleibt für mich die beste Parthie' ['Regina, the old spinster, with her wealth is the most suitable marriage partner for me'] (p. 78). It could hardly be stated more directly. During the celebrations of her birthday – she maintains it is her twenty-ninth – he proposes to her, and is refused on account of the difference in their ages. Producing her baptismal record, which reveals that she is the same age as he, namely fifty, he attempts to shame her into marrying him. But she does not give up easily; only if she fails to gain a young and handsome spouse within the space of a year, will she consider Hirschwald as her prospective husband. As Siegfried Diehl remarks, 'Weder Liebe noch Vernunftgründe drängen sie zur Heirat, sondern allein die verlorene Wette' ['Neither love nor reason urges

120

her to marry, but only the lost wager'].[13] One should not forget, however, that she enters the wager above all to save face and to conceal her weakness and embarrassment.

Nestroy's play is based on traditional comic motifs. The old spinster who tries to fish for a young spouse is part of the stock-in-trade of comedy.[14] Regina's desire to appear younger makes her ridiculous, but does not justify the hoax played upon her by Hirschwald. With all the funny business going on, the serious aspect of the situation should not be overlooked. Regina's wealth secures her privileged position but, given the pressures to which unmarried women were subjected at that time, it also makes her the object of blackmail – without her wealth she would have been the object of derision and the butt of jokes. As a child of his era, Nestroy could hardly be expected to express the feminist concerns of today but, as a keen observer of the social life of his day, he clearly shows the harsh social reality faced by women. 'Any attempt to claim Nestroy for the feminist cause [...] is bound to be an uphill job,' W. E. Yates states, but he also concedes, 'Nestroy's work [...] shows considerable understanding of the social position of women in Austria of the *Biedermeier*'.[15]

The main part of *Das Verlobungsfest im Feenreiche* (and of *Die Gleichheit der Jahre*) again shows that marriage belongs to the category of financial transactions, not only in aristocratic circles but equally in the world of the petty bourgeois. We find ourselves in the home of a customs collector (Christoph Schlagmayer in the *Zauberspiel*, Christoph Strizl in the *Posse*) in the small town of Kobelsbach – Nestroy specifically stresses the provincial aspect of the place.[16] The action starts with the discovery that 1000 silver guilders of official monies have been stolen from the customs collector's desk.[17] The old state official, whose yearly income would amount to a tiny fraction of the missing sum, feels 'ruinirt [...] tod [...] umgebracht [...] zu Tod karbatscht' (p. 18) ['ruined – dead – murdered – whipped to death']. (Whipping, though officially banned as a form of punishment in Austria, was actually still practised.) He is in no state for rational action. It takes the entry of his brother-in-law Zettermann (a word derived from *zetern*, 'to raise a hue and cry') to show the only reasonable course to follow. He tries to ascertain who was in the house, how the thief entered, and how the theft was committed. It later transpires that he was on the right track, but has been prevented from pursuing his ideas by the customs collector. The theft has to be kept secret, otherwise he, the customs collector, could be accused of negligence in the performance of his official duties (p. 19). Although he does not expressly say so, he sees his superior authorities as hostile forces, from whom he cannot expect understanding. He feels helplessly exposed to his fate and already imagines threatening consequences: 'Dienstes entlassen [...] Schand, Spott, Armuth, vielleicht auch die Festung stehen mir bevor' ['dismissed from service, [...] disgrace, derision, and poverty, perhaps even detention in a fortress await me'] (pp. 19, 21).

Only one way out presents itself: his rich neighbour Mamsell Regina Geldkatz[18] could possibly provide the money for him. When she seems prepared to do so, the customs collector asks his subordinate Schladriwux, the

Schrankenwärter [turnpike attendant], to kneel down before her. Regina has only to hint at the possibility of her marrying one of the local youths for the customs collector immediately to offer her his own son Eduard (Nestroy here closely follows his source). The father's reaction is especially significant. He is the real main character in the play (in the *Zauberspiel*, at least, he has the most lines to deliver). In the course of the action he develops character traits one would not have expected of him. We are unaware of the experiences to which this loyal servant of the state has been subjected throughout the course of his life; all we can see is how his attitude towards his superiors mirrors that towards his family and his subordinate. The name that Nestroy gives him, Schlagmayer (derived from *schlagen*, 'to beat', the name could be translated as 'Thrashman'), aptly reflects his choleric nature. When his son fails to arrive at the appointed time – for good reasons, as we later learn – he wants to 'inscribe a lesson on paternal authority in Gothic script on the son's back' ['ein Capitel über die väterliche Auctorität mit Fracturbuchstaben auf den Buckel schreiben'] (p. 17).[19] When the worried mother protests against the marriage plans of her husband, he brushes her objections aside: 'Weib, wann du noch ein Wort in Geschäfte drein redst' ['Woman, don't interfere in business matters, or else ...'] (pp. 25–26, 95). Here the threat is not articulated but, when confronting his brother-in-law, he threatens him with physical force: 'Schwager, wenn mir der Schwager den Plan verdirbt, so bring ich den Schwagern um' ['Brother-in-law, if you, brother-in-law, thwart my plan, I'll kill you, brother-in-law'] (p. 97). The tender feelings of his son are shamelessly exploited. The 'misbegotten' son, who earlier was to have been *zerrissen* ['torn apart'] and *karbatscht* ['horse-whipped'],[20] suddenly turns into a *Herzenssohn* ['son of his heart'], *Rettungsengel* ['rescuing angel'], *Helfer in der Not* ['helper in time of need'], and even earns the name *Goldmenschen* ['golden boy'], as he is supposed to procure the necessary silver. The betrothal is celebrated and the union secured by a contract drafted by a notary; the wedding, however, is postponed for one year until Eduard has finished his studies. Regina obtains leave for Schladriwux, the turnpike attendant, to accompany Eduard on his journey into the capital. He is to spy on Eduard and keep him within bounds.

The introduction and the first act clearly show the authoritarian, patriarchal society depicted in a critical light. In terms of Reichmann's interpretation, only the second act could be interpreted as presenting the rural estate of the Count of Steinthal as a positive counterpoint. Eduard, who has saved the life of the count's son, is made welcome in the count's house. He, Eduard, falls in love with Amalie, the daughter of the steward, Miller, and believes that she returns his love. But the thought of the marriage contract with Regina nips his beautiful hopes in the bud; he becomes melancholic. All the members of the aristocratic family feel for him and set about putting things right. As a first step, Captain Brand, a relative of the house, has the turnpike attendant removed. Naturally there is a happy ending. In the last act, the stipulated year has passed and the time for the wedding has arrived. Parents and bride long for the appearance of the bridegroom. Instead of a timid youth, however, a brawling, unkempt, dishevelled lout with sabre, pipes, a collection of bottles, and two large dogs appears. He treats everyone roughly, threatening them with his stick. This threat of force is more persuasive than Regina's money. She rejects him, tears up the marriage contract and, in the end, even confesses to having misappropriated the money herself. She now wants to give her hand to Kandidat Schwarz (an applicant for public office), who for some months has admired her from afar. Schwarz now declares himself to be the son of the count, who has pretended to be Regina's suitor to liberate Eduard from his shackles. In the *Zauberspiel* Regina accepts Tranquillus, in the *Posse* she marries the Chief Forester to conceal her embarrassment. Hirschwald's superior social position has gained him Regina's wealth.

A happy ending: all's well that ends well, or is it? Through fortuitous circumstances Eduard escapes the clutches of Regina and is able to marry his young beloved. Much, however, remains unsolved. Regina's crime cannot be made public for it would incriminate the customs collector. She has to marry the Chief Forester, the lord of the manor house, the chief authority in the village. Is it a punishment that fits the crime? Hirschwald is the real winner, for he takes possession of her wealth. That his bride has committed a crime hardly concerns him. That he, the instigator of the whole train of events, is in one sense also a guilty party, is not even mentioned. All this has nothing to do with the choice of marriage partners of suitable age, of course; essentially, it concerns the exploitation of human beings by other human beings. Everyone uses and abuses his or her position without scruples and often without punishment. Women are desirable because of their dowry; children represent capital on the marriage market. Inasmuch as in the main plot it is not the daughter but the son who is on offer, Nestroy's plot constitutes a reversal of the old comic motif that the highest bidder will get the bride.[21] In comedy such actions are rarely born out of sheer necessity and desperation, as is the case here, and are rarely expressed so crudely: '[...] um Tausend Gulden verkauffst du deinen Sohn an die Schachtel?' ['You are selling your son for a thousand guilders to the old hag?'] (p. 97), exclaims Zettermann. The son, however, does not question the wisdom of the action of his *Herren Ältern* ['venerable parents']. The father has drawn blood and has even grander aspirations: the connections with the *Geldkatze* should enable the son to obtain the stewardship of Kobelsbach. This is why, in the final scene, he is not glad that his son has escaped the dreaded marriage; on the contrary he feels cheated because, 'die Verwaltersstell fürn Eduard, die is halt weg' ['the position of steward is gone'] and, furious, he chides Eduard: 'Verdammte Maskerad, durch die hast du dich um Amt und Braut gebracht.' ['Damned mummery, it lost you your bride and your position'] (p. 63). Only after Eduard has introduced himself as the steward of Count Steinthal's estates, and disclosed that he is to marry the daughter of the previous steward and to receive a rich dowry, is the father consoled, 'Eduarderl' ['Little Eduard'] is allowed back into the bosom of his family – the diminutive clearly expresses the son's station in the eyes of the father. The son's subordinate position is made clear in the first act: 'Ich hab keinen Willen, als den meiner Herrn

Ältern' ['I have no will but the one of my venerable parents'] (p. 32) the son says in the *Zauberspiel*; in the *Posse* he concedes with comic exaggeration: 'Ich heurath alles, was der Papa schafft' ['I'll marry anything my papa orders me to'] (p. 99). The name of Schlagmayer characterises the father for what he is: a tyrant in the guise of a paterfamilias. His position as customs collector (admittedly derived from the source) also seems significant, for it is his duty to control traffic and trade of all kinds.

Where the Spirit King is able to order his subjects about and even to banish them, the Chief Forester has to engineer an intrigue. Because Regina in the *Posse* is much more typical of the comic old maid, the pressure exerted on her seems to be less obvious. When challenged, she feels entitled to steal the official monies, and, in the end, speaks of this as an innocent prank (pp. 61 and 137). Small wonder that the customs collector assumes that his superior office, which never acquires a human face, will not treat him with justice; this is why he prevents his brother-in-law from publicising his plight. 'Richtig, richtig!' the latter agrees, ''s laute Schreyen, verdirbt noch mehr in der Sach; ganz in der Still muß man da schreyen' ['Absolutely right. [...] Crying out loud can only make things worse; crying out in silence is all that one can do'] (p. 19). This paradoxical formulation has attracted some critical interest. Siegfried Diehl sees in it the 'tortured cringing of the exploited petty bourgeois' (p. 92). Franz H. Mautner writes about the corrupting influence of money in Nestroy's comedies;[22] in fact, Eduard and his family face a different problem. As Nestroy says in *"Nur keck!"*: 'Die Macht des Geldes [...] Ist nichts, aber die Macht des Keingeldes ist furchtbar' ['The power of money is nothing compared with the power of (having) no money'].[23] This dictum rules in Kobelsbach.

From the oppression of Kobelsbach – doubtless an allusion to *Kobel* ('pigsty') – Eduard manages to escape into the wholesome world of the count's estate. Financial security protects this aristocratic family from all oppression. Here the plan for Eduard's liberation is hatched. According to Reichmann, Nestroy intended this household to be seen as a model of a patriarchal society. But this counterpoint to the previous scenes also warrants closer examination. The plan succeeds only because of the use or, rather, abuse of power, of superior social position, and of authority. To be rid of Eduard's guard, Schladriwux, Captain Brand blatantly abuses his military authority and has him arrested as a deserter. The turnpike attendant is to be held for five days and then set free again. In addition, he is tricked out of his travel pass. To Nestroy's audience this must have seemed considerably more alarming than it does to us today. Even a short journey of 5 Austrian miles (about 35 kilometres) could be undertaken only with the prior approval of the police authorities. Desertion, even today no small matter, was then punishable with death. Convinced of his innocence, he believes that this must be a case of mistaken identity, but this may be of only small consolation to him. In the actual performance (a production probably directed by the theatre manager Karl Carl himself) an exchange of shots occurred during Schladriwux's arrest, thus emphasising the seriousness of the situation (see the text of stage version of this scene, pp. 219–20).

124

In the *Posse* version we find yet further instances. One may well ask how the Chief Forester managed to get hold of Regina's baptismal record. This is an obvious misuse of official power. We may cite also the example of the steward's daughter Amalie. The Count and the Countess, who are indebted to Eduard for saving their son, take great pains, together with the Captain, to persuade the steward to promise his daughter to Eduard. He is reluctant to do so because he has come to know Eduard as a hard-drinking, card-playing young man who defaults on his debts and forever chases girls. At first the steward does not see that he should repay the services Eduard has rendered to his employers, by granting him the hand of his daughter. As Amalie happens to be in love with Eduard this motif is not further developed. Finally, in the *Posse* a judge appears who is open to bribes; 'Impertinentes Volck!' ['Impertinent mob'] (p. 86), he snaps at the people, having accepted a monetary reward.[24]

Seen in this light, the title of our play is nothing if not misleading, but it may well have been part of Nestroy's strategy to get his concerns on to the stage. It appears to be a deliberate device to deflect attention from what the play is really about, which is not the equality of age, but the inequality of the social classes, social inequality that divides people into perpetrators and victims, into those who exploit and those who are exploited, and which results in corruption and venality. Kurt Kahl summarises the play as a 'bestiary of bourgeois society',[25] a bestiary that contains some very unpleasant specimens.

In Nestroy's plays, 'fate' is often addressed and made responsible for the human condition. In the play *Die Familien Zwirn, Knieriem und Leim*, Fate appears personified on the stage in his favourite 'occupation': he is asleep. In another play written about the same time and performed earlier in the same year, *Müller, Kohlenbrenner and Sesseltrager* [Miller, Charcoal-burner, and Sedan-chair Bearer], the main figure, the sedan-chair carrier, portrayed in performance by Nestroy himself, quarrels not only with his own fate but with fate in general. But he also makes the *Macht des Blutes* ['the power of the blood']²⁶ responsible for his lowly state, because his forebears carried out the same trade as he does. This is a thinly veiled attack on the hierarchical order of society. Similarly, Eduard suggests that he would gladly reject Regina if his uncle were rich enough to come up with the money. Thus, we have to differentiate the concepts of fate in Nestroy: in many cases the term is used as shorthand to describe machinations that are clearly the work of human beings. The dependencies depicted in *Die Gleichheit der Jahre* cannot be ascribed simply to the weaknesses and faults of individuals. Responsibility rests with the organisation of society in general. For these reasons, even if everything ends well, this work cannot be seen as embodying a conservative outlook.

The *Zauberspiel* version is not normally regarded as an independent creation, chiefly because the origin of both works is generally misunderstood.[27] The reworking was completed by October 1833,[28] yet the play was not performed until October 1834. This delay (most likely caused by the outstanding success of another play, *Lumpacivagabundus*, which within the space of twelve months ran to 100 performances) has created the impression that the earlier version was discarded on account of the extraordinary rejection by critics and audiences alike of two *Zauberspiele* at the beginning of 1834, *Müller, Kohlenbrenner und Sesseltrager* and *Der Zauberer Sulphur* [...].[29] But both these plays were written *after* Nestroy had adapted our play as a *Posse*. And later in 1834, possibly as late as the beginning of 1835, Nestroy initially conceived his parody of Holtei's *Lorbeerbaum und Bettelstab* [Laurel Wreath and Beggar's Staff] as a *Zauberspiel*.[30] It cannot therefore have been the hostile reaction to his other plays that motivated Nestroy to rework his earlier version and to write a completely new introduction for the revised text.

It is reasonable to infer that discarding the unfashionable supernatural framework was not foremost in Nestroy's mind. What differences between the two versions might give us a clue to Nestroy's reasons for reworking the text? On a pragmatic level, the *Posse* probably incurred lower production costs than the *Zauberspiel*. One might also point to the imperial aura surrounding the spirit king, a possible source of offence to the monarchy. He is replaced by the *Oberforstmeister* (Chief Forester), who, while socially on a much lower level, still resides in a *Schloß* [palace or manor house]. The major difference, however, is in the figure of Eduard. In the first version he is clearly an innocent victim of the circumstances in which his father finds himself. He is an honest and assiduous student, a dedicated son who takes it upon himself to marry Regina when he realises that the money his parents need cannot be procured by decent means: ' – meine Ältern in solcher Noth – ich muß das Opfer seyn' ['my parents in such distress – I have to sacrifice myself'] (p. 31). The father is certain of his son's loyalty: 'Das habe ich gwußt, du bringst mir das Opfer' ['I knew all along that you would make this sacrifice'] (S. 29).

In the *Posse* Eduard also accepts the marriage arranged by his father, but he is not a victim, he cynically joins in the proceedings. In a series of new scenes he is shown to be a frivolous ne'er-do-well (the change of surname from Schlagmayer, which characterises the father, to Strizl, an allusion to the Viennese term 'Strizzi' – a young rascal – indicates the greater prominence the son now has). Given to drink, cards, and chasing girls, he is unlikely to win the sympathy of the audience, which the Eduard of the *Zauberspiel* enjoys. More importantly, we do not feel that this Eduard has been hard done by. The innocent victim has been transformed into a speculator on the marriage market: 'ihr Geld – meine Schulden – dem Papa sein Malör – das saubere Stubenmädl – ich laß [s'] halt doch nit aus.' ['her money – my debts – Papa's bad luck – the pretty parlour maid – I won't let her go.'] (p. 101). Marriage to the wealthy spinster is an easy way to secure the financial future of this irresponsible good-for-nothing. In the stage version he praises the advantages of such a union in a song with the refrain 'I heirath a Alte mit Geld' ['I'm going to marry an old hag with cash'] (p. 142) while making eyes to the pretty parlour-maid, even during the engagement party. Nestroy's play thus reverts to traditional comedy patterns. The sacrifice of the son has lost its preposterousness, and Regina's intrigue seems to carry with it its own punishment.

The last scenes of the *Posse* abound in cheap slapstick elements. To cite

Friedrich Walla

just one instance, the turnpike attendant, played in the first production by the short and fat Wenzel Scholz, dresses up in a cupid's costume, with a skirt that is far too short, and hides in the chimney of the open fireplace, tumbling down from it, completely covered in soot. It may be a consequence of censorship, which regularly objected to the mention of students, that in the final act Eduard appears, not as a depraved member of the Halle student association, but as the leader of a gang of robbers. This affords Nestroy an opportunity to parody the hackneyed situations of the pseudo-romantic robber dramas that were performed with great success in the Theater an der Wien (including Schiller's *Die Räuber* [The Robbers], to which he makes frequent reference). Here social satire is overshadowed by parody. In other plays of this period, Nestroy camouflages his social criticism behind literary satire. For example, in *Weder Lorbeerbaum noch Bettelstab* (1835), in the guise of parodying a sensationally successful play of the day Nestroy attacks public taste and critical response. The parodistic elements increase the force of the gratuitous comic elements. 'Die Posse verdeckt ihre Ansprüche mit Klamauk und Kostüm' ['The play covers its serious concerns behind slapstick and costume'] writes Kurt Kahl.[31] But there is nevertheless a suggestion that, in the society of Kobelsbach, only criminal force can overcome the power of Regina's money.

In the canon of Nestroy's works *Die Gleichheit der Jahre* occupies a modest place. First produced anonymously in 1834, it did not find favour with the press. In 1839 it was revived in the Theater in der Leopoldstadt, and Wenzel Scholz chose it for a benefit performance. In all, there were twenty-two performances: it was no great sucess, but neither was it a complete flop. The work has almost certainly not been staged since that time. Several of Nestroy's works that initially received a cool reception have since been successfully revived. In an age of increasing social pressures *Die Gleichheit der Jahre* has much to offer; if suitably adapted and appropriately performed, it would certainly arouse critical interest.

Notes

1. A play with supernatural elements, including either allegorical figures (Greed, Hate, etc.) or folklore figures (e.g. Rübezahl) who are perceived as influencing human behaviour.
2. See the new edition of the work in the HKA, *Stücke 7/1*, ed. Friedrich Walla (Vienna, 1987). All quotations from the plays are taken from this edition.
3. W. E. Yates, 'Nestroys Komödie der Freundschaft', *Österreich in Geschichte und Literatur*, 23 (1979), 43–48 (p. 43).
4. Prätzel's story is reproduced in HKA, *Stücke 7/1*, pp. 231–66.
5. W. E. Yates, *Nestroy: Satire and Parody in Viennese Popular Comedy* (Cambridge, 1972), p. 152; Yates also points out, however, that Nestroy regards all progress with a critical eye.
6. Ernst Fischer, 'Johann Nestroy', in: Fischer, *Von Grillparzer zu Kafka* (Vienna, 1962).
7. Rio Preisner, 'Der konservative Nestroy. Aspekte der zukünftigen Forschung', *Maske und Kothurn*, 18 (1972), 23–37; Friedrich Sengle, 'Johann Nestroy (1801–

1862)', in: Sengle, *Biedermeierzeit*, 3 vols (Stuttgart, 1980), vol. III, pp. 191–264.

8. Eva Reichmann, *Konservative Inhalte in den Theaterstücken Johann Nestroys* (Würzburg, 1995).

9. Reichmann labels the bankrupt aristocratic family of Stoppelbach (*Die Familien Zwirn, Knieriem und Leim*) as *nouveau riche* (p. 167), when the very name ('stubble creek') indicates their precarious financial position. She repeats this erroneous characterisation in a further paper (Eva Reichmann, 'Gebrauch und Funktion von Klischees im Wiener Volkstheater und bei Johann Nestroy', *Nestroyana*, 15 (1995), 122–30 (p. 126), where she describes Madam Leim as the embodiment of the cliché of a bourgeois woman who covets a higher social status, one that she wants to gain through the marriages of her children. In fact, the opposite is the case. True, Madam Leim defers to her husband's wishes concerning the children, but she steadfastly refuses to speak *hochdeutsch* ('standard High German') and to give up her *gemeine* ('common') friendships (HKA, *Stücke 8/I*, ed. F. Walla (Vienna, 1996), pp. 15 and 41).

10. Interestingly, when commenting on this scene Reichmann remarks that the employer in a patriarchal household had the right to exercise punishment, hardly something that can be read as a recommendation of patriarchal society ('Der Dienstherr hat in einem patriarchalisch strukturierten Haushalt ja das Züchtigungsrecht', p. 166) (the term *Züchtigung* implies corporal punishment).

11. An almost identical example is to be found in Nestroy's first full-length play *Dreyßig Jahre aus dem Leben eines Lumpen* [Thirty Years in the Life of a Scoundrel] with its subtitle *Die Verbannung aus dem Zauberreiche* [The Exile from the Spirit Kingdom].

12. In her desire to show that Nestroy criticises the newly emerging bourgeoisie, Reichmann completely ignores the significance of the fact that so many of Nestroy's plays are set in palaces and manor houses ('Schlösser'). Clearly, even where names and titles suggest a bourgeois background, Nestroy has the ruling class in mind (this practice was doubtless forced upon him by the censorship regulations). The financially strapped Hirschwald could hardly be classified as *nouveau riche*, the term Reichmann often employs to characterise the inhabitants of the manor houses.

13. Siegfried Diehl, *Zauberei und Satire im Frühwerk Nestroys* (Bad Homburg, 1962), p. 91.

14. In Nestroy's plays we find Madam Speer (*Dreyßig Jahre aus dem Leben eines Lumpen*), Frau Lärminger (*Heimliches Geld, heimliche Liebe*) and Frau Groning (*Nur Ruhe!*).

15. W. E. Yates, 'Nestroy, Grillparzer and the Feminist Cause' in W. E. Yates and John R. P. McKenzie (eds) *Viennese Popular Theatre. A Symposium* (Exeter, 1985), pp. 93–108 (pp. 94 and 92).

16. He prescribes 'kleinstädtische' ('small town, provincial') clothes for the customs collector and his wife, thus stressing their limited horizons and sphere of action (pp. 17 and 87).

17. The mentioning of the silver guilders is significant. The hard currency was worth several times the value of the same sum in paper money (usually referred to as *Wiener Währung* [Viennese currency]).

18. The name actually means 'money bag' or 'money belt'.

19. The pun is particularly apt in German: *Fractur* signifies not only Gothic script but also a broken bone or limb. Note also the old-fashioned spelling of *Auctorität* [authority].

20. Significantly, he uses the same word to describe his own state after discovering the theft.

21. Nestroy uses this motif in *Nagerl und Handschuh* [Buttonhole and Glove] (a Cinderella story), *Glück, Mißbrauch und Rückkehr* [Good Fortune, Misuse, and Return].

22. Franz H. Mautner, 'Geld, Nestroy und Nestroy-Interpretationen', in: Jürgen Hein (ed.), *Theater und Gesellschaft. Das Volksstück im 19. und 20. Jahrhundert* (Düsseldorf, 1973), pp. 113–18.
23. *"Nur keck!"* (HKA, *Stücke 34*, p. 15). This invites comparison with Lips's statement in *Der Zerrissene*: 'Armuth is ohne Zweifel das Schrecklichste. Mir könnt' einer Zehn Millionen herlegen, und sagen, ich soll arm seyn dafür, ich nähmet's nicht' ['Poverty is beyond doubt the worst thing that could happen to one. If somebody offered me ten million on condition that I'd be poor, I wouldn't take it.'] (HKA, *Stücke 21*, p. 34).
24. For censorship purposes this was changed in the stage version, where only the peasants receive a tip.
25. Kurt Kahl, *Johann Nestroy oder Der wienerische Shakespeare* (Vienna, 1970), p. 100.
26. This was also intended as an allusion to a play by the contemporary writer Ignaz Jeitteles.
27. 'Der Zauber ist Nestroy selbst schon lästig, und so bleibt von der Zauberposse "Das Verlobungsfest im Feenreiche oder Die Gleichheit der Jahre", [...] nur der zweite Teil des Titels übrig.' ['Nestroy was weary of magic effects, and of the Zauberposse *Engagement Party in the Spirit Realm or the Equality in Years* only the second part of the title remains'], Kahl, *Johann Nestroy*, p. 98.
28. HKA, *Stücke 7/I*, pp. 152–54.
29. The full title of this play is *Der Zauberer Sulphurelectrimagneticophosphoratus und die Fee Walpurgiblocksbergiseptemtrionalis.*
30. Contrary to Rommel's opinion, the *Zauberspiel* version was actually completed; see *Stücke 8/II*, ed. F. Walla (in preparation).
31. Kahl, *Johann Nestroy*, p. 100.

Nestroy's *Zwey ewige Juden und Keiner*: a Tale of Three Cities

John R. P. McKenzie

ROSAMUNDE. Ich streich mir die Hälfte weg. [...]
MUMMLER. Wenn's von so einen hungrigen Dichter wär da kann man
   streichen nach Gusto. (*Zwey ewige Juden und Keiner*, II, 16)

[ROSAMUNDE. I'll cut the text by half. [...]
MUMMLER. If it was written by some starving poet you could cut as
   much as you liked.]

Nestroy's *Zwey ewige Juden und Keiner* [Two Wandering Jews and None], a
burlesque that he based on a Parisian *comédie-vaudeville*, was first produced in
August 1846. In fact, it was the subject of two simultaneous, wholly distinct
first productions: the one in Vienna, the other in Pest. This theatrical tale of
three cities is a remarkable story and, in terms of theatre history, of
considerable significance. In this article I wish to summarise the preliminary
findings I have made while editing the text for the new critical edition of
Nestroy's works (HKA). In addition to the unusual circumstances of the first
productions, I concentrate on the following topics: the genesis of *Zwey ewige
Juden und Keiner*, Nestroy's debt to his French *vaudeville* source and to
Eugène Sue's novel *Le Juif errant*; secondly, Nestroy's characteristic process
of creative adaptation;[1] and finally, the ironic and satirical force of the work –
his satire of the world of the theatre, of the dominant role of money in human
affairs, and of popular superstition, and the self-referential nature of his
burlesque.

 Zwey ewige Juden und Keiner is normally dismissed as an insignificant piece
sandwiched between two important works, *Der Unbedeutende* and *Der Schützling*
[The Unimportant Man and The Protégé]. It has been largely neglected by
Nestroy scholarship even though the text was included in the first major
collected editions of Nestroy's works, Chiavacci and Ganghofer (1891) and
Rommel (1929).[2] Those who mention the play regard it as little more than a
curiosity, in Mautner's phrase, a piece of 'turbulent nonsense'.[3] It has suffered
a worse fate in the theatre: apart from one production in Prague in October
1846 there is no record of its having been staged since the productions in
Vienna and Pest.[4]

130

The surviving autograph manuscript material for *Zwey ewige Juden und Keiner* is relatively thin. As Nestroy's fair autograph copy is lost, I have had to base my edition of the text on a prompter's book; originally in the archive of the Carl-Theater, it is now housed in the library of the Austrian Theatre Museum (formerly the Theatersammlung of the Austrian National Library). The prompter's book, a copy-writer's manuscript, is a fascinating document in its own right.[5] It allows us to reconstruct several stages in the genesis of the text: the original version, 'precautionary' pre-censorship, official censorship, and the resulting revised version.

The simultaneous staging of two productions that compete for the description 'first production' constitutes a unique event in Nestroy's career. The premières of both took place on 4 August 1846: the one took place in Vienna in the Theater in der Leopoldstadt, Nestroy's home base; the other in the Königlich Deutsches Theater in Pest. Karl Carl, owner-director of the Theater in der Leopoldstadt, played the leading role, Kranz, in the Viennese production; Nestroy played the same part in Pest, where he was making guest appearances (Nestroy normally undertook a summer tour; in 1846 he also visited Prague and Graz but did not perform in the play in either city).[6] Remarkably, the work was given in two distinct versions and with different titles. The original version, *Zwey ewige Juden und Keiner*, was given in Pest, while the Viennese production used a heavily censored text with the title *Der fliegende Holländer zu Fuß* [The Flying Dutchman on Foot].[7] The change of title indicates the degree of censorship to which the text was subjected; indeed, the whole concept of the play suffered radical alteration. Even if neither version was a box-office success – there were only six performances in Vienna and four in Pest – the work has considerable historical significance. Censorship in the Austrian Empire was a complex, cumbersome process. Once a play was passed by the Viennese censor, approval elsewhere in the Empire was normally a formality but there was no guarantee that the Viennese authorities would endorse approval given elsewhere. Thus, it comes as no surprise that a work which was heavily censored in Vienna could be considered acceptable in Pest. This does not necessarily mean that the two offices were working to widely different standards; the decisive factor in this case was doubtless one of language. German was the first language of the vast majority of the citizens of Vienna while, in Pest, it was a minority language. The performance of a German-language comedy in Pest was unlikely to cause the kind of stir that such works commonly provoked in the popular theatres of Vienna. Why the two versions were produced simultaneously is unclear.[8] The most likely explanation is that Nestroy's contract obliged him to provide Carl with a play for the summer months and that he was all too happy to avoid appearing in the emasculated Viennese version.

As *Zwey ewige Juden* is virtually an unknown piece it may be helpful to provide a summary of the action. There are two acts: the first takes place in a country inn, the second in the country seat of Herr von Auerhahn, a landed gentleman. The plot is complex, consisting of three interwoven strands of action. The first strand concerns the seven descendants of a silk merchant

131

called Stern who married his seven daughters to men of different social and economic status living in the far-flung quarters of the world. Stern's brother emigrated to India where he died childless, having amassed a huge fortune. The terms of his will stipulate that it shall be published twenty-five years after his death and that the whole of the fortune shall be inherited by whichever of his heirs is penniless on that date. The duties of trustee and executor have passed to Wandling, a millionaire; he is bound by oath to keep silent about the will and the fortune, which now amounts to three million, until the twenty-five years are up. As the play opens, the date on which the will is to be published is fast approaching and Wandling has arranged for all seven heirs to assemble on the appointed day.

Five of the potential heirs play a significant role in the action: von Auerhahn; Kranz, an elderly, impecunious landscape painter; Holper, a rich merchant; Mummler, leader of a troupe of wandering players; and Chevalier Distelbrand, adventurer and cad (to make up the numbers and to avoid cluttering up Act I, Nestroy has two further heirs put in their first appearance in the final scenes of Act II). Wandling's task is complicated by his reunion with Kranz, the man who saved his life in America (the reunion occurs at the beginning of Act I). We learn that Kranz shot a panther that was about to attack Wandling (the fact that the natural habitat of the panther is Africa and Southern Asia simply adds to the general dottiness of the work). As a belated reward for Kranz's heroic act of mercy, Wandling offers him an annuity of 3000 francs but, on learning Kranz's surname, Wandling is forced to rescind his offer as it would make Kranz ineligible as heir and, sworn to secrecy as executor, Wandling cannot explain his motives (cast in the role of knight errant, Wandling has determined that Kranz shall inherit). Until the grand dénouement at the end of Act II, Kranz assumes that Wandling is deliberately hostile towards him.

By a series of highly unlikely coincidences of the kind regularly encountered in Nestroy's farces, Wandling and all seven heirs find themselves in Auerhahn's house three days before the appointed date. After a further series of apparently chance occurrences, many of which are orchestrated by Wandling, Kranz emerges as the only penniless heir; he divides the three millions between himself and his nephew, Wilhelm, who is now able to marry the woman of his heart, Auerhahn's daughter Pauline.

The liaison between Wilhelm and Pauline constitutes the second strand of the action and maintains the conscious lack of realism evident in the main action. This romantic sub-plot takes the characteristic form of 'eine Heirat mit Hindernissen', the rocky road to matrimony, without which no Viennese *Posse* [farce] would be complete. The obstacles strewn along this road include the machinations of a ruthless rival, Distelbrand, a duel between Wilhelm and Distelbrand that results in a highly improbable exchange of identities between them, and the intervention of a fictitious Spanish marchioness – supposedly Distelbrand's crazed former lover – who threatens to set fire to Auerhahn's house (the role is given a ham performance by Mummler's daughter, Rosamunde). Unbeknown to Kranz and Wilhelm, this intrigue has been engineered by

Wandling to smooth the path of true love for Wilhelm and Pauline; Kranz
interrupts Rosamunde's pyromanic histrionics and thereby earns Auerhahn's
gratitude.

The third strand of the action concerns a troupe of strolling players.
Mummler, an actor-manager, arrives at the inn, intent on staging a dramatised version of the the legend of the Wandering Jew. Unable to do so because
the two leading members of his troupe have decamped, he persuades Kranz
and Wilhelm to take over the roles at short notice: Kranz is to play Ahasverus,
the Wandering Jew, and Wilhelm the role of Rennepont (according to the
legend, one of the heirs to a huge estate). The arrival of Auerhahn and
Pauline throws Kranz and Wilhelm into confusion: if they are recognised on
stage, Wilhelm's chance of marrying Pauline will be wrecked. Accordingly,
they decide to leave and, at the end of Act I, are seen fleeing in their stage
costumes. After a further series of unlikely adventures, Mummler and Kranz
appear at the end of Act II each in the costume of the Wandering Jew.
Mummler announces his intention of finally staging the play: he and Kranz
will share the role. As will be all too clear from this brief résumé, we are
dealing with a self-ironising fictive world.

Since the first production of *Zwey ewige Juden*, commentators have assumed
– wrongly – that Nestroy based his play primarily on the novel *Le Juif errant*
[*The Wandering Jew*] by Eugène Sue (1804–57), which was published as a
serial novel in the Parisian newspaper *Le Constitutionnel* between June 1844
and July 1845.[9] The identity of the actual source has remained a mystery,
although it is revealed in one of Nestroy's autograph manuscripts (this
consists of what appear to be the first two pages of the original text). The first
page shows the title, as follows:[10]

Zwey ewige Juden (× für Einen ×) (+ und Keiner +)
(× Posse ×) (+ Burleske +) mit Gesang in Zwey Acten v. J. Nestroy
(die Handlung ist theilweise Varners "   " nachgebieldet)

[Two Eternal Jews (× instead of One ×) (+ and None +)
(× A Farce ×) (+ A Burlesque +) with Songs in Two Acts by J. Nestroy
(the action is based partly on Varner's "   "]

Clearly, Nestroy intended to insert the title of Varner's work in the blank
space.[11] The play in question, *Le Nouveau Juif errant* [The New Wandering
Jew], was first performed on 28 March 1846 in the Théâtre du Palais Royal in
Paris, that is, just over four months before Nestroy's version; it is billed as
'comédie en trois actes, mêlée de chant' ['comedy in three acts with songs'].[12]
The name of the author, the French *vaudevilliste* François-Antoine Varner
(1789–1854), is now all but forgotten but in his day he was a well-known
figure. He wrote a large number of plays for the Parisian popular theatre,
many in collaboration with other playwrights, such as Bayard, Dupin, Imbert,
Mélesville, and Scribe. His works were known also in Vienna: between 1826
and 1846 no fewer than ten of his plays were given in French in the

Kärntnerthortheater and the Kleiner Redoutensaal by visiting French actors, and two were produced in translation in the Theater in der Leopoldstadt.[13]

Ignorance of the French source has inevitably led commentators to attribute to Nestroy ideas that in fact derive from his source. For example, Rommel speculates that Nestroy set out to make his adaptation of a French comedy of intrigue more attractive by simultaneously parodying Sue's novel (see SW XIII, 620). In one sense he was right: the play introduces a parodistic element into a traditional comedy of intrigue, but this was not Nestroy's doing; the combination of parody and intrigue is already present in Varner. Reaching a similar conclusion, Mautner maintains that Nestroy varied his parodistic technique by introducing new *vaudeville* motifs, and by adding a surprising new element to Sue's theme: the stipulation that the whole inheritance is to go to the poorest heir. Together with the introduction of a troupe of wandering players and the in-jokes about the theatre, this innovation, Mautner asserts, turned the farce into a burlesque.[14] In identifying the undoubted strengths of Nestroy's burlesque Mautner, like Rommel, could not know that Nestroy had taken them from Varner.

Varner's play is itself a burlesque treatment of Sue's *Le Juif errant*. In assessing its impact we must bear in mind the way in which Sue adapted the theme of the Wandering Jew, the enormous popularity of the novel, and the reasons for its success. With *Le Juif errant* Sue breathed new life into a legend that was first recorded in England in the thirteenth century, the story of the Wandering Jew who is condemned to wander the Earth eternally because he refused to allow Christ on the way of the cross to rest on his doorstep, and of his companion Herodias who was responsible for the death of John the Baptist. Often interpreted as an explanation for, and metaphor of, the Jewish Diaspora, the legend is marked by a distinct anti-Semitic bias, which varies in degree from version to version. The action of Sue's novel is set in contemporary times, beginning in 1831. Though Sue's novel rehearses the main events of the legend, his primary aim, as in *Les Mystères de Paris*, was to present a liberal critique of social conditions in contemporary France. His depiction of the Jews is relatively positive; the main target of his criticism is the Church, in particular what he sees as an international Jesuit conspiracy. It was this heady mix of supernatural legend, social reportage, and anti-clericalism that intoxicated the readership of *Le Constitutionnel*.

Given the huge popularity of Sue's novel, Varner could take for granted his audience's familiarity with its plot – in outline at least – as also could Nestroy. In adapting the work, Varner and Nestroy concentrate on the following aspect of the novel, the story of the inheritance of the Rennepont family. Marius de Rennepont, descendant of the sister of Ahasverus, the Wandering Jew, leaves a fortune of 50,000 écus on his death in 1682, which he asks a trusted Jewish friend to invest. His will is to remain secret until the 150th anniversary of his death in 1832. Rennepont's seven heirs – none of whom is aware of the others' existence – are invited to attend the reading of his will on the appointed day, when they will personally receive their share of the fortune which, invested in government bonds, has grown to 212 million francs. A group of conspirators, members of the Society of Jesus, hatch a plot to prevent six of the seven from attending and to misappropriate the funds of the only heir who is able to attend, Abbé Gabriel de Rennepont, a 'good' priest and Jesuit. But they have not reckoned with Ahasverus, the Wandering Jew who, for over 1800 years, has closely followed the family's fortunes. Following his intervention, a codicil is produced that postpones the reading by a few weeks. During this period further nefarious intrigues lead to the death of all the heirs but Gabriel de Rennepont. Rennepont inherits the fortune but is forced to make it over to the Jesuits. They are prevented from acquiring it, however, when, on the orders of Ahasverus, the title-deeds are burned.

To what extent do Varner and Nestroy exploit this source material? In essence *Le Nouveau Juif errant* is a lightweight *comédie-vaudeville*, a typical product of its time. But the work distinguishes itself in one important respect: it provides a burlesque treatment of the main theme in Sue's novel, the disbursement of a huge fortune among a number of heirs. This story-line functions as a vehicle for a love intrigue and for a benevolent satire on the world of the theatre. Unlike the heirs in the novel, who inhabit a quasi-fantastic world, Varner's heirs have their feet firmly planted in contemporary France. The supernatural motifs, social criticism, and anti-clericalism that feature prominently in Sue's work are absent from Varner's play. In comparing Nestroy and Varner one is struck by the extent to which Nestroy's text closely follows the original (the two plays are roughly equal in length). Nestroy took over the three main strands of the action but, while he introduced no major changes, he elaborated the following themes: the staging of the play-within-a-play, the lot of a theatre-manager, and the role of money. He omitted several tedious sections in Varner and, in accordance with established practice in adapting contemporary French comedies for the Viennese stage, he deleted the numerous short musical numbers that punctuate the dialogue in *Le Nouveau Juif errant* (a typical feature of mid-nineteenth-century French *comédie-vaudeville*), and inserted in their place two lengthy satirical songs, characteristic ingredients of the *Posse mit Gesang*.

In adapting *Le Nouveau Juif errant*, Nestroy departed from his usual practice in one significant respect. The characteristic feature of his method of creative adaptation is *Verwienerung* (a process that involves the translation of the action of the original to a Viennese setting and the reworking of the text in a Viennese idiom). He made significantly less use of *Verwienerung* in *Zwey ewige Juden* than in most of the plays that he based on foreign sources. It is reasonable to surmise that Nestroy's deviation from normal practice has to do with the nature of his subject matter. In the *Vormärz*, the era of Metternich's rule before the outbreak of the Revolution in March 1848, references to the Jews in dramatic works were normally banned by the Austrian censor's office. Nestroy could hardly transpose the legend of the Wandering Jew to a Viennese setting without inviting the censor to issue the judgement *damnatur*. This inhibition could explain why the action takes place in an unspecified setting and why there are no references that link the play specifically to Vienna, except for the satirical comments in the songs which, in any case, do not form part of the action. This is also true of the dialogue: for the most part, it is cast not in Viennese dialect but in High German with an Austrian colouring.

With one exception, Nestroy's main characters are taken directly from Varner: they are characterised in a similar way and they fulfil similar functions. The main difference is the division into two of Varner's lead juvenile role: Oscar Durand, a newly qualified physician, is transformed into the middle-aged Kranz and his youthful nephew Wilhelm, both landscape painters. This change may well have been prompted by a desire on Nestroy's part to reinforce one of the themes of the play, the meagre lot of the artist: Varner's hard-pressed director-actor is now joined by two struggling painters.

A comparison of motifs that Nestroy took directly from the opening scenes of Varner's first Act, serves to demonstrate the extent to which Nestroy freely borrowed his material (in each case, Varner's scene number is followed by its equivalent in Nestroy):

> I, 1 (I, 1; 2; 4) Geneviève (Babett), servant in an inn, expresses her great enthusiasm for Sue's novel *Le Juif errant* [*Der ewige Jude*];
>
> I, 2 (I, 10) Saltzbourg (Holper), a wealthy merchant, believes that Oscar Durand (Kranz), one of his creditors, committed suicide in America;
>
> I, 3 (I, 11–13) Oscar (Kranz) and Bertrand (Wandling) meet; it emerges that Oscar saved Bertrand from an attack by a wild animal in America;
>
> I, 4 (I, 15) Bertrand (Wilhelm) relates how he encountered a young girl, Henriette (Pauline), on the banks of a river, helped her to recover a gold medallion she had lost, but was unable to speak to her before she left the scene;
>
> I, 4 (I, 15) Bertrand (Wandling) offers Oscar (Kranz) an annuity in recognition of Oscar's having saved his life;
>
> I, 5 (I, 19) Bertrand (Wandling) withdraws the offer on learning Oscar's (Kranz's) surname;
>
> I, 5 (I, 16) Duramberg (Mummler), the leader of a troupe of itinerant players, bemoans the fate of artists and expresses his anger at the innkeeper's demand for advance payment for the use of a barn in which he wants to stage a dramatised version of *Le Juif errant* [*Der ewige Jude*].

The prompter's book, on which I have based the main text of *Zwey ewige Juden*, provides considerable evidence of the second stage in the genesis of the play, the 'precautionary' pre-censorship with which Nestroy attempted to second-guess those sections of the text to which the censor would object (he indicated these sections with spiral rings written over the existing text, often supplying an alternative text above). W. E. Yates summarises the process as follows:

> Nestroy generally wrote in the 'precautionary' rings and alternative wordings in his own autograph fair copy of the text. [...] His revisions –

rings and alternatives – were copied into the manuscript used by the producer or the prompter, for use at rehearsals. [...] But only the revised text was written out for the censor. [...] It seems, then, that all the passages omitted in the text submitted to the censor were smuggled back for the performance. [...] The police spies attending the performance can, of course, only have been checking that what the censor had rejected was definitely left out. [...] this helped get approval quickly, as there was normally next to nothing left that the censor could possibly object to. [...] For obvious reasons, published memoirs of the time do not contain accounts of this precautionary 'pre-censorship', so that the practice has to be pieced together from surviving manuscripts.[15]

The success of pre-censorship relied upon a basic flaw in the procedure: the police spies attending performances in the theatre possessed a list of censored material but not a copy of the whole text. There are over seventy examples of precautionary substitutions in *Zwey ewige Juden*, of which all but a couple were found acceptable by the censor. To this extent Nestroy's subterfuge had worked once again, but the story does not end there for, as far as this particular text was concerned, the focus of the censor's attention was directed elsewhere.

The interventions of the censor's office determined the third stage in the genesis of the work. In the case of *Zwey ewige Juden*, the censor outlawed all references to the Wandering Jew. The censor's practice of deleting from a play any references that made fun of the Jews or were hostile to them had nothing to do with social or religious enlightenment; it was motivated by fear that the performance of a play with such sentiments would provoke public disorder. This is why in the first half of the nineteenth century Viennese popular theatre largely ignored the situation of the Jews.[16] Given this state of affairs, why did Nestroy decide to adapt such a theme and how did he depict the Jews? One can only surmise that the absence in *Le Nouveau Juif errant* of any 'real' Jewish characters led him to believe that his adaptation would not fall victim to censorship. That said, it has to be admitted that *Zwey ewige Juden* contains several references which, while not downright hostile, nevertheless reveal a stereotype image of the Jews – and one must remember that, comparatively bland though Nestroy's version may be, the legend of the Wandering Jew itself has a long anti-Semitic pedigree.

Whatever Nestroy's calculations were, the censor's harsh reaction meant that the title *Zwey ewige Juden* had to be abandoned and the text radically altered. It has not been possible to establish who undertook the revision of the text and to what extent Nestroy was consulted, nor is it known for sure why *Der fliegende Holländer* was chosen as an alternative title; it is likely, however, that the substitution was thought to be appropriate in view of the many references in the text to eternal wandering. In part, at least, the choice of alternative title may also be attributed to the contemporary revival of interest in the legend of the Flying Dutchman: a folk ballad 'Die treue Braut' recorded by Wilhelm Grimm (1811), Heine's version of that poem (1834), and Wagner's opera (1843), inspired by his reading of Heine.[17]

In accordance with the censor's decision, over forty references to the
Wandering Jew were deleted in the version produced in Vienna. In the
majority of cases this consisted simply in the substitution of one phrase for
another but in four instances it involved longer passages. One of these is of
particular interest: in an unconvincing attempt to justify the full substitute
title, *Der fliegende Holländer zu Fuß* (prompted doubtless by the fact that the
character does not fly), the following change was made:

HOLPER. Haben Sie keine Ahnung wer der is (*geheimnisvoll auf* KRANZ
   zeigend.) Dieser rastlos Wandernde(+×˙, der den Tod sucht und
   nicht finden kann? ×+).
BABETT (*gespannt*). No?
HOLPER. (× Der ewige Jud. ×) (+ 's [is] der fliegende Holländer˙+)
(+BABETT. Aber er fligt ja nicht. +)
(+HOLPER. Weils Sommer is, in Sommer geht er zu Fuß, und im
   Winter, weil die Wege zu schlecht sein, fliegt er, darum heißt er der
   fliegende Holländer zu Fuß. +) (*Zwey ewige Juden*, I, 18)

[HOLPER. Have you no idea who that is (*pointing mysteriously at* KRANZ)?
   This restless wanderer (+× who looks for death and cannot find
   it. ×+)
BABETT (*intrigued*). Well, then who is it?
HOLPER. (× The Wandering Jew. ×) (+ It's the Flying Dutchman. +)
(+BABETT. But he's not flying. +)
(+HOLPER. That's because it's summer time. He goes on foot in summer
   and, in winter when the roads are bad, he flies – that's why he's
   called the Flying Dutchman on foot. +)]

The main consequence of the change of title and central motif was a
weakening of the web of cross-references on which the integrity of the play
depends. The separate strands of the action are bound together by the motif
of the Wandering Jew, which provides a conceptual framework for the whole
action: it is introduced in the opening scene, and it provides a serviceable
comic ending. Parallel motifs are established by several characters who refer
to their constant journeying: Mummler, the itinerant actor, Kranz and
Wilhelm who travel abroad in search of new subjects for their painting,
Wandling who travels the globe to escape from the ennui of the rich man's
life. Describing his travels as a merchant, Holper makes the most direct
reference: '[...] ich bin schon ein zweiter ewiger Jud' [I'm already a second
Wandering Jew'] (I, 5). He provides a second link to the legend when he
develops an irrational belief that Kranz in theatre costume is the real
Wandering Jew; this persuades Mummler to advertise the play accordingly
and the audience takes his barnstormer's patter at face value. The closing lines
of the final scene return to the theme of the Wandering Jew: both Kranz and
Mummler appear dressed for the role, and Mummler, still intent on staging
his production, must decide who shall play the part; undeterred, he suggests a

solution: 'Zwei ewige Juden sind da, wir theilen die Roll' ['There are two Wandering Jews here; we'll share the role'] (II, 30). This completes the frame and explains the wording of the title, *Two Wandering Jews and None*: there are two of them but neither is the 'real' Wandering Jew. The force of this final connection is destroyed by the substitution of the Flying Dutchman.

Nestroy changed the designation of his play on the title page of his putative fair copy from farce (*Posse*) to burlesque (*Burleske*) (see the transcription above); this change does not appear to be of great taxonomic significance, except inasmuch as it may well have been an attempt to forestall the habitual criticism from reviewers: 'One of the most consistent points in contemporary Nestroy criticism was the demand for "original" material rather than plots borrowed from the French; and this criticism was sharpened by the competition between the *Posse* and the imported *comédie-vaudeville*, which is documented in the reviews Nestroy received in 1843 and 1844 [...]. In [1846] Nestroy delighted the critics: *Der Unbedeutende* answered their criteria and in particular presented an unmistakable "moral"'.[18] Writing *Zwey ewige Juden* immediately after *Der Unbedeutende*, Nestroy may well have hoped that the term 'burlesque' would encourage critics to take the play for what it is, a comedy of intrigue in which he caricatured the central event in one of the most popular works of fiction of the time and, with his band of wandering characters, Holper, Mummler, Kranz, and Wandling, exploited the comic potential of the theme. If this was Nestroy's hope, his strategy failed: with the exception of the critique in the *Oesterreichischer Courier* (see note 8), the reviews in Pest and Vienna range from lukewarm to downright hostile. In many respects the reviewers wholly misunderstood the play or were inhibited by inflexible aesthetic assumptions: to demand, as many did, a well-made piece with a neatly developing plot is to miss the point of Nestroy's burlesque, for, as the title suggests, *Zwey ewige Juden* is a deliberate trivialisation of the legend of the Wandering Jew.[19]

Although Nestroy's text conforms closely to Varner's it would be wrong to dismiss it as no more than a German-language version; Hein's summary of Nestroy's process of adaptation could have been formulated with precisely this work in mind:

> Even when he virtually translates his source material, bringing out no new features, when he produces a text to order at speed, Nestroy does not surrender to the triviality of his source. Rather, by stressing its theatricality he manages to distance himself from the original. Of particular importance in this context are Nestroy's songs, which provide him with opportunities for satirical comment, as does the juxtaposition of the fictive world of the play and the reality of the contemporary world.[20]

Indeed, *Zwey ewige Juden* contains a number of these ingredients: an ironic awareness of genre, social comment, and an extended satire on the world of the theatre. In other words, we are dealing with a work in which the action is intentionally disorganised and the motivation consciously unbelievable. On one level *Zwey ewige Juden* is a burlesque of Sue's novel, on another it mocks the genre of farce itself. The unlikely story of an inheritance left by a rich uncle in India not only provides the happy ending, it also determines much of the action, and, in so doing, provides a burlesque of Sue's tale and an ironic comment on the nature of farce. Such self-referential irony calls for deft handling: the skill with which Nestroy controls his material prevents the irony from becoming a form of self-indulgence, which is often the case with lesser writers.

Secondly, the play is rich in comic allusions to the theatre: Mummler bemoans the lot of the actor-manager in charge of a rebellious troupe of strolling players: he discusses the lack of patrons willing to buy season tickets (I, 9), the mania for free tickets ['Freibillietmanie'] (I, 6–8), the cavalier manner in which actors approach their roles (I, 21), and stage-fright (I, 40) – in-jokes that reflect Nestroy's personal experience. One reference in particular, the question of theatre contracts (I, 22), could well be read as a veiled allusion to the plight of his colleagues at the hands of Karl Carl, a manager renowned for his parsimony; Mummler gives Kranz the following ironic assurance: ''s Wort gilt bey mir so viel als ein Theater Contract, denn man halt't ihn auch nur, so lang man will' ['One's word is as good as a theatre contract: you keep it only as long as you want to'] (I, 22). As Carl played Kranz in Vienna, the line would have acquired added poignancy and it prompts the question: was he oblivious to the jibe or did he not care? One of the most significant innovations in Nestroy's version is the staging of Mummler's play, which occupies a large section of Act I. This is a minor *tour de force* on Nestroy's part: the play-within-a-play turns into a fiasco, reminiscent of Tieck's *Der gestiefelte Kater* [*Puss in Boots*] and Grabbe's *Scherz, Satire, Ironie und tiefere Bedeutung* [Jest, Satire, Irony and Deeper Meaning].

Thirdly, Nestroy also introduces some trenchant social comment. A couple of examples stand out. The story of the inheritance, fundamental to Varner's and to Nestroy's versions, is developed by Nestroy into a major satirical theme. Money is seen as the governing force in all human relations. There is constant talk of bills for food and drink in the inn (Act I): Holper and Wandling can afford to pay, while the impoverished artists, the actor-manager and the painters, fail to make ends meet. On the other hand, Wandling's wealth brings him no pleasure; on the contrary, it burdens him with *Weltschmerz*. The details of the inheritance dominate Act II, where the prospect of monetary gain outweighs all other considerations: the heirs show no interest in their dead relation until they hear he has left a huge fortune, Auerhahn's attitude towards Wilhelm is transformed when he realises that Wilhelm will share half his uncle's inheritance of three million.

Finally, the scene in which Kranz appears as the 'real' Wandering Jew (I, 31) provides Nestroy with the opportunity to introduce a short monologue of the kind usually spoken by his main character, who half steps out of his role to deliver philosophical observations on the state of the world. Here Wandling expresses his amazement at the susceptibility to superstition and the primitive gullibility of the audience: 'Aber merkwürdiger is doch noch der Aberglaube, Anno, was wir jetzt schreiben, und ein ewiger Jud! Wo is denn die Wacht daß man so Leut z'sammfangen und einsperren laßt!?' ['Superstition is even stranger: a Wandering Jew in this day and age! Call the guards! People like that should be rounded up and put away!'] (I, 34). This episode is significant also in terms of the genesis of the play, for Nestroy is drawing here on his 'Reserve' (a list of witty formulations that he collected for use in future works).[21] Entry no. 54 in the 'Reserve' consists of the ironic nonce-word 'Aberglaubologie' – the term is impossible to translate effectively, it combines 'Aberglaube' ['superstition'] and the suffix '-ology' to construct a pseudo-scientific concept. Dressed in the theatre costume of the Wandering Jew, Kranz comments 'So hat der ewige Jud ausg'schaut nach der Geschichte, und so schaut er *noch* aus nach dem Kostümbuch der Aberglaubologie' ['This is what the Wandering Jew looked like according to history, and this is what he *still* looks like in the role-book of the incurably superstitious'] (I, 35). Clearly, it was anticipated that this speech would offend the censor because the words 'der Aberglaubologie' are marked with a spiral line (see the description of provisional self-censorship above). Nestroy may originally have intended to make use here of a further entry in the 'Reserve'; no. 231 reads: '*Lied* über den Aberglauben' ['song about superstition'] and the introduction to Wandling's song (I, 34) suggests that this was indeed his original intention. It, too, may well have fallen victim to the censor's pencil, for the version of the song contained in the prompter's book is a relatively mild satire on social pretensions. Alternatively, Nestroy may have written a sharper version of the song which has since disappeared.

In conclusion I should like to illustrate the effectiveness of Nestroy's text by quoting an extract from the duet between Mummler and Wandling (II, 10), in which Nestroy plays upon two homonyms: 'jemandem einen Possen spielen' [to make a fool of somone, to play a prank on someone] and 'Posse' (plural 'Possen') ['farce']:[22]

WANDLING. 's gibt Ehleut die hab'n sich so überhapps gern,
MUMMLER. Und im Grund thut sich doch keins ums andre viel schearn.
WANDLING. Bald steckt sie in Intrign, bald kommt er in a Wäsch,
MUMMLER. All's, was [s'] reden und thun, is halb deutsch, halb französch –
WANDLING. Oft sein s' sentimental, und hab'n doch ka wahres G'fühl,
MUMMLER. Solche Leut sind ja selbst ein lebendigs Vaudevill –
WANDLING. In ein andern Haus habn s' einen Sohn, einen großn,
    Der nix lernt, theils sich selbst, theils den Ältern zum Possen.
WANDLING. Der Mann sagt: Madam, ich komm heut nicht zu Haus,
    Und sie thut ihm den Possen und macht sich nix draus,
WANDLING. Die Frau wünscht den Mann a paar Stunden weit weg,
MUMMLER. Jetzt thut er ihr den Possen und geht nicht von Flek.
WANDLING. Thäten solche Leut Possen anschaun, wär' das klug?
MUMMLER. Sie spieln sich ja Possen – z'Haus mehr als genug.
WANDLING. So thut's in Privatlebn zugehn,
MUMMLER. Ja da kann kein Theater bestehn,
    Ja da kann kein Theater bestehn.

[WANDLING. Some married folk are madly in love
MUMMLER. But neither bothers about the other much.
WANDLING. She gets involved in intrigues, he gets into scrapes.
MUMMLER. Everything they say and do is half German, half French –
WANDLING. They often get sentimental but have no real feelings.
MUMMLER. Such people are a real-life vaudeville.
WANDLING. In another play they have a son who's grown up,
　　He neglects his studies, makes a fool of himself and a fool of his parents.
MUMMLER. The husband tells his wife he's not coming home that night,
　　She plays a trick on him – although she couldn't care less,
WANDLING. She's glad to have her husband out of the house for a few
　　hours.
MUMMLER. Now he tricks her by refusing to budge.
WANDLING. If people like that went to see a farce would it be wise?
MUMMLER. They stage their own farces (*or:* they trick one another) – at
　　home and to excess.
WANDLING. If that's the way things are in private life
MUMMLER. There's no hope for the theatre,
　　There's no hope for the theatre.]

Nestroy's use of specialised terminology as a satirical weapon is a regular
feature of his style. Here he employs the language of the theatre to satirise the
pretentious aspirations of certain well-to-do Viennese citizens for whom the
reality of everyday life has been supplanted by a theatrical, self-regarding
existence, one in which they reveal themselves as buffoons, unwittingly acting
out a farcical existence. The extract from the duet demonstrates Nestroy's
burlesque intention with his characteristically deft presentation of self-
referential material and it exemplifies the interplay of the real world and the
world of theatre; these are, arguably, the two most appealing features of *Zwey
ewige Juden*.

Notes

1. Nestroy's process of creative adaptation is treated in detail in the ground-breaking
study by W. E. Yates, *Nestroy. Satire and Parody in Viennese Popular Comedy*
(Cambridge, 1972), pp. 120–48.
2. CG V, 125–72 (1891), and SW XIII, 93–192 (1929).
3. 'Turbulenter Unsinn', see Franz H. Mautner, *Nestroy* (Heidelberg, 1974), p. 274.
4. The Prague production, given in the uncensored version, had no connection with
either of the other two; a characteristically incisive review is provided by Bernhard
Gutt in *Bohemia*, 23 October 1846 (no. 157).
5. The MS contains 226 pages. The hands of four different copy-writers can be
distinguished. A label on the cover bears the revised title *Der fligende Holländer zu
Fuß* [*sic*], together with the catalogue number Cth H 43a and the reference
'Souflirbuch No. 13351' (prompter's book).
6. See Jolán Pukánszky-Kádár's brief history of the German-speaking theatre in Pest
and Ofen (= Buda), 'Geschichte des deutschen Theaters in Pest und Ofen' (1923)
in: *Deutsche Theater in Pest und Ofen 1770–1850. Normativer Titelkatalog und*

John R. P. McKenzie

Dokumentation, ed. Hedvig Belitska-Scholz & Olga Somorjai, 2 vols (Budapest, no date (1995)), vol. 1, pp. 11–35; she demonstrates (p. 33) the importance of such summer tours for the German-language theatrical life of Buda and Pest, pointing out that there was no authentic German culture in Hungary in which a German-speaking theatre could take root; thus, the German theatre in Pest simply provided a venue for imported German drama. A definitive study of German-speaking theatre in the polyglot Austrian Empire has yet to be written.

7. Subsequent references to these titles are normally given in an abbreviated form: *Zwey ewige Juden* and *Der fliegende Holländer*. The text of *Der fliegende Holländer*, which can be pieced together from the prompter's manuscript of *Zwey ewige Juden*, is confirmed by the text of a theatre manuscript (also entitled *Der fliegende Holländer*) housed in the library of the Austrian Theatre Museum.

8. The simultaneous performances in Pest and Vienna led to considerable speculation in reviews in the Viennese press. *Der Wanderer* of 5 August 1846 (no. 186, p. 740) claims that it was the result of Carl's suggestion: ' "Sie, lieber Nestroy, will ich wohl für einige Wochen entbehren – aber Ihren Geist muß ich hier behalten, den brauche ich nothwendig." Und so geschah es, daß Nestroy nach der Idee eines vom Director Carl ihm übergebenen französischen Stückes seine neueste Posse verfaßte' ['"I can manage without you for a few weeks, my dear Nestroy, but I cannot do without your spirit in Vienna." And so Nestroy wrote his latest farce after a French play given to him by Director Carl']. L. Raudnitz, writing in the *Oesterreichischer Courier* of 6 August 1846 (no. 187, p. 747), speculates about Nestroy's intentions: 'Ob Hr. Nestroy die Hauptrolle, einen alten Maler [...] für sich selber geschrieben hat, kann man nicht ganz bezweifeln, ich glaube sogar, daß sie ihm sehr zusagen müßte: doch läßt der Zuschnitt vermuthen, sie sei für Hrn. Carls Individualität berechnet, welcher sie auch mit seiner bekannten, außerordentlichen Lebhaftigkeit und Wirksamkeit spielt, und damit einen großen Erfolg erringt.' ['It is not clear whether Herr Nestroy wrote the part of an old painter [...] for himself, I am sure it would appeal to him; however, it would appear to be tailor-made for the particular acting skills of Herr Carl: he played the part with characteristic liveliness and effectiveness and thus ensured that the play was a great success'].

9. *Le Juif errant* enjoyed huge popularity in France and was published in translation in several European countries: between 1844 and 1846 it appeared in ten different German translations and in eighteen editions. Recent discussions of Nestroy's debt to Sue's works include the following: Hugo Aust, 'Einige Überlegungen zum Problem der Literaturnutzung am Beispiel von Eugène Sues *L'Orgueil* und Johann Nestroys *Kampl*', in: Gerald Stieg and Jean-Marie Valentin (eds), *Johann Nestroy 1801–1862. Vision du monde et écriture dramatique* (Asnières, 1991), pp. 9–22; Susan Doering, *Der wienerische Europäer. Johann Nestroy und die Vorlagen seiner Stücke* (Munich, 1992); John R. P. McKenzie, 'Les Mystères de *Lady und Schneider*: Johann Nestroy und Eugène Sue', *Nestroyana*, 11 (1991), 51–66.

10. The surviving autograph manuscript material for *Zwey ewige Juden* is relatively thin; it consists of a number of preparatory notes and drafted dialogue, together with the drafts of the two songs; the MSS are housed in the manuscript collection of the Vienna City Library. The musical score by Adolf Müller has also survived (Music Collection of the Vienna City Library). Transcriptions of MS material are given in this article in accordance with the conventions of the HKA, deletions are indicated by (× ×) and additions by (+ +); (+× ×+) indicates deleted text that has been restored.

11. Gladt transcribes the reference as follows: 'Die Handlung ist theilweise Varnecs nachgebieldet'; he appears to have overlooked the gap after Varner's name and to have mistaken Nestroy's lower-case latin 'r' for 'c' (Karl Gladt, *Die Handschriften Johann Nestroys* (Graz, Vienna, Cologne, 1967), p. 49); the transcription of the

143

name is incorrect also in Bernhard Gutt's review of the Prague production of *Zwey ewige Juden* (in which Nestroy did not perform) in *Bohemia*, 23 October 1846 (no. 157), where he writes 'Narner'.

12. The text of Varner's play is included in a volume in the series entitled *Französisches Théâtre* (Paris, n.d.), a copy of which is held in the Music Collection of the Austrian National Library.

13. See Franz Hadamowsky, *Das Theater in der Wiener Leopoldstadt 1781–1860. Bibliotheks- und Archivbestände in der Theatersammlung der Nationalbibliothek Wien* (Kataloge der Theatersammlung der Nationalbibliothek in Wien, vol. 3) (Vienna, 1934), and F. H., *Wien. Theatergeschichte. Von den Anfängen bis zum Ende des Ersten Weltkrieges* (Vienna, Munich, 1988), pp. 342–52.

14. See Mautner, *Nestroy*, p. 275.

15. W. E. Yates, *Theatre in Vienna. A Critical History, 1776–1995* (Cambridge, 1996), pp. 40–41. See also Johann Hüttner, 'Selbstzensur bei Johann Nestroy', *Die Presse*, 13–14 September 1980: Literarium, pp. iv–v; Johann Hüttner, 'Vor- und Selbstzensur bei Johann Nestroy', *Maske und Kothurn*, 26 (1980), 234–48; Friedrich Walla, 'Johann Nestroy und die Zensur, *Nestroyana*, 9 (1989), 22–34; W. E. Yates, 'Das Werden eines (edierten) Nestroy-Textes', in Yates (ed.), *Vom schaffenden zum edierten Nestroy* (Wiener Vorlesungen. Konservatorien und Studien, vol. 3) (Vienna, 1994), pp. 11–30.

16. The representation of the Jews in the Viennese popular theatre is discussed in the following articles: Jürgen Hein, 'Judenthematik im Wiener Volkstheater', in Hans Otto Horch and Horst Denkler (eds), *Conditio Judaica. Judentum, Antisemitismus und deutschsprachige Literatur vom 18. Jahrhundert bis zum ersten Weltkrieg*, 2 vols (Tübingen, 1988), vol. 1, pp. 164–86; Jürgen Hein, 'Unfreiwillige Zwillinge? Christen und Juden im Wiener Volkstheater', *Nestroyana*, 8 (1988), Heft 1/2, 21–28; Friedrich Walla, 'Johann Nestroy und der Antisemitismus. Eine Bestandsaufnahme', *Österreich in Geschichte und Literatur*, 29 (1985), Heft 1, pp. 37–51. In view of its theme *Zwey ewige Juden* invites comparison with Nestroy's *Judith und Holofernes*, first produced some three and a half years later, in March 1849. It remains a mystery how the censor can have condoned the process of *Verwienerung* in *Judith und Holofernes*, which involved the transformation of the biblical Hebrews into Viennese Jews (see John R. P McKenzie, 'Die Wiener Juden 1848–1849' and 'Zensur', HKA, *Stücke 26/II*, 343–78; 379–91).

17. Heine's poem appears in Chapter V of *Schnabelewopski*. Although Wagner's opera did not receive its first full production in Vienna until 1863, its fame had gone before it.

18. W. E. Yates, *Nestroy and the Critics* (Columbia, SC, 1994), pp. 8–9. Some sixty per cent of Nestroy's eighty plays are described as *Possen*; only two carry the label *Burleske*: *Zwey ewige Juden* and the hugely successful work *Die schlimmen Buben in der Schule*, first produced in the following year (1847).

19. The inability of reviewers to see the wood for the trees is discussed by Louise Adey Huish, 'A Source for Nestroy's *Gegen Thorheit gibt es kein Mittel*', *Modern Language Review*, 87 (1992), 616–25 (p. 618), and W. E. Yates, 'Nestroy und die Rezensenten', *Nestroyana*, 7 (1987), 28–40 (p. 31).

20. Translated from Jürgen Hein, *Johann Nestroy* (Sammlung Metzler vol. 258) (Stuttgart, 1990), pp. 103–04.

21. Three notes in the 'Reserve' were incorporated in *Zwey ewige Juden*: nos 51, 54, and 59. The 'Reserve', missing since the 1930s, was discovered in 1996 among uncatalogued material in the Deutsches Theatermuseum in Munich by Birgit Pargner, head of the manuscript collection. It is intended that the 'Reserve' will be published in the final volume of the HKA; Rommel's transcription appears in SW XV, 680–703 and GW VI, 560–77.

22. The text of the duet, written in another hand, is contained in an insert in the manuscript. Where appropriate, 'missing' punctuation has been supplied.

Friedrich Halm and the Comic Muse

Peter Skrine

It must be a very long time since a Friedrich Halm play was last performed. The repertoire of twentieth-century German drama can find little or no place for him and the other once-famous playwrights of his generation, and chances of a revival in the twenty-first century are slight. But if, in 2006, Halm's bicentenary year, a theatre director were to contemplate a revival, he or she would be well advised to turn to one of the two plays that form the central focus of this essay; for these are the plays that represent Halm at his best. Each of them in its unique way is marked by that deftness of structure and fluency of line and language that form the essential element of his charm, and each is brought to life, even on the printed page, by the human themes – political, social and sexual – that smoulder more or less overtly in their texts, themes that, even now, still make them interesting. Halm's name may no longer be a familiar one to theatre-goers, but in his day, between 1835 and 1900, matters were very different. He was not only a leading Viennese dramatist but also one whose popularity spread far beyond the Austrian capital, thanks in particular to the two plays with which this discussion begins and ends.

From 1835, the year which saw his first triumph, to his death in 1871, Halm's reputation was closely bound up with the official Vienna stage or *Hofbühne*, and depended largely on his serious verse dramas such as *Griseldis*, the early feminist play with which he first attracted public attention (its première took place at the Hofburgtheater on 20 December 1835) and the controversial anti-nationalistic masterpiece, *Der Fechter von Ravenna* [The Gladiator of Ravenna], which called into question the validity of the Hermann myth as a paradigm for nineteenth-century German unity. Premièred anonymously on 18 October 1854, probably because Halm wanted to see whether it could win approval on its own merits, it was not acknowledged by him until April 1856, by which time the controversy concerning its authorship, and turning on an accusation of plagiarism, had begun to abate. *Der Fechter von Ravenna* was not published until 1857. In the interim, the theatre-going public, with its shrewd eye for a winner, had been particularly quick to applaud a play of a rather different kind: *Der Sohn der Wildnis* [The Son of the Wilderness]. Its première had taken place at the Hofburgtheater on 28 January 1842, with Ludwig Löwe, the creator of Grillparzer's Rustan and Leon, in the leading male role, supported by Karl La Roche, and with Julie Rettich, an actress as intimately bound up with the author's private life as her name on play-bills was with his reputation as a dramatist, in the star role of Parthenia, its heroine.

Part *ingénue*, part emancipated young woman of the *Vormärz* kind, and not without a touch of the Viennese 'sweet young thing' beneath her Graeco-Austrian charm, Parthenia in *Der Sohn der Wildnis* was a role created to please, and please it did in a play whose popularity made it one of the three highest earners in the first half of the century.[1] It owed this popularity far beyond the orbit of Vienna not so much to the critics as to the reassuring fact that it was an entertaining piece pre-eminently suitable for all the family. Soon *Der Sohn der Wildnis* was established in the repertoires of theatres throughout the German-speaking world. Unlike any of the plays of Grillparzer or Nestroy, the two Austrian contemporaries whose talents outweighed his, Halm's play seems to have become quite a favourite on the Victorian stage, too.[2] An English version by William Henry Chalton, entitled *The Son of the Wilderness*, was published in London in 1847 and reappeared at intervals in 1852 and (as *Ingomar*) in 1860, but, more often than not, the favoured English rendition was the one by Maria Lovell, called *Ingomar the Barbarian* after its amiable hulk of a hero. Editions of both were numerous: the *Union Catalog* carries twelve different British and American editions of the Lovell translation and two editions of the Chalton version (and one purporting to be the work of 'Charles Edward Anthon' published in New York in 1848), and adds the anonymous *The Son of the Desert* published in Denbigh in 1849, while the British Museum catalogue gives a not dissimilar distribution, adding N. A. Faber's *The Child of the Wold: A Dramatic Poem* (London, 1867) for good measure. French (1846), Italian (1854 and 1856), Danish (1843) and Swedish (1848) translations reinforce a picture of international success.

There can be no doubt that Halm, today all but forgotten, was a name to be reckoned with in his own lifetime; indeed his success at home and abroad lasted at least until 1897. In that year, as James Joyce reminds us in *Portrait of the Artist as a Young Man*, young Stephen Dedalus won a prize for an essay he had written:

> For a swift season of merry-making the money of his prize ran through Stephen's fingers. Great parcels of groceries and delicacies and dried fruits arrived from the city. Every day he drew up a bill of fare for the family and every night led a party of three or four to the theatre to see Ingomar or The Lady of Lyons.[3] In his coat pockets he carried squares of Vienna chocolate for his guests.

The reference to chocolate reinforces the allusion – at least for those who can pick it up already! – and the dating is plausible, too, for in the year of that Dublin production, Halm's *Der Sohn der Wildnis* seems to have enjoyed a theatrical *Nachsommer*. In November 1897 it ran for a week at Wallack's Theatre in New York,[4] and, in the same year, it was issued as No. 3665 in

Reclam's *Universal-Bibliothek*. On 2 March 1902 it achieved its 134th performance at the Burgtheater before sinking into twentieth-century oblivion as the *fin de siècle* fondness for the make-believe of neo-Romanticism faded, and with it that brief valedictory revival.

Der Sohn der Wildnis is clearly important in terms of theatre history. But what made it so popular? It exerted an appeal that was probably more widespread than that of any German play since the assassination of Kotzebue, and should therefore play a key role in any attempt to gauge the shifts and fluctuations of taste in the theatre and among readers throughout the Victorian era, so why is it still neglected by theatre and literary historians alike? The most obvious reasons for its success and subsequent oblivion are, perhaps, not far to seek. With it, Halm had created a paradigmatic prototype for a genre of drama that has failed to arouse the interest of literary historians, especially those working in a German tradition that tends to concentrate its attention on a canon emphasising seriousness of moral or philosophical purpose at the expense of popularity and entertainment value, two qualities which the theatre also needs, as the Elizabethans and Jacobeans knew. To underrate these aspects is an approach inimical to the comic traditions of metropolitan cultures such as those of Vienna, Paris or London, and it is bound to be unsympathetic, if not hostile, to the type of play *Der Sohn der Wildnis* represents. Halm's play, like many another neglected favourite of the mid-nineteenth-century theatre, belongs to a genre of semi-serious drama that allowed the comic muse her place alongside poetry and idealism. It shuns collisions between crass reality and incongruous make-believe. It may lack satirical bite. But then its *raison d'être* is to give pleasure. Halm, with his rare gift for creating a tone deliciously poised between pathos and farce, was ideally suited to this kind of drama, and it happened to be one to which mid-nineteenth-century audiences were particularly responsive.

Der Sohn der Wildnis is a verse play, but its blank verse avoids the stylised formality of the Weimar tradition by audibly imitating instead the example of Grillparzer's *Sappho*, clearly Halm's main stylistic model. But, unlike Grillparzer's tragedy, Halm's drama does no more than flirt with tragedy. However dire its dramatic situation may seem to be (as, for instance, when Parthenia bravely sets out into the unknown to rescue her father when he has been kidnapped by barbarians), the Muse of Comedy is never far away: indeed, sometimes she makes her presence felt by raising a laugh that was not, one suspects, the playwright's intention. Mirth and seriousness are held in delicate balance. A delightful instance of this occurs at the end of Act II. Parthenia, the daughter of the blacksmith of a Greek colony somewhere on the French Riviera, having tired of the attentions of an elderly but wealthy suitor, has set off into the dark forest with the bright idea that she would make an excellent ransom for her elderly father, Myron, held captive by a tribe of savage Tectosagen. Needless to say, when she locates him, her father has misgivings about the wisdom of her action. But when he tells her he is loath to leave her ('Wo Tod dein harrt, ja Schlimmeres noch als Tod' ['where death awaits you, maybe something worse than death']) the phrase he uses provokes something between a chuckle and a frisson that neatly turns to suspense when Parthenia, having ransomed her father and set him free, is left, alone and sobbing, and at the mercy of Ingomar, the barbarians' leader. He regrets the exchange he has agreed to: Myron would have been more useful because he could make weapons: but what's the use of women? This is too much for Parthenia. She scornfully rejects his uncivilised view that women are mere chattels.

> Wie? Ihr werbt
> Mit Gold, mit schnödem Gold um eure Bräute?
> Ihr kauft sie, tauscht sie ein, sie selber Sklaven,
> Um Sklaven so wie sie? Ihr ew'gen Götter,
> Sind Weiber Waren? (p. 102)[5]

[What, you woo your brides with gold, with filthy gold? You purchase them, you barter them like slaves for other slaves like them? Ye gods eternal! Are women wares?]

No, she says, with a note of pride worthy of Elizabeth Bennet, 'Uns führt dem Freier nur die Liebe zu!' ['We are led to our suitors by love alone']. The barbarian Ingomar, who has never heard anything like this, is puzzled: 'Ihr freit aus Liebe? Ei, wie macht ihr das?' ['You marry for love? How do you manage that?'] (p. 103). From this moment on, the play, which seemed to be developing into a tense hostage drama, turns into an *ars amandi*, dramatised with an almost child-like innocence, yet not without its decorous use of *double entendre*. It is a style that harks back to Renaissance pastoral, Guarini's *Il Pastor Fido*, and that whole rich tradition of European comedy – Italian, French and Elizabethan English – which has seldom been recognised as a major formative element in more modern traditions of drama such as the semi-serious romantic mid-nineteenth-century one that *Der Sohn der Wildnis* represents. Before Ingomar knows what is happening to him, Parthenia has him picking flowers for her in a forest glade. It is a foretaste of the play's most amusing scene.

This comes in Act III. By now, Ingomar is love-sick, though he does not realise it. He finds Parthenia attractively unlike barbarian women while she, for her part, is not in the least intimidated by his rough barbarian ways, quite the contrary. She offers him wild strawberries (a strange inversion of the scene in Storm's *Immensee*!), but he rudely rejects them, wanting only to be alone to sort out his disordered thoughts and emotions, yet he also wants her near him: 'Nach Stille lechzt mein Herz und träumt und träumt, / Errötet seines Traums und träumt ihn wieder ...' ['My heart pants for calm, it dreams and dreams, blushes at its dream but dreams it again'] (p. 109). The words hardly prepare us for what now happens – an incident that provides a wonderful example of the humour, half deliberate, half not, that brings the textual fabric of this play to life. After a pause Ingomar comes out with it:

Parthenia, ich wollt', du wärst ein Mann –
PARTHENIA. Ein Mann?
INGOMAR. O dann wär' alles gut!
Du wärst mein Jagdgenoß, mein Waffenbruder,
Ich ginge wie dein Schatten neben dir,
Ich wachte, wenn du schliefst, ich trüg' dich, wärst
Du müde! (p. 109)

[Parthenia, I wish you were a man – PARTHENIA. A man? INGOMAR. Then everything would be all right. You'd be my hunting companion, my brother in arms, I'd walk beside you like your shadow, I'd keep watch while you slept, I'd carry you if you were tired.]

It is an exchange that amuses at whatever level, provoking smiles or laughter that range from childish amusement to adult knowingness, and reminding us that the text – or, rather, the subtext – of this nineteenth-century Austrian drama – the kind of drama watched by Leutnant Gustl – is shot through with insights that anticipate ideas which only came into the open as the century ended and the generation of Freud and Schnitzler revealed the hidden depths of the psyche and the subconscious. But in 1842 Halm's play veers deftly away from the as yet unsayable. Instead, Act III entertains us with some action, as a group of Ingomar's barbarian companions attempt to carry off its hapless but resourceful heroine ('Ins Dickicht fort mit ihr!') ['Away with her into the thicket!'], a plan scotched by their chieftain's sudden resolve to swap her for ten head of cattle and twice as many of sheep. This is, of course, an elaboration of one of the play's more serious satirical underlying themes, namely the place and role of women in a male-dominated patriarchal society caricatured by the barbarians and by Parthenia's wealthy but obnoxious suitor. Once again, the barbs of social satire and contemporary relevance are withdrawn, however, so that the act can end with the most memorable scene in the whole play. Parthenia, now 'won' by the love-lorn Ingomar, persuades him to grant her her freedom, and is all ready to set off home. But her influence has already made him quite a gentleman and he finds himself saying: 'Ich will dich selbst geleiten' ['I'll accompany you myself']. And why not? 'Was siehst du mich so forschend an? – Du meinst, / Ich wär viel besser nicht als jene? – Nein, / Parthenia, ich bin nicht, der ich war!' (p. 118) ['Why do you look at me so searchingly? You're thinking I'm not much better than the rest, aren't you? But no, Parthenia, I'm not the man I was']. She accepts the offer, adding mischievously:

Und daß du nicht mit leeren Händen gehest,
So nimm das Körbchen mit den Erdbeern dort!
INGOMAR. Das Körbchen –
PARTHENIA. Ja, das Körbchen – Willst du nicht?
INGOMAR. Ich will, gewiß, ich will –
PARTHENIA. Ich aber – Sieh'
Ich will dagegen Speer und Schild dir tragen – (p. 119)

[And so that you don't go empty-handed, carry that little basket with the strawberries! INGOMAR. The basket? PARTHENIA. Yes, the basket, Don't you want to? INGOMAR. Yes, I do, I do... PARTHENIA. And I – let's see: I'll carry your spear and shield for you.]

As the curtain falls, a stage direction translates the dialogue into visual terms: *Ingomar, das Körbchen tragend, geht rechts im Vordergrunde ab; Parthenia, den Schild am Arm, den Speer in der Rechten, folgt ihm.* [Exit Ingomar, downstage right, carrying the basket. Parthenia, his shield on her arm and his spear in her right hand, follows him.] Thanks to their own youthful spontaneity and naturalness, Halm's socially ill-assorted couple have achieved an ideal balance. And, with this touch, Halm's art disarms the tendentious muses of *Vormärz* tragedy and social drama on their home ground.

Halm's plays are often close in feel and technique to that other great artistic tradition, light opera and operetta, which is an equally important component of Viennese nineteenth-century theatre. This is abundantly evident in the two plays that he explicitly described as 'Lustspiele' [comedies]: *König und Bauer* [King and Peasant] and *Verbot und Befehl* [Prohibition and Compulsion]. *König und Bauer*, his first attempt at comedy, was premièred at the Hofburgtheater on 4 March 1841. If not a triumph, it was at least a considerable success, with thirty performances there up to 1856 and a short revival in 1867–69; in common with Halm's work in general, it received a new lease of life in the years leading up to the turn of the century, with twenty-nine Burgtheater performances between 1888 and 1900. Unlike *Der Sohn der Wildnis*, however, it seems not to have travelled outside the German-speaking theatrical world, a world much wider and more 'international' in those days, it should be remembered, than it is today. It was closely modelled on *El villano en su rincón* (1617), a *comedia* written between 1611 and 1616 by Lope de Vega with whom Halm, like his great contemporary Grillparzer, felt a particular affinity and to whose model of swift word- and action-packed drama he felt drawn. It is a comedy in the sense that it ends happily with a double marriage, and depends for its momentum on a cleverly devised and deftly handled plot; but it is a comedy of smiles and general *joie de vivre* rather than of satirical bite and open laughter. Its 'Spanish' origin is less evident than might be expected: this is largely due to the fact that the action takes place in France – a France of no particular historical time, ruled by an intelligent, personable and popular king renamed Charles in Halm's adaptation.[6] In contrast to *Der Sohn der Wildnis*, in which the central scenes are essentially comic in spirit, here, what comedy there is is relegated to the intrigue. King Charles, whose equerry, Graf Armand, has fallen in love with the beautiful Rosanna, hears that her father, Jean Gomard, a wealthy farmer, has never been to Paris nor set eyes on him.[7] Finding such conduct inexplicable – as would most Viennese in the audience! – he resolves to beard him *incognito* in his country retreat. This leads to the first of the play's two great *scènes à faire*. Pretending to be 'Denis, Schultheiß von Paris', Charles interviews Jean in Act II and discovers that his peasant subject knows a contentment that he, the sovereign, can only envy. He then decides to test him by commanding that he send his son and daughter to court and lend his sovereign the vast sum of 100,000 *livres*, a monarch's ransom. The second of the two great scenes occurs in Act IV. Once again king and peasant confront each other, but this time there is no disguise. Just as Jean had made his visitor accept the customs of his farmhouse, the king now makes the peasant accept royal hospitality on its own terms. Thus, king and commoner discover that, underpinning the social contract between lord and subject, there is a deeper human one, and we recall that *Der Sohn der Wildnis* was equipped with an epigraph from Rousseau which would really be more applicable here: 'Les hommes sont méchants, cependant l'homme est naturellement bon! – Qu'on admire tant qu'on voudra la société humaine, il n'en sera pas moins vrai, qu'elle porte nécessairement les hommes à s'entrehaïr à proportion que leurs intérêts se croisent' ['Men are wicked, yet man is naturally good – admire human society as much as you will, it is nevertheless true that it is bound to lead men to hate each other in proportion to how much their interests overlap']. The earlier play was essentially make-believe. Here, however, only the appellation 'Lustspiel' and the distancing effect of the 'safety label' beneath the title indicating that it is 'from the Spanish of Lope de Vega' ('Nach dem Spanischen des Lope de Vega Carpio') could deafen the reader to the political message of this apparently harmless play or blind the spectator to its topical relevance.

Verbot und Befehl was premièred at an inopportune moment. The Hofburg-theater staged it on 29 March 1848! Rettich, Löwe and La Roche were once again involved, but their histrionic talents were impotent in the face of public and political events. In such an atmosphere there was no hope of such a play having a proper hearing. A mere four performances were all that it was given, and publication was deferred until 1856. Yet Halm had surpassed himself. As with his Novelle *Die Marzipan-Lise*, published the same year, a writer more noticed in his own lifetime for his large-scale serious dramas had produced a greater masterpiece in a different genre. The curtain goes up to reveal the office of Antonio Tentori, Secretary to the Venetian Council of Ten, and he takes us into his confidence, telling us with pardonable self-pity:

Ja, ich bin Sekretär – das will was sagen,
Und dennoch – unter uns gesagt – es ist
Ein Mummienleben, dies Beamtenleben,
Ein streusandtrockenes Registerleben,
Ein Leben, grau von Aktenstaub, gesprenkelt
Mit Tintenflecken, ein fortwährendes
Halbtrauerleben... (p. 157)

[Yes, I am a secretary – and that says it all, and yet – between ourselves – it's the life of a mummy, this civil servant's life – a life of registers, as arid as writing-sand – a life grey with the dust of documents, spattered with ink-blots, an existence of continual half-mourning.']

From this moment we know that we are in the presence of great comedy. This quality is immediately evident in the handling of words and metre. It is evident, too, in Halm's ability to create a rounded comic character who, though plausibly Venetian, is immediately recognisable as the quintessential Austrian civil servant, harnessed body and soul to the vast bureaucracy that kept the Empire going. And it is also evident in the agile handling of a complicated plot in the Goldoni manner which turns on Antonio's momentary lapse of professional conduct, or, rather, on the paradox that this lapse brings about the happy outcome. Only a successful civil servant such as Baron Münch-Bellinghausen could bring off a comedy in which muddling through pays off and in which any references to Austria's political situation in 1848 are 'entirely coincidental'. As one of the characters remarks: 'Wer denkt an Politik? / Von einem Liebeslied ist hier die Rede, / Von einem harmlos heitern Maskenscherz' ['Who's thinking about politics? We're talking here about a song of love, a harmless, happy masquerade'] (p. 179).

Halm generates the action of his comedy by allowing Antonio, his desiccated but devoted civil servant, before the curtain rises, to befuddle himself by drinking too much wine at the solitary *Jugendfest* he celebrates each year, and then to address the audience thus:

> Denn wißt, ich war auch jung zu meiner Zeit,
> Und lebt' ich auch von Klostersuppen nur
> Und kargem Bettelbrot, ich war auch jung
> Und wild und lustig, bis im Arsenal
> Als Registrant ich später Dienste nahm:
> Dann war's vorbei, dann galt es schreiben nur,
> Und was sonst Reiz und Schmuck verleiht der Jugend,
> War wie ein unnütz Schlagwort weggestrichen
> Aus dem Register meines Lebens. (p. 157)

[I'd have you know I too was young once and lived on convent pottage and meagre beggar's bread; I too was young and wild and merry, until I took up service in the Arsenal as clerk there. Then it was over; from then on it was just a matter of writing, and everything else that gives delight and joy to youth was crossed out like a useless heading in the register of my life.]

When he finds himself having to take the minutes at an emergency meeting of a Council committee in his office, he dozes off. The garbled notes he takes are all he later has to go by, so he can reconstruct only a partial version of the truth: to whom the order went, and to whom the prohibition, he can only guess. As in an episode of *Yes, Minister*, the comedy generated in this way shows that muddle can create results and that the happiest are not necessarily the direct result of implementing the policy originally decided. Thus bureaucratic incompetence ignites and, indeed, becomes synonymous with the intrigue of a comedy of errors in which a high-born man and woman, whose marriage is seen as essential to the good working of the Republic, are given instructions to 'cool' it, whereas a happily married couple, notorious for their embarrassing public displays of mutual affection, are told to 'warm' things up. Being human beings, Halm's characters react as humans tend to do: they object to being told how to behave, and promptly do the opposite, responses that allow Halm to explore a chain of reactions ranging from straightforward farce to that near-tragic confusion of emotions that is always present in great comedy.

There is another dimension to Halm's comic masterpiece. Just as *König und Bauer* is built up on a scheme that applies the structures and forms of light opera – solo aria, duet, ensemble – to straight spoken drama, so here, too, we meet a type of literary comedy born 'aus dem Geiste der Musik'. In this case, however, the musical spirit that inspired it is no longer that of Scribe and Auber – all the rage in the 1840s – so much as an anticipation of the more 'serious' and 'durchkomponiert' conception of operatic comedy associated with *Der Barbier von Bagdad* (1858) by Peter Cornelius, Berlioz's *Béatrice et Bénédict* (1862) and the new wave of comic operas in German that followed them in Germany, such as *Der Widerspenstigen Zähmung* (1874) [The Taming of the Shrew] by Hermann Goetz. Ernst Alker was surely right in describing *Verbot und Befehl* as 'an achievement wrongly overlooked by the theatre of today, and full of Venetian atmosphere' ('eine vom Theater heute zu unrecht vergessene Leistung voll venezianischer Stimmung').[8] It is a work that should rank high in the long list of German masterpieces associated with, or set in, Venice.

The Muse of Comedy had been kind to Halm, as *Verbot und Befehl* proved. But sometimes she was mischievous. This was the case with *Wildfeuer* [Wildfire], a work calling itself a 'dramatic poem' and prefaced by an all-too-familar quotation from I Corinthians 13 which, in the context, totters uneasily on the brink of irreverence. The difficulty of pin-pointing Halm's true place in the development of nineteenth-century Austrian drama is evident here. Halm's play about the boy who did not know he was a girl, was one which, in pre-Wedekind and pre-Schnitzler days, enjoyed a certain notoriety among *habitués* of the theatre, and aroused a natural, if prurient, curiosity especially among the young because of its decidedly odd, not to say *risqué*, subject. In our more liberal and, we like to think, more sensible climate, adults and adolescents would probably be more likely to reject it out of hand as warped or sentimental nonsense, or to see it as a clumsy expression of its author's hang-ups in an age not yet ready for such topics or at ease in dealing with them in artistic terms. Yet, even more surprisingly, Halm's contemporaries seem on the whole to have enjoyed the play (though there were of course objections in the press). This is interesting as further confirmation of his ability to entertain even when rashly dramatising a situation whose improbability might perhaps have been acceptable if narrated in a Novelle, but which must have stretched credibility to the limit when presented on stage.

The action, set in Savoy during the Middle Ages, revolves around the only child of the late count of Dommartin who, for dynastic reasons, has been brought up by his mother as a boy – René – in a desperate attempt to prevent the title passing to Gerard von Lomménie, her nephew. Gerard, for his part, has been brought up by an old retainer, Pierre, to believe that he is the latter's foster-child, Marcel. Early in Act I, in dialogue with his putative father, he sets the key-note for the play, which is to turn on the nature of identity:

> Der Ärmste weiß: Das bin ich und so heiß' ich!
> Ich geh', ein Schemen, in der Welt umher,
> Mir selbst nicht bloß ein Rätsel, eine Lüge!
> Ich bin nicht wahrhaft ich! (p. 86)

[The poorest person knows: this is me, and this is my name. But I go about the world, a spectre, not just a riddle to myself but a lie! I am not really me.]

The identity crisis being suffered by twenty-year-old Gerard is compounded by the fact that he feels himself increasingly attracted to his young charge and pupil, René, nicknamed 'Wildfeuer' because of his volatile personality:

> Wenn
> Im Feld zum Beispiel wir spazierenreiten,
> Da hält er plötzlich still auf einer Wiese
> Und spricht: 'Die schönen Blumen! Rote, blaue,
> Auch gelbe dort! O pflück' mir welche, bitte!'

[When, for example, we go riding, he will suddenly stop in a meadow and say, 'Look, what lovely flowers: red, blue, and there, look, yellow ones! Oh, pick some for me, please!]

When Pierre points out that he should scorn the boy's demands, Gerard counters: 'Nein, das ist's eben! / Ich kann ihm nichts verweigern, wenn er bittet: / Ich pflück' die Blumen...' ['No, that's just it! I cannot refuse him anything he asks for: so I pick the flowers...'] (p. 87). The boy's emotional hold on him is thus expressed in terms reminiscent of Ingomar's 'taming' by Parthenia in *Der Sohn der Wildnis* as they begin to fall in love. More problematic is the ever more obvious fact that René is drawn to him. In Act III, a mild flirtation between Gerard and a peasant girl is enough to bring the already tense situation to a head. The emotional and stylistic temperature of the drama rises as the act builds up into a large-scale love scene of a kind unique perhaps on the nineteenth-century stage. René chides Gerard for having embraced the peasant girl in his presence – something which he himself would never ever do; perhaps, says Gerard, that's because, though you have already turned sixteen, you've never kissed a woman other than your mother or your nurse. But what's the point of kissing, René asks? The great speech beginning, 'Verurteilt nicht, was Ihr nicht kennt! / Ein Wunder, ein Geheimnis ist der Kuß' ['Do not condemn what you do not know! A kiss is a miracle and a mystery'] (p. 114) glows with an ardour reminiscent of Johannes Secundus and of the Elizabethan theatre which Halm's concept of drama so often resembles. Yet still René cannot comprehend what his companion is trying to say. Is there really a magic on our lips, he asks? There is indeed, says Gerard:

Ein Zauber ist es, zwischen Männern selbst
Allmächtig wirkend! Denkt Euch beispielsweise
Wir wären Freunde, und ein Streit verstörte
Entzweiend unsern Bund!

[It is a magic which, even between men, has an all-powerful effect.
Imagine for instance we were friends, and a quarrel were to sever our
bond.]

What would I do to make it up? 'Nun, was tätet Ihr?' asks René. Gerard replies:

Ganz einfach dies! Ich träte zu Euch hin
Und legte still den Arm um Euren Nacken
Und drückte Euch an mich und tauchte forschend
Des Blickes Strahl in Eure Augen, bis
Halbträumend sie, wie eben jetzt, sich schlössen,
Bis Purpurglut die Wangen Euch umflammte,
Bis zitternd Ihr im Arm mir lägt, wie jetzt,
Und dann – dann beugt' ich mich zu Euch herab
Und küßt' Euch – (p. 115)

[Quite simply this: I'd go up to you and put my arm around your
shoulder and press you to me and plunge my questioning gaze into your
eyes, until, half dreaming, as they are now, they'd close, and a crimson
glow would blaze upon your cheeks, and you would sink trembling into
my arms, as now, and then – then I'd bend down to you and kiss you –]

With a cry René tears himself away, and then, the stage direction tells us,
nearly faints. Yet still he has not awakened to the fact or even the idea that he
is a girl. Such ignorant innocence would be oddly out of place in a Shakespeare
comedy and is a good deal less plausible than Wendla Bergmann's in *Frühlings
Erwachen* [*Spring Awakening*] – a title that would have suited *Wildfeuer* well.

Gerard, it is true, has already begun to wonder what sex René really is or,
rather, to hope that the general assumption, which he shares, may be
mistaken. In Act II he says to himself (and us):

Ich fass' es nicht!
Voll Launen wie ein Weib, ist dies ein Knabe,
So trotzig knabenhaft, ist dies ein Weib? -
Zwar weib'sche Knaben gibt's, und wilde Hummeln
Von Mädchen! – Auch Gestalt und Wuchs und Stimme,
Das flaumlos glatte Kinn! – Doch das ist Jugend! —
Wer löst dies Rätsel auf? (p. 104)

[I cannot comprehend it! As moody as a woman, yet a boy? So defiantly
boyish, yet a woman? There are effeminate boys, I know, and some girls
can be tomboys – stature, figure and voice, the smooth and downless
chin – but that's youth. Who can solve this riddle?]

In Halm's late play such questions seem to suggest – in anticipation almost of Pirandello – that characters are looking for their author to explain the underlying purpose of the drama they are caught up in. But before falling into the temptation of interpreting the play in modern terms, it should be remembered that the role of Wildfeuer was a breeches part specifically written with the famous soubrette actress Friederike Gossmann in mind. Unfortunately, she withdrew from the Burgtheater in 1861 on marrying an aristocrat, and the role was created instead by Louisabeth Röckel when the play was premièred in Schwerin, not Vienna, on 30 November 1863, two weeks before the death of Friedrich Hebbel. Röckel also played René when *Wildfeuer* was introduced to the Viennese public on 18 October 1866 with Adolf Sonnenthal as its male lead, Marcel/Gerard, and Hebbel's widow Christine Hebbel-Enghaus as the Countess, René's mother. Four parodies were soon being performed, so Rudolf Fürst tells us.[9] This confirms that, initially, it scored considerable success, and this despite – or perhaps because of – the mood of depression in Vienna following defeat in the Six Weeks War and Austria's final reluctant acceptance that it no longer had a role to play in the new Germany, an acceptance already implicitly foreseen by Halm in *Der Fechter von Ravenna* ten years earlier.

Part pseudo-medieval costume drama, part romantic verse play and part psycho-drama, whatever it may be, there can be no doubt that *Wildfeuer* relies heavily on its author's command of the techniques and conventions of comedy to weld its disparate elements into a theatrical entertainment that pleased contemporaries even when it shocked them.[10] The result is a variation on the stock theme of mistaken identity poised tantalisingly, even uncomfortably, between insight and inanity. As Gerard sets out to solve the mystery of Wildfeuer's sex, and of his own sexual identity, he asks:

> Er oder Sie? –
> Jetzt trotzig wilder als der tollste Knabe,
> Jetzt weich und innig, wie nur Mädchen sind,
> Was ist er und was nicht? – Ich weiß es nicht!
> Ich weiß das eine nur! Nichts wünsch' ich mehr
> Fürs erste mir, als daß er Mädchen wär'! (p. 107)

[He or she? Now obstinate and wilder than the wildest boy, now soft and intense as only maidens are: what is he, and what is he not? I do not know. I know only one thing: there's nothing I wish more than that he were a girl!]

The implication is, of course, that love transcends such simplistic distinctions. The Act ends with a curtain line – rhyming couplet, rather – that demonstrates how there are times when the Comic Muse can move a drama on if only because she is bold enough to utter things that might embarrass her more serious tragic sister: 'Doch weigert das Geschick mir diese Gabe, / So möcht' ich Mädchen sein, ist er ein Knabe' ['But if destiny denies me this gift, I'd gladly be a girl if he's a boy'] (p. 107). Yet smile as we may, how can we as spectators or as readers forget the awkwardly painful dialogue some minutes before, in which René complained to his mother's personal physician, Etienne, that at sixteen he is still so underdeveloped?

> Bin
> Ich nicht ein Zwerg beinah' für meine Jahre
> Und zum Abbrechen dünn wie eine Gerte?
> [...] Ihr habt
> Nicht viel an mir gestärkt und nichts gekräftigt! (p. 101)

[Am I not almost a dwarf for my age, and slim enough to be broken like a reed? You haven't done much to toughen me up or make me any stronger!]

Etienne's reply sounds almost naturalistic, as if out of Ibsen or early Hauptmann: 'Kein Arzt kann geben, was Natur versagt; / Vermögen wir auch oft ihr nachzuhelfen!' ['No doctor can provide what nature withholds, though we are often able to assist her']. But this is before the days of cosmetic surgery. René replies:

> Ihr helft ihr nach! Nun ja, ich hab's erfahren!
> Wie oft nicht bat ich Euch, ein bißchen nur,
> Ein ganz klein bißchen Schnurrbart mir zu schaffen,
> Wie jedem doch in meinem Alter sproßt!
> Wie fleißig rieb ich Eure Salben ein
> Und Eure Wässer, und nichts kam hervor.
> Jedweder Pfirsich hat mehr Flaum als ich!
> Nachhelfen der Natur! Ihr möchtet wohl,
> Wenn Ihr's verstündet nur! [pp. 101–2]

[You assist her, do you? Yes, I've experienced that. How often have I implored you to provide me with a little, just a very little moustache, such as everyone grows at my age. How diligently I rub your ointments and your lotions in, but nothing's sprouted. Any peach has more down on it than I do! Assist nature! You'd like to, if only you knew how!]

In this absurd exchange the pretty reference to a peach cannot conceal the presence of a cruel subtext, or dim the likelihood that the audience's reactions to it ranged from chuckles to embarrassment. But the ignorance in which René has been kept would be even more disturbing were it not that even in the late 1860s spectators must have asked themselves how it was possible, on the long days of hunting, horse-riding and the martial sports, for no male in Schloss Dommartin to have noticed! Built on such a preposterous premiss, the play, for all its romantic *élan*, was bound to sink into bathos.

The mystery of Wildfeuer's gender is not resolved until almost the end of Act V. By then, however, the love between René and Gerard has been sealed so passionately and solemnly that his/her sexual identity scarcely seems to matter. Indeed it is revealed to him in so perfunctory a manner as to suggest an afterthought rather than a *coup de théâtre*. Or could it be that we are caught up in a play in which we have taken the theme too seriously because it seems to anticipate the anxieties and the stock themes of our post-Freudian age? There is certainly a note of burlesque as well as a cry for help in the exchange that articulates the anagnorisis of this non-tragedy. Gerard addresses his loved one, who has followed him at great risk, disguised in women's clothing, with the following words: Und wenn ich nun begehrte, daß du immer / Dein Leben lang die Tracht und Kleidung tragest, / Die jetzt du trägst? ['And what if I now requested you always to wear, all your life long, the clothing which you are now wearing?']. René, still ignorant of the truth about himself, indignantly responds:

> Wie, was? Mein Leben lang
> In Weiberkleidern, ich? Du bist von Sinnen!
> Ein Mann in Weibertracht!
> MARCEL.   René! Und wenn
> Nur eben diese dir geziemte, wenn
> Du nicht ein Knabe, nein, ein junges, holdes,
> Unschuldig, reizumblühtes Mädchen wärst?
> RENÉ. Ein Mädchen, ich? – Was siehst du mich so ernst,
> So seltsam an? – Herrgott im Himmel! – Wie,
> Wär's Ernst? – Ich wär' nicht wahrhaft ich, wär' nur
> Ein Blendwerk, eine Lüge! (p. 142)

[What? all my life? Me? – in women's clothing? Are you out of your mind? A man in women's clothes!' – 'René! What if that were all that befitted you? What if you were not a boy, but a young and lovely, innocent, delightful girl?' – 'What? Me a girl? – Why are you looking at me so solemnly and strangely? Lord God in heaven! What? Are you serious? – You mean that I'm not really me, that I'm just an illusion, a lie?]

But it is too late for another crisis of identity. The stereotypes of nineteenth-century gender definition, announced here for the first time in all their simplistic clarity, descend on the dénouement of the drama so rapidly that some minutes later René can say to Marcel with sentimental and conventional pathos: 'Du Einziger! Da bin ich, nimm mich hin!' ['Beloved! Take me! Here I am!'] (p. 143). Surely Halm cannot really have hoped that his audience would have more or less forgotten that in Act III they had heard and felt the immediacy of misconstrued but genuine passion?

A convincing explanation of Halm's most enigmatic play is impossible. Is it a romantic melodrama that somehow goes off the rails? A personal confession in disguise? Or could it be a pre-echo of Krafft-Ebing, Otto Weininger,[11] and the Viennese preoccupation with the psychology of sex at the turn of the century? Or is it just a very bad play? In the light of Halm's development as the major Austrian poet-playwright to fill the long years of Grillparzer's silence (he died on 22 May 1871: thus Grillparzer outlived him) it may be truest to say that on this occasion his sometimes helpful ally, the Muse of Comedy, gave it the kiss of death.

Notes

1. W. E. Yates, *Theatre in Vienna: a Critical History, 1776–1995* (Cambridge, 1996), p. 66. The other two were Bauernfeld's *Ein deutscher Krieger* (1842) and *Großjährig* (1846).
2. A stage history of Halm's plays in and outside Vienna has yet to be written: a catalogue of Halm performances on the British stage would make an interesting start.
3. *The Lady of Lyons, or Love and Pride* was a romantic comedy by Bulwer-Lytton first performed in 1838.
4. Peter Bauland, *The Hooded Eagle; Modern German Drama on the New York Stage* (Syracuse, 1968), p. 240.
5. All quotations are taken from Friedrich Halm, *Werke*, ed. Rudolf Fürst (4 parts in 2 vols, Berlin, n.d.). *Der Sohn der Wildnis* and *Verbot und Befehl* are to be found in Part II, *Wildfeuer* in Part III.
6. In Lope's original the French setting reflects the Spanish-French dynastic marriages of the day, notably that of Anne of Austria to Louis XIII, the monarch indirectly depicted in Lope's play. See *El villano en su rincón*, ed. by Juan María Marín (Madrid, 1987), p. 16.
7. Lope's name for him, Juan Labrador, makes the social scenario of the comedy clearer, but it is far from hidden in Halm's *Vormärz* version.
8. Ernst Alker, *Die deutsche Literatur im 19. Jahrhundert*, 3rd edn (Stuttgart, 1969), p. 164.
9. Halm, *Werke*, Vol. I, p. lxiii.
10. Edward Henry Siebert, 'A Typology of Friedrich Halm's Drama' (University of Connecticut Ph.D., 1973) is disappointing when analysing the play.
11. Weininger's influential *Geschlecht und Charakter* appeared in 1903, but his outlook, like that of all his generation, was at least partly formed by the 'classics' of the previous generation, such as the dramatic works of Halm.

Bloodshed in the Balkans: Robert Scheu, Karl Kraus and a Question of Satire

Gilbert J. Carr

Robert Scheu was a contemporary of Karl Kraus with a radical political background. His significance in the social networks of Vienna has long been neglected. As founder of the *Kulturpolitische Gesellschaft* [Society for Cultural Politics] in 1901, he demanded direct social action to reform Austrian society, and initiated public debate about key institutions in a series of inquiries. He later remarked that the *Gesellschaft* could have been more productive than parliament as a forum for arbitration of the ethnic conflicts that were to rend Austria apart.[1] As a writer, his critical views on topical social issues in Kraus's periodical *Die Fackel* provided a counterpoint to the political aloofness of the editor, before he succeeded Kraus as the prominent satirist of *Simplicissimus* in 1911. What is scarcely known, however, is that, as a youth, Scheu had been fêted in the salon of the powerful newspaper editor, Moriz Benedikt, as a new Raimund or Anzengruber and that, even after his breakthrough as co-author of a 'Wiener Stück' ['play in the Viennese style'] in 1897 had been prevented by censorship and a speculative theatre director, he continued to look for inspiration in the Viennese comic tradition. One neglected example of this, which will concern us here, is his *Der Staatsstreich. Burleske Posse mit Gesang in fünf Aufzügen* [The Coup d'État. Burlesque Musical Farce in Five Acts], based on the Belgrade coup of 1903. It was never staged but, on 26 February 1904, it was read by three performers at the third of Scheu's 'Rezitationsabende' [soirées] to the *Kulturpolitische Gesellschaft* in Vienna – the audience being exhorted to imagine the music. According to the *Arbeiter-Zeitung*, Scheu with his 'impudent humour' had avoided the pitfalls of 'satiric brazenness' descending into tastelessness: '[...] er hat aus der jämmerlichen serbischen Königstragödie eine unblutige, stellenweise sehr lustige Satire hervorgeholt.' ['out of Serbia's wretched royal tragedy he has created a bloodless, at times very amusing, satire'].[2] Kraus, who at the time was also exploring the resonances of the comic tradition for contemporary satire,[3] was 'hochbegeistert' ['highly enthusiastic'] about the play.[4] The manner of its performance before an independent forum is also significant, for Kraus himself later adopted public recital of dramatic and satirical works as a means of circumventing the clique-ridden Viennese press and theatre. The possibility, however, of a *Posse*

160

about a bloody coup meeting with Kraus's approval raises questions about the scope of satire, given his strictures on the literary violation of the dead.[5] Finally, the recourse to comic tradition in the face of potentially tragic subject matter will necessitate a brief consideration of the relation of satire to the depiction of modern warfare.

The generic tensions in Kraus's *Die letzten Tage der Menschheit* [The Last Days of Mankind], his monumental tragedy of the First World War played by 'Operettenfiguren',[6] are exemplified in the *Vorspiel* [Prelude], in the last scene of which all figures are designated as 'Marionetten' (Kraus, p.14), yet where the funeral of Archduke Franz Ferdinand is surrounded by court and social treachery construed in Shakespearean vein. At the height of his 'reactionary' phase, Kraus had polemicised against the radicals who were behind the assassination at Sarajevo in 1914, in the essay 'Franz Ferdinand und die Talente', an obituary for the murdered Archduke as a Fortinbras who might have been Austria's saviour (F 400–3, 2).[7] The tone of Kraus's reaction here is characteristic of the pathos which, in its alternation with his mocking satire, creates the dynamic of his work.[8] The pathos of tragic grief marks the exemption of death from journalistic or satirical commentary, in a similar way to his taboo on any investigation of an individual's sexual privacy.

It may just be an historical coincidence that these two taboos had been infringed in the satirical journal *Simplicissimus* only a few months before the assassination at Sarajevo, by the author Roda Roda, who in the anecdote 'Barta und die Hetäre' [Barta and the Courtesan] had named Queen Draga of Serbia – victim of assassination in 1903 – as the 'whore' of his eponymous officer-narrator's 'true' encounter. For this slur, Kraus had called Roda Roda to account publicly in Munich in February 1914.[9] The Belgrade coup of 11 June 1903, in which King Alexander Obrenović, Queen Draga and her two brothers, along with a minister and officials, had been assassinated in the plot by some 120 army officers and supporters of his Russophile heir Peter Karadjordjević, had brought about the 'radical shift' in Serbian policy which – politically welcomed in Serbia in a carnival atmosphere – eventually led to war in 1914.[10]

Dynastic struggles and bloodshed would scarcely seem to combine into a subject for comedy. While European opinion was shocked by the brutality of the coup, however (Jelavich, p. 32), a cartoon by Thomas Theodor Heine in *Simplicissimus* mocked the 'Serbian Coronation' with the caption: 'Die Zeremonie wird mit Insektenpulver vorgenommen' ['The ceremony is conducted with insect powder'].[11] This barely surpasses the – supposedly fitting – vulgarity and heaviness of the accompanying 'Serbisches Heldenlied' ['Serbian Heroic Lay'] in six stanzas by Peter Schlemihl (Ludwig Thoma), which contained the caricature:

> Jeder sprach: Ich bin ein freier Sr̆b,
>   Bin ein freier Sr̆b,
> König Alexander, du mußt str̆b,
>   Du mußt str̆b.

Und sie schlachten ihn und seine Frau
  Und seine Frau
Ab wie eine fette Sȑbenszau,
  Sȑbenszau.[12]

[Each one spoke: I am a free Sȑb, am a free Sȑb, King Alexander,
  thou must die.
And they slaughter him and his wife, and his wife, like a fat Sȑb sow,
  Sȑb sow.]

The humourless chauvinism here anticipates First World War jingles like
'Serbien muß sterbien' ['Serbia must die'] which, in *Die letzten Tage der
Menschheit*, particularly typifies the barbarism of indoctrinated street crowds
(Kraus, p. 72). It could not have contrasted more with the reaction of
Simplicissimus to the assassination of Franz Ferdinand – a sombre cartoon by
Heine, 'Im Balkan-Blutmeer' ['In the Balkan sea of blood'], with the caption
'Steuermann über Bord!' ['Helmsman overboard!'].[13] *Die Muskete*, too, while
damning Serbian cynicism in training assassins,[14] reacted with a sub-Shake-
spearean lament 'Franz Ferdinand†' by 'Jeremias': 'Ein Schandmal brennt auf
dem Gesicht der Welt: / Es ward ein Mann von Bubenhand gefällt [...]' ['A
stigma burns on the face of the world: knavish hands a man have felled'] –
which spares a thought for the Archduchess and demands retribution on the
con-spirators: 'Dann wird dies Volk, im Königsmord erfahren, / Dich
hündisch lieben, wie vor hundert Jahren [...]'.[15] ['Only then will this people,
versed in regicide, love thee slavishly, as a hundred years ago'.] This
stereotype of Serbians has persisted,[16] and had already been articulated by the
verdict of *The Times* in 1903: 'Serbia, the land of assassinations, abdications,
pronunciamentos and *coups d'état*, has surpassed itself and caused all previous
achievements to pale into insignificance [...]'.[17]

What political pressures had led to that earlier assassination? After years of
misrule King Milan Obrenović had abdicated in 1889. His son Alexander,
once of age, had arrested the regents and dissolved the constitution. Unrest
was exacerbated by his exiled father's return in 1897 as Commander-in-Chief,
and by Alexander's marriage in 1900 to his notorious mistress, Draga
Maschin, who was believed infertile and whose family's public influence was
resented (Danby, p.127; Jelavich, p. 32). From the start *Die Fackel* had been
well informed on Serbian affairs, and, while the anonymous articles it
published between 1899 and 1903 were not necessarily by Kraus, they had –
despite shifts of emphasis – voiced consistent criticism of Milan's tyranny and
corruption and of the protection afforded him by Austrian government and
press. Robin Okey's remark that 'Austria's non-official media did not offer an
alternative perspective on the South Slav lands' therefore needs some qualifi-
cation.[18] Given Milan's sleazy connections, an alleged assassination attempt
was discredited, the execution of the suspect Knezevics being a miscarriage of
justice (F 18, 11), after a 'despicable court-room comedy' (F 38, 3). Indeed,
the incident is presented as a political manoeuvre of Milan's to bring variety
'in seine Freudenhäuslichkeit' ['into his pleasure-house domesticity'] (F 11,

20). The censure of the ex-King's dubious morals in this pun also contrasts with Kraus's treatment of the 1903 assassination, and the incongruity between Milan's status and lifestyle is treated less in burlesque manner than as cause for indignation about Europe's monarchs allowing an insult to 'a pimp somewhere in Europe' to be deemed a *lèse-majesté* (F 17, 25). The lack of Austrian and international concern about the unjust imprisonment of highly regarded opposition figures like Vesnić is contrasted to the outrage over the Dreyfus proceedings (F 17, 24). In other protests against political persecution by the regime (F 12, 16f.), *Die Fackel* castigates Austria for failing to realise 'daß Kartenkönige in der Politik keine Trümpfe sein können' ['that in politics playing-card kings cannot be trumps'], and for antagonising 'ascendant nations' – unlike opportunistic Russian diplomacy, Austrians remained 'die "Wurzen" des Legitimitätsprincips' ['suckers for the legitimacy principle'] (F 12, 17f.). The card metaphor already suggests the potential of this puppet regime as a subject of satire, but the Austriacism 'Wurzen' recalls the tradition of vernacular humour bringing statesmen down to earth.

One of these contributions was 'Goluchowski und Milan', an anonymous open letter of April 1900 (F 38, 1–9) from Milan Milovanović, a moderate in the Serbian Radical Party. The author appealed to Austria to strengthen Alexander's hand against the monster ex-King, who had surpassed Nero and Caligula in poisoning public life with his 'Schändlichkeiten, all die Niederträchtigkeiten, Erbärmlichkeiten und Schreckensthaten' ['ignominies, despicable abuses, wretched tricks and acts of terror']. Serbia needed another palace revolution, which might then turn Alexander into a constitutional monarch (F 38, 4–8). Despite the promise of reform after the exile of Milan in 1900 (F 65, 19f.), Alexander remained a weak ruler, playing off political factions against each other, and the elections and new assembly in 1901 were shams (Jelavich, p. 32).

In 1899 *Die Fackel* had satirised Alexander, who, having failed to gain an audience with Kaiser Franz Josef, wipes bloodstains from his fingers in an ante-room while a journalist wipes the ink-stains from his: 'Und so ließ die eine Hand die andere ungewaschen' ['And thus one hand left the other unwashed'] (F 22, 1). Here combined with an inverted proverb, the motif of stained hands recurs in Kraus's later indictments of war reporters. In 1901, *Die Fackel* exposed the Viennese press's belated criticism of Milan, now dead, as hypocritical and relativistic. The ethical strictures of Kraus's critique of war are anticipated when the fault is seen in Austria's failure to apply civilised European standards to judge Milan: 'Sie [= die liberale Presse, *G.C.*] wusste: wenn ein orientalischer Herrscher wie Milan ein paar hundert Unterthanen niedermetzeln lässt, so "spürt" er's so wenig, wie Offenbachs Bobèche; er ist eben ein Barbar' ['(The liberal press) knew: when an oriental ruler like Milan orders a few hundred subjects to be butchered, he is as "impervious" as Offenbach's Bobèche; he is, after all, a barbarian'] (F 68, 2). This view of Bobèche, the scheming king from Offenbach's *Barbe-bleue*, signals a (temporary) distancing from Kraus's early theatrical view of politics (Carr, pp.116f.). 'Operettenpolitik' continued to provide targets for satire before 1914, as catalogued by Thoma in *Simplicissimus*,[19] and thus construing the Serbian turmoil certainly provided the paradigm for Scheu's *Der Staatsstreich*.

Austria's failure to intervene after the 1903 coup was compounded by its hypocritical indignation and premature recognition of a Russophile regime in which the assassins were represented.[20] After June 1903, *Die Fackel* adopted a sarcastic tone towards Austrian self-interest and remoteness from Serbian politics, and used varied devices in a sequence of critical glosses on the news reports. Austria's hope for continued good relations with the new regime is presented as a statement by the Austrian Prime Minister von Koerber 'after the victory of the Serbian army over a sleeping couple'. There follows a press cutting, given the laconic title: 'Ein Raubmord?' ['Murder by robbers?'], because it relates to the looting of the royal couple's jewellery by the assassins (F 141, 1). Typical of this transition to the *Glossen* of Kraus's later satire are the shifts of perspective from the full pathos of horror at the bloody deed to bitter irony at peripheral events. Thus, two glosses construing 'the events in the light of the *Neue Freie Presse*' quote, in turn, a Viennese fashion firm's advertisement of the costumes recently ordered by Queen Draga, and the report of a shop-keeper thwarting a madman's alleged assassination attempt on the Kaiser (F 141, 2). Under the guise of an 'editor's reply' to a reader, a newspaper report of the murders is quoted, which records melodramatically that international recognition will be accorded to the new king on the bloodstained throne, but then evokes the 'lavish' nocturnal meal of the couple oblivious of their doom (F 141, 22). More important is another 'reply', an early critique of empty clichés in a woman journalist's smug condemnation of Draga's morals and Alexander's gullibility. Kraus's satirical vengeance takes the laconic form of glossing the veritable hotchpotch of mixed metaphors used to metamorphose Draga successively into an Eve beguiling her Adam, Autumn wedding Spring, Circe ensnaring her bird, calling the tune, crushing maternal values with her dancing shoe, a Siren deafening her victim to duty (F 141, 22f.).

On 1 August 1903, when relaying his greetings to Robert Scheu on a postcard to his friend Otto Stoessl, Kraus took issue with an article by Vladan Djordjević, former Serbian Prime Minister: 'Mit Georgewitsch's Aufsatz war ich gar nicht einverstanden, am allerwenigsten mit den "pikanten" Stellen. Die Attentatsversion ist natürlich Quatsch. Scheu möge den – ebenso pathetischen – Aufsatz eines serbischen Ministers in "Fackel" 1899 oder 1900 nachlesen.' ['I was not at all in agreement with Djordjević's essay, least of all with the "spicy" passages. The assassination attempt theory is obvious nonsense. Scheu might care to re-read the – equally melodramatic – article by a Serbian minister in *Die Fackel* from 1899 or 1900'] (Kraus / Stoessl, *Briefwechsel*, p.39). Kraus here reiterates the denial in *Die Fackel* of Alexander's implication in the Knezevics affair (F 38, 8). Djordjević, after an earlier sensational attack on the living Draga,[21] did not spare her retrospectively: 'Ihr Leib war Gemeingut [...] eine hitzige Dirne' ['Her body was common property (...) a hot slut']; she was '[das] unglückselige Weib, das soviel Unglück und Schande über uns aufgethürmt und reichlich verdient hatte, vom Throne herabgerissen und in eine Klosterzelle eingesperrt zu werden' ['the unfortunate female who had brought down so much misfortune and disgrace upon us and had amply deserved to be dragged from the throne and locked away in a nunnery cell'].[22] The objection to such 'spicy passages' – which precedes Kraus's break with Maximilian Harden for his censorious prying in *Die Zukunft* into the bigamy of Frau von Hervay (F 168, 12f.) – is characteristic of polemics in *Sittlichkeit und Kriminalität* [Morality and criminality] (1908) against journalists and judges in scandalous court cases who abused sexual privacy. One continuation of this campaign was the Roda Roda affair of 1914.

The contrast of Kraus's outrage at Roda Roda with his enthusiasm for Scheu's handling of this subject matter suggests that *Der Staatsstreich* overcame his often expressed scepticism about an authentic revival of the comic tradition (Carr, pp. 111–16). The play raises another question about what has been deemed the 'decline' of the Viennese popular theatre after Nestroy's death, when Anzengruber and his contemporaries preached 'old Enlightenment truisms'.[23] A sign of the detachment of the popular theatre from its heritage is the use of ethnic stereotypes around 1900. Nestroy's wealth of social types includes Bohemian artisans and tradesmen, but very few of these are caricatured as Slavs – even the political stereotype created when Ultra impersonates a Russian Prince in *Freiheit in Krähwinkel* [Freedom in Krähwinkel] is secondary to the satire on the gullible local townspeople (see HKA, *Stücke 26/I*, 42–5). Edgar Yates has supported the view that such ethnic images cannot be extracted from the satirical context, that mockery and conscious prejudice are by no means to be equated.[24] As Austria's internal ethnic tensions around the turn of the century became entangled with the political struggles of neighbouring states and regions, however, there are signs of a narrower political agenda in the popular theatre.[25]

In an anonymous newspaper article in 1896, too, one finds a caricature of South Slav rulers. The title 'Das liederliche Kleeblatt' [Three Ne'er-do-Wells] announces a parody of Act I, 4 of Nestroy's *Lumpacivagabundus* (see HKA, *Stücke 5*, 141–43) – the meeting of the three journeymen Knieriem, Leim and Zwirn in search of their fortune. Ending with a trio modelled on that of the original scene, the parody presents an hypothetical meeting in Sofia between the Prince of Montenegro, the King of Serbia and the Prince of Bulgaria respectively in the guise of a drunken Nikita Knieriem, Alexander Leim I and an opportunist Ferdinand Zwirn, on the way to seek 'Protection' in Russia. Alexander Leim enters with crown and sceptre in his knapsack, using the journeyman's metaphors while recounting his earlier disappointment in Russia:

> [...] ich bin a ausg'lernter König und alle Augenblicke fallt mir die Legitimität aus der Kron'. [...] Diese Leut' da haben ja Herzen, so beweglich wie a russische Knuten. Woher kommt das aber? Weil die Leut' keine Bildung hab'n auf'n Balcan! Und warum hab'n's auf'n Balcan keine Bildung? Weil sie auf ihre ewige Balcanfrage nie a rechte Antwort krieg'n.[26]

> [I'm a fully trained king and every moment my crown is brimming with legitimacy. These people here have hearts that can only be moved the

way a Russian knout is. And why? Because people in the Balkans have
no education. And why is that? Because they never get a proper answer
to their eternal Balkan question.]

Such parody claims continuity with a 'traditionally' down-to-earth Viennese
model of construing situations and – as it is the Serbian king who shares the
Vormärz cobbler's detachment, if not his wit – it privileges a 'modern' view of
the Balkans, characteristic of the Viennese press before 1914, as 'extremely
unfree' and intellectually backward (Okey, p. 53). The same may be said of
the underlying conception of Scheu's *Der Staatsstreich* as well as of contemporary operettas of the 'silver era', however much it may be argued that their
subtext challenges Austrian institutions too.[27]

Der Staatsstreich emphatically adopts the conventions of *Posse* and operetta
in some highly implausible plot constructions, scene changes and motivations.
The language ranges from parodies of Goethean verse drama to wooden prose
dialogues, but the obvious 'ethnic' caricature of *Simplicissimus* is avoided. At
best the song parts come close to the style of Offenbach's librettos, and the
satire on institutions is well accomplished in verbal virtuosity.

The play begins in the operetta setting of an inn with the cloak-and-dagger
conspirators Gorski, Zarizow, Lenkowitsch and Kaskitsch rolling their eyes
while singing their Chorus, before revealing that they have all been proscribed
by royal decree.[28] The poet Fantaskowitsch presents himself in an *Auftrittslied*
[solo on entering] as a master of disguise, deceit and intrigue. Though
apparently lacking political awareness, he is their natural ally – albeit
intellectually superior (11). In his recognition of a potential use for his
'brotlose Kunst' ['unlucrative art'], the culinary metaphors: 'Wie wünschen
Sie die Revolution, blutig oder durchgebraten?' ['How would you like the
revolution, bloody or well-done?'] (12) echo Klaus's order to the waiter at the
'Heerd der Revolution' ['hearth', i.e. 'hot-bed of the revolution'] in Nestroy's
Freiheit in Krähwinkel (HKA, *Stücke 26/I*, 15). As appropriate to the genre,
Fantaskowitsch is in love with a down-to-earth servant-girl at the inn, Bianka,
'Amor' thus vying with the God of Thieves (12). Her prophetic dream,
however – of becoming Queen within three days (14) – promises a coincidence
with the planned *coup d'état*. *Hamlet* travesties such as Nestroy's *Die Papiere
des Teufels* [The Devil's Papers][29] are recalled when a peasant play provides
exposition on the state of the royal marriage, and the performer Tschoggel
proves to be a double of King Fedor (18) – giving Fantaskowitsch the idea of
outwitting the authorities with stagecraft, by creating enough confusion at
court to foil Fedor's coup and to put the disguised Tschoggel on the throne
and the conspirators in power. The revolution is to be bloodless and its
metaphorical form is satire:

So wird der Staatsstreich pariert,
Und das Volk amüsiert,
Ein Riesengelächter
Entwaffnet die Wächter,
Die Autorität,

Gilbert J. Carr

Wird hingemäht. –
[...]
Dann will ich versprechen
Euch glänzend zu rächen,
Ohne Blutvergießen,
Ohne Stechen und Schießen,
Durch Witz und Intrige
Euch führen zum Sieg! (19f.)

[Thus the coup is countered, and the people amused, gales of laughter disarm the guards, authority is mown down. Then I shall promise to avenge you handsomely, without bloodshed, without stabbing and shooting, by wit and by intrigue, lead you to victory!]

Political upheaval is construed in the tradition of Nestroy – it recalls Ultra's song in *Freiheit in Krähwinkel* (HKA, *Stücke 26/I*, 15–17) and particularly *Judith und Holofernes*, with the use of disguise as a foil to bloodshed (HKA, *Stücke 26/II*, 107–14) – as well as of Offenbach's conspirators in *Madame l'Archiduc*.

The second act introduces the King and his entourage, and the priest Kanalles. In a burlesque *Quodlibet* – punctuated by the chorus's refrains – Fedor, in turn, holds court with Queen Knautscha and his ministers Plutzki, Kroda and Lonzef. In his *Auftrittslied* the vain Fedor presents himself as a pseudo-liberal and patron of arts and science, whose thick skull is necessary to bear the weight of the crown (21f.). The former lady-in-waiting ·Knautscha boasts her ignoble origins and her advancement at court – 'der Minne Lohn' ['the wages of courtship'] for having exploited men's weakness (23) – and then forces King and courtiers into a ritual kissing of her garter:

Das war ein Knix?
Das war nix!
Ich werde euch lehren!
Mich zu verehren! (25)

[Was that a curtsy? That was nowt! I'll teach you! To adore me!]

Foreign Minister Plutzki reports first:

Unsere Lage ist kritisch,
Unsere Haltung ist soldatisch.
Unsere Diplomatie ist politisch,
Unsere Politik diplomatisch.
Der Friede ist gesichert –
Wenn wir nachgeben [...]. (26)

[Our situation is critical, our stance is soldierly, our diplomacy is political, our policy diplomatic. Peace is agreed – if we concede.]

– adding the consolation that the interior situation is even worse. Interior Minister Kroda responds:

Die Industrie wird gefördert
Durch weise Besteuerung,
Die Sterblichkeit mindert
Die Lebensmittelteuerung.
[...]
Die Polizei funktioniert,
Die Sicherheit ist garantiert -
Den Arrestanten
Und Defraudanten. (27)

[Industry is promoted by wise taxation, the death rate minimises food price increases. (...) Police force is operational, security guaranteed – to persons arrested and to defrauders.]

War Minister Lonzef continues: 'Es lebe die Autorität, / Besonders wenn sie besteht!' ['Long live authority, especially if it survives!'] – and, after apostrophising cannons and bombs in typical martial bombast, concedes: 'Besonders gegen den inneren Feind / Die Armee sehr nützlich erscheint.' (28) ['Especially against the enemy within, the army appears very useful.']

In the following council of state Fedor is not altogether reassured that every hair on his head is protected by 100 marksmen and that half of the population are informers – since a single traitor can outwit the secret police (29). Neither Plutzki's proposal of a mass distribution of postcards of the royal couple, nor even the prospect of having three-quarters of the population hanged satisfies Knautscha, so Lonzef recommends a different cure to Fedor:

Hoheit, reisen Sie auf sechs Wochen ins Blutbad. Ich verordne Ihnen Stahlbäder, Blutbäder, Aderlässe, Eisenpillen. Hier habe ich eine Liste der Staatsautoritätsanzweifler, der Königshausscheelbetrachter, der Steuererhöhungantipathischgegenübersteher, der Militärhoheitüberdieachselschauer, der Polizeiüberwachungsabholdlinge, der Nichtjedeköniglicheweisheitsäußerungsbewunderer, der Handkußverweigerer, der Stillegrollnährer und noch vieler anderer Verdachtsverdächtiger. (31)

[Highness, go on a six-week cure in a blood bath. For you I prescribe iron-impregnated baths, blood baths, blood-letting, iron pills. Here is a list of doubters-of-state-authority, askance-lookers-at-royal-family, tax-increase-regarders-with-antipathy, down-their-nose-lookers-at-military-superiors, police-surveillance-averselings, not-every-royal-pearl-of-wisdom-admirers, bow-and-scrape-refusers, silent-grudge-nursers and many others suspected of suspicion besides.]

This parody of bureaucratic bombast uses cumulative syntax and lexical inventiveness in the manner of the 'bortirte Befehlerfüllungs-Maschine' ['braided command-carrying-out-machine'] of Titus Feuerfuchs in *Der Talisman* (HKA, *Stücke 17/I*, 76) to comment on a transition to modernity the complexity of which defies autocratic categorisations. Behind this absurdity lurks the sinister role reversal of the 'cure', as well as further, ominous subdivision of the list of subversives according to fit punishment – from bribery, dungeon, gallows, to 'eligible to be a missing person' (31). Further satire on professions comes in the *Auftrittslied* of the aptly named Kanalles – who blesses all and sundry for a fee: 'Ich segne hin, ich segne her' ['I bless them here, I bless them there'] (32f.) – and where Fantaskowitsch imbues his role as prompter for Tschoggel, during the conspirators' preparations, with a symbolic importance:

Ein edler Stand ist der Souffleur,
Er findet jederzeit Gehör [...]
Und was da oben glänzt und gleißt,
Ob's König oder Bettler heißt,
Von seinen Lippen wird's versorgt. (37)

[A noble trade is the prompter's, he at all times enjoys an audience (...), and whether the dazzling show put on is of kings or of beggars, from his lips it is supplied.]

Another virtuoso satire of corruption opens Act III when, outside the royal bathroom, the disguised Fantaskowitsch has to convince Hölzel, the head valet, of his credentials in an expansive curriculum vitae, namely of the connections (the 'protection in style') that qualify him as (alleged) new appointee to second valet. Hölzel boasts his command of excuses for exemption from duty (40), before initiating Fantaskowitsch into the secret of the King's impotence. Lonzef is another example of a self-revealing reactionary, reassuring the King that once the coup d'état 'constitutionally' enacts absolute rule, *lèse-majesté* will include thought-crime (42). The King, however, is Tschoggel in disguise, who promptly has Lonzef and the other ministers arrested and proclaims the counter-coup (45f.). When Fedor re-appears, outraged but underdressed, the dispute about the identity of the true King begins. Lenkowitsch, who quells the commotion, disingenuously calling it 'a scoundrel's trick' (47), orders a formal inquiry, headed by 'General' Zarizow. In the meantime, Fedor is put into ridiculous clothes, and Knautscha is 'sequestered' to avoid her involvement.

In Act IV the parliament is now dominated by the conspirators – the name *Reichsrat* hints that Austrian institutions are the butt of this Serbian farce. Ignoring the view of one member that, because there was little to choose between the two pretenders, they should govern alternately (51), this body proceeds to an identity test, for which purpose the two – after reviling each other in a duet (52) – are distinguished as Wurscht and Durscht and by one being shaven clean. Such duplication, familiar from comic operetta, fits a scene construction in which their alternating claims are echoed by the chorus, all of which predictably levels any individuality. Their fatuous definitions of the constitution, their programmes of government (53–5) and their predictably callous proposals for 'Das Budget / U je' ['The budget – Oh no'] (56), belong within the convention of satirical unmasking, retarding the plot, until, when evidence from the public is invited, Fantaskowitsch, now disguised as a peasant, claims Fedor as his impotent son. The pragmatic priest, now called

169

upon temporarily to annul the King's marriage for the test of the pretenders' virility, prides himself on his power to 'join and dissolve, for better or worse, release from oaths, condemn and forgive, on demand' (61).

Inevitably, the maiden enjoined to co-operate is Bianka, who, at first, believes a future queen has nothing to lose (63). Promptly 'married' to Wurscht/Fedor for the duration of the test, she requires advance absolution after all, given her doubts about forfeiting her virginity (65), and Fantaskowitsch realises how the political snare for Fedor will also defeat his own romantic aspirations – calling himself 'ein dummer Dichter / Ein Sichselbstzugrunderichter' ['a stupid poet / An own-downfall-causer'] (71). But the process is irreversible, and in the bridal chamber – a setting mimicking *Lohengrin* – neither Bianka's 'dance of the seven veils' (68) nor the fetish of Knautscha's garter arouses Fedor, who fails the test. He is not unduly surprised to discover an undisguised Fantaskowitsch in the chamber, who brokers a solution: Fedor and Knautscha are to abdicate in return for a state pension, and it is now Fantaskowitsch who consummates the 'test' with Bianka, who consents in the knowledge that she is to be queen. In the public dénouement, Fedor is quickly disabused of his presumption about being reinstated and is shamed when the garter is produced. Thus the conspirators, the state and the deposed monarchs survive this bloodless coup and the people exult, as Fantaskowitsch and Bianka are pronounced king and queen, man and wife, by the hypocritically rueful priest (76f.).

Scheu's burlesque alternative to the bloodshed of politics is partly modelled on an earlier work with a plot of improbable alacrity, with inn and court scenes, ridiculous type-cast conspirators, bloodless coups and extra-marital flirtations: Offenbach's *Madame l'Archiduc*, which Kraus later adapted and read at his recitals.[30] Lacking in Scheu's plot is the way the operetta's many role-reversals not only hint at a need for revolution, but – threatened as the heroine is by the Archduke's unwelcome advances – create an hypothesis of women's liberation. Offenbach's music and the libretto encapsulate these themes with a lightness lost on today's more earnest feminists. In a *burleske Posse*, one may expect 'arrest' and 'marriage' to be equated or a 'blood-relationship' between 'Krieg und Eh'stand' ['war and matrimony'] to be traced, in the words of Gertrud's and Kilian's duet in Nestroy's *Der Färber und sein Zwillingsbruder* [The Dyer and his Twin Brother].[31]

In *Der Staatsstreich* the critique of marital relations is closer, in one respect, to the modern male identity crisis – but it may be no more than a farcical sense of the gossip over Alexander's and Draga's inability to produce an heir that the political eligibility of an anachronistic monarchy to rule over an unstable society turns on proof of Fedor's sexual impotence. However, the play evidently contains authorial comment. It is Fantaskowitsch, a variation of the 'trouble-maker' common in the popular theatre,[32] who is a persona and mouthpiece for Scheu, who adopted the name in his socially critical articles in these years.[33] Like his author, the play's Fantaskowitsch does not recoil from self-advertisement of his Odyssean armoury of 'several thousand ideas' (12). The manipulations of marital status in the play certainly have functions for the comic plot and for Scheu's anti-clerical satire, aimed at the priest's unprincipled, ultimately self-serving pragmatism and hypocrisy. However, given Scheu's ambivalence towards marriage before and after his 'stürmische Ehemonate' in 1902–3 ['stormy first months of marriage'] and his contacts with the Verein der Katholisch-Geschiedenen [Club of Catholic divorcees],[34] the plot's mock suspension of marital status is an authorial subtext on the arbitrary constraints of (Austrian) marriage law. Indeed, between 1904 and 1907, Scheu himself claims to have spearheaded a marriage-law reform movement that snowballed into a popular political initiative with four million signatures, thereby sustaining the militancy with which he had founded the Kulturpolitische Gesellschaft.[35] Therefore, despite the sometimes gratuitous comedy in *Der Staatsstreich* at the expense of Balkan backwardness, there is more justification in construing this play as an oblique comment on Austrian institutions than the 'silver era' operettas reclaimed by Moritz Csáky (Csáky, pp. 89ff., 98f.).

Around 1906, just as Scheu viewed *Die Fackel* as a forum for publicising his reforming ideas, Kraus in his 'aesthetic phase' had adopted a demonstratively apolitical stance. Scheu's successful *Simplicissimus* rubric 'Chronik der Weltereignisse' [Chronicle of World Events] was a continuation of the satirical *feuilleton*, such as Kraus's early 'Wiener Briefe' [Letters from Vienna], bred on the same Viennese tradition of theatrical wit. In endless permutations, the privileged narrator appears to make light of world events, bringing leaders down to the level of local mentalities and mocking them as examples of folly. Although the inter-textual play of documented banality and literary pathos in Kraus's *Glossen* produced a much more varied response, they still used the method of the 'Chronik'. One of Scheu's 'Chroniken' from 1914, on the 'Mexican War', begins: 'Gegen unsympathische Menschen gibt es oft nur ein einziges Mittel: den Weltkrieg' ['There is often only one means to deal with unpleasant characters: World War']. This supercilious assertion is then mock-justified by citing diplomatic antipathies, before petroleum is given as the real cause, and the territory's desolation is construed as a deterrent against American invasion.[36] Scheu's satire during the World War continued in this vein of 'cynical' detachment and proportional inversion. One 'Rückblick' [Retrospect] begins typically: 'Als die Kultur ihren Höhepunkt erreicht hatte, brach der Tango und bald darauf der Weltkrieg aus' ['Just as culture had reached its apogee, the tango erupted, and then, soon after, World War'].[37] Of interest here are two of these wartime satires.

'Couplet der Triple-Entente. Neue Strophen zu einem alten Refrain von Nestroy' of October 1914 parodies Federl's *Auftrittslied* from *Die Papiere des Teufels*.[38] As a propagandistic response to the outcry over German 'atrocities' in Belgium, Scheu's 'Couplet' adopts an ironic posture, that of the Entente's 'alarm' at its drubbing at the hands of the Germans, and of its wish for the alternative: of Russian occupation of Austria, French encirclement of Berlin, and St Stephen's rather than Rheims Cathedral being attacked. All that remains of the clerk Federl's wishful role reversal in his 'traurige Wirklichkeit' ['sad reality'] is this structure of inversion and the (freely quoted) refrain: "'s ist zwar nur Schimäre, aber mich unterhalt's...' ["Tis but a chimera, but it keeps me amused...']. These mock fantasies include the notion of the Serbs as 'a noble race'. This sarcasm may conform to the Austrian interpretation, but the uncanny feature of such propagandistic use of a mock-Entente perspective, a catalogue of the unthinkable which is then dismissed in the refrain, is the unwitting prophecy it contains – for example, of the whole of Germany becoming 'ein einziges Leichentuch' ['a vast shroud'], the Entente dictating peace terms and

> In Berlin, da haben sie die Hungersnot,
> Man zahlt vier Mark für ein trockenes Brot,
> In Wien hab'n s' kein Mehl mehr, kein Fleisch und kein Schmalz –
> [...]
> In Preußen und Bayern Revolution!
> [...]
> Oesterreich, weil's zu lang besteht,
> Durch innere Wirren in Fransen geht. (Scheu, 'Couplet ...')

> [In Berlin they have starvation, they're paying four Marks for dry bread, in Vienna they've no more flour, no meat and no lard (...) In Prussia and Bavaria revolution! (...) Austria, for having existed too long, is going to pieces through internal strife.]

This structure of inversion, which echoes Scheu's earlier 'revolutionary' sympathies and his assimilation of popular theatre conventions, unintentionally subverts the propaganda it serves. The second, more unusual piece, from 1915, comprises three brief scenes entitled 'Ex'zellenz Tod. Groteske' [His excellency Death. Scenes grotesque] (*Die Muskete* 20/509 (1.3.1915), 106–10). In this macabre dialogue the traditional allegorical death figure appears in the role of a high-ranking bureaucrat revealing the cynical calculation behind the mass slaughter to an obsequious interviewer 'Fix', who has bribed his way past an officious attendant. Both the social roles depicted and the traditional device of a metaperspective strikingly anticipate the satirical conception of *Die letzten Tage der Menschheit*, but Scheu's cynical insider, while comparable to figures of Kraus's who are the echoes of the corridors of power, could scarcely have been sustained beyond these scenes, in the way that Kraus's sceptical outsider, the *Nörgler* [the 'grouse'], is the omnipresent conscience recording a whole range of atrocities in despair at the human condition.

Scheu was certainly concerned not only with the human cost of war, but with questions of its portrayal. In a *feuilleton* of March 1916, referring to the way a few sentences of a recent official front-line report constituted 'eine Ballade', he construes the significance for posterity of a single, apparently banal day of the war, supplemented as it will be by memoirs and official records:

> Was wir heute in seiner bildhaften und tragischen Gewalt kaum beachten, wird künftigen Malern, Balladendichtern und Dramatikern geläufiges Material sein. [...] Der ganze Weltkrieg ist ein Monster-Epos in

ungezählten Gesängen. Es braucht nur erzählt zu werden, wie sich die Dinge zugetragen haben, so nüchtern und gedrängt als möglich, und es wird eine packende Dichtung sein, ein zweites Nibelungenlied![39]

[What we barely notice today in its graphic and tragic force will be the material for future painters, balladeers and dramatists. (...) The whole World War is a monster epic in innumerable cantos. It needs only a plain narration of how things came to pass, as sober and concise as possible, and it will be a powerful poem, a second Song of the Nibelungs!]

Likening stories of freed hostages and escaped prisoners-of-war to *Odysseys*, and conceiving an air-raid as a monumental painting, Scheu's aesthetic concern with epic subjects betrays a fascination with the war. We may well see his insight into the poetological challenge of the enormity of war being fulfilled – rather differently – by *Die letzten Tage der Menschheit*, but the primacy of poetics and genre prevents Scheu from perceiving the whole reality. The 'tragedies' of individual leaders he singles out as potential 'Königs-dramen' [that is, Shakespearean 'history plays'], 'König Viktor Emanuel' of Italy and 'Venizelos', Prime Minister of Greece: 'König und Minister, diese repräsentativen Figuren mit ihrer ewig typischen Schicksalsverknüpfung stehen in beiden Tragödien im Mittelpunkte der Handlung' ['King and minister, these representative figures, eternally typified by their linked destinies, are at the centre of the action in both tragedies']. In both cases, the fate of the hero, however tragic, can remain meaningful because, Scheu argues, the course of history can at certain points still be influenced by individuals, as in the struggle between Venizelos and King Constantine of Greece. These were, however, exceptions, like Scheu's own personal influence in diplomatic missions in the Succession States after 1918. This conception had easily enough served a comedy of opportunism like *Der Staatsstreich*, but, as *Die letzten Tage der Menschheit* demonstrates, the war saw the last days of such traditional individualism. Kraus's 'monster epic' with its modernist fusion of 'Königsdrama' and operetta turns the initial homage to Austria's lost Fortinbras into a decisive break with Shakespearean or Schillerian heroics.

Notes

1. Robert Scheu, 'Kulturpolitische Gesellschaft', *Arbeiterzeitung* (8.11.47). I am grateful to Dr Egbert Steiner, Vienna, for access to newspaper cuttings and unpublished biographical material from Robert Scheu's Nachlass.
2. *Arbeiter-Zeitung* 58 (27.2.04); Archiv der Kammer für Arbeiter und Angestellte, Vienna.
3. Gilbert J. Carr, 'Karl Kraus's reception of satire in his early career', in: Sigurd P. Scheichl/Edward F. Timms (eds), *Karl Kraus in neuer Sicht. Londoner Kraus-Symposium* (Munich, 1986), pp. 112–14.
4. Robert Scheu, letter to Otto Stoessl, 11.11.03; Karl Kraus/Otto Stoessl, *Briefwechsel 1902–1925*, ed. Gilbert J. Carr (Vienna, 1996), p. 184.
5. Paul Schick, 'Der Satiriker und der Tod. Versuch einer typologischen Deutung',

in: *Festschrift zum hundertjährigen Bestehen der Wiener Stadtbibliothek* (Vienna, 1956), pp. 200–31.

6. Karl Kraus, *Schriften. Bd.10. Die letzten Tage der Menschheit. Tragödie in 5 Akten mit Vorspiel und Epilog*, (ed.) Christian Wagenknecht (Frankfurt, 1986), p. 9.

7. *Die Fackel* 400–03, 1914, 2; hereinafter referred to as F + issue no., page nos.

8. Sigurd P. Scheichl, 'Stilmittel der Pathoserregung bei Karl Kraus', in: Joseph P. Strelka (ed.), *Karl Kraus. Diener der Sprache – Meister des Ethos*, Edition Orpheus, vol. 1 (Tübingen, 1990), pp. 167–81.

9. Paul Schick, *Karl Kraus in Selbstzeugnissen und Bilddokumenten* (Reinbek, 1965), pp. 61f.; Sigurd P. Scheichl, 'Roda Roda in der *Fackel* – ein durchschnittliches Objekt der Satire', in: *Zagreber Germanistische Beiträge*, Beiheft 4, 1996, 39–53.

10. Henry C. Danby, 'Serbia', in: Stephen Clissold (ed.), *A short history of Yugoslavia from early times to 1966* (Cambridge, 1966), p. 127; Barbara Jelavich, *History of the Balkans. Vol.2. Twentieth Century* (Cambridge, 1983), pp. 30–3.

11. 'Serbische Königskrönung', *Simplicissimus*, VIII/15 (7.7.1903), 115.

12. *Simplicissimus*, VIII/15 (7.7.03), 115.

13. *Simplicissimus*, XIX/15 (13.7.14), 248.

14. 'Serbisches Regierungs-Princip', *Die Muskete*, 18/458 (9.7.14), Beiblatt I.

15. *Die Muskete*, 18/458 (9.7.14), 114.

16. Zoran Konstantinovic, 'Das österreichisch-serbische Verhältnis in der deutschen Literatur zum Ersten Weltkrieg', in: Klaus Amann / Hubert Lengauer (eds), *Österreich und der Große Krieg. 1914–1918. Die andere Seite der Geschichte* (Vienna, 1989), p. 241.

17. *The Times* (12.6.03), 5.

18. Robin Okey, 'Austria and the South Slavs', in: *Austrian Studies*, 5 (1994), 53.

19. Ruprecht Konrad, 'Politische Zielsetzungen und Selbstverständnis des *Simplicissimus*', in: *Simplicissimus. Eine satirische Zeitschrift. München 1896–1944*, Ausstellungskatalog Haus der Kunst [Munich, n.d. (1977)], p. 99.

20. Francis Roy Bridge, 'Österreich(-Ungarn) unter den Großmächten', in: Adam Wandruszka/ Peter Urbanitsch (eds), *Die Habsburgermonarchie. 1848–1918. Bd. VI/1. Die Habsburgermonarchie im System der internationalen Beziehungen* (Vienna, 1989), pp. 301f.

21. Vladan Georgewitsch, 'Die Frauen der Obrenowitsch', *Die Zukunft*, 42 (7.2.03), 209–21.

22. Vladan Georgewitsch, 'Der letzte Obrenowitsch', *Die Zukunft*, 44 (18.7.03), 113, 107.

23. W. Edgar Yates, 'Das Vorurteil als Thema im Wiener Volksstück', in: Jürgen Hein (ed.), *Theater und Gesellschaft. Das Volksstück im 19. und 20. Jahrhundert*, Literatur in der Gesellschaft, vol. 12 (Düsseldorf, 1973), p. 77.

24. Yates, p. 74, quoting an argument of Jürgen Hein's.

25. Richard S. Geehr, *Adam Müller-Guttenbrunn and the Aryan theatre of Vienna 1898–1903. The approach of cultural Fascism*, Göppinger Arbeiten zur Germanistik, vol. 114 (Göppingen, 1973).

26. 'Das liederliche Kleeblatt', *Wiener Allgemeine Zeitung*, 5479 (4.6.1896), p. 2.

27. *Der Staatsstreich*, however, is far less 'romantic' than Lehár's *Die lustige Witwe* (1905), which epitomises the way the 'silver' era of operetta thematised Balkan politics; Moritz Csáky, *Ideologie der Operette und Wiener Moderne. Ein kulturhistorischer Essay zur österreichischen Identität* (Vienna/Cologne, Weimar, 1996), pp. 89ff., 98f.

28. Robert Scheu, *Der Staatsstreich. Burleske Posse mit Gesang in fünf Aufzügen* (Vienna, 1904), p. 8. Hereinafter referred to by page no. only.

29. Johann Nestroy, *Gesammelte Werke*, ed. Otto Rommel (Vienna, 1948–49), vol. 4, pp. 64–71.

30. Karl Kraus, *Schriften. Bd.13. Theater der Dichtung. Jacques Offenbach*, ed. Christian Wagenknecht (Frankfurt, 1994), pp. 7–118, 411–502.

31. Johann Nestroy, *Werke. Komödien 1838–1845*, ed. Franz Mautner (Frankfurt, 1970), vol. 2, pp. 240–41.
32. Volker Klotz, *Bürgerliches Lachtheater. Komödie – Posse – Schwank – Operette* (Munich, 1980), pp. 62f.
33. Open letter and 'replies' by Fantaskowitsch appeared in: *Der Weg. Wochenschrift für Politik und Kultur*, ed. Friedrich Hertz/Richard Charmatz, I/2–6 (1905–06).
34. Robert Scheu, 'Tagebuch. VI. Heft'; Nachlass Robert Scheu.
35. Scheu, 'Kulturpolitische Gesellschaft' (see note 1).
36. *Simplicissimus. 1896–1914*, ed. Richard Christ (Berlin, n.d. (1972)), p. 380.
37. Robert Scheu, 'Rückblick', *Die Muskete* 21/535 (30.12.15), 98. Similar examples in *Die Muskete* include: 'Kriegschronik', 21/548 (30.3.16), 202–03, and 'Rückblick 1916', 23/587 (28.12.16), 98–101.
38. Robert Scheu, 'Couplet der Triple-Entente. Neue Strophen zu einem alten Refrain von Nestroy', *Die Muskete* 19/474 (29.10.14), Beiblatt, III. Cf. Johann Nestroy, *Gesammelte Werke*, vol. 4, p. 15.
39. Robert Scheu, 'Stoffe und Motive', *Pester Lloyd* (15.3.16); Nachlass Robert Scheu.

The Aristocratic Philanderer: Reflections on Hofmannsthal's *Der Schwierige*

Martin Swales

One of the chief virtues of the Hofmannsthal sections of W. E. Yates's study, *Schnitzler, Hofmannsthal, and the Austrian Theatre*, is that they inject a note of scepticism and interpretative differentiation into what often strikes outsiders as the insufferable blandness of critical writing devoted to Hofmannsthal. Yates, for example, warns us against an all-too-deferential reading of some of Hofmannsthal's key statements of retrospective self-analysis (the *Ariadne-Brief* and *Ad me ipsum*). And, in a telling comment on *Der Schwierige*, a play for which, as we all know, he has the highest regard, he indicates a particular problem to do with the representative stature of Hans Karl. Yates writes: 'His function as a representative of threatened values combines uneasily with the implications of his characterization as a (more or less reformed) philanderer.'[1] That is well said – and this article is an attempt to address the problematic issue of Hans Karl's representativeness.

As anyone who has tried to write or lecture on the play will know, there is an acute dilemma of interpretative tact that the text poses at every turn. Manifestly, Hans Karl is the all-important central character. Yet it is very difficult to get hold of that all-importance. There is an indeterminacy – and, indeed, an undeterminedness (in almost every conceivable sense of the word) – that constantly informs the Hans Karl figure. If we are not careful, we as interpreters run the risk of doing what so many of the other characters in the play do – of talking endlessly about him, of defining and delimiting him, without in the process coming anywhere near to an adequate understanding of what it is that makes him so important.[2] Yet in the last analysis, *Der Schwierige* is a play, and not a mystical nostrum; and presumably some interpretative headway can be made even with this most elusive of texts.

Perhaps, in our quest for some understanding of the resonance of the Hans Karl figure, we can take our cue from two moments, one at the beginning of the play and one at the end – and both of them have to do with Hans Karl's aristocratic position. In the second speech of the play, Vinzenz, the new servant, asks what the aristocrat actually *does*: 'Was arbeitet er? Majoratsverwaltung? Oder was? Politische Sachen?'(7) ['What kind of work does he do?

Manage his estate? Or what? Political affairs?]. No answer is forthcoming, of course. Later, we are given a gentle hint as to what these 'political matters' might be. Stani says the following:

> Deswegen find ich auch ganz natürlich, worüber sich so viele Leut den Mund zerreißen: daß du im Herrenhaus seit anderthalb Jahren deinen Sitz eingenommen hast, aber nie das Wort ergreifst. Vollkommen in der Ordnung ist das für einen Herrn wie du bist! Ein solcher Herr spricht eben durch seine Person! (26)

> [Hence I find quite natural what so many people talk about constantly: that, for the past year-and-a-half you have taken your seat in the Upper House, but you never speak. Absolutely right for a gentleman such as yourself. Such people speak by virtue of what they are!]

And at the end of the play, we return to the matter of the aristocrat's political persona; Hans Karl desperately tries to avoid getting into conversation with Poldo Altenwyl because he knows full well that the latter will seek to persuade him to make his maiden speech in the Upper House:

> Ich soll aufstehen und eine Rede halten, über Völkerversöhnung und über das Zusammenleben der Nationen – ich, ein Mensch, der durchdrungen ist von einer Sache auf der Welt: daß es unmöglich ist, den Mund aufzumachen, ohne die heillosesten Konfusionen anzurichten! Aber lieber leg ich doch die erbliche Mitgliederschaft nieder und verkriech mich zeitlebens in eine Uhuhütte. (106)

> [I am supposed to get up and give a speech about reconciliation of peoples, the coexistence of nations – and yet I am somebody who is utterly persuaded of one thing in this world: that it is impossible for anyone to open their mouth without producing irreparable confusion. I'd rather lay down my hereditary title and crawl away for the rest of my life to some primitive hut.]

Hans Karl's aristocratic rank confers on him the expectation of political representativeness. It is, admittedly, a public function that does not sit easily on him. But, if Stani is to be believed, that public function will not go away – even if Hans Karl declines to carry it out. His representativeness, it seems, is less a matter of doing than of being. Whatever he does or does not do, his public role is simply given – it is inherited ('erblich'). He is in no sense an elected representative of the people; membership of the Upper House is, quite simply, his birthright. Yet, as the play constantly suggests, that birthright is earned, earned by the fact that those around him constantly seek him out and look up to him. Hans Karl's aristocratic being, one both inherited and endowed, is, then, at the very heart of his representative stature.

There is in the play a whole thematic nexus that derives from Hans Karl's identity as an aristocrat. One strand, which has attracted much critical comment, has to do with the politico-historical specification of the play's temporal location. There are indications that the play is set just after the end of the War – yet, in Hofmannsthal's text, there is still an Upper House where people (and peoples) are represented.[3] I shall return later to the particular aspect of the play's political implications. All I want to register at this stage is its complex aesthetic of redundancy. The aristocrat may be politically, thematically, we might say, redundant; but that redundancy, that very non-functionalism is inseparable from his aesthetic resonance as a publicly representative figure – and from the play's aesthetic celebration of him. It is, I think, helpful in this context to remember Jürgen Habermas's discussion of the thematics of aristocrat and bourgeois in Goethe's *Wilhelm Meister* project.[4] In their various ways, the novels address the emergence of a new mercantile class (and ethos) – one that calibrates achievement in terms of manifest, measurable productivity. Wilhelm hopes to reconcile such entrepreneurial energy with the aristocrat's serene, many-faceted, aesthetically sustained way of life. The bourgeois has always to be doing and making; whereas the aristocrat can be content with what he is, portrays, represents. Goethe's novel articulates the ways in which, and the extent to which, in a culture of increasing specialisation and of productive drive and directedness, there is an immense longing for forms of social existence that have the aesthetic dimension of 'interesseloses Wohl-gefallen' [disinterested pleasure] built into them. Paradoxically, the aimless-ness of the aristocratic way of life is its very (representative) point. We recall the all-important themes of aims and aimlessness in Hofmannsthal's *Der Schwierige*.[5] Hans Karl's charm is unintended and unintentional. As Stani puts it:

> Du hast doch das Wunderbare, daß du mühelos das vorstellst, was du bist: ein großer Herr! Mühelos! Das ist der große Punkt. (31)

> [That is the fantastic thing about you, that you effortlessly represent what you are: a supreme gentleman! Effortless – that's the key factor.]

This is the charm of *Absichtslosigkeit* (aimlessness). Its redundancy is the secret of its social role – and also of its questionableness. One finds oneself asking whether the aristocratic way of life is all style and surface, or whether it truly (whatever that might mean) stands for something.(Precisely this dialectic informs Evelyn Waugh's *Brideshead Revisited* and Kazuo Ishiguro's *The Remains of the Day* – and it is worth noting that both highly successful film versions of these novels engage fully with the interpretative dilemmas posed by the aesthetics of aristocracy.) It is part of the complex rhetoric of *Der Schwierige* that it acknowledges the questionableness of Hans Karl's aristo-cratic aimlessness while, at the same time, investing it with a complex of values – moral, erotic, existential and historical-cultural.

I want to begin with the moral issue, which is manifestly linked to the central linguistic theme on which countless commentators have reflected.[6] Let me briefly review the terrain once again in the context of that dialectical illumination implicit in the following remark from Hans Karl:

Durchs Reden kommt ja alles auf der Welt zustande. Allerdings, es ist ein bißl lächerlich, wenn man sich einbildet, durch wohlgesetzte Wörter eine weiß Gott wie große Wirkung auszuüben, in einem Leben, wo doch schließlich alles auf das Letzte, Unaussprechliche ankommt. Das Reden basiert auf einer indezenten Selbstüberschätzung. (73)

[It is by speaking that everything in this world comes about. Admittedly, it is a shade ridiculous if anyone imagines that they can achieve some immense effect by a few well-chosen words – whereas, in this life, everything depends on the ultimate, unsayable things. Speaking rests on an indecently inflated sense of one's own importance.]

Hans Karl recognises here the humanly creative potential of language – and its sheer *dirigiste* indecency. We recall the remark from the end of the play that I have already quoted, in which Hans Karl reacts with horror and incredulity at the prospect of having to make a speech on 'Völkerversöhnung'. Once again, in that context, he invokes the notion of the indecency of words. The theme sounds constantly throughout the play – not least because those figures in the play who speak easily and confidently are shown to be guilty of manipulative crudity and unreflectivity in respect of the otherness of their fellow human beings. The linguistic issue interlocks with the moral one: those who are unaware of the indecency of language are guilty of self-aggrandisement, because they believe that they have the right to impose their voices on the world.[7] Hence, Hans Karl's silences are not just an absence of utterance, a lack. Rather, they have to do with an ethos of moral reticence and scrupulousness. At one level, the play confirms this strand of language scepticism, for it highlights the confusions and misunderstandings that can occur when human otherness disrupts the attempt at communication (the implications of this issue extend from Hans Karl's desperately scrambled telephone conversation with Ado Hechingen, via the cross-purposes and mistaken identities at the party, to the human pain of the conversation with Agathe). Yet – and here the linguistic and ethical dialectic run in parallel – the play also insists that language is the supreme medium of relatedness and communion between people. In the process, language is shown to function at a number of levels. It is at its most complex in the scenes between Hans Karl and Antoinette and between Hans Karl and Helene, or when Hans Karl speaks of Furlani, or of his trench experience. At such moments one registers an interplay of metaphorical and literal statement, of conceptual and concrete registers. But there are also moments of piercing simplicity. One thinks of Hans Karl's responses in the scene with Stani (Act I, scene x) where the discussion turns to Ado Hechingen – 'Sein Schicksal geht mir nah' ['His fate touches me deeply'], 'Ich habe ihn gern' ['I like him'], 'Aber ein innerlich vornehmer Mensch' ['But an inwardly distinguished person'], 'Er braucht eine Flasche Champagner ins Blut' ['He could do with a bottle of champagne inside him'], 'Ich hab ihn gern' ['I like him'], 'Aber er ist ein so guter, vortrefflicher Mensch' ['But he is such a good, excellent person'], 'Es nützt nichts, ich hab ihn gern' ['It's no good, I like him'] (30). It is perfectly clear that Hans Karl means everything that he says here – just as he means his rejoinder to Stani in the following exchange:

> STANI. Er nimmt alles wörtlich, auch deine Freundschaft für ihn.
> HANS KARL. Aber er darf sie wörtlich nehmen. (30)
>
> [STANI. He takes everything literally – even your friendship for him.
> HANS KARL. But he is entitled to take it literally.]

Or one could think of the radiant immediacy of Helene's declaration of love: 'ich bin in dich verliebt, und ich will...von deinem Leben, von deiner Seele, von allem – meinen Teil' ['I am in love with you, and I want my share of your life, your soul, of everything'] (98–99). Such moments all have to do with language as a moral agency, one that acknowledges, but also builds bridges to, the alterity of other people. Hence Hans Karl's centrality to the moral universe of the play; his combination of kindliness and aloofness, his mistrust of 'Absichten' yet his preparedness to take on the 'Absichten' ['intentions'] of others make him representative of human relatedness. He is unfailingly generous about those who are awkward and clumsy – even about the ghastly Neuhoff ('Er will sehr freundlich sein, er will für sich gewinnen' ['He wants to be friendly, he wants people to like him'] (35)). What makes Hans Karl such a supreme mediator is the disinterested courtesy of the impeccably trained aristocrat, his ability to attend to the wishes and aspirations of others, to be at all times, and with all sorts and conditions of men and women, the tactful and attentive interlocutor.

Something of the same ethos informs Hans Karl's relationship with women, and generates the problem to which Yates draws our attention – namely that a barely reformed philanderer would seem to be endowed with a representative status far in excess of his moral deserts. In the context of erotic relationships, Hans Karl's reputation as supreme mediator gives rise to a multiplicity of problems. The chief difficulty arises with respect to traditional notions of the centrality and sanctity of marriage. Hans Karl's goodwill and friendliness can easily transform themselves (and be transformed by the perception of others) into the endless dalliance of the confirmed bachelor. Another has to do with the dialectic of aristocratic semblance to which I have already drawn attention. Hans Karl's courtesy and readiness to respect the plans and intentions of others can, at one level, entail no more than the skills of the proverbial 'good listener'. But the good listener can find himself or herself invested with a greater degree of emotional attachment than is welcome or justified. Suddenly the patient interlocutor is (or is held to be) involved. The well-turned phrase, the tactful negotiation can produce consequences other than those intended. One thinks, for example, of the moment when Hans Karl returns Antoinette's letters to her maid Agathe with the following words:

> Sagen Sie der Frau Gräfin, daß ich mich von diesen Briefen darum trennen kann, weil die Erinnerung an das Schöne für mich unzerstörbar ist; ich werde sie nicht in einem Brief finden, sondern überall. (38)

[Tell the countess that I can part with these letters only because the memory of beauty is for me indestructible; and I will find it not in letters, but everywhere].

The aristocrat's ability to find assuaging and beautiful words may be a prized skill; but it makes him less knowable as an individual than his fellow men and women, who lack his social and linguistic endowment. We would do well in this context to recall Stani's epithet of adulation for his uncle – 'mühelos' ['effortless']. That 'mühelos' quality inherent in the aristocrat's capacity for self-representation may help less articulate humanity to find expression for its feelings; but the aesthetic gain may entail a corresponding human loss. Once again, in the erotic sphere no less than in the political one, style may be bought at the cost of substance, representation at the cost of human authenticity. Antoinette is not far from the truth when she says:

> Ja, das ist dein Kunststück, damit hast du mich herumgekriegt, daß du kein Verführer bist, kein Mann für Frauen, daß du nur ein Freund bist, aber ein wirklicher Freund. Damit kokettierst du, so wie du mit allem kokettierst was du hast, und mit allem, was dir fehlt. (65)

> [Yes that is your great trick, that is how you won me round – because you are not a seducer, not a ladies' man, but rather a true friend. You flirt with that, as you flirt with everything you have – and with everything you lack.]

Antoinette is not exactly a dispassionate witness here; but she is a witness nonetheless, and we sense that she speaks much that is true.

All these remarks bring me to the issue of Hans Karl's existential importance (or lack of it). And here, clearly, his experience of the war is of overriding significance. At one level, what is entailed is fear and comradeship, is a sensitisation to pain, to the hurt in the self and in others. As Hans Karl says to his sister Crescence, 'das macht einen ja nicht weniger empfindlich, sondern mehr' ['it makes you not less sensitive but more'] (11). At the heart of Hans Karl's time 'draußen' is the terror and the epiphany of the moments spent buried when a trench collapses on him. As he makes clear to both Antoinette and to Helene, the upshot is a heightened sense of the value of personal relationships – above all of marriage as the paradigm for commitment and permanence. Although he believes that this is a 'Glück, [...] das ich mir verscherzt habe' ['happiness that I have thrown away'] (77) the insight remains generally and existentially valid. In this sense, the aristocrat's courtesy, his disinterested availability to all comers, have been deepened by a sense of existential priority. The mastery of modes of social intercourse is now something ontologically underwritten. In this context, surface and depth, manner and substance, triviality and profundity interlock. The man who came close to death in the trenches does, after all, go to the Altenwyl party. And he does so in spite of, and because of, the conversations that will inevitably occur there. As the final two acts of the play show us, conversations can be trivial and profound. But in any event, as long as they are conversations and not monologues, they provide some measure of assurance to the participants that they are not alone in the world. Poldo Altenwyl regrets that the 'Direktheit' (51) of the modern world has inevitably taken its toll of a culture in which conversing had everything to do with making the world a slightly more habitable place, with making individual human beings members of a slightly more caring community:

> In meinen Augen ist Konversation das, was jetzt kein Mensch mehr kennt: nicht selbst perorieren, wie ein Wasserfall, sondern dem andern das Stichwort bringen. Zu meiner Zeit hat man gesagt: wer zu mir kommt, mit dem muß ich die Konversation so führen, daß er, wenn er die Türschnallen in der Hand hat, sich gescheit vorkommt, dann wird er auf der Stiegen mich gescheit finden. (48)

> [In my eyes conversation is something that nobody knows about any more: not talking endlessly about oneself like a waterfall, but giving a cue to the other person. In my time it was said – whoever comes to me should find himself having the kind of conversation after which, when he is about to leave, he regards himself as clever – and then, when he is on the stairs, he will find me clever.]

To the moral and existential ramifications of this modest image of human togetherness *Der Schwierige* bears moving witness; and it does so chiefly by persuading us that Hans Karl is to be seen as representative of the human need and capacity for connectedness.

Poldo Altenwyl's denunciation of the modern world as a place bereft of conversation brings me to a further strand of the play's rhetoric of representativeness that I wish to consider: its historical–cum–cultural agenda. The play manifestly is a valedictory tribute to the 'Vielvölkerstaat' of Old Austria, and contributes powerfully to that 'Habsburg myth',[8] which invests the paralysis and decline of the last century or so of the Danube monarchy with a rhetoric of meta-national nobility. In a sense, the ethos of muddling through, of indirection and reticence, is at the heart of Hofmannsthal's play – and it is his tribute to what he perceived as the political legacy of Old Austria, the (Hans-Karl-like) aimlessness of which may be construed as a politically tolerant mentality. In any event, the new world that is poised to take over is a very different place – one that is awash with fervently sought aims and goals, with quests for spiritual profundity that leave the obsolete culture high and dry, marooned in the willed superficiality of its delicate reticence and irrelevance.[9] Clearly, the chief spokesman for the new age is Neuhoff, a man of strenuous will and purpose, contemptuous of, yet also helplessly in love with, the density of the outmoded (Austrian) culture. For him, people are not people; they tend to be 'Wesen' ['beings']. And the new culture is not confined to this fairly traditional (Austrian) caricature of the North German. It can also be heard in Neugebauer, the secretary whose emotional and professional life is sustained by a prickly rectitude; even his recent engagement is sustained by ideological commitments that Hans Karl seeks to undercut with the radiantly

Martin Swales

understated remark – 'Ich habe gemeint, wenn man heiratet, so freut man sich darauf' ['I thought that when people got married, they looked forward to it'] (23). The secretary's name, Neugebauer, aligns him with the new (the allegorical force of the contrast of *Neu*hoff with *Alt*enwyl is obvious). The new seems poised, then, to infiltrate Hans Karl's world; Vinzenz, the servant, is in love with 'Absichten' – particularly his own. Stani, like Crescence, adores 'den Entschluß, die Kraft, das Definitive' ['decision, strength, decisiveness'] (10), and has a baleful tendency to put people into categories. Even the hapless Edine is in quest of a culture transfigured by redemptively higher things. Hofmannsthal's matchless text, by contrast, cherishes lower things – the modest propitiations and conciliations of the comic tradition. Even the perfect aristocrat speaks the humble prose of comedy.[10] Beyond and behind his allegorical function as the spirit of a historically obsolescent culture, Hans Karl, by virtue of the indirection of his way of life, seems representative of simple, often comic and, by that token, unideological humanity and tolerance.

Der Schwierige, as part of its intertextual sophistication, abundantly evokes and acknowledges the Austrian comic tradition; and this is the final level of representation I wish to consider. Critical literature concerned with European comedy often distinguishes between the punitive (Molièresque) mode and the regenerative mode (of, for example, the late Shakespeare romances). Hofmannsthal was very much aware of these two strands – also in their Austrian incarnation (the redemptiveness of Raimund, on the one hand, and the punitive ferocity of Nestroy on the other). Perhaps it is not too fanciful to claim the co-presence of both traditions in his masterpiece in the comic form; *Der Schwierige* acknowledges the redemptive possibility in Hans Karl's trench experience, yet it also has the sheer pace of socially engineered comedy in the dizzying coming and going of characters that is worthy of Nestroy at his most creatively acerbic. The erstwhile philanderer and aristocratic ditherer need 'only connect', and thereby the play connects with, and represents, the conciliations of a rich comic tradition.[11] In the process, that tradition is validated, modified and transfigured.

Notes

References throughout are to Hugo von Hofmannsthal, *Der Schwierige, Der Unbestechliche: zwei Lustspiele* (Fischer Taschenbuch Verlag, Frankfurt, 1984).

1. W. E. Yates, *Schnitzler, Hofmannsthal, and the Austrian Theatre* (New Haven and London, 1992) p. 198.
2. On the configuration of characters see Benno Rech, *Hofmannsthals Komödien* (Bonn, 1971).
3. See Martin Stern, 'Die Entstehung von Hofmannsthals anachronistischem Gegenwartslustspiel *Der Schwierige*' in Joseph P. Strelka (ed.), *'Wir sind aus solchem Zeug wie das zu träumen'*: *Kritische Beiträge zu Hofmannsthals Werk* (Berne, 1992), pp. 257–81; and Stern, 'Wann entstand und spielt *Der Schwierige*?' in Karl Pestalozzi and Martin Stern (eds), *Basel Hofmannsthal-Beiträge* (Würzburg, 1991), pp. 203–15.
4. Jürgen Habermas, *Strukturwandel der Öffentlichkeit* (Neuwied and Berlin, 1962), pp. 25–28.

5. See Erwin Kobel, *Hugo von Hofmannsthal* (Berlin, 1970), pp. 295–313.
6. See Gerhard Austin, *Phänomenologie der Gebärde bei Hugo von Hofmannsthal* (Heidelberg, 1981), pp. 228–37; Donald G. Daviau, 'Hofmannsthal's language – a positive view', in Strelka (ed.), *Kritische Beiträge*, pp. 285–304; Glenn A. Guidry, *Language, morality, and society: an ethical model of communication in Fontane and Hofmannsthal* (Berkeley, Los Angeles, and London, 1989); Jürgen Schwalbe, *Sprache und Gebärde im Werk Hugo von Hofmannsthals* (Freiburg im Breisgau, 1971), pp. 129–63; Heike Söhnlein, *Gesellschaftliche und private Interaktionen: Dialoganalysen zu Hofmannsthals 'Der Schwierige' und Schnitzlers 'Das weite Land'* (Tübingen, 1986); Lothar Wittmann, *Sprachthematik und dramatische Form im Werk Hofmannsthals* (Stuttgart, 1966), pp. 137–70.
7. See Wilhelm Emrich, 'Hofmannsthals Lustspiel *Der Schwierige*' in Sibylle Bauer (ed.), *Hugo von Hofmannsthal* (Wege der Forschung) (Darmstadt, 1968), pp. 434–47.
8. Claudio Magris, *Der habsburgische Mythos in der österreichischen Literatur* (Salzburg, 1966).
9. See Gerhart Pickerodt, *Hofmannsthals Dramen: Kritik ihres historischen Gehalts* (Stuttgart, 1968), pp. 213–32.
10. See J. B. Bednall, 'From high language to dialect: a study in Hofmannsthal's change of medium', in F. Norman (ed.), *Hofmannsthal: Studies in Commemoration* (London, 1963), pp. 83-117.
11. See Jean Wilson, *The Challenge of Belatedness: Goethe, Kleist, Hofmannsthal* (Lanham, New York, and London, 1991), especially p. 206.

'Stop all the Clocks': Time and Times in the 'Vienna Operas' of Hofmannsthal and Strauss

Robert Vilain

Towards the end of Act I of *Der Rosenkavalier* the Marschallin sings of time flowing past as an almost tangible presence, like the sand in an hour-glass, and of how she sometimes gets up at night to stop all the clocks. At its high point Strauss accompanies Hofmannsthal's text with ethereal chimes on the celeste and harps playing harmonics to produce a magical aria of great lyric intensity. If Hofmannsthal had had his way, however, 'Die Zeit, die ist ein sonderbar Ding'[1] ['Time – what a curious thing it is'] would have been cut, as 'a passage that is poetically quite pretty but not indispensable'.[2] The aria's theme saturates the whole work, and arguably its omission would not have robbed the argument of the opera of more than a reiteration of some of its main deliberations. Written nearly twenty years later, another comedy set in Vienna, conceived explicitly as a second *Rosenkavalier*, *Arabella* is less obviously permeated by reflections on time, but Hofmannsthal's near-obsession with the theme has hardly cooled. In both works reference is made to time at nearly all the crucial structural points, and a defining characteristic of all the main characters is their attitude to time. Almost all of them dream of 'stopping the clocks' in one way or another, and, in his choice and combination of historical settings, Hofmannsthal, too, can be said to be dreaming of suspending time. This essay will attempt to justify these contentions, to account for Hofmannsthal's lasting preoccupation with the theme, and to relate it to the dramatic, specifically comic, genre of the two works.

The opening words of *Der Rosenkavalier* record Octavian's consciousness of time and his attempt to ignore it. His 'Wie du warst! Wie du bist!' ['How you were! How you are!'] (XXIII, 9) subtly anticipates the Marschallin's later reflections on time and identity, suggesting that the 'real' Marschallin revealed in their love-making remains just the same now that it is over: the past tense of 'wie du *warst*' establishes an invalid temporal boundary corrected by the universalising present tense. By juxtaposing past and present tenses to make this point, Octavian effectively seeks to annihilate the difference between them. He is equally resentful of the obstinately persisting difference between *du* and *ich*, wishing for the fusion of lover and beloved (an ironic echo of Wagner's Tristan and Isolde questioning the 'and' between their names, underlined by hints of the chromatic *Tristan* theme in the music). His passion, however, has already been parodied by the consciously excessive whoops and sighs of Strauss's orchestral introduction, so his railing against the irruption of 'public' daytime (another echo of *Tristan*) is robbed of all philosophical significance.

The Marschallin is tolerant and tender, but puts an end to Octavian's posturing; her gentle put-down – 'Don't philosophise, Darling Sir, it's time for breakfast. There is a proper time for everything' (11) – is almost maternal, and Octavian sits with his head on her knee to have his hair stroked as a child might. The arrival of Ochs shatters the peace of the Marschallin's temporally ordered world, because he is as insouciant of time as Octavian was intolerant, casually asking 'what does the early hour matter among persons of rank?' (16). Socially he is what Octavian is psychologically – spontaneous, unselfconscious to the point of selfishness, amiably irresponsible – and both are attempting to preserve what, in the terms of *Ad me ipsum*, would be called a pre–existential state of being, Octavian like a child, and Ochs like an animal.[3] Ochs imagines himself as the god Jupiter 'in a thousand forms, with a use for them all' (24) and his very name reminds one of the bull that pursued Io.[4] Jupiter's self-seeking metamorphoses betoken an identity without boundaries, and Ochs's capacity for adaptation in the course of an endless series of conquests has the same existential flexibility presupposed by the self-forgetting that Octavian prizes.

The Marschallin is irritated by Ochs's insensitivity because she is so aware of the resemblance between herself and Sophie von Faninal, both married 'fresh from the convent' (18 and 36). Marie-Thérèse is not old – Strauss suggested no older than thirty-two, so hardly even middle-aged[5] – but she is old enough to be conscious of ageing. Her probing of the mystery of how time and identity interact echoes Hofmannsthal's *Terzinen* 'Über Vergänglichkeit' [On Transience] where he asked 'Wie kann das sein, daß diese nahen Tage / Fort sind, für immer fort, und ganz vergangen?' ['how can it be that days so near are gone, gone for ever, completely past?'].[6] Quoting Villon's 'Ballade des dames du temps jadis', the Marschallin registers the same sense that the passage of time makes one's experience irrecoverable, but is not satisfied. She also asks the opposite question, about how an identity can persist *despite* time: 'Wie kann das wirklich sein, / Daß ich die kleine Resi war / und daß ich auch einmal die alte Frau sein werd!' ['How can it really be that I was once little Resi, and that I shall be an old woman some day?'] (36). It is how one copes with the pain of passing time that is the measure of that identity, and, temporarily, the Marschallin's poise is shaken. These questions are a magnification of Octavian's worries, and it is significant that they occur after the Marschallin has had to show her public face at the levée. Like Octavian, she investigates the relationship between herself and another: linguistically she may formulate this other as the third person ('little Resi' and 'the old woman'), but the fact that she is looking in the mirror as she sings makes it clear that the *ich-du* problem has been retained and internalised.

When Octavian returns he cannot fully understand her new mood, and suggests she has been exchanged for someone else (38), unwittingly pin-pointing the reason for the Marschallin's sadness. As she tries to explain how time unsettles her, that she feels the world slipping through her fingers, her metaphors are prompted by Octavian's insistence on embrace and physical possession ('I want to hold you and squeeze you') (38). By reasserting the oppositional status of 'I' and 'you' Octavian betrays the loss of his earlier vision of Romantic unity. He tries to counter her worries by saying that, far from slipping through her fingers, he is bound to her, his fingers intertwined with hers. The fact that dialogue fails to establish communication here prepares the ground for Octavian's emotionally more binding lyric bond with Sophie in Acts II and III.

The Marschallin is so preoccupied with the strength of passing time that she uses it to drive Octavian away despite herself. Sometime, 'heut' oder morgen oder den übernächsten Tag' ['today, or tomorrow, or the next day'] (39), he will find someone else. 'The day will come without being called', for 'everything in the world has its time and its rules' (39). The Marschallin understands how time and social existence are interdependent; only in the asocial, lyric world, or in the extra-social world of the bedroom at night, is time suspended. But Octavian resists this insight, angrily defying time to interfere.[7] Marie-Thérèse reflects sadly that she is consoling her lover for the fact that 'sooner or later' *he* will leave *her*, but Octavian winces at the repeated temporal phrase 'über kurz oder lang', and she is forced to explain again. This is the famous reflection on the flowing of time conceived as a compound of air, dust and water, within which she and Octavian have to live, and which not only links them but *separates* them as if it had spatial properties, too.

In the libretto, this set piece is placed as a lyric interlude between two of Octavian's tantrums, and before the angry outburst referred to above, which enhances the link to the opening of Act II. In invoking the day of Sophie von Faninal's betrothal, the time references are insistent, showing how inevitable it was that Octavian's dreaded day would dawn sooner or later: 'A solemn day, a great day, a day of honour, a holy day' (43). Octavian's encounter with Sophie revolves around the contrast of the earthly and the heavenly, the real and the symbolic, the temporal and the timeless. As Sophie takes the rose, she declares herself 'deeply obliged for all eternity' (46), feeling herself lifted from the worldly excitement of marriage preparations to the level of a bond in perpetuity. The rose mediates between the two levels, its scent being 'like living roses' *and* 'like heavenly, not earthly roses', roses from paradise (46). It pulls her onwards towards heaven and also reminds her of a place where she once felt 'so selig' ['blissfully happy'], and which she now feels compelled to seek out again even at the cost of her earthly life. Octavian is similarly lifted beyond the temporal, and in a manner reminiscent of his opening scene with the Marschallin, for his imagined memory is of a time neither 'yesterday' nor 'an eternity ago', but when he was a child. Temporal suspension is accompa-nied by an evocation of bewildered lyric self-sufficiency, because this blissful state was one where Octavian was not aware of being differentiated from the object of his love: ·

Da hab' ich *die* noch nicht gekannt.
Die hab' ich nicht gekannt?
Wer ist denn *die*?
Wie kommt sie denn zu mir?
Wer bin denn ich? Wie komm' ich denn zu ihr? (46)

[I did not know *her* there. I did not know *her*. But who is *she*? And how did she reach me? Who am I? How did I reach her?]

Octavian again uses the language of grasping and possessing (46), this time of his own senses in an effort to preserve the epiphanic insight he has been granted. His final words in the duet are 'das ist ein seliger, seliger Augenblick, / den will ich nie vergessen bis an meinen Tod' ['this is a blissful, blissful moment, and I will never forget it until I die'] (47). In the full text that Hofmannsthal sent to Strauss on 26 June 1909, Sophie sings almost the same words, preceded by a phrase that Hofmannsthal was later to use in modified form in *Arabella*, 'ist Zeit und Ewigkeit in einem seligen Augenblick' ['I can feel time and eternity both at once in a single blissful moment'].[8] The baroque formality of the silver rose ritual encapsulates this blend of time and eternity. The ritual has a local social function (emphasising the dignity of the union and the social standing of the husband), yet there is also a spiritual dimension, because the timeless symbol of love is not presented by the husband-to-be in person and the marriage offer is thus purified of the sensuality with which the opera began. The mystical fusion of time and eternity here differentiates such a love from the escapist passion with which the opera began.

The events in the inn in Act III represent a different kind of timelessness, a carnival *Walpurgisnacht* in which identities and status are exchanged, and where the plans of the day are overturned. The confusion is resolved only when the Marschallin intervenes and imposes the rule of time and its allies, social order and decorum, insisting that the whole affair is 'mit dieser Stund' vorbei' ['with this hour over and done with'] (94) – sung no fewer than four times, before being echoed twice more as 'is' halt vorbei'. The Marschallin laughs angrily at Octavian as she has to tell him to go to Sophie (96). Yet she has to wipe a tear from her eye as she quotes the words of her own prediction, 'today, tomorrow or the next day' (97), and when she observes Octavian still hesitating between them this modulates to 'a sad smile' (98). Her sadness derives not so much from losing Octavian as yet again from her consciousness of passing time for, despite her mental preparations, she confesses that she had not imagined having to cope with losing him so soon (98). By the time she talks to Octavian, her expression is described simply as 'indefinable' (99); she is composed again, remarking defensively that Octavian will be only as happy with Sophie as the limited male understanding of happiness permits (99).[9] The negative component of the Marschallin's gesture of renunciation – sensed instinctively by Sophie (100) – is often understated. Yet her mixed motivation is no more than an acknowledgement of what she has already told us, namely that the passage of time is painful, however sovereign the manner in which we manage in public.

The lovers look forward to 'alle Zeit und Ewigkeit' ['all time and eternity'] – the words with which the comedy ends[10] – and back to that place of bliss 'remembered' at their first meeting. Hofmannsthal is aware here, as he was to be in *Arabella*, that this is an unstable compound: both of them sing of their feelings as dream-like in their penultimate lines, 'everything is passing by as if it were a dream' and 'it must be a dream, it cannot be real' (101). Just as one is torn between admiring the Marschallin's maturity and simultaneously regretting that she has lost forever the uncomplicated freshness that constitutes a capacity for this kind of love, one admires the young lovers' lyric intensity while registering some doubts about its ultimate durability. But Hofmannsthal does not raise the issue of their future – which is an extraordinary way to end an opera whose most noble character is so acutely conscious of how exaltation must cede to time and of the need to prepare oneself. It is as if the temporal irrelevance characteristic of a lyric poem is reasserting itself after the characters have been put through the mill of the drama's concerns with progression. It does so, moreover, within the context of a stock comedy closure, the eventual marriage of the lovers. Strauss's simple melody for the final duet is reminiscent of Pamina's duet with Papageno towards the end of Act I of *The Magic Flute*, 'Könnte jeder brave Mann / Solche Glöckchen finden' ['If only every good man could find such bells'],[11] and the lurch back to the eighteenth century after the contemporary tonalities of the trio makes a similar gesture of retraction.

Arabella is set on *Faschingsdienstag* (Shrove Tuesday), the last day of disorder before the regulated period of Lent.[12] As a symbolic border between two states of existence, it is analogous to many other such days in Hofmannsthal's works, but by choosing, exceptionally in *Arabella*, a day with a wider cultural significance, Hofmannsthal allows its religious overtones to resonate within the opera, overtones of a change in mode of life and focus of thought, from self-indulgent and worldly to reflective and other-worldly.

In their various ways, all the members of the Waldner family in *Arabella* are trying to resist time. They perpetually defer the reality of having to pay their creditors; Countess Adelaide ignores the present and is devoured by impatience to know what the cards prophesy for the future (XXVI, 7–8); Waldner's perpetual gambling is another symptom of the inability to face the here-and-now: 'they're sitting down and starting to play again', he tells himself, and 'everything else is a waste of time' (25). Waldner has a capacity to live purely in the future when present difficulties will surely have been resolved, and Adelaide's ludicrous day-dream about her daughter marrying into the Imperial family (24) is another symptom of the same malaise; both are always a step ahead in imagination, always a step behind in matters of brute financial fact.

Zdenka is a victim of her parents' desperate attempts to dodge time, vowing to sacrifice herself and to dress up in men's clothes forever if it will put off the day when they are forced to move away and leave Matteo (11). She reflects on what might happen if her plan to convince Arabella does not come off, and her conclusion is as impractical as her father's usually are, and couched in the same language: 'wenn's mir nicht gelingt – hab ich verspielt' ['if I don't succeed – well, I have played my cards wrong'] (13). The masquerade of Zdenka's disguise is contingent upon the atmosphere of misrule and disordered roles that characterises her family's lifestyle and Fasching. In the original version of Act I her character is quite different and she demands her true identity back by invoking time: 'Carnival is over now! Mama, I insist on being allowed to be what God made me – and that this play-acting stop' (79). In the final version Zdenka is determined *not* to resume her female identity, and her attitude is imbued with her parents' habit of postponing the day of reckoning.

When Arabella uses the gaming metaphor, it is deflected on to someone else. Matteo is not 'der Richtige' ['the right man'] (15) for her: 'Wer das nicht ist, der hat bei mir verspielt!' ['Anyone who is not the right man has played his cards wrong with me'] (15).[13] She is the only one who thinks that it is high time for Zdenka to become a girl again (15). Yet her attitude to time is not unproblematic: her dilemma consists in the clash between a powerful sense that time is irrelevant in her true choice of husband and an equally strong sense that time is running out. On the one hand, if there is a true husband for her at all, she is convinced he will appear suddenly and she will be transformed, 'der wird auf einmal dastehn, [...] und selig werd ich sein und ihm gehorsam wie ein Kind' ['he will suddenly be there in front of me, [...] and I will be blissfully happy, and as obedient to him as a child'] (16). She imagines an epiphanic moment of perfect mutual recognition, borrowing her memory of childhood to project a state similarly characterised by unself-consciousness (reversing the vision in *Der Rosenkavalier*, where the lovers project a childhood state of bliss from their present experience). On the other hand, however, Arabella accepts that today is her last chance to decide on a husband and break the trend of her family's decline: 'Carnival comes to an end this evening. This evening I must make up my mind' (17, repeated 20).

Arabella's defiant rejoinder to Count Elemer's aggressively proprietary behaviour, however, makes it clear that she intends to keep control of her future as far as she can: 'I am going to taste to the full the only bitter-sweet advantage that a girl has: to be hidden and floating, not giving herself to anyone entirely! and prevaricating still' (19). Zdenka ruefully comments that it is for men to choose, for women to wait until they are chosen, which is precisely what Arabella resists.[14] She remembers it in her monologue at the end of Act I, a reflection, not unlike the Marschallin's at a similar point in *Der Rosenkavalier*, on her relationship to her surroundings, on her identity as an individual, and on the sources of her feelings and instincts. When, like the Marschallin, she registers a sense of strangeness, 'Mein Elemer! – Das hat so einen sonderbaren Klang' ['My Elemer! – That sounds so curious'] (33), what puzzles her is the word 'mein'; she ponders the implications of the personal pronouns and possessives, 'Er mein – ich sein' ['He mine – I his'), in an echo of Octavian's philosophising with its Wagnerian subtext. She has no problems with the use of the possessive 'mein' for the stranger, however, and he is fascinating because no such relationship of mere personalities exists between them. Arabella has no power to bring about an encounter with him, which she first associates with Zdenka's point about society's refusal to allow women self-determination. But this also characterises her dream of 'der Richtige' (the motif associated with which is strongly present again in the music accompanying her wish to see the stranger), who appears 'auf einmal' ['suddenly']. This apparently innocuous temporal phrase is modulated effectively in Arabella's wish to see the stranger 'noch einmal' ['once more'] and hear his voice 'einmal' ['just once'], all of which amounts to an attempt to isolate the imagined moment from the context of time. The shadow of eternity then falls across her emotions, for she feels 'as if [she] were walking over someone's grave' (33), a shadow with which she associates the stranger once more, and a prefiguration of her promise to Mandryka in Act II, 'I want to be buried alongside you in your grave' (38).

In contrast, Mandryka is comfortable with time in all its aspects. Continuity has endowed him with his lands and fortune and will do the same for his children and grandchildren; his characterisation of these lands and their inhabitants has an air of timelessness underscored by Strauss's use of traditional folk-song motifs in the Mandryka music. He is just as comfortable with chance, taking in his stride the significance of how his encounter with the bear coincided with the arrival of Arabella's portrait. Nor does change upset him, and he is able to regard the conversion of ancient woodlands into a wad of cash without the goggle-eyed amazement that seizes Waldner. This relaxed relationship with time is disturbed only by the periodic discomfort that results from the contrast of his world with that of the Waldners. The peace of the world he has left to come to Vienna is associated with a difference in pace that occasionally makes him feel awkward, disturbing the smoothness of what is essentially a lyrical existence.[15]

When Mandryka and Arabella regard each other properly for the first time at the ball, they both use the image of a flowing river. Arabella repeats part of the Act I duet with Zdenka in which she evoked the imagined encounter with her true partner ('he will suddenly be there'), adding that 'everything will be bright and open, like a pale river on which the sun is sparkling' (37); for Mandryka it is as if she has been brought into his world by the bright, gently flowing Danube. The superimposition of a strong image of progression on an imagined moment that is specifically hoisted *out* of the normal progression of time is a prefiguration of the combination of time and eternity that they are about to evoke and with which Arabella's last aria will end. Mandryka tells Arabella about a local betrothal custom from his lands which, in its new context, is laden with temporal and spatial symbolism:

> heute abend noch, vor Schlafenszeit –
> wärst du ein Mädchen aus der Dörfer einem meinigen,
> du müßtest mir zum Brunnen gehen hinter deines Vaters Haus
> und klares Wasser schöpfen einen Becher voll
> und mir ihn reichen vor der Schwelle, daß ich dein
>   Verlobter bin vor Gott
> und vor den Menschen, meine Allerschönste! (38)

[this very evening, before going to sleep – if you were a girl from one of my villages, you would have to go to the well behind your father's house for me and draw a glass of water, and hand it to me before the threshold, to show before God and man that I am your betrothed, fairest lady.]

The binding of the lovers into marriage begins at the close of the day, symbolising the end of Arabella's girlhood, underpinning the symbolism of the end of Fasching and the start of Lent. The glass of water is handed over at the threshold of the house, also marking the threshold into the new stage of life. Syntactically, semantically and musically, Mandryka's words flow towards closure and unity, the complexity of the long sentence culminating in the bond of the betrothed and the partnership of humankind and God, rounded off by an apostrophe to Arabella's beauty; the musical motifs that are associated with Arabella and Mandryka combine and move together towards E major, the 'love key' of the opera.

Mandryka and Arabella evoke a traditionally ordered world in a further series of spatial and temporal metaphors. Mandryka sees a partnership of man and wife ruling equally, subject only to the Emperor; yet he says he can live like this only 'wenn ich etwas Herrliches / erhöhe über mich' – if he elevates something marvellous above him (38). But 'herrlich' literally means 'masterful', and Mandryka paradoxically implies that he must elevate what is of its nature already superior. The equality of master and mistress that he then evokes is immediately contradicted by Arabella, who chooses to subjugate herself to her husband in the duet 'Und du wirst mein Gebieter sein und ich dir untertan' ['And you will be my lord and I will be in thrall to you'] (38). Furthermore, she has made her declaration of love only after being chosen by Mandryka, which apparently contradicts her reluctance to accept the social restriction articulated by Zdenka in Act I. The contradiction is resolved, however, when the appropriate temporal perspective is applied. Arabella's reluctance was felt within the oppressive context of time running out; her self-abasement before Mandryka takes place when her dream of a timeless encounter with the right man has been realised, when her identity is securely established *vis-à-vis* his, and she is free from the temporal and concomitant social pressures that make resistance to convention a necessary part of self-determination. She attempts to fuse time and the timeless as she promises herself to him 'auf Zeit und Ewigkeit' ['for time and eternity'], but the compound is unstable. Her almost peremptory instruction immediately after this – 'jetzt fahren Sie nachhaus' ['go home now'] – reminds him that the time component has a starting point, and that it cannot begin until she has properly said farewell to girlhood.

In fact, Mandryka stays: time for him is a flowing continuum, and he cannot easily come to terms with the way that, in Arabella's 'girlhood' conception, it still has the character of a sequence of different, demarcated stages. This is why her farewells are so certain and firm. Dominik is told that the waltz they have just danced was 'our last dance for all time' (43); she bids Elemer 'Adieu' ['farewell'] not 'Auf Wiedersehen' ['until we meet again'], and thanks him for 'many lovely moments' (44); Lamoral is given his first and last kiss, offered a final dance and the prospect of 'Nimmerwiedersehn' ['never meeting again'] (45). Her note to Mandryka also stresses closure heavily – 'for today I shall say good night. [...] From tomorrow I am yours' (50) – and leaves him with the impression that the last hour of Shrove Tuesday is to be used for something more concrete than synchronising their senses of time.

Zdenka's plan threatens to prolong the play-acting of Fasching, because Mandryka feels he has been made to take on a role in an 'ugly comedy' (58) and Arabella feels equally miscast, asking 'Wie reden Sie zu mir! Wer bin ich denn?' ['How dare you speak to me like that! Who do you think I am?'] (58). Mandryka's reply – 'Sie sind halt eben, die Sie sind' ['You are who you are'] – is a mirror of Octavian's plea to Sophie, 'Sie muß [...] bleiben, was Sie ist' (57). Sophie is urged to acquire self-possession, Arabella is accused of having too much of it.[16] But, as Mandryka and Arabella feel their identities threatened, Zdenka emerges as her real self, re-establishing order, and turning the hour of closure into the pivotal moment of continuation. The phrase 'was jetzt noch kommt' (like 'mit dieser Stund' vorbei' in *Der Rosenkavalier*) is passed around, from Zdenka to Mandryka, Waldner and Arabella, as an object clause, a subject clause, an exclamation and a question, to be sung seven times in all. Arabella forgives Mandryka by consigning the misunderstandings to the past and focusing on the future, and this is the context in which the modest ritual of the glass of water takes place. It, too, designates closure, symbolising 'den Abend, wo die freie Mädchenzeit zu Ende ist für mich' ['the evening when the freedom of girlhood comes to an end for me'] (69) and the end of her virginity, for the water she hands Mandryka is untouched and after drinking it Mandryka smashes the glass. But it also symbolises their bond 'für ewige Zeit' ['for eternal time'] (69), marking the lovers' accession to a purer, less worldly relationship with time, in which Arabella may, and must, preserve her identity despite her voluntary submission to Mandryka. Strauss was afraid that they would be accused of overdoing the Wagner echoes with yet another love potion,[17] but the open presentation of pure H_2O instead of the secret administration of a murky compound not only repudiates the complaint but confirms that, in marrying Arabella, Mandryka gets exactly what he sees. The opera ends with 'Ich kann nicht anders werden, nimm mich wie ich bin!' ['I cannot be otherwise, take me as I am'] (70).

In both operas the characters' various attitudes to the passing of time are anchored in clearly depicted historical settings, the specificity of which was extremely important to Hofmannsthal. He explained to Strauss that, just as the 'indestructible reality' of Wagner's *Mastersingers* derives from its revivification of 'a genuine, closed world that once actually existed', here 'it is Maria Theresia's Vienna – a whole real and therefore convincing city environment with a network of living interconnections [...] – that actually supports the whole, and it is through this whole that the figures come alive'.[18] Linguistically, Hofmannsthal did not claim to have imitated eighteenth-century

Viennese vocabulary and diction precisely but made what he called the 'imaginary language of the time' fictionally plausible, 'at once genuine and made-up', by creating a range of mutually consistent tones, registers, colourings and degrees of sophistication.[19] Further historical colour is applied for the most part without direct reference to historical events or the appearance on stage of real historical figures. Yet the names of all the characters in *Der Rosenkavalier* derive from eighteenth-century sources, including every one of Octavian's names that Sophie's bedtime reading of *Österreich's Ehrenspiegel* has so assiduously uncovered.[20] There is even a Freiherr von Faninal, the second husband of a widow first married – appropriately enough, in the light of Act III – to Freiherr von Chaos,[21] and one of the models for Ochs, Graf von Rosenberg-Orsini (a Freiherr von Lerchenau) has as his coat of arms a red rose on a silver background.[22]

Arabella was also conceived as the evocation of a particular period in Viennese history: first the 1840s but eventually the 1860s.[23] Hofmannsthal was pleased with the choice, partly because it was more original than the *Rosenkavalier* epoch (he described the 1860s as a period 'due for some attention'), and partly because it was such a good contrast, 'more ordinary, more natural, more vulgar'. He wanted a down-to-earth foil for Arabella's courage and independence of spirit, and, at the same time, something decadent and frivolous as a foil for Mandryka's world, 'the purity of his villages and of his oak forests untouched by the axe, [...] the sheer breadth of great, half-Slavic Austria'.[24]

Der Rosenkavalier and *Arabella* are both set at times of change and, in each, Hofmannsthal is intent on showing both 'Sein' and 'Werden'. *Der Rosenkavalier*'s clearest historical anchor is the Austrian Empress Maria Theresia, after whom the Marschallin is named. Hofmannsthal's 1917 essay on Maria Theresia identifies the fundamental tension that made her an ideal monarch and on which the resemblance between her and the Marschallin is based: ' "Great individuals," says Jakob Burckhardt, "are the coincidence of constancy and mobility within a single person." This dictum might have been coined for her.'[25] Similarly, in renouncing Octavian, the Marschallin gives and withholds something (XXIII, 100); she sanctions change and is herself not changed. Franz Tumler and Michael Hamburger see *Der Rosenkavalier* as depicting a specific historical change, namely the rise of the modern state and what Ochs dismisses as the 'Bagatelladeligen' [petty nobility] symbolised in the union of blue blood and *parvenue*.[26] This involves not only a shift in socio-economic conditions but a radical change of sensibility. When Sophie cries for help and protection from the uncouth Ochs, Octavian tells her she must stand fast for both their sakes, 'Für sich und mich muß Sie das tun, / sich wehren, sich retten, und bleiben, was Sie ist!' ['You must do this for yourself and for me, defend yourself, save yourself, remain what you are!'] (57).[27] The old aristocracy's stress on the defining qualities of rank is giving way to a distinctly modern demand for self-determination as an individual. Ochs, however, is so completely defined by his class that even the very personal tricks played on him in Act III do not elicit the personal response they intended; he is told by the Marschallin to give in gracefully and he retires more as a representative of his rank than as an individual. Hamburger comments, 'At the same time we know that a whole social class is being asked to retire decently, [...] it has come to the end of its predatory reign'.[28] This is perhaps overstated, for Hofmannsthal takes pains to distinguish this from the 'disintegration of a feudally structured society' presented in another of the most notable eighteenth-century influences on *Der Rosenkavalier*, Hogarth's *Marriage à la Mode*: 'Hogarth goes to extremes in depicting not only a prearranged match [...] but a cynical barter – the very desecration of marriage which Hofmannsthal shows us'.[29] Ochs does plan something akin to a barter, but it is less cynical than selfish and out-of-date. He is neither stupid nor wicked, merely greedy, self-obsessed and pompous, and, if Ochs does embody 'cryptically mythologized'[30] social comment in *Der Rosenkavalier*, the socio-critical thrust of Hogarth has been much tempered.

Tumler reads a similar historical allegory into *Arabella*, which he interprets as depicting Austria after 1866: Arabella is a 'daughter of Austria', Matteo her German (military) suitor, their potential liaison therefore the possibility of *Anschluß*; Mandryka is the symbol of the Eastern provinces and his union with Arabella becomes representative of *Ausgleich*.[31] Hofmannsthal may not have encrypted history so deliberately, but the contrasts contribute nonetheless to the historical verisimilitude on which he laid such weight, and which, like *Der Rosenkavalier*, derives from a collage of sources. Elements of the supposedly Croatian folk-songs that help to develop the atmosphere around Mandryka are taken from Bulgarian, Russian and Serbian sources as well as genuine Croatian songs, all subject to modification and extension by Hofmannsthal. The *Fiakerball* in Act II is a combination of two distinct periods, the opulent happy-go-lucky atmosphere of the 1860s, and the more restrained atmosphere after the stock-market crash of 1873. Hans-Albrecht Koch argues that setting the ball in *Arabella* on Shrove Tuesday, rather than during Lent itself, makes it characteristic of this later period; when Mandryka loses his cool, it turns into something more typical of the 1860s.[32] The latter epoch dominates the rest of the opera, however. *Lucidor*, the prose text out of which the opera developed, was set in the late 1870s, but the *Gründerjahre* provide a more fitting context for the Waldners' difficulties and the lifestyle out of which Arabella has to grow. The Waldner family represents a further stage in the social development whose inception was depicted in *Der Rosenkavalier*. The hotel in which the outside acts are set is a solid structure housing a collapsing class, and the glamour of the ball is not the reflection of deep-seated and dignified Imperial wealth but of a socially indeterminate gathering in which Mandryka's rather showily deployed cash, exploited by the exuberant Fiakermilli, has the greatest influence.

Historical drama characteristically investigates a historical setting in such a way that the personal or contemporary interests of the dramatist are explored at the same time. Hofmannsthal's two Vienna opera librettos are no exception, and together they form a context for the question 'How could Vienna once have been so different from what it is now and still be the same place, the same city?'[33] Vienna is a convenient symbolic focus for Hofmannsthal's imaginative understanding of the role of the past in defining the epoch that he experienced as present – and it is the historical equivalent of the Marschallin's attempts to understand identity across time. The much criticised anachronistic presence in *Der Rosenkavalier* of the music that more appropriately characterises the period of *Arabella* – the waltzes – merely shows that the problem of how a single place is defined cumulatively by different times is being posed *within* the one opera as well as *between* the two. Musically, too, Strauss attempts to answer the question of how the single genre of opera can reconcile Mozart and Wagner, and the self-consciousness with which he approaches it matches Hofmannsthal's in his relationship with literary tradition.[34] The motifs and images in both operas are from sources as diverse as they are in any of Hofmannsthal's works, ranging from the medieval, through the Baroque and Rococo, Romanticism and Realism, to the *fin de siècle*.[35] Hofmannsthal's eclecticism makes his technique a form of pastiche, an attempt to define a present stylistic identity via the appropriation of fragments of the past, again the stylistic equivalent of the characters' attempts to come to terms with the combination of moment and continuum in time.

Yet the reasons for Hofmannsthal's consistent preoccupation with time are rooted less in the familiar problematic of 'tradition and the individual talent' than in his own personal struggles with genre, most particularly in the limitations of his dramatic imagination.[36] The Strauss-Hofmannsthal correspondence largely confirms the superiority of Strauss's feel for drama.[37] There is more to this than mere value judgement, and Peter Conrad has argued that Hofmannsthal 'saw opera as a musical novel rather than musical drama, dealing in psychological change and shifts of consciousness, not endeavour and achievement'.[38] Hofmannsthal's librettos contributed towards the development in opera, initiated by the Romantics, away from drama and towards the novel, the genres respectively characterised by 'external action in a crampingly compact form and subjective exploration in a limitlessly ramifying form' (p. 112). The importance of dramatic characters is thus less in their individual activity than in their participation in the 'Musik des Ganzen' ['music of the whole'].[39] Yet precisely this musical dimension is achievable in comedy. As Hofmannsthal explains in the 'Unwritten Afterword' to *Der Rosenkavalier*, the characters of comedy are figures whose action is half-way between the infinite potential of real human beings and the rigidly delimited scope of puppets:

> The Marschallin is not there for herself alone, and neither is Ochs. They stand opposite each other and yet belong to each other; the boy Octavian is between them and links them. Sophie stands against the Marschallin, girl against woman, and again Octavian steps between them and separates them and holds them together. [...] Whatever else Ochs may be, he is nonetheless a kind of nobleman; Faninal and he are mutually complementary, the one needs the other not only in this world

but also, so to speak, in a metaphysical sense. [...] Thus groups are ranged against other groups, those bound together are separated, those separated are bound together. They all belong together, and the best of it lies between them: it is both momentary and eternal, the space for music ['Raum für Musik'].[40]

For Hofmannsthal, comedy almost inherently undermines existential stability for, if it derives meaning from the musical space created by the distribution of characters relative only to each other, it therefore also strongly undermines the independent identity of all those characters.[41] That this is not also true of tragedy is explained in an essay entitled 'The Irony of Things' (1921):

> Tragedy gives its hero, the individual, artificial dignity ['künstliche Würde']; it makes him into a demi-god and lifts him up and beyond the conditions of bourgeois existence. [...] True comedy, however, sets its individuals into a relationship with the world consisting of thousands of interlocking strands. It sets everything into relations with everything else.[42]

This condition, whereby meaning is determined by a plethora of mutually defining and interdependent perspectives, is identified as the condition of irony, the natural element of comedy. This conception makes comedy almost the only possible genre in which to articulate social and political concerns such as those of *Der Rosenkavalier* and *Arabella*. Tragedy, by lifting its protagonists out of this network, assigns semi-absolute values to them and their actions. Irony is inherent to comedy because of comedy's dependence on the structural configurations of its characters, and this makes it the ideal vehicle for dealing with periods where traditional values are gradually disintegrating and identities are felt as increasingly unstable.

If in Hofmannsthal's view it is the comic genre that helps his drama tend towards the condition of music, there is nonetheless a high degree of subjective exploration in the comic opera librettos that would justify seeing a novelistic dimension to them. This may after all explain why he could countenance cutting the Marschallin's time aria. But his literary practice had previously been as a lyric poet rather than as a novelist, and his librettos also continually demonstrate a productive nostalgia for the lyric. This happens on a relatively simple level from the first page of *Der Rosenkavalier* to the last page of *Arabella*. The directionless (e)motions in Octavian's passion for the Marschallin echo the poem 'Wolken' from 1891,[43] and the ritual of the glass of water in *Arabella* is a reversal of the poem 'Die Beiden' (I, 50). Hofmannsthal himself recognised the congruence of his work as a librettist and his early lyric poety in an essay on *The Egyptian Helen*:

> People talk of poets and musicians who work together in collaboration [...] but they have hardly any idea of how necessary a development it was for *me* to arrive at this form. I found the following in the paragraph relating to me in Nadler's History of Literature: my very first dramas, he writes, have a subconscious craving for music, and the word 'lyrical'

indicates this only very imprecisely. He is quite right, but to my mind the word indicates it perfectly adequately. The French call an opera a 'drame lyrique', and perhaps in this respect they have always been more instinctively close to classical antiquity than we have; they have never quite forgotten that classical tragedy was a sung form of tragedy.[44]

Beyond motivic, terminological or historical similarity, however, it is the temporal distinctiveness of the lyric that pervades the operas. If drama and the novel present development and the succession of feelings and events as they are affected by the actions of others, the lyric deals essentially with timeless or eternal moments of concentrated sensation, where all is always intensely and suddenly now. It is precisely such moments in which *Der Rosenkavalier* and *Arabella* culminate. Despite their dramatic structure and the extended exploration of the characters' various subjectivities, both focus on, conjure up and seek to preserve moments outside time. The Marschallin half-understands but sometimes tries to stop time; Ochs ignores it; Sophie is innocent of it; Octavian initially resists it and, with Sophie, steps outside it, keeping it suspended for them until the end of the opera. The process is similar in *Arabella*: Mandryka is exotically a-temporal; Zdenka is in limbo until the end of Fasching; and Arabella fears the moment of decision that will mark the end of her girlhood – she, too, moves from a stormy relationship with time to security within eternity, when she is given a promise of love 'für ewige Zeit' ['for eternal time'] (XXVI, 69). Stopping all the clocks is the equivalent of trying to preserve the relationships that obtain at any given time – freezing the 'space for music' into a permanent snapshot – and thus, while not approaching the absolute nature of tragedy, the opera librettos here at least leave drama and the social suspended and move towards the realm of lyric. The forthcoming marriages that both operas announce at the end are staples of comedy, and, in the context of Hofmannsthal's view of the genre, the promise might be felt to be insecure; but, by lifting them out of one generic framework and into another, Hofmannsthal is also able to preserve the moral status of marriage.

Despite being operas in the shadow of Wagner, both the Strauss–Hofmannsthal compositions celebrate these moments of extra-temporal longing or fulfilment in short arias like lyric poems. Unlike the limitless subjective ramifications that characterise the novel, the essence of these dense, charged moments lies in their being devoid of 'ramification' – roses, so to speak, neither dramatically at war nor novelistically climbing and covering, but single buds, so distinct from the reality surrounding them that they are not always even organic. 'Das Gespräch über Gedichte' [Conversation about Poems] (1903) makes it clear that Hofmannsthal did not reject the lyric after he stopped writing poems: 'jedes vollkommene Gedicht ist Ahnung und Gegenwart, Sehnsucht und Erfüllung zugleich' ['every perfect poem is anticipation and presence, longing and fulfilment at the same time'].[45] We might add, in the words of Sophie and Arabella, 'Zeit und Ewigkeit', for it looks very much as if opera is Hofmannsthal's excuse to return to the lyric by the back door.

Robert Vilain

Notes

1. Quoted from Hugo von Hofmannsthal, *Richard Strauss, Der Rosenkavalier: Fassungen, Filmszenarien, Briefe*, ed. Willi Schuh (Frankfurt am Main, 1971) [= Libretto], p. 62. Except where the libretto differs significantly, the text of *Der Rosenkavalier* will be quoted from the 'Comedy for Music' or so-called 'book version', Hugo von Hofmannsthal, *Sämtliche Werke. Kritische Ausgabe*, XXIII, *Operndichtungen 1, Der Rosenkavalier*, ed. Dirk O. Hoffmann and Willi Schuh (Frankfurt am Main, 1986) [= comedy], here p. 40. The textual relationship is discussed by Joanna Bottenberg, *Shared Creation: Words and Music in the Hofmannsthal–Strauss Operas*, German Studies in Canada, 6 (Frankfurt am Main, etc., 1996). *Arabella* is quoted from *Sämtliche Werke*, XXVI, *Operndichtungen 4, Arabella, Lucidor, Der Fiaker als Graf*, ed. Hans-Albrecht Koch (Frankfurt am Main, 1976). Page numbers only will be given, in the text, except where a volume number from the Critical Edition is needed for clarity. All translations are my own.
2. Richard Strauss, Hugo von Hofmannsthal, *Briefwechsel*, ed. Willi Schuh (Zurich, ⁵1978), p. 80 (15 August 1909), henceforth cited as *BW*.
3. For an analysis on these lines, see Ewald Rösch, *Komödien Hofmannsthals. Die Entfaltung ihrer Sinnstruktur aus dem Thema der Daseinsstufen* (Marburg, 1963).
4. A draft specifies 'a beautiful Io, after Correggio' for the Marschallin's room, an idea inspired by Hogarth. See Mary Gilbert, 'Painter and Poet: Hogarth's "Marriage à la Mode" and Hofmannsthal's "Der Rosenkavalier"', *MLR*, 64 (1969), 818–27 (pp. 821, 823).
5. 'Erinnerungen an die ersten Aufführungen meiner Opern', in Richard Strauss, *Betrachtungen und Erinnerungen*, (ed.) Willi Schuh (Zurich, 1949), p. 193.
6. *Sämtliche Werke. Kritische Ausgabe*, I, *Gedichte 1*, ed. Eugene Weber (Frankfurt am Main, 1984), p. 45.
7. See Libretto, p. 63 (refs 12–18), an expanded version of the comedy text, XXIII, 39, ll. 13–14.
8. Libretto, p. 71, cf. XXIII, 315.
9. Earlier versions make much more of this (see XXIII, 492).
10. Strauss has Octavian and Sophie sing 'Spür' nur dich allein' ['I can only feel you'] once more (Libretto, p. 137).
11. Lewis Lockwood, 'The Element of Time in *Der Rosenkavalier*', in Bryan Gilliam (ed.), *Richard Strauss. New Perspectives on the Composer and his Work* (Durham and London, 1992), pp. 243–58 (p. 256).
12. See also Rudolf H. Schäfer, *Hugo von Hofmannsthals 'Arabella'* (Bern, 1967), pp. 57–58.
13. This phrase was not set by Strauss.
14. XXVI, 21. Cf. *Der Rosenkavalier*, XXIII, 48 (Sophie's words, 'You are a man and can be what you remain, but I need a man in order to become anything at all').
15. For an account of how Mandryka is counter-modelled on Ochs, see Dugald Sturges, *The German Molière Revival and the Comedies of Hugo von Hofmannsthal and Carl Sternheim* (Frankfurt am Main, etc., 1993), pp. 130–31.
16. Arabella's shaken reaction is another mirror: she wonders if Mandryka is really the right man after all and turns to God like Sophie early in Act II of *Der Rosenkavalier* and in similar terms. Compare XXVI, 62, ll. 29–30 and XXIII, 44, ll. 2–8.
17. There is a magic potion in *Die Ägyptische Helena* and when, in *Ariadne auf Naxos*, 'Circe's magic drink' is mentioned Strauss has the *Tristan* chord sound in the orchestra. Cf *BW*, p. 623 (30 April 1928), pp. 643–44 (23 July 1928), and p. 658 (5 August 1928).

18. *BW*, p. 578 (1 July 1927). See also the 1927 essay '*Der Rosenkavalier*: Zum Geleit' (reproduced in XXIII, 548–50), and *BW*, p. 613 (22 December 1927): 'Everything is proper 1740s Vienna'. For Hofmannsthal's view that the Marschallin was analogous to Hans Sachs in *The Mastersingers*, see Hugo von Hofmannsthal, *Gesammelte Werke*, ed. Bernd Schoeller (Frankfurt am Main, 1979–80), *Reden und Aufsätze III, 1925–1929, Aufzeichnungen*, p. 504 and Sturges pp. 16 and 179.
19. See XXIII, 549–50 and 715–16, Adam Wandruszka, 'Das Zeit-und Sprachkostüm von Hofmannsthals "Rosenkavalier"', *ZfdPh*, 86 (1967), 561–70 (pp. 568–70), and Andreas Razumovsky, 'Über den Text des Rosenkavalier', in *Zeugnisse. Theodor W. Adorno zum sechzigsten Geburtstag*, edited by Max Horkheimer (Frankfurt am Main, 1963), pp. 225–40 (p. 226).
20. See Wandruszka, pp. 561–70 and XXIII, 708–709.
21. See XXIII, 710–11.
22. See Wandruszka, p. 566 and Razumovsky, p. 240.
23. For the development of Hofmannsthal's ideas on the period see *BW*, p. 494 (22 September 1923), p. 578 (1 July 1927), p. 587 (1 October 1927) and pp. 612–13 (22 December 1927).
24. *BW*, pp. 637–39.
25. 'Maria Theresia', in *Gesammelte Werke, Reden und Aufsätze II, 1914–1924*, p. 444.
26. Franz Tumler, '*Rosenkavalier* und *Arabella*', *Neue Deutsche Hefte*, 3 (1956/1957), 359–78; Michael Hamburger, 'Plays and Libretti', in *Hofmannsthal: Three Essays* (Princeton, NJ, 1972), pp. 109–14. See also C. E. Williams, *The Broken Eagle: The Politics of Austrian Literature from Empire to Anschluss* (London, 1974), pp. 25–26.
27. An earlier version is quoted by Hamburger, 'Plays and Libretti', p. 112.
28. Hamburger, p. 113. See also Tumler, p. 365.
29. Gilbert, p. 826.
30. Hamburger, p. 110.
31. Tumler, pp. 370–71. For reservations and objections, see Rösch, pp. 205–06 (note 228) and Schäfer, pp. 17–18.
32. Hans-Albrecht Koch, 'Die österreichische Ballkultur des 19. Jahrhunderts im Werk Hofmannsthals', in *Hofmannsthal-Forschungen*, II, ed. Wolfram Mauser (Freiburg, 1974), pp. 23–38 (pp. 31–33).
33. Lockwood, pp. 247–48.
34. See Leon Botstein, 'The Enigmas of Richard Strauss: A Revisionist View', in Bryan Gilliam (ed.), *Richard Strauss and his World* (Princeton, NJ, 1992), pp. 3–32 (esp. pp. 18–19).
35. See XXIII, 701–17, XXVI, 190–99, and Peter Branscombe, 'Some Observations on the Sources of the Strauss–Hofmannsthal Opera Librettos', in W. E. Yuill and Patricia Howe (eds), *Hugo von Hofmannsthal: Commemorative Essays* (London, 1981), pp. 86–95 (pp. 86–87). Sturges shows how *Arabella* is not only indebted to Molière, but synthesises modes of Molière reception characteristic of Hofmannsthal's early 'direct' borrowings and the later technique of *gegenentwerfen* (pp. 128–32).
36. Perhaps the most trenchant formulation is Harry Kessler's during their dispute: 'Hofmannsthal has absolutely no constructive talent [...]. If he has an effective scenario he can bring it to life lyrically in a marvellous way'. See Eberhard von Bodenhausen, Harry Graf Kessler, *Ein Briefwechsel 1894–1918*, ed. Hans-Ulrich Simon (Marbach am Neckar, 1978), p. 94 (letter of 24 March 1912).
37. Hofmannsthal betrays his own uncertainty when he writes of having read Act I to a number of people who have a feel for the dramatic; Strauss was still unhappy with Act III, however, requesting 'conflicts and tensions that are completely absent at the moment', describing it as 'lyrical burbling' (*BW*, pp. 638 and 647, 13 and 23 July 1928).

38. Peter Conrad, *Romantic Opera and Literary Form* (Berkeley, Los Angeles and London, 1977), pp. 112–43 (p. 122).
39. 'Shakespeares Könige und große Herren', *Gesammelte Werke, Reden und Aufsätze I, 1891–1913*, pp. 33–53 (p. 37).
40. 'Ungeschriebenes Nachwort zum *Rosenkavalier*', XXIII, 547–48 (p. 547).
41. See also Paul Stefanek, 'Zur Theorie und Praxis der Komödie bei Hofmannsthal', in Yuill and Howe (eds), *Hugo von Hofmannsthal: Commemorative Essays*, pp. 112–22.
42. 'Die Ironie der Dinge', *Gesammelte Werke, Reden und Aufsätze II*, pp. 138–41 (p. 138).
43. Compare XXIII, 9, l. 26 and I, 23, ll. 1–4.
44. 'Die Ägyptische Helena (1928)', *Gesammelte Werke, Dramen V: Operndichtungen*, pp. 498–512 (p. 498).
45. 'Das Gespräch über Gedichte', *Gesammelte Werke, Erzählungen, Erfundene Gespräche und Briefe, Reisen*, pp. 495–509 (p. 507).

The Significance of the Irrational in Horváth's *Geschichten aus dem Wiener Wald*

Alan Bance

'Ein wahrhaftiges Volkstheater, das an die Instinkte und nicht an den Intellekt des Volkes appelliert'[1] ['An authentic popular theatre, appealing to the instincts and not the intellect of the people']: what aspects of the old Viennese stage does Horváth have in mind when he invokes the *Volkstheater* [Austrian popular theatre] tradition? Edgar Yates has already told us what Horváth was *not* doing: his type of *Volksstück* [popular play] has nothing to do with the Viennese dialect drama, 'the "humorous", idealizing, moralistic, and specifically *not* satirical "Volksstück" as the mid-nineteenth century conceived of it'.[2] By Horváth's time, neither the 'Volk' nor the 'Stück', the play nor the people, remained what they had been in the days of Raimund or Nestroy.

To deal first with the 'Volk': Horváth's dramatis personae are no longer simple artisans, but belong to the ranks of the deracinated, urban *Kleinbürger* or petty bourgeois, among whom the new type of inter-war citizen and the majority of Weimar play-goers must be numbered. Any discernible affinity with the old Nestroyan *Volksstück* lies in Horváth's continuation of the tradition of Austrian language consciousness through his satire on the everyday language of this new class.

To go on to the 'Stück', the nature of the theatre itself: another aspect of the old *Volksstück* – and the nineteenth-century debate about the genre – to which Horváth can be related is the combination of comedy and morality. As Edgar Yates has shown ('The Idea of the "Volksstück" ', p. 469) it was around the supposed incompatibility of these two concepts, and Nestroy's relationship with them, that debate raged in the turbulent 1840s. This nineteenth-century dispute about the desirability, or otherwise, of separating 'comic' and 'serious' genres was as antiquated by the 1920s as the assumption that there was still a healthy and innocent 'Volk' ('gesunde Auffassung des Volkslebens').[3] It is true that there is a serious moral purpose in Horváth's comedic *Volksstück*; 'to describe and expose the hypocritical and self-deceptive norms of his day' is one way in which it has been defined.[4] But Horváth's modern fusing of comedy with seriousness is radically different from any nineteenth-century combination of these qualities. In the age of modernism, comedy had become the only remaining viable genre which, from then on, had to do the work of all the others. Traditional qualities of tragedy, for example, are recalled in tragi-comic mode in *Geschichten aus dem Wiener Wald* [*Tales from the Vienna Woods*] (first produced in Berlin in 1931) by Valerie's comment on the heroine Marianne's fall from grace: 'die hat sich eingebildet, die Welt nach ihrem Bild umzuformen' ['she deluded herself that she could shape the world according to her image'] – a verdict that, with a change of pronouns, could equally apply to Hamlet or to Goethe's Egmont. In Horváth's tragi-comic world, Marianne can, of course, be no pure tragic heroine; her fate is a part of the play's wider import. But her function is highly significant as an indicator of the degree of Horváth's seriousness. (This is something he signals directly just once in the play, at the moment of Marianne's despairing appeal to God in the cathedral scene, a self-consciously 'literary' moment with echoes of Gretchen in Goethe's *Faust*. It is characteristic of the modernist mode that the overt and affective expression of seriousness is, so to speak, possible only in quotation marks.) With typical prescience – for these characters are the recognisable precursors of Hitler's willing subjects – Horváth uses Marianne's fate to show how dangerous his otherwise comically self-deluding figures can be. Marianne's tragi-comic role tempers with sympathy and humanity the impact of a play that might otherwise be seen as an exercise in pure (if enjoyable) malice.

Horváth never ceased to believe in the role of the theatre as a 'moralische Anstalt' ['moral institution'], but needed a new dramatic practice to renew the moral appeal of the stage under modern conditions. Part of that practice was his exploitation of his characters' irrationality. The irrational in Horváth's *Volksstücke* has been well-charted territory since 1975 at the latest, when Herbert Gamper made the uncanny the central focus of his interpretation of the playwright.[5] But it has never been obvious what Horváth had in mind when he declared in the famous *Gebrauchsanweisung* ['instructions for use'] in 1932 that it was to the unconscious depths of his audiences' minds he was speaking rather than to their reasoning powers. In view of the date of his statement, and the current of irrationality that was running deep on the eve of the Nazi takeover, 'instinct' seems an unlikely addressee for a left-of-centre writer to prefer.

Instinct and the irrational do not have a very good political record, from the excesses of the French Revolution to the fanatical nationalisms of the twentieth century; no matter that in both cases the irrationality is a perversion of enlightenment thinking, about the universal rights of man and the organisation of the nation state respectively. It may be the very fact that rationalism can so easily lead to its opposite that moves Horváth to appeal directly to a (healthy) instinct rather than to such a treacherous faculty as the intellect. But in this he is fairly exceptional among 'progressives'. (Other exceptions, however, were Wilhelm Reich and Ernst Bloch.)[6] The climate of inter-war irrationalism created by radical right-wing movements such as National Bolshevism and the 'conservative revolution' generally evoked from their opponents an equal and opposite stress on reason and suspicion of emotionality. The recent experience of defeat in The First World War was one that reactionaries strove to assimilate by playing upon emotive and mystical values such as *Kameradschaft* [comradeship] which, to the left, were simply manipulative devices. When Ernst Jünger declared that 'Jeder Versuch, das Schicksalhafte durch Denkresultate zu korrigieren, ist von vornherein zum Scheitern bestimmt' ['Every attempt to correct fate by the power of thought is condemned to failure in advance'], the typical reply from the left was, in J. R. Becher's words, 'Macht euch gefeit gegen idealistischen Aberglauben, Jenseitstaumel und gegen jede Art von noch so interessanten Mystifikationsversuchen' ['Arm yourselves against idealistic superstition, otherworldly delirium, and every kind of attempt at mystification, however interesting'].[7] Brecht's demystification of Hitlerism in *Arturo Ui* by presenting the phenomenon simply in terms of a 'racket' or crooked business consortium brilliantly typifies the left-wing application of reason to unmasking the 'real', economic motives of apparent unreason but, of course (and this may be Horváth's instinctive perception), it leaves out of account some less easily explained, irrational aspects of the motivation – and appeal – of National Socialism.

One of the central paradoxes of 'völkisch' [nationalistic] ideology is that its representatives were not only anti-parliamentary and undemocratic as well as irrationalist and romantic; they also despised the *Volk*.[8] (The arrogance of the German logocracy goes back at least to Nietzsche's advocacy, in *Beyond Good and Evil*, of a social system in which a small number of superior beings employ all the rest as slaves; and it finds its vulgar apotheosis in Hitler.) In appealing to instinct, Horváth by contrast is stressing his understanding of ordinary people and his intuitive conviction that they are capable of sharing his insights. It was an understanding that arose out of awareness of his own emotionality, his susceptibility to superstition, forebodings, and prophecies, and his preoccupation with death, all of which are well attested. He never claimed to be stronger than the average weak human beings he portrays, and shared their wish-projections and their strategies for escape into a world of irrational causality. It is, if anything, an understatement to suggest, as Horst Jarka does, that 'It is possible that Horváth took more than just a sociological interest in the escape of his pathetic Volksstück characters into fatalism and the occult'.[9] Certainly there is an ambivalence in his attitude to humanity in all its frailty and stupidity. One of his favourite comments on the behaviour he observed in fellow humans was a delighted 'san's net tierisch?' ['ain't they animals?'].[10] And yet an appropriate epitaph for himself is contained in another line of his: 'Ich habe nie politisiert. Ich trat ein für das Recht der Kreatur' ['I never went in for politics. I stood up for the rights of my [human] fellow-creatures'].[11] This mixture of malicious humour and compassion is one that encompasses him as much as others. All of Horváth's characters abuse language and are simultaneously abused by it; but, by the same token, like them we are all to varying degrees victims and culprits, 'tierisch' and 'Kreatur'; 'jeder Mensch begeht aber täglich durchschnittlich zehn Schweinereien, zumindest als Gedankensünde' ['but on average, every human being is guilty of doing ten rotten things a day, at least in the form of thought-crimes'].[12]

Horváth's implicit view of the intellect is that it is a precarious achievement always subject to subversion by the wrong instincts, to be kept in line only by the right ones: 'the view that the intellect is a hard-won achievement of civilisation, conducive to self-deception and constantly in danger of being reabsorbed by the life of the instincts, is completely in accord with Horváth's fundamental convictions'.[13] His Utopia would be one in which goodness and instincts can coincide, or at least not collide. In the seventh 'Bild' [scene] of Horváth's *Italienische Nacht* [Italian Evening], the innkeeper, Josef Lehninger, laments that the graffiti in his lavatory have now become political in content; 'glaubs mir: solangs nicht wieder erotisch werden, solang wird das deutsche Volk nicht wieder gesunden' ['believe me, the German people won't get back to health until they [the graffiti] get smutty again'], he declares. The erotic drive that produced the graffiti is all too easily subverted into a different kind of libidinous impulse. The innkeeper can be understood as the mouthpiece of Horváth, however, in suggesting that the way back to political-psychological health is through reason – but reason can best be reached via an appeal to the very instincts that have been perverted. To ignore the positive power of irrationality is to hand over the realm of the instincts to the fascists:

> ... irrationalities must not be thrown out with the bath water of irrationalism. They can reinforce reason's arguments [...] with self-determining longings and intimations. If this connection with reason is not made, then propaganda can do anything it wishes with the longings and intimations denounced by rationalism.[14]

In other words, it was a mistake for the left wing in Weimar to insist that 'the only enemy of irrationalism was the rationality of socialist optimism' and assert 'an orthodox categorical imperative whereby any rationality is preferable to the incomprehensible dangers of the irrational' (Schmidt, p. 87). A rough and ready distinction between Brecht, representing 'the rationality of socialist optimism', and Horváth, representing the analysis of irrationality in the name of reason, is that Brecht wants to talk his audience *into* his own version of reason, Horváth merely to talk them *out of* unreason via a sympathetic understanding of their proneness to irrationality. The very form he chooses, the *Volksstück*, and the provocative use he makes of it, are evidence of his desire to train his audience by way of the familiar to see the seriousness of their flight from reality: his expectations of the audience, and his trust in their sound instincts, are inscribed in his frustrating of their normal expectations by his deconstruction of a traditional genre.

Horváth's great insight, and what gives him the status of a twentieth-century classic, is his recognition – and presentation in a new dramatic form – of the intermediate stage of development reached by the 'Volk' who are his subject, and by the evolving social structures in which they are embedded. What makes people vulnerable to political exploitation and manipulation is a combination that arouses Horváth's satirical sense of humour and his compassion at the same time: his characters continue (like the author himself) to be prone to irrational fears, and unconsciously seek ways to shore up their egos against such underlying panic; and equally they live in what Adorno called a climate of semi-erudition where 'primary naïvety, the unreflecting acceptance of the existent has been lost whereas at the same time neither the power of thinking nor positive knowledge has been developed sufficiently'.[15] This intermediate position is expressed in linguistic terms by Horváth's notion of the decline of dialect and its replacement by what he calls *Bildungsjargon*, a half-educated ('semi-erudite') style of speech meant to demonstrate the status. of the speaker. A clear grasp of the underlying psychological dependency and dispossession revealed in this language is reflected in Horváth's summary in the *Gebrauchsanweisung*: 'Es darf kein Wort Dialekt gesprochen werden! Jedes Wort muß hochdeutsch gesprochen werden, allerdings so, wie jemand, der sonst nur Dialekt spricht und sich nun zwingt, hochdeutsch zu reden' ['Not a word of dialect must be uttered! Every word has got to be standard German, although German as it would be spoken by someone who normally only speaks dialect and is now making himself speak the standard language'] *(GW,* XI, p. 219). It is a style intended to assert the speaker's control over his or her own situation, but in reality displaying – just as it displays undeniable traces of the dialect the characters are attempting to overcome – the depth of the speaker's unease or even anguish about a lack of personal control in an increasingly complex world. 'Psychological dependency' is the key term here: where individuals are unable to achieve any kind of overview of the world they inhabit, they are vulnerable to the power of irrational pseudo-explanations, whether political or occult. Since 'the social system is the "fate" of most individuals independent of their will and interest' (Adorno, p.42), they are apt to equate the social system with an abstract 'fate':

> Naïve persons fail to look through the complexities of a highly organized and institutionalized society, but even the sophisticated ones cannot understand it in plain terms of consistency and reason, but are faced with antagonism and uncertainties, the most blatant of which is the threat brought to mankind by the very same technology which was furthered in order to make life easier. Who wants to survive under present conditions is tempted to 'accept' such absurdities, like the verdict of the stars, rather than to penetrate them by thinking which means discomfort in many directions. (Adorno, p. 42)

The *Bildungsjargon* in Horváth is the linguistic equivalent of a general tendency to assert individuality the more it is actually negated by the social structure, in accordance with 'the pattern of modern mass culture which protests the more fanatically about the tenets of individualism and the freedom of the will, the more actual freedom of action vanishes' (Adorno, p. 44).

For interpersonal relations, the result of all these pressures is that Horváth's characters exhibit to the audience a drastic reduction in any sense of authenticity, reliability or responsibility. Their supposed individualism tends towards solipsism and intensifies the sense of insecurity and isolation they convey, the underlying violent intent of one person against another, and an existential fear expressing itself in the reinforced awareness of death which thrusts itself into the foreground even (or particularly) at seemingly unselfconscious or carnivalesque moments. An obvious example of such a moment occurs in the first scene of Part Three of *Geschichten aus dem Wiener Wald*, 'Beim Heurigen' ['At the Heuriger'] (inn where new wine is drunk), after the line of the song 'Da draußen in der Wachau' ['Out there in the Wachau'] which runs 'Und wir werden nimmer leben –' ['we'll no longer be alive']: the stage-direction states *Jetzt wirds einen Augenblick totenstill beim Heurigen – aber dann singt wieder alles mit verdreifachter Kraft* [And now for a moment the inn falls dead silent – but then everybody starts singing again, three times as heartily] (*GW*, IV, p. 170).[16] In Maximilian Schell's film version of the play, made in 1979, the 'Totentanz' [dance of death] theme beloved of Horváth – he subtitled the Volksstück *Glaube Liebe Hoffnung* [Faith, Charity, Hope] 'a little dance of death' – which lies behind this moment, is brilliantly brought out by making the ensemble, carrying open umbrellas, abruptly freeze in the midst of a lively waltz; the canopy of black umbrellas, shot from above, suddenly assumes a sinister air, as a pall is literally cast over the scene. Another example is in the operetta-style love scene between Alfred and Marianne 'an der schönen blauen Donau' ['by the blue Danube']:

MARIANNE. Oh Mann, grübl doch nicht – grübl nicht, schau die Sterne – die werden noch droben hängen, wenn wir drunten liegen –
ALFRED. Ich laß mich verbrennen.
MARIANNE. Ich auch – du, o du – du –
Stille. (p. 136)

[MARIANNE. Oh my love, don't brood – don't brood, look at the stars – they'll still be hanging up there above when we're lying down below –
ALFRED. I'm going to have myself cremated.
MARIANNE. Me too – you, oh you – you –
Pause.]

It is not fortuitous that it is Marianne who introduces the note of mortality here: females are even more precariously placed in this society than males, and their added awareness of ageing also brings a heightened consciousness of death.

The determination to assert control over one's own fate is paradoxically strengthened by the overwhelming power of the forces (social and existential) one is confronted with. The inter-war years are the period when, for the first time, the self became recognised as a commodity. In *Geschichten aus dem Wiener Wald* most of the main characters are in commerce, and some are in the business of selling themselves through their ability to charm and to exploit their connections; others, like Marianne (but also, more willingly, Alfred, in his gigolo-like exploitation of Valerie) directly sell their bodies. In reality, all are in the same boat; their illusion of control is a pseudo-individualism, at its most strident in the case of the Viennese-American 'Mister', the so-called self-made man, beloved of inter-war inspirational literature of the Dale Carnegie type. The self-made man betrays an underlying insecurity; he feels the need to enhance his self-creation a little by adding a fashionable Freudian 'interestingness' ('ich bin kompliziert' ['I'm complicated']). Nonetheless, 'self-made' is a term that implies a kind of solipsistic self-sufficiency and denies dependency (while it makes psychological dependency all the more obvious): it detaches the sphere of the individual artificially from that of the 'world' – just as the predictions of palmistry or astrology conveniently make the individual the centre of the world and exclude all reference to 'the major and mostly solemn speculations about the fate of mankind at large' (Adorno, p. 49). The inherent narcissism of the control myth creates another homology between inter-war popular culture and the attractions of fascism: it generates the potential for identification with a leader figure, who by presenting himself as the 'great little man', projects his understanding of the fears of the little man and of the self-aggrandisement of the latter, a 'mixture of "pettiness and grandeur" which encourages two levels of narcissistic identification'.[17]

In relations between people, the desire to establish control expresses itself in *Geschichten aus dem Wiener Wald* in the constant jostling for a position that will enable the individual to maintain self-respect. The struggle for personal supremacy acquires national and generational dimensions in the dealings between Erich, the National Socialist Prussian student from Kassel, and the retired Rittmeister (Captain of cavalry), who embodies the old days of the Habsburg monarchy. All transactions are part of a generation war or a battle of the sexes, or both, and are conducted by negotiation of one kind or another, often with an underlying and unspoken hint of violence or existential fear. The sparring between Alfred and his grandmother at the beginning of the play brings out the fact that all dialogues are about relations of exchange, where control and not money is the real currency (even if money often features as the ostensible focus of friction):

> DIE GROSSMUTTER. Wann kommst du denn wieder? Bald?
> ALFRED. Sicher.
> DIE GROSSMUTTER. Ich hab so Abschiede nicht gern, weißt du. –
>   Daß dir nur nichts passiert, ich hab so oft Angst –
> ALFRED. Was soll mir denn schon passieren?
>   *Stille.*
> DIE GROSSMUTTER. Wann gibst du mir denn das Geld zurück?
> ALFRED. Sowie ich es hab. (p. 109)

> [GRANDMOTHER. When are you coming back again? Soon?
> ALFRED. Sure.
> GRANDMOTHER. I don't like all these partings, see. – As long as
>   nothing happens to you – I'm always getting frightened –
> ALFRED. What could happen to me?
> *Pause.*
> GRANDMOTHER. When are you going to give me the money back?
> ALFRED. As soon as I've got it.]

The grandmother's fear on behalf of Alfred is really fear for herself, ostensibly concerning her anxiety about the return of the money he owes her, which she claims she needs to pay for her funeral ('ich möcht um mein eigenes Geld begraben werden') ['I want to be buried at my own expense'], but in reality connected with her fear of death. He brutally emphasises her proximity to death ('Was soll *mir* denn passieren?') ['what could happen to *me*?'] [my italics], and after a *Stille* to allow this menacing signal to be decoded, she brutally returns to the one instrument she can use to remind him of her control – her money, which is later to play a fateful part in the destruction of Marianne. Relations of exchange often appear, in this psychological power game, in the guise of religious or ethical concern to uphold the status quo, as in Part III, Scene iii, where Alfred and Oskar have successfully negotiated the return of Marianne – no better than a commodity – to Oskar's clutches, and need to put a 'civilised' moral gloss on the deal:

> ALFRED. Nein, soviel Leut ins Unglück zu stürzen! Wirklich: wir
>   Männer müßten mehr zusammenhalten.
> OSKAR. Wir sind halt zu naiv.
> ALFRED. Allerdings.   (pp. 194–95)

> [ALFRED. No, I mean – making so many people unhappy!
>   Us men really ought to stick together more.
> OSKAR. We're just too naïve.
> ALFRED. That's for sure.]

Later in the same scene, Valerie plays upon the Zauberkönig's fear of death to persuade him to accept his illegitimate grandson, before it is too late. No doubt with a view to paving the way to her own 'reconciliation' with Alfred (i.e. her no-holds-barred negotiation to take him back, provided he humbly submits to her dominance), which immediately ensues, after playing on the theme of mortality, she shrewdly pursues tactics that show her knowledge of his *kleinbürgerlich* [petty bourgeois] sense of priorities, deploying in turn the chance to save his business if he allows Marianne to return; then a salve to his hurt pride as she represents Marianne as 'nur ein dummes Weiberl' ['just a daft female']; and finally an appeal to his narcissism by slyly addressing him as 'Großpapa' ['Grandad'].

The negotiations between Marianne and Alfred at the beginning of her seduction of him are equally complex. When she asks him 'Können Sie hypnotisieren?' ['Are you a hypnotist?'], she unconsciously makes him responsible for the consequences of their burgeoning affair. She is attributing to him a hypnotic sexual power (the only basis of which in fact lies in his ability to turn his superficial 'charm' on and off at will) while flattering his ego. She implies that he possesses a big personality, to which she is prepared to submit her own ego; although actually her suggestion that he exercises exceptional power over her is a way of manipulating him. Lurking beneath the dialogue, however, is another psychological reality, conveyed by the uncanny images of penetration that spring to her mind, such as that of hypnotising (reminiscent of Oskar's frustration at not being able to penetrate his fiancée's skull; p. 117) and of a lightning strike ('wie der Blitz hast du in mich eingeschlagen und hat

209

[*sic*] mich gespalten') ['you struck into me like lightning and you've split me apart'] (p. 136). Her psychosocially-conditioned need to submit to some male imago – and failing anybody else, Alfred will do – is met by his equally conditioned acceptance of her subservience, although it is clearly going to burden him with responsibilities he does not want. It is not primarily their linguistic ineptitude that leads them on to act out Marianne's fantasies; language is merely the outer sign of their lack of control over their existence, a control that, in desperation, Marianne attempts to recuperate for herself. Alfred is ostensibly the passive partner, but both act irrationally.

Valerie, as the older woman who is financially independent, would seem to be in a stronger position with regard to Alfred and, indeed, she does triumphantly reassert her (entirely financially based) power over him in the end. But the point is that, though economically independent, she still regards herself as possessing nothing until she has a man to valorise her existence, stave off the thoughts of death inseparable from awareness of ageing, and suppress the *Torschlußpanik* [panic about being left on the shelf] to which she would otherwise be subject in a world where time is against her and her financial power will bring diminishing returns.

When control is pathetically 'seized' by Marianne, she covers up this doomed attempt to assert herself with threadbare notions of 'predestination' ('Gott hat mir im letzten Moment diesen Mann zugeführt'; 'dich hat mir der Himmel gesandt, mein Schutzengel') ['God sent me this man here in the nick of time'; 'you were sent to me by Heaven, my guardian angel'], which passes responsibility for her move on to some higher power. Among the most cynical characters, who are the ones who present themselves as the most convention-ally respectable and pious, resorting to 'divine intervention' as an explanation is transparently a hypocritical move, most blatantly in the sadistic letter of the murderous old grandmother informing Marianne of the death of baby Leopold: 'Gott der Allmächtige hat es mit seinem unerforschlichen Willen so gewollt, daß Sie, wertes Fräulein, kein Kind mehr haben sollen' ['the unfathomable will of all mighty God has ordained that you, my dear Miss, should not have a child any more'] (p. 204). Similarly, Oskar's 'consoling' of Marianne, 'Gott gibt und Gott nimmt' ['the Lord gives and the Lord takes away'], reveals his satisfaction at the death of the child. The *obvious* insincer-ity of these sentiments in the mouths of the most culpable helps to expose the complicity of others who cite divine will or parade their religiosity merely to justify their mindless complacency. As always with Horváth, conscious heir to a fine Austrian theatrical tradition of gesture, incidental stage business conveys as much as words as, for example, by the lax manner of Havlitschek, the butcher's assistant who is Oskar's sinister *alter ego*, in continuing to chew his sausage while uttering pious sentiments: 'geh, bittschön, betens auch in meinem Namen ein Vaterunser für die arme gnädige Frau Mutter selig' ['hey, if you don't mind, say an "Our Father" on my behalf as well for your poor dear mother, God rest her soul'] (p. 116). As a natural scapegoat, only Marianne pays the price for the criminal complacency of the others, and her words cut through their linguistic armour and their comfortably fitting mediated view of the world to confront them, as this society is rarely confronted, with the real-life results of their attitudes and with the callousness of their platitudes. An example is Marianne's flat reply to Oskar's 'pieties' at the end of the play about the God who takes as well as gives: 'Mir hat er nur genommen, nur genommen –' ['he's done nothing but take from me, nothing but take']. Even more telling is the dialogue between Marianne and Valerie in the 'great reconciliation' scene of Part III, Scene iii (p. 201):

> VALERIE. Zu guter Letzt ist bei einer solchen Liaison überhaupt nie jemand schuld – das ist doch zu guter Letzt eine Frage der Planeten, wie man sich gegenseitig bestrahlt und so.
> MARIANNE. Mich hat man aber eingesperrt.
>
> [VALERIE. In such an affair nobody's to blame at all in the end – in the end it's all a matter of the planets, the way they influence each other and all that.
> MARIANNE. But they locked *me* up in jail.]

That the victim here happens to be female is no coincidence – but the astrological nonsense that insults her suffering comes from a female, too, indicating that Horváth, though clearly a feminist by disposition, is under no illusion about the complicity of females in the repression of their own sex.

When 'Schicksal', 'die Planeten', or 'Naturgesetze' ['fate', 'the planets', 'laws of nature'], or the notion of life as a game of chance or a lottery, are invoked by the characters in the play, as they frequently are, these concepts of course represent an escape from responsibility (the male figures in particular tend to cite 'Schicksal' ['fate'], when they find their dominant role becoming too much for them), but they are also concepts that are ideologically suspect. The psychological syndrome expressed by dependence on 'higher forces', including astrology, is only a means to an end, the promotion of a social ideology:

> It offers the advantage of veiling all deeper-lying causes of distress and thus promoting acceptance of the given. Moreover, by strengthening the sense of fatality, dependence and obedience, it paralyzes the will to change objective conditions in any respect and relegates all worries to a private plane promising a cure-all by the very same compliance which prevents a change of conditions. (Adorno, p. 121)

Adorno goes further in linking irrational beliefs to ideology: 'the claim of something particular and apocryphal to be all-comprehensive and exclusive, is indicative of a most sinister social potential: the transition of an emasculated liberal ideology to a totalitarian one' [ibid.].

The invocation of war as 'Naturgesetz' ['a law of nature'] in *Geschichten aus dem Wiener Wald* is one of the best examples in the play of irrationality dressed up as scientific fact; this pseudo-fact is then blamed in advance for the inevitably catastrophic outcome of abdicating responsibility – the next war (p. 196). Blind subservience to 'nature' means in fact abdicating control to other human agencies which, as likely as not, will be totalitarian. 'War is a law of nature' has a pedigree in Germany going back to Clausewitz and Treitschke, but continuing casual acceptance of such a 'law', despite the experience of the First World War, seems a particularly good example of the endless stupidity that Horváth evoked in the motto of his play, 'Nichts gibt so sehr das Gefühl der Unendlichkeit als wie die Dummheit' ['There's nothing like stupidity for giving you a sense of infinity']. Equally casual is Valerie's absent-minded comment, 'Aber das [i.e. Krieg] wär das Ende unserer Kultur' ['But a war would be the end of civilisation as we know it'] (p. 195).

The casualness with which ideological stupidities are mouthed, and are simply subordinated to more important private preoccupations, is likewise shown in Valerie's throw-away line, directed at Erich: 'Ja glaubens denn, daß ich die Juden mag? Sie großes Kind – ['Come on, you don't think I like the Jews, do you? You big kid'] (p. 127). Any utterance of Horváth's figures has more or less the character of a *Verlegenheitseinfall* [a spur-of-the-moment idea]; their words are tactical moves, and do not carry the weight of reflection or conviction. There is an eerie playfulness about these characters that surely reflects Horváth's general sense of foreboding: 'Warum fürchten die Menschen sich im finsteren Wald? Warum nicht auf der Straße?' ['Why are people afraid in dark woods? Why not in the street?'] (Pauli, p. 56). The terrifying unseriousness and infantilism of the characters prefigures (as does the centrality of the Zauberkönig's 'magic' shop) the Magic Realism of Angela Carter's 'toyshop' themes, or, even more appropriate, Günter Grass's oblique treatment of the banality of Nazi horrors through the *enfant terrible*, Oskar, in *The Tin Drum* and the vicious *Spieltrieb* [play-drive] of the SA men he depicts there, or the dismembered–doll drawings that appeared in the original edition of his volume of poetry, *Gleisdreieck*, in 1960.

The 'big kid', Erich, with his military obsession and his target-practice, as well as the Gnädige Frau's order for 'fallende und verwundete' ['dying and wounded'] toy soldiers that she has placed for her spoilt son and is anxious to pursue with the Zauberkönig, reinforce the message of the dangers of infantilism, especially taken in conjunction with the puerile – and, no doubt, in inter-war Austria and Germany, very widespread – assertion that, as Valerie puts it, 'Wenn der Krieg nur vierzehn Tage länger gedauert hätt, dann hätten wir gesiegt' ['If only the war had only lasted a fortnight longer, we'd have won'] (p. 113). For good measure, the Rittmeister calculates that the 'premature' end of the war was an unfortunate throw of the dice which has cost him his 'Majorspension' (another example of the divorce of personal concerns from the larger sphere of affairs). All this irresponsibility and play with war leaves no doubt that war continues to be seen as a game, and renders unpleasantly convincing the Zauberkönig's assertion that 'morgen gibts wieder einen Krieg' ['another war's not far off'] (p. 195).

Males in the play have all too often been reduced to an infantile state of frustration through their losses in the class, sex, and international wars, so that they resemble 'der Bubi' ['the little lad'] who will cry if he does not receive for his birthday the dead and wounded toy soldiers he has set his heart on. Moreover, to add to the impression that war is inevitable, it can be observed that for males to act upon their frustrations is sanctioned by society through the assumption of a 'drive-discharge' model of behaviour that makes it 'natural', and even manly, for the Zauberkönig to vent upon his daughter Marianne the pent-up rage of his patriarchal class at no longer being able to afford even one servant ('Nicht einmal einen Dienstbot kann man sich halten' ['you can't afford even one servant nowadays'] (p. 115)), which, in turn, justifies his deliberate refusal to allow her any career training, so that she remains his surrogate servant, and unemployable except by selling her body. It is also acceptable (to her father at least, if not to the women present) for Oskar to demonstrate his masculine prowess at ju-jitsu by flooring Marianne in a sadistic display that symbolically shows her where she belongs (p.129). Havlitschek, the lowest form of life in the play, accurately formulates the 'drive-discharge' theory when he wonders how his boss Oskar now works off his frustrated rage during the absence of Marianne in the short-lived menage with Alfred: 'Ich meine das so, daß man es nicht weiß, wo er es hinausschwitzt' ['What I mean is, nobody knows where he sweats it out of his system'] (p. 141). When Alfred, with his grandmother's encouragement and with her money to support him, leaves Marianne and their baby to their fate, he is advised to go off to the notoriously libidinous joys of France to sow some wild oats (i.e. discharge his sexual drives), while Marianne by contrast is ostracised as a whore and the mother of a bastard.

If Horváth's fictive world accurately mirrors the real world of 1930, no-one can be surprised at the triumph of fascist demagogues who have the gift of expressing people's hysteria to themselves, or that pent-up grievances and feelings of persecution are channelled into the paranoid projection of anti-Semitism. It is a climate, too, in which the sado-masochistic 'authoritarian personality' thrives, combining, as Oskar does, the conviction of absolute moral rectitude with the most murderous transgressive instincts. The objective corollary of this combination is to be found in Horváth's scene settings, whether it be the façade of the respectable 'stille Straße' ['quiet street'] masking brutality behind closed doors (its undisturbed 'Stille' or quietness contributes to that sense of immutability or infinity that, according to Horváth's motto for his play, can best be imagined by contemplating stupidity); or the more cosmopolitan veneer of Maxim's nightclub, which is built upon the exploitation of females by the sinister impresario and (probably) white-slave trader, the Baronin, but also by 'respectable' males like the Zauberkönig; or the tranquil bucolic landscape of the Wachau with its picturesque 'heritage' associations, a landscape that harbours, however, a brutal peasant mentality, embodied in the grandmother, which breeds the greatest savagery of all.

What is surprising, but is probably historically accurate, is the 'Ungleich-zeitigkeit' [nonsynchronism or non-simultaneity] (to use the well-known term theorised by Ernst Bloch)[18] which allows the vicious application of pre-war morality, by the priest in the Stephansdom scene (II, vii) and by the old grandmother in condemning Marianne, when the reality was that the old moral order had collapsed – so that, for example, the German State had found it expedient to legitimise wartime babies born out of wedlock (illegitimacy would surely never again bear the same stigma); there were 2.8 million 'surplus' women in post-World War I Germany, with the result that extra-marital liaisons became commonplace; and, by 1925, 40 per cent of pregnancies in Germany ended in abortion. It is, indeed, probably because of these momentous changes in German and Austrian society that, in those backward areas where it is still possible, characters cling all the more obsessively to traditional mores. In doing so, though, they subject themselves to an inauthentic (because superannuated) way of living that invites exploitation by those who appear to reconcile modernity with traditional values – above all the Nazis.

The same non-simultaneity is presented graphically in the scene in Maxim's where uninhibited postwar hedonism is celebrated in the revue tableau featuring naked girls entitled 'Die Jagd nach dem Glück' ['the pursuit of happiness'] (ironically, 'happiness' is portrayed by the miserable Marianne), followed by one in which the modern technological pride of Germany, represented by the Zeppelin, is likewise paraded by naked females; incongruously, the delighted customers leap to their feet to celebrate their nationalistic tradition by singing the first verse of 'Deutschland über alles'. In fact, though, this German jingoism is not 'their' nationalist tradition; which underlines even more heavily the special confusion and desperation of post-war German-speaking Austria. If the older generation was confused and disoriented by the radical changes they had experienced in their lifetime, the generation born at the turn of the century and later (Erich the Nazi student is a 'Neunzehn-hundertelfer', born in 1911) had never known peace and stability, and had even greater reason for psychological dependency creating susceptibility to irrational politics. Horváth's description in 1929 of Sladek the member of the 'schwarze Reichswehr' (an illicit army raised secretly in defiance of the conditions of the Versailles treaty) covers the type:

> Sladek ist als Figur ein völlig aus unserer Zeit geborener und nur durch sie erklärbarer Typ; [...] der Typus des Traditionslosen, Entwurzelten, dem jedes feste Fundament fehlt und der so zum Prototyp des Mitläufers wird. Ohne eigentlich Mörder zu sein, begeht er einen Mord. Ein pessimistischer Sucher, liebt er die Gerechtigkeit – ohne daß er an sie glaubt (*GW*, II, p.148).

> [As a figure Sladek is completely a child of our time and can only be explained by that fact [...]; he is the typical example of those without roots and traditions, lacking any firm basis and so becoming the prototype of the time-server. Without really being a murderer he commits a murder. He is a pessimistic seeker who loves justice – without believing in it.][19]

Sladek's age-group was, of course, also Horváth's own, and he had good reason to fear the generation that was produced by the war, without ever having experienced war itself at first hand. In a sketch for the novel *Ein Kind unserer Zeit* [A Child of our Time],[20] one character puts it well when he says 'In der heutigen Zeit sind wir alle Findelkinder' ['In this day and age we're all foundlings']. For those 'orphaned by the times', war really is 'der Vater aller Dinge' ['the father of all things'], as the title of the first chapter of *Ein Kind unserer Zeit* has it. With grievances to settle, they are likely to turn to the 'father' they have never known, above all to revenge themselves on the generation of the real fathers who have supposedly betrayed them.

As the motto of the play indicates, with its approximation of 'stupidity' to 'infinity', Horváth knows what he is up against in attempting to recreate the *Volksstück* as a moral institution for his time. To this end, he purposely evokes responses – by the use of irresistible Viennese music, for example – to frustrate them; in other words, he proceeds according to the method by which all serious literature evolves. In the language of reader-response theory, he creates 'parole qui doit, en même temps qu'elle lui parle, créer un interlocateur capable de l'entendre' ['words that must, at the same time that they speak to him, create an interlocutor capable of listening'].[21] His novelty lies in 'creating his interlocutor' by appealing to his or her instinctual life. Old conventions of the *Volksstück* are made to play their part. The recognition scene (III, i) carefully set up by the Rittmeister confounds the Raimund tradition of 'recognition as synonymous with reconciliation': the Zauberkönig rejects Marianne. But the principle of recognition is now perhaps applied to the instincts of the interlocutor, the audience, in place of the stage character; it is for them to recognise Marianne and the Zauberkönig for what they are, and to see the seriousness of such an abdication from instinctually recognisable moral reality. It is characteristic of Horváth that it is just when his characters are most sure that they have escaped responsibility into a world of distraction and entertainment (the fairground in *Kasimir und Karoline*; the Italian Evening in the play of that name) that they encounter reality. The 'stage within a stage' device makes the scene at Maxim's a triple escape for Horváth's audience; within the theatre, they are transported to another location, and then presented with 'tableaux vivants' by the Conferencier. Maxim's is in itself a 'Steigerung' [intensification] of the stage-characters' would-be escapist evening, for they progress at one bound and without difficulty from the kitsch of old Vienna at the Heuriger to that of brash new Weimar cabaret, which might as well be taking place in Berlin – a progression that surely represents a comment in itself. The frustrated escapism and the inverted recognition scene at Maxim's are a figure for the role of theatre and for the function of Horváth's reconstructed version of the *Volksstück* convention. In this version, as in the old, recognition is not primarily a function of the intellect, but of the heart.

Notes

1. Quoted from Ödön von Horváth, 'Gebrauchsanweisung', *Gesammelte Werke: kommentierte Ausgabe in Einzelbänden*, ed. by Traugott Krischke in collaboration with Susanna Foral-Krischke (15 vols, Frankfurt, 1983–88), XI, p. 218. This edition will subsequently be referred to in the text as *GW* with volume number.

2. W. E. Yates, 'The Idea of the "Volksstück" in Nestroy's Vienna', *German Life and Letters*, 38 (1984–85), 462–73 (p. 471).

3. W. E. Yates, 'The Idea of the "Volksstück"' (p. 464), quoting Franz Wiest, *Theater-zeitung*, 8 May 1837, 365.

4. See Gerd Müller, *Das Volksstück von Raimund bis Kroetz* (Munich, 1979), p.96.

5. See Herbert Gamper, *Ödön von Horváth. Geschichten aus dem Wienerwald*. Hrsg. Württembergisches Staatstheater Stuttgart. Programmbuch 7. 14.3.75.

6. Wilhelm Reich's *Mass Psychology of Fascism* (New York, 1970) recognises the power of fascist ideology in terms of unconscious sexual strivings; Ernst Bloch in *Erbschaft dieser Zeit* (Heritage of our Times, Zurich, 1935) indicts the Left for abandoning the terrain of fantasy to fascist colonisation, and shows how fascism filled a void at the heart of Enlightenment rationality. See Anson Rabinbach, 'Unclaimed Heritage: Ernst Bloch's *Heritage of our Times* and the Theory of Fascism', *New German Critique*, 11 (1977), 5–21, especially the aphoristic quotation from Bloch: 'The Nazis speak falsely, but to people, the communists truthfully, but of things' (p. 19).

7. Ernst Jünger, Vorwort to *Der feurige Weg*, by Franz Schauwecker (Leipzig, 1926), VII–X, p. x; Johannes R. Becher, *(CHCl=CH)3 As (Levisite) oder Der einzig gerechte Krieg, Gesammelte Werke*, ed. by the Johannes-R.-Becher-Archiv of the Deutsche Akademie der Künste zu Berlin (Berlin, Weimar, 1966–), x, pp. 347–48. See the recent (unpublished) University of Nottingham thesis by Thorsten Bartz, ' "Allgegenwärtige Fronten" – Sozialistische und linke Kriegsromane in der Weimarer Republik 1918–1933' (Ph.D., 1997), pp. 49–50.

8. See e.g. Jeffrey Herf, *Reactionary Modernism: Technology, Culture and Politics in Weimar and the Third Reich* (Cambridge, 1984), p. 81: '[Jünger] was contemptuous of "the masses" and celebrated a myth of a charismatic elite, a community born of the trenches that prefigured a more extensive national authoritarian community. In his view, the "experience" of the war ought to take precedence over intellectualistic haggling over political programs and ideologies.'

9. Horst Jarka, 'Horváth und der Traditionalismus', lecture given in 1975 on the thirtieth anniversary of the liberation of Austria, to the 'Internationales Symposium zur Erforschung des österreichischen Exils von 1934–1945, vom 3.–6. Juni in Wien', p. 4. (Text lodged in the Ödön von Horváth Archive at the Akademie der Künste, Berlin.)

10. Hertha Pauli, *Der Riß der Zeit geht durch mein Herz* (Vienna, Hamburg, 1970), p.25, recalling Horváth's comment on his own characters: 'San's net tierisch? fragte er immer wieder' ['Ain't they animals? he kept on saying'].

11. 'Adieu Europa', *Neue Wellen*, in Ödön von Horváth, *Die stille Revolution. Kleine Prosa*, (ed.) Traugott Krischke (Frankfurt, 1978), p. 88.

12. Horváth, unidentified newspaper cutting in the former Horváth Archive, Akademie der Künste, Berlin.

13. Postscript by Ansgar Hillach to Suhrkamp edition of *Mord in der Mohrengasse* and *Revolte auf Côte 3018* (Frankfurt a. M., 1981), p. 100.

14. Burghard Schmidt, 'German Irrationalism during Weimar', in *Telos*, 65 (1985), 87–96 (p. 91).

15. Theodor Adorno, 'The Stars down to Earth: the *Los Angeles Times* Astrology Column', originally published in *Telos*, 19 (1974), 13–90; reproduced in *The Stars down to Earth and other Essays on the Irrational in Culture*, (ed.) with an Introduction by Stephen Crook (London and New York, 1994), p.45. References to this publication will subsequently be indicated in the body of the text by 'Adorno' and page number.

16. Subsequent references to *Geschichten aus dem Wiener Wald* in the edition cited (see Note 1) will be given in the text as page numbers only.

17. Stephen Crook, 'Introduction' to Theodor Adorno, *The Stars down to Earth*, p. 11.
18. See Ernst Bloch, 'Nonsynchronism and the Obligation to its Dialectics', trans. Mark Ritter, from *Erbschaft dieser Zeit*, in *New German Critique*, 11 (1977), 22–38 (p. 22): 'Not all people exist in the same Now. They do so only externally, by virtue of the fact that they may all be seen today. But that does not mean that they are living at the same time with others.'
19. Translation by Ian Huish, *A Student's Guide to Horváth* (London, 1980), p.26.
20. Formerly to be found in the Horváth Archive in the Akademie der Künste, Berlin.
21. G. Picon, *Introduction à une ésthetique de la littérature* (Paris, 1953), p. 34. Quoted by Hans Robert Jauss, 'Literaturgeschichte als Provokation der Literaturwissenschaft', in *Literaturgeschichte als Provokation* (Frankfurt, 1970, pp. 144–207 (p. 172)). For a translation of the Jauss essay, see R. Cohen (ed.), *New Directions in Literary History* (London, 1974).

Part Two
Review Article

Viennese Theatre History

John Warren

W. E. Yates, *Theatre in Vienna: A Critical History 1776–1995* (Cambridge: Cambridge University Press, 1996), 328 pp., £35.00

A history of Viennese theatre in English has long been needed, and one could have thought of no-one better qualified for the job of writing it than W. E. Yates, whose published work, in addition to numerous articles and reviews, includes *Grillparzer: A Critical Introduction* (1972), *Nestroy: Satire and Parody in Viennese Popular Comedy* (1972), *Schnitzler, Hofmannsthal and the Austrian Theatre* (1992), and *Nestroy and the Critics* (1994). That such an exercise would pose considerable problems is clear to anyone who read his review of Franz Hadamowsky's attempt in 1988.[1] The problems facing the author of an English history are perhaps even greater. How broad a readership can one expect? Readers with an academic interest in Austrian culture will be delighted with a volume marked by scholarly clarity of vision and factual presentation, a mastery of the widest range of source material, and the avoidance of confusing lists of long-forgotten personalities. For those whose knowledge of Viennese theatrical history is limited to the first half of the nineteenth century and to the Schnitzler and Hofmannsthal years, Yates's excellent account of those years and, indeed, the intervening period, will prove of inestimable value and at times perhaps a necessary corrective, as will his fair and balanced account of theatre since World War II. The latter section includes the case for and against Claus Peymann and references to Vienna's recent attempt to emulate London under the slogan 'Vienna, the Metropolis of Musicals'.

The nuts and bolts of theatrical life are clearly presented: theatres and their administration; new buildings (not to forget those destroyed by fire); the relationship of the state theatres to private theatres; the repertoire; an assessment of the key theatre directors, producers and actors; and an account of the politics of theatre and the interaction of politics and theatre. When one considers that opera and operetta are also included within the scope of this ambitious, and, compared to Hadamowsky's 700-page work, relatively slim volume, one can only marvel at Yates's organisational powers.

All this brings me back to the question of the readership. An English-speaking theatre practitioner wanting to know what characterises 'Viennese' theatre, as opposed to the theatre of Berlin, Paris, London or New York, may find the reading of this scholarly and concise work slightly harder going than those already well acquainted with Vienna and the Viennese, despite some cogent contrasts (particularly with Paris and London). But, before attempting to define the essence of Viennese theatrical life, let me first briefly survey Yates's achievement.

The narrative account begins with the two decrees promulgated on 23 March 1776 by Joseph II. One of them elevated one of the two court theatres, the Burgtheater, to the status of a 'National Theatre', while the second broke the monopoly previously enjoyed by the court theatres by allowing 'Spektakelfreiheit' or 'Schauspielfreiheit' (a new liberty for theatrical performance that permitted the building of new theatres outside the walled inner city). This first chapter elegantly indicates the main threads of theatrical development in Vienna prior to this event, with the almost obligatory references to the splendours of baroque opera (Cesti's *Il pomo d'oro* of 1668) and to Lady Mary Wortley Montagu's reports on a baroque opera (*Angela Vincitrici di Alcina*) and on Stranitzky's version of the Amphitryon story (*Amphitrio*) which she saw in 1716. The suppression of extemporised comedy and the figure of Hanswurst (seen as a part of that enlightened despotism – and here Sonnenfels is a key figure – which introduced censorship for printed books) are covered, but the decisive changes to theatrical life in Vienna begin after 1776. We see the establishment of the theatres that were to form the basis for Viennese theatre for over fifty years: the Burgtheater and Kärtnerthortheater, which were controlled and financed by the court, and the three 'commercial' theatres situated outside the walled city. Yates sees this structure as the basis for 'the most remarkable half-century of theatre in the history of German-speaking Europe', and few (apart from devotees of Berlin's theatrical life between 1918 and 1933) will challenge this claim.

No-one working in Austrian theatre studies can fail to recognise that censorship has been a vital factor, particularly in the period from Joseph II to the revolution of 1848. The question is well aired in the second chapter as a necessary prerequisite to an understanding of the problems faced by directors and playwrights alike, and key documents are provided, in German, in Appendix 1. The threat of censorship produced pre-censorship, which helped dramatists, especially in the popular theatre, to refine their work and avoid the worst excesses of crudity witnessed by Lady Mary (Yates spared us her report that 'the two Sosias fairly let down their breeches in the direct view of the boxes ...'). There were, and are, other sorts of censorship in Vienna not mentioned by Yates: that exercised by the court, which meant that the first performance of Richard Strauss's opera *Salome* had to take place in Graz; and an unofficial political censorship that did not allow the performance of Stefan Grossmann's *Die beiden Adler* nor (more recently, on the fiftieth anniversary of the 1934 civil war) Friedrich Wolf's *Floridsdorf*.

222

The next two chapters cover that 'golden half-century'. Chapter 3, on the 'old' Burgtheater, provides a lively account of Vienna's pre-eminent stage until the move to the new building designed by Semper on the Ringstrasse (originally a design for Wagner's Bayreuth). From the positive work of Schreyvogel, particularly with young dramatists such as Grillparzer and Bauernfeld and in establishing a repertoire, we trace the downward path to 1849 and the accession of Heinrich Laube, the German who revived the theatre's fortunes, hiring new acting talent and putting into place a repertoire of which any European theatre would have been proud. The revolutionary year of 1848 is featured (very interesting are the details of the performance of Benedix's play *Das bemooste Haus*, an illustration of which adorns the front cover) and the problems associated with the unpopular and difficult move to the new theatre are covered. We also learn something of actors' salaries in the Biedermeier period, generous when compared to the relatively modest sums paid to dramatists (no royalties until 1844).

The account of the commercial theatres in 'Old Vienna' (chapter 4) which parallels the above is, as was to be expected, a lively and well-balanced *tour de force*. I recommend it as background reading for all who study the work of Raimund and Nestroy. Five sections take us from an account of the three 'popular theatres', through an excellent assessment of the leading director Karl Carl (Yates is kinder to his business practices than many commentators), to a general survey of the cultural climate and working environment, the debate on 'popular drama' and finally to an examination of the decline of dialect comedy and its replacement by operetta. Having introduced the arrival of operetta from France, Yates now (chapter 5) provides a brief excursus into the world of opera and operetta, ending with a description of the move and early years of the new opera house on the Ring.

Two solid chapters now take us through the new changes to Vienna's theatrical life in the late nineteenth century and on to what Yates terms 'Modernism at the end of the monarchy'. These are informative and worthwhile chapters, providing many insights into territory that had not hitherto been sufficiently explored in English. We learn much about Laube's second career in the private sector and of his rivalry with the Burgtheater under Dingelstedt (another German) exemplified by the two rival productions (1872) of Grillparzer's *Ein Bruderzwist in Habsburg*. Much valuable information is given about new theatrical enterprises and how theatre reflected the age of Makart and what is known as the 'Ringstraßenstil'. Of greatest interest, perhaps, is the account given of the journalist Adam Müller-Guttenbrunn (for a brief period director of the Raimund Theatre), a man who, in his journalistic attempts to infect the Viennese theatre with anti-Semitism, matched the worst efforts of Vienna's Christian Social Mayor Lueger. Vienna's uncertain approach to early theatrical modernism, as seen in the reception of Ibsen, Hauptmann, Schnitzler and others, is well documented. While Max Burckhard, director of the Burgtheater from 1890 to 1898, increased the acting strength and welcomed the new drama, championing Ibsen, Anzengruber and Schnitzler, his successor, the Berliner Paul Schlenther, though starting well, proved 'cautious and indecisive'. There is also a brief mention of the establishment of cabaret in Vienna (although I find no mention of Rudolf Weys's excellent short account, *Cabaret und Kabarett in Wien*, in the otherwise very comprehensive bibliography).

The period of the First Austrian Republic, when the two court theatres became state theatres and were placed under the direct control of the Ministry of Education, is extended to cover the National Socialist years. They were not good years for Vienna: the severe financial problems of the impoverished new republic did not make for a thriving theatrical scene although there were some notable productions, and the opera continued to provide evenings to match the finest in the world. Anti-Semitism was strong, the most notorious example being the attack on the first performance of Schnitzler's *Reigen*. Another decisive factor was that many leading actors and dramatists, who would normally have made Vienna their home, were forced to find fame and fortune in Berlin.[2] There is also the case of Max Reinhardt to consider. Intrigues were mounted to prevent his involvement with the Burgtheater (though many wished that he should become its director) but, in 1924, he did find a temporary home in the Theater in der Josefstadt, bringing with him a superb team of actors, including many Viennese, from Berlin. Reinhardt was a figure of world renown, who had made his name in Berlin and, despite his activities in Vienna and Salzburg, was unable to resist the lure of Berlin and, indeed, of productions throughout Europe and eventually the United States. But there were others in pre-war Vienna worthy of note, among them Rudolf Beer, called by Hofmannsthal 'the youngest, most active and indeed most talented theatre director in Vienna' – the unkind might say that was because he staged the dramatist's *Der Unbestechliche*. He controlled Vienna's largest theatrical empire for several years, providing valuable links with Berlin through co-operation with the producer Karlheinz Martin and many guest actors. Nor must the German Hermann Röbbeling be forgotten. He did much in the 1930s to restore the fortunes of the Burgtheater, mounting major cycles of classical drama, as well as staging over forty Austrian dramatists, including many contemporary writers.

This compact and well-balanced survey ends with a chapter on the Second Republic: from post-war rebuilding to the situation today where, once again, the Burgtheater is controlled by a German, Claus Peymann. Peymann shows little or no respect for the Austrian tradition and, in spite of great directorial skill, remains a highly controversial figure. While focusing perforce on the major theatrical institutions, Yates still manages to find space for reference to the achievements of the smaller independent theatres, including Hans Gratzer's Schauspielhaus with its programme of contemporary drama and the tiny theatre of the 'Gruppe 80' that cultivates the Viennese repertoire.

A useful appendix of documents from the earlier years of Viennese theatre, and a clear guide to 'Research Resources', are followed by a comprehensive bibliography. There are thirty-one illustrations and a useful map of Vienna in 1845 showing the five theatres and the sites of other post-1776 foundations. A reviewer may suggest that a list of available sound recordings and videos (of which there are many, though commercial availability fluctuates wildly) could be added, should the book be reprinted.

'... aber Wien ist die Stadt der feinsten Theaterpsychologie des breiten Publikums... Wien erkennt den Schauspieler wie keine zweite Stadt.'
Max Reinhardt[3]

Now we may ask wherein lies the specific quality of Viennese theatre. How does it differ from theatre in Berlin, Paris, London or New York? Considering the position of Vienna at the centre for so many years of a multi-national empire, the outsider might look for a lively multi-ethnic theatre – the strong influence from Czechoslovakia, from Hungary, Galicia and the Balkans. He would look in vain, for Vienna's only concession to its subject states lay in the use of nationalistic musical forms, such as the polka and the csárdás, in operetta. Over the years, Viennese theatre has fostered only two traditions. One is its dialect theatre (popular or 'Volkstheater'), a tradition that lived on after Raimund and Nestroy in the work of Anzengruber and Schönherr and is not entirely extinguished today, even though, as Yates suggests, it was eclipsed by operetta in the 1870s and now (unfortunately) by the musical. It lived on, too, in revivals of the work of the two greatest 'Volksdichter', Raimund and Nestroy, especially once they became accepted by the Burgtheater, though I fear that tradition looks weaker now, after the arrival of Peymann and especially after the deaths of so many great exponents of a tradition of comic acting that went back to Stranitzky. It is sad that Josef Meinrad receives no mention in this volume. Meinrad, holder of the Iffland Ring, along with Erich Kunz (who claimed he made a new extempore joke in every performance of *The Magic Flute*), surely gave the Viennese public enormous pleasure over the years. The second, of course, is the Western tradition that looks to the European classics (Shakespeare and the German classical dramatists as cornerstones) and to comedy and the lighter French and English farces, the influence of which on Viennese theatre Yates so skilfully indicates. Another crucial element of Viennese theatre is that provided, naturally enough, by Viennese authors. Ample reference is made to them but they do not seem to travel well and are not often to be found in theatres outside the German-speaking areas. As for Austria's former subject states, it was not until Röbbeling's cycle 'Stimmen der Völker im Drama' (introduced in part for political reasons) that the classic works of the Poles, the Hungarians and the Czechs were seen in Vienna.

Crucial to Vienna is the relationship with Germany, particularly with Berlin and Hamburg. Austria's theatrical life (dialect comedy apart) has been intricately interwoven with German actors, directors and dramatists in a way seen in no other theatrical centre (not even in the interaction between London and Dublin). From the Austrian Schreyvogel (who gained much from years spent in Jena and Weimar) through Laube, Dingelstedt, Schlenther, Karlheinz Martin, Röbbeling and now Peymann, German directors and producers have played a vital role in directing Viennese theatrical affairs. German actors, too, from Schröder and Sacco through Costenoble, Mitterwurzer, and the great Werner Krauss, contributed to the dignity and fame of the Burgtheater, alongside much excellent local talent.

Great acting and great actors, too, have fascinated the Viennese. Stefan Zweig, as Yates reminds us, bore witness in his autobiography to the esteem in which the great thespians were held. Symbolic of that reverence was the funeral of Max Devrient in 1929 (complete with lying in state in the Burgtheater and the final procession along the Ring). It is interesting to note, by contrast, that in Berlin in 1929 Albert Steinrück's death was celebrated by a charity performance of Wedekind's *Marquis von Keith* in which every major actor was allotted a role, right down to Fritzi Massary's non-speaking chambermaid (according to Ihering, 'the glory of the evening'). Many who read this volume will have their own memories. Josef Meinrad and Attila Hörbiger in the post-war years might come to mind but, as an example of the impact of an actor on a Viennese audience, I remember on one of my first visits to the Burgtheater the palpable frisson of excitement that ran round the theatre when Boy Gobert (a German actor) appeared on stage in the minor role of Chevalier Dumont in Raimund's *Der Verschwender*.

The influential Berlin theatre director and producer Leopold Jessner remarked: 'Theatre does not just mirror its age, it also mirrors the way that age changes.'[4] It may seem difficult to apply that judgement to Vienna when comparing the reflection, for example, of the political situation in the interwar period (a time in Berlin where the stage was like a seismograph measuring every ripple of the social and political atmosphere), but this book shows that, in a very Viennese way, the theatre over 200 years has reflected the concerns, strengths and limitations of its inhabitants. From the early nineteenth century one remembers two worlds: the young Bauernfeld and his friends in the Burgtheater cheered the lines in *Torquato Tasso* that condemn as barbarians those who reject poetry, while, in the 'Vorstadt', pomposity was deflated in the numerous parodies (particularly effective was Nestroy's later demolition of Hebbel's *Judith* and of two Wagner operas), and it is good to see that some of these parodies are appearing again, staged by smaller companies. From the security of Raimund's Biedermeier world, the theatre moved, with Nestroy, into the more turbulent waters of the Vormärz (much, of necessity, had to be read between the lines), and on into the era of the 'Ringstraßenstil'. After 1918, the post-war trauma was marked by a nostalgic return to historical romances but, as Josef Gregor perceptively noted, the repertoire did include references, however oblique, to the political situation.[5] One such play was Hofmannsthal's *Das Salzburger große Welttheater*, where the beggar was depicted as the threat of world communism. Another was Csokor's *3. November 1918*, performed shortly before the Anschluss. It is a superb example of Viennese ambivalence, managing to please everyone; from the left (at that time disenfranchised) through the 'Vaterländische Front' to the National Socialists (Fred Hennings, who played the young Carinthian, was already a member of that party).

Karl Kraus (whose idiosyncratic efforts at one-man drama Yates charts) once remarked that the Burgtheater was capable only of looking to the past

('... hat nur Vergangenheit und keine Zukunft') and, for Vienna, tradition has always been more important than the latest literary fashion; Klinger's *Die Zwillinge* (a fiery drama of 'Sturm und Drang') was rejected under Joseph II and, in the 1920s, the avant-garde made little impact on Vienna (at best in guest productions from Berlin). Brecht, for example, was almost totally ignored. The more traditional forms favoured by the Viennese public, in addition to the dialect drama, which had one of its finest later manifestations in Horváth's *Geschichten aus dem Wiener Wald*, include the 'Konversationsstück' pioneered by Bauernfeld and continued with considerable popular success by Hermann Bahr and also by Hofmannsthal (a comparison of Bauernfeld's *Aus der Gesellschaft* with the latter's *Der Schwierige* would make an interesting study).

Tradition, a strong German influence, local and European comedy, a reverence for good acting, a fostering of the West European dramatic repertoire: these have been the hallmarks of Viennese theatre over the years. Let me conclude by citing Austria's greatest dramatist Franz Grillparzer. He once maintained that there were three vital elements for successful theatre: 'Schauspieler, Dichter und ein Publikum'. Looking at 200 years of Viennese theatre (and despite the Zasche cartoon that adorns the back page of the cover – an anti-Semitic attack on the *nouveaux riches* at the opera in the early 1920s) one realises that Viennese theatre, notwithstanding its ups and downs, has had its fair share of all three: great actors and great authors matched by a knowledgeable and appreciative audience. This excellent volume provides a rich account of the diversity of Vienna's theatrical life extending for well over two centuries in an authoritative, excellently balanced and concise survey. It will certainly be essential reading for all specialists in Austrian theatre for years to come.

Notes

1. Franz Hadamowsky, *Wien. Theatergeschichte* (Vienna, 1988) reviewed by W. E. Yates in the *Modern Language Review*, 85 (1990), 515–18.
2. 'Ernst Krenek and Max Brand – two Austrians at the "court" of Weimar', *German Life and Letters*, 41 (1988), 467–78.
3. Max Reinhardt, *Schriften*, ed. Hugo Fetting (Berlin, 1974).
4. Leopold Jessner, *Schriften*, ed. Hugo Fetting (Berlin, 1979), p. 126.
5. Josef Gregor, *Geschichte des österreichischen Theaters* (Vienna, 1948), pp. 270–71.

Part Three
Reviews

Mauriz Schuster and Hans Schikola, *Das alte Wienerisch. Ein kulturgeschichtliches Wörterbuch* (Vienna: Deuticke, 1996), 350 pp., 398 Sch./DM 56.00.

Das alte Wienerisch is a revised edition of *Sprachlehre der Wiener Mundart*, which was first published in 1956 and again in 1983. It was then, and to some extent still is, an exceptionally thorough description of the Viennese dialect, the particular virtue óf which lies in the fact that it is not merely a dictionary of dialect words (of which there are a number, all of them aimed squarely at lay readers) but devotes a substantial section to a description of the phonology of Viennese, together with a brief explanation of the processes of diachronic change that account, to some extent, for the phonological deviations from standard German. It also contains a short description of aspects of Viennese dialect grammar, including a detailed discussion of the pronoun system and of verb forms. There is remarkably little published work on the grammar of the dialect and, for this alone, the book is worth reading, though its approach, as in the other sections, is purely descriptive.

The impetus for issuing a new edition of the work was the discovery of a large body of unpublished notes Schuster had made prior to his death which enabled the dictionary section to be substantially expanded. It is unfortunate, however, that the editors of the new edition have contented themselves with merely tacking these additional items on to the dictionary without undertaking any further updating whatsoever. Quite aside from the fact that modern research into Viennese phonology has rendered some of Schikola's explanations of particular forms wholly out of date, it is regrettable that the opportunity was not taken to replace his old-fashioned transcription conventions with IPA notations, which are no less accessible to the general reader and would have greatly increased the work's usefulness to linguists.

It is, in general, hard to tell at which readership the book is aimed. The majority of dialect dictionaries are intended for native speakers of the dialect, or at least those with a passive competence in that variety, and so are structured as monolingual reference works. This is not a dictionary of contemporary Viennese, however, but of Viennese as it was spoken before the war, indeed as it was spoken in Schikola's own childhood. The quality of personal reminiscence in the entries is so strong that the editors are obliged to admit 'Fast möchte man meinen, der riesige wissenschaftliche Aufwand hätte letztlich dazu gedient, die Atmosphäre der eignen Kindheitsjahre festzuhalten' (p. 8). The dictionary thus contains lengthy descriptions of 'längst verschwundenen Straßentypen und Vertretern ausgestorbener Berufe', and includes lexemes such as 'Vatermörder' which are manifestly not Viennese. The dictionary, then, is not aimed at the long-dead native speakers of this variety, but at those interested in Vienna's past, and hence the editors have termed it 'Ein kulturgeschichtliches Wörterbuch'.

It is frustrating that a work that calls itself a dictionary, but whose readers are not native speakers, provides no means of looking up the dialect equivalent of a word known in standard German. A reader interested, for instance, in knowing the pre-war term for 'Straßenbahn' has to plough through almost the entire lexicon to discover that it was 'Tramway' rather than the modern Viennese 'Bim'. It is also regrettable that the editors did not take the opportunity to remove the irritatingly self-pitying references to the achievements of the Viennese after World War II, a pity that is not extended to the city's Jewish citizens, of whose sufferings no mention is made, and whose contribution to the dictionary is startlingly out of proportion to their influence on the dialect (a swift read through produced a total of eleven items that are derived from Hebrew or from Yiddish and only three, 'Jud', 'Binkljud' and 'Körberljud', that refer explicitly to Jews). That a work that calls itself a 'kulturgeschichtliches Wörterbuch' should ignore the traces left on the language by Jewish culture is peculiar, and it is particularly regrettable given that this is an aspect of Viennese cultural history that is irrevocably lost. It is hard to believe that, in pre-Nazi Vienna, there was no dialect word for synagogue or for Sabbath, or that there were not more than three words for Jews, but, because they would almost certainly have been pejorative, they presumably did not fit Schikola's vision of a Viennese past, full of 'Humor und Gemütlichkeit' (p. 12). Schikola died in 1952, but it is remarkable that his editors in 1996 did not seek to rectify this glaring omission.

VICTORIA MARTIN

Konrad Küster, translated by Mary Whittall, *Mozart. A Musical Biography* (Oxford: Clarendon Press, 1996), xviii + 409 pp., £25.00.

Vjera Katalinić (ed.), *Off-Mozart. Musical Culture and the 'Kleinmeister' of Central Europe 1750–1820*, Croatian Musicological Society Series (Stuyvesant, NY: Pendragon Press, 1996), 240 pp., $36.00 (paper).

Konrad Küster's *Mozart. Eine musikalische Biographie* (1990) struck me as one of the most valuable studies from the period of the anniversary celebrations. I frequently take it down from the shelf to see what its author has to say about a work or a topic of immediate concern to me, and am hardly ever disappointed. A warm welcome, then, to the elegant volume that Oxford University Press has produced, in Mary Whittall's stylish translation. It reads very well, though comparison with the original edition shows the occasional altered emphasis, and odd minor departures from the German. These may indicate that Küster has taken advantage of recent research, and of the opportunity occasionally to modify his opinions.

This will for many readers prove to be the ideal single-volume study of Mozart's life and works: reliable, stimulating, easily handled, uncantankerous. There are forty mainly short chapters, each devoted to a work or group of works typical of a particular event or period of Mozart's life: there are copious footnotes (of far greater use to the reader than the endnotes of the German edition); fifteen well-chosen and reasonably well-reproduced illustrations; music examples; select bibliography; and indexes of works, persons and

places. As in the original Deutsche Verlags-Anstalt edition, the endpapers –
many-coloured facsimiles of the slow movement of the Horn Concerto K495 –
are of particular beauty. What is new about Küster's book is the successful
attempt to draw out the general implications from particular examples; in the
best sense it is indeed a 'musical biography'.

The Croatian volume, with its oddly endearing title, comprises the
proceedings of the International Musicological Symposium held in Zagreb on
1–3 October 1992. It is a handy little paperback volume, its front cover
decorated with hasty drawings from Mozart's letters. The seventeen papers
are the works of authors mainly from east and south-east European regions;
two come from Italy, one each from France, Austria, Germany (and one,
though working in the United States, has a local name). All the essays are in
English or German (apart from two in Italian and one each in French and
Serbo-Croat; the latter has a summary in Italian). An admirable touch, too
rare in publications of this kind, is a full index of names.

As the title implies, the subject matter is music and musicians from the
fringes of Mozart's field of activity. A few of the contributions are general in
subject matter; most are devoted to an interesting minor figure (František
Dusík's orchestral music, masses by Haibel and Schwerdt, sacred compositions and piano works by Ebner, new research on Maria Theresia Paradis) or
to the music of a particular locality (Zagreb, with Croatia more generally;
Ljubljana, Trieste, Bratislava, Warsaw). Two essays are, as it were, *On-
Mozart*: a study of early editions of works by Mozart that are preserved in the
library of the Croatian Music Institute in Zagreb, and a chapter on Leopold
Mozart and the 'mannered Mannheim Goût'. This is a valuable publication,
very different from, yet in its own way quite as useful as, Agnes Ziffer's
Kleinmeister zur Zeit der Wiener Klassik (Tutzing, 1984).

PETER BRANSCOMBE

Hartmut Laufhütte and Karl Möseneder (eds), *Adalbert Stifter: Dichter und Maler,
Denkmalpfleger und Schulmann. Neue Zugänge zu seinem Werk* (Tübingen: Niemeyer,
1996), 590 pp., DM 142.00.

This volume had its origin in a symposium held in Passau in April 1994.
Though clearly very much a local occasion – no less than eight of the
contributors are Passau academics – one still finds such famous names of
Stifter scholarship in the German-speaking world as Alfred Doppler and
Johann Lachinger represented. As is suggested by the title of the book and by
the fact that the editors are a Germanist and an art historian respectively, both
well known for their contributions to early modern studies, the symposium
had as its aim an examination of all spheres of Stifter's activity. The Preface
tells us that interdisciplinarity was the other aim. The twenty-six contributions are divided into four sections which follow these two aims to varying
degrees. The first two of them, 'Kunsttheoretisches, Poetologisches und
andere werkübergreifende Konzepte', and 'Zu größeren Werkzusammenhängen',

include articles on all aspects of Stifter's work but usually from the perspective of a single discipline. Thus, for instance, Stifter's painting is discussed by an art historian. The third and longest section, entitled 'Zu einzelnen Werken', concentrates on analyses of individual literary works, but applies a range of methodologies to them in a much more interdisciplinary fashion. The fourth is a mini-section consisting of only two articles dealing with Stifter's reception.

The following can do no more than pick out some individual articles for comment. In Section I, Karl Möseneder provides an interesting overview of the iconology of Stifter's landscape paintings and Ferdinand van Ingen brings all his knowledge of seventeenth-century thought and imagery to bear in an illuminating contribution on Stifter's concept of fate. Two further contributions in this section, by Jörg Kästner and Joachim W. Storck respectively, deal with 'Liebe' and 'Eros' in Stifter's work. Wilfried Lipp, in discussing Stifter as a 'Denkmalpfleger', puts his ideas in the context of contemporary thinking about older architecture and how to preserve it, comparing his ideas in particular with those of Ruskin, Stifter's contemporary. In Section II, Alfred Doppler makes most welcome comparisons between Stifter's stories and the popular 'Novellen' of the day by such writers as Betty Paoli and Walter Tesche, while Martin Lindner discusses the transformation in Stifter of the Goethean concept of 'Bildung'. In Section III, Marianne Wünsch, Michael Titzmann, Wolfgang Lukas and Wilhelm Kühlmann make use of anthropological theory; Christian von Zimmermann applies psychological methodology; Hans-Werner Eroms uses linguistic analysis; and Birgit Ehlbeck investigates how the scientific thinking of Stifter's day influenced *Kalkstein* and *Witiko*. Other works covered in this section are *Der Hochwald, Die Narrenburg, Die Mappe, Abdias, Brigitta, Zwei Schwestern, Turmalin, Der Nachsommer* and *Nachkommenschaften*. The final section consists of an interesting account of Stifter's reception in Bohemia by Václav Maidl and of the fascinating tale of how Stifter's bust was finally allowed into Valhalla as told by Emanuel Schmid.

This is a handsomely produced and well-edited volume with useful indexes and forty illustrations, of which two are in colour. It is a useful addition to Stifter scholarship, even though one wonders if the contributors live in a hermetically sealed German-speaking world. Apart from the art historians, no one seems interested in attempting to see Stifter within a wider European context. Scholarship on Stifter that is not published in Germany or Austria is ignored. Symptomatic of this is the astonishing fact that the monograph on Stifter by Erika and Martin Swales which appeared in 1984 does not receive so much as a mention from any of the contributors. Neither do the current critical concerns of the French and English-speaking scholarly communities seem to have pierced this seal. It seems to me we do Stifter an injustice if we do not give him his rightful place in a European pantheon as well as in a German Valhalla.

HELEN WATANABE-O'KELLY

Gabriele von Glasenapp, *Aus der Judengasse: Zur Entstehung und Ausprägung deutsch-sprachiger Ghettoliteratur im 19. Jahrhundert*, Conditio Judaica 11 (Tübingen: Niemeyer, 1996), vi +320 pp., DM 152.00.

German literary criticism has perpetuated a misleading image of ghetto fiction as a sentimental genre that idealised ghetto life and shrank from a more naturalistic representation of its frequently harsh reality. The truth is more complex and, as Glasenapp's immensely wide-ranging and informative study demonstrates, infinitely more interesting. It is the first comprehensive analysis of the nineteenth-century German-language ghetto literature of Central Europe. As ghetto fiction assumed a multiplicity of forms, ranging from the historical novel through the village tale to the memoir, Glasenapp abandons any attempt to define the formal characteristics of the genre. Instead she concludes that ghetto fiction is best characterised as a medium through which Jewish writers could explore their identity and work through their response to the challenges of modernity. Analysing the work of well-known ghetto authors, such as Leopold Kompert and Karl Emil Franzos, but also looking at a host of lesser-known authors of ghetto fiction, Glasenapp offers valuable insights into the often openly ideological function of ghetto literature. The ghetto fiction of the orthodox writers, Herz Ehrmann, Isidor Borchardt and Arthur Kahn, for example, articulated a newly assertive neo-orthodox consciousness by presenting orthodox life in a positive light. The ghetto novels of the enlightened Jewish writer, Berthold Auerbach, by contrast, demonstrate that his main concern was to explore the contemporary challenges of assimilation and emancipation. Later in the century, as the growth of anti-Semitism forced many Jews to take refuge in a renaissance of Jewish consciousness, ghetto fiction played a role in the rediscovery and re-evaluation of Eastern European Jewry and more traditional Jewish ways of life. By focusing on the function of ghetto fiction as a response to contemporary Jewish problems, Glasenapp ably demonstrates its significance, not so much as representations of life in the ghetto, but as a reflection of the quest for a viable Jewish identity in the post-ghetto world.

Glasenapp's stimulating analysis also brings out the peculiarities of German, Bohemian and Galician ghetto literature while providing a clear exposition of the political, social and religious developments in each of these regions. She highlights the particular intensity of ideological conflict in Galicia between enlightened, orthodox *and* Hasidic Jews. Inter-Jewish conflict was not so pronounced in Bohemia and so, unlike in Germany and Galicia, the fierce battles between orthodox and modern Jewry find little reflection in the ghetto fiction of the region. Instead, Bohemian Jews, such as Leopold Weisels and Salomon Kohn, drew on the legends of the famous Jewish ghetto of Prague as a source of pride and identity.

Inevitably, a pioneering study of this nature raises many questions that deserve further attention. One of the most fascinating, not to say controversial, aspects of the study that would merit further research is the extent to which Jewish authors engaged in inter-Jewish ideological conflict contributed unwittingly to the construction of Jewish cultural stereotypes in fiction. As Glasenapp offers an historical rather than a literary evaluation of ghetto fiction, there is plenty of work to be done on the language and literary form of ghetto writing. Finally, by drawing attention to the link between ghetto fiction, the genre of autobiography and the search for identity, Glasenapp's study indicates that the concept of ghetto fiction as a form of covert Jewish autobiographical writing is something that would merit further research.

ANITA BUNYAN

Mark H. Gelber, Hans Otto Horch, Sigurd Paul Scheichl (eds), *Von Franzos zu Canetti: Jüdische Autoren aus Österreich. Neue Studien*, Conditio Judaica 14 (Tübingen: Niemeyer, 1996), ix + 428 pp., DM 198.

In their preface, the editors identify the reconstruction of a lost Jewish world and culture as the overriding aim of their publication. Calling for a revision of the common approach to Austrian literature and its emphasis on universal aesthetic qualities, they argue for the recognition of the historical and cultural uniqueness of the works of Austrian-Jewish writers. The volume, which is dedicated to Margarita Pazi, thus marks a gradual change in a critical tradition that has tended to marginalise the category of Jewishness until recently. By loosely grouping articles on authors from the same region, the editors attempt to create a sense of regional Jewish literary histories covering mainly writers from Bohemia, Moravia, the Bukovina, Galicia, Vienna and diverse parts of Austria and Germany.

Some contributions are devoted to forgotten authors: Dieter Sudhoff adds to the rediscovery of Franz Janowitz; Armin A. Wallas introduces the life and work of the expressionist and pan-Asiatic writer Eugen Hoeflich; Harry Zohn offers a survey of the dramatic works of Frank Zwillinger; and finally, Harro H. Kühnelt attempts a rediscovery of Joseph Wechsberg in a rather unstructured, and at times anecdotal and opinionated article.

A second group deals with various symbolisations of a Jewish consciousness: in a very thorough article Florian Krobb explores two examples of the articulation of a Jewish national consciousness in nineteenth-century Prague: the popular *Sippurim* collections and Salomon Kohn's stories. Ehrhard Bahr tries to re-establish Max Brod as a Zionist novelist; Hans Otto Horch places Kisch's ghetto stories in the context of the tradition of German-Jewish ghetto writing; Joseph A. Kruse highlights the importance of Yiddish for Rose Ausländer; and Amir Eshel and Thomas Sparr jointly analyse metaphors of origin in poems by Paul Celan and Dan Pagis in their excellent contribution. While Stefan H. Kaszynski diagnoses a collective consciousness in the works of Galician writers, Itta Shedletzky traces an intertextual dynamic in the literature from Heine to Roth and its influence on the stereotype of the Eastern European Jew. Introducing four autobiographies by Galician women, Maria Klanska focuses on the female experience of Jewishness. Finally, Sigurd Paul Scheichl analyses Jews who are not Jewish in Schnitzler's *Fink und Fliederbusch*, and Sigrid Bauschinger looks at exile and memory in Richard Beer-Hofmann's *Paula. Ein Fragment.*

A third group studies the reception of German-Jewish writing: Jeffrey L. Sammons examines Franzos' and Gustav Karpeles' Heine-reception; Mark H. Gelber analyses the Roth-reception in Zionist journals; Hans-Peter Bayerdörfer compares the reception of Schnitzler's *Professor Bernhardi* in Berlin in 1912 with productions in the early 1930s; and Gerald Stieg looks at aspects of Canetti's reception of Nietzsche.

While most contributions focus on Jewish themes and traditions, some articles, such as Norbert Oellers', Bernard Greiner's and Paul Michael Lützeler's, deal with other aesthetic or ideological aspects not directly addressing Jewish issues. The inclusion of these otherwise stimulating articles weakens the methodological repositioning of German studies towards its German-Jewish heritage as mentioned in the preface. In addition, Leah Hadomi's final contribution on two plays by Franz Csokor and Martin Walser seems somewhat displaced in a volume that is explicitly committed to highlighting the literary achievements of *Jewish* writers from *Austria*. A clearer focus on the articulation of a Jewish consciousness and its symbolisation would have been desirable for the volume as a whole. Many of the above-mentioned articles reflect, however, an increasing critical awareness of the category of Austro-Jewishness and its varied expressions. This alone makes the volume a welcome contribution to Austrian literary histories.

ANNE FUCHS

Lorna Martens, *Shadow Lines. Austrian Literature from Freud to Kafka* (Lincoln and London: University of Nebraska Press, 1996), xii + 291 pp., £35.00.

Katherine Arens, *Austria and Other Margins: Reading Culture* (Columbia, SC: Camden House, 1996), 263 pp., £40.00.

———

Shadow Lines is a handsome book with an eye-catching title, mentioning in one breath two of the biggest 'names' in world culture of the early twentieth century. The now common assumption that Freud was a literary figure, rather than an exceptionally literate scientist, is never here challenged, and the assumption of Kafka (and also Rilke) into the Austrian canon also goes unquestioned. Further, because the book's subtitle suggests something in the nature of literary history, it apparently presents us with a model instance of the issues and problems recently addressed by Wendelin Schmidt-Dengler and his team debating the notion of an Austrian literary history and the contents of the canon.

On closer inspection, the book reveals itself in quite large measure to be the republication and/or reworking of a series of free-standing essays first published between 1982 and 1990. Many readers will be acquainted with at least some of this work, and will not be surprised to find that, out of it, Martens has fashioned a lucid and cogent book. It is, however, in no sense a work of literary history but rather an often densely argued examination of the 'dark area' of the irrational, of memory and dreams, consciousness and the unconscious, concentrating on such writers as Beer-Hofmann, Hofmannsthal, Musil, Rilke and Schnitzler. Aided by Martens's quiet command of psychoanalytic and literary theory, the book deepens our awareness of authors and issues often considered central to turn-of-the-century Austrian literature. Indeed, for long it was the obsessive concentration on the minutiae of the psyche that many regarded as the defining feature of the culture. To that extent, the book reveals nothing new about the *nature* of Austrian literary culture in the early twentieth century. Through the quality of its analyses, however, it demonstrates the deeper structures linking so many of the classic texts of the period. Works examined include examples of the lyric (Hofmannsthal, Rilke), the drama (Hofmannsthal, Schnitzler), shorter prose (Schnitzler, Kafka) and the novel (Musil, Beer-Hofmann) as well as texts by Freud and Breuer. On occasions Martens's prose can be hard going but, in general, her style responds well to the considerable challenge of the material she is dealing with.

This is, then, a generously proportioned book with a consistent theme, one dealing with well-known texts by major authors. Its stated purpose is 'to show how a reorientation in epistemological concerns took place specifically in Austrian culture around 1900, and in what ways Austrian literature from about 1890 to 1924 participates in this reorientation' (p. 1), and in this it succeeds. The book's title is ultimately misleading, however. Above all, one questions the scope of a work bearing this title and concluding with a chapter 'Language Crisis and Literary Form' in which Karl Kraus is mentioned once in the body of the text, Altenberg warrants a solitary mention in a footnote, and Georg Trakl is never mentioned at all. Yet each of these writers addresses the dualisms of known and unknown, order and chaos, language and the inexpressible, and is central to 'Austrian Literature from Freud to Kafka' in a way that Rilke is probably not. Their absence serves merely to perpetuate a schism in the historiography of Austrian literature based on conflicts existing during the lifetimes of the authors themselves. We now know, however, that a concern with the expression of the irrational transcended the squabbles of the day. To have included these missing figures would have made for a still richer book. As it is, Martens reveals deep knowledge of authors and texts, and her work shows none of the signs of hasty thought and production now abounding in an environment that calls for instant returns from scholars and critics.

Katherine Arens's collection of essays is rather different. Unlike *Shadow Lines*, there is no overall theme to *Austria and Other Margins*. Indeed, only four of the eight chapters refer specifically to Austrian literature, the authors treated being Doderer, Schnitzler, Stifter and Grillparzer. Other topics include the literary treatment of Mozart by Mörike, Hildesheimer and Shaffer, and essays on John Irving and Günter Grass, the playwright/director/designer Robert Wilson, Christo (of Reichstag-wrapping fame) and Judy Chicago.

This is a well-meaning book, attempting to perform what Jost Hermand described as 'disquieting criticism', that is, to provide a 'critical reading of culture without asserting the privilege of any particular school of criticism over any text but rather based on the primacy of the text's position *vis-à-vis* a reader in context' (p. 228). Many readers of *Austrian Studies* will warm to these sentiments, and indeed to the sections where Arens displays a lively but attractively undogmatic awareness of theoretical issues. Her close reading of texts may also prove rather disquieting, but not in the manner intended. The opening chapter on the politics of Doderer's *Die Dämonen* already gives grounds for disquiet. It is largely a competent *Forschungsbericht*, but with a shaky grasp of detail. It was to the *Reichsschrifttumskammer* and not the *Reichsschriftstellerkammer* that Doderer's work was unacceptable (p. 15); the novel *Die Strudlhofstiege* was begun in the 1940s, not in the 1930s (p. 15); the consistent misspelling of the translated title as *The Strudelhof Steps* irritates, as does the spelling of the author of *Là-Bas* as J. K. Huysmann (p. 19). Although this essay has valid things to say about Doderer's treatment of history, it is plainly wrong to say that nothing in *Die Dämonen* is 'proto-Nazi' (p. 31).

This tendency to turn a work on its head is far more pronounced in Arens's account of Schnitzler's *Leutnant Gustl*. She claims that a Viennese audience of 1900 would have seen Gustl as the victim of 'an army with excessively high standards' (p. 145), suffering in that institution because of 'suspect lineage, possibly even partially non-Germanic – a member of a questionable element in the Empire's structure' (p. 145). Although Schnitzler has Gustl say that he has been to a dozen performances of *Lohengrin*, Arens contends that 'anyone who had never been to the opera would of course have problems dealing with bakers and other tradesmen' (p. 146). In a novel misreading of the text, where Schnitzler shows Gustl shoving his way to the front of the queue, Arens has the Bäckermeister bump into Gustl, this precipitating Gustl's crisis and emphasising his passivity. Her final assessment of Gustl's situation as conceived by Schnitzler and his position *vis-à-vis* the military is almost perverse:

> [Schnitzler] was countering [the army's] official policy of ethnic diver-
> sity and somewhat open access and suggesting that some officers didn't
> deserve the respect due to an army that should recruit and promote
> better candidates than Gustl (p. 146).

Overall, this section betrays an insecure grasp, not only of *fin de siècle* Viennese literature but also society, for example, attributing 'Red Vienna' to the early 1900s, the time of Christian Social dominance of metropolitan politics (p. 147). In sum, this is an odd book: a pot-pourri which, unlike Martens's meticulous study, one would hesitate to recommend to students.

ANDREW BARKER

Reviews

Anton Mayer, *Theater in Wien um 1900. Der Dichterkreis Jung Wien*, 'Maske und Kothurn', Beiheft 17 (Vienna, Cologne, Weimar: Böhlau, 1997), 174 pp., 298 Sch.

This is an unlikely book to have appeared under the auspices of *Maske und Kothurn* because, despite the title, it is not principally concerned with theatre. Nor, indeed, is it about a 'Dichterkreis'. After beginning with an introduction to 'Jung Wien', it surveys the contemporary issues reflected more or less directly in the dramatic works of five writers from the 'Jung Wien' generation who remained in touch for the rest of their lives: Schnitzler, Hofmannsthal, Bahr (the self-styled 'new Bauernfeld'), Beer-Hofmann and Salten. The last two chapters treat the 'impressionism' of the Viennese 'moderns', and the reputation and standing of the 'Jung Wien' circle, with special emphasis on their traditionalism. The method followed throughout is one of collage rather than of argument. Many pages consist mainly of quotations, not just from the five playwrights and their contemporaries (Wengraf, Wertheimer, Rudolph Lothar), but also from later commentators: Broch, Nadler, Kindermann, Hederer, Renate Wagner, Althaus, and – repeatedly – *Kindlers Literatur Lexikon* (the 1970s edition). There is relatively little evidence of engagement with specialist research published in the last twenty years or so, and even the authentic contemporary evidence used appears to be patchy: much of that cited – even material from Schnitzler's diaries – is excerpted from modern anthologies; Hofmannsthal's 'Ad me ipsum' is referred to as a 'volume'.

Of course, there is some interesting and even – to a lesser extent – some unfamiliar material here. But on the impact of 'Jung Wien' on the theatre there is much more to be said. Theatre was at the heart of Viennese cultural life and, as Mayer points out, actors and actresses feature prominently in the work of his five playwrights. It would be possible to examine the development of the Griensteidl circle in relation to their practical connections with the theatre. This would need to take in the complex relation between the theatres and the whole spectrum of the press, and the relation between traditional theatre and cabaret, and might also be extended to include an examination of the playwrights' contrasting relations with Max Reinhardt, on which Mayer touches briefly. On their engagement with contemporary issues, it would be possible to relate their work to issues of feminism and gender, taking up a point made by Wengraf in 1891 and quoted by Mayer (though he gets Wengraf's name wrong) about the detrimental effect of the coffee-house as an exclusively male preserve. If Schnitzler's early plays show that what was wrong in erotic relations between the sexes was that they were unable to speak openly (Fritz in *Liebelei*, the married couple in *Reigen*), so in the intellectual and cultural fields there were structural obstacles, not least in the universities, in the way of fruitful communication between the sexes. It would also be important to probe, in the theatrical context, the distinctive avoidance of specifically political issues characteristic of this generation, their general unawareness of the political upheaval threatening – a phenomenon that might be explored in comparison with contemporary developments in Berlin and especially in Munich.

239

Readers of this review will doubtless think of other useful angles to probe. It could make a good book, and I hope someone may be stimulated to write it. The field is free.

W. E. YATES

Karin J. Jušek, *Auf der Suche nach der Verlorenen. Die Prostitutionsdebatten im Wien der Jahrhundertwende* (Vienna: Löcker, 1994), 295 pp., 348 Sch.

Karin Jušek's book is far more than a discussion of the debate on prostitution in *fin-de siècle* Vienna. In the first 100 pages she seldom mentions Vienna, but engages in a very detailed and energetic criticism of debates on prostitution, starting with the nineteenth century and ending with more recent feminist debates. Why, she asks, is prostitution always seen as a 'woman's question', when it involves only a small number of women (the prostitutes) and a larger number of men (the clients)? Jušek's answer is that attitudes towards prostitution reflect attitudes towards female sexuality. This, she contends, has always been the case. Sexuality is still seen as being gender-specific, the major division being between male and female sexuality. In the nineteenth century, men alone were thought to have a sexual drive: women were passive or temptresses. This theme was continued by Freudians, who identified the male drive for sexual satisfaction and the female need to be loved. Modern feminists also accept the gender divide, the most radical rejecting heterosexual love as part of male dominance of women. The female sexual libido is seen by all as weaker or less important than that of the male. Throughout the book, Jušek challenges this view, arguing that we do not know enough about our own sexuality to be sure that the gender divide is that important. We assume that men and women have different sexual drives. This, she believes, has seriously distorted the debates on prostitution. Other factors, such as race, class and religion, may also influence sexuality.

It is at this stage that Jušek returns to the studies of nineteenth-century sexuality, repression and prostitution. If sexual drive was/is low, what drove women into prostitution? It is not a simple question to answer, for the prostitutes themselves were never asked; they remain mute and invisible for the historian. Instead, the debates on prostitution have been conducted by bourgeois critics, and their most common answer is economic need – prostitutes were/are 'fallen women' who had no other alternative: they were the lowest of the low. According to Jušek, this argument is based on bourgeois morality. Not all 'fallen women' went into prostitution. Upper-class women went abroad to give birth to illegitimate children. The notion of the irredeemable 'fallen woman' depended on class. Not all women who became prostitutes did so for the same reason and not all remained in prostitution. For some, prostitution was a short-term solution. More important, she argues, some chose prostitution, for it was preferable to the appalling living and working conditions that were the alternative for working-class women.

The second part of this book is a detailed account of the debate on prosti-

240

tution in Vienna at the turn of the century. It covers the introduction of public regulation of prostitution, the attitudes of the bourgeois women's movement, the Social Democratic Party and the Roman Catholic Church. Jušek argues that the laws that were introduced in the second half of the nineteenth century were designed to protect morality rather than to control venereal disease. The bourgeois women's movement and the SDAP were also more concerned with the effect that prostitution had on the family than with the plight of the prostitutes. She quotes Rosa Mayreder and Irma Troll-Borostyani at length, examining the attitude of these Austrian feminists to female sexuality. The SDAP, she argues, was intent on defending itself against conservative allegations of licentiousness. Her discussion of the party covers many aspects of its curious attitude to women, not all of which seem entirely relevant. This is also the case in the section on the Roman Catholic Church.

The book is not easy to read. Its scope is vast, covering sexuality, morality and historical debate, as well as a detailed study of the specific arguments in Vienna at the turn of the century. The division between the two parts is abrupt and both needed serious editing. But the questions that Jušek has raised, albeit in a very personal style, are important.

JILL LEWIS

Beatrix Hoffmann-Holter, '*Abreisendmachung*': *Jüdische Flüchtlinge in Wien 1914 bis 1923* (Vienna: Böhlau, 1995), 302 pp., 476 Sch./DM 68.

The rapid Russian advance into Galicia in the early months of World War I prompted a mass exodus of Jews. Familiar with tsarist anti-Semitism, hundreds of thousands fled into the interior of the Empire, with over 100,000 making their way to Vienna, hoping to find support from friends or relatives among the capital's already substantial Galician Jewish community. While most returned to Galicia during the course of the war, some 25–30,000 remained in the city in the post-war period. In '*Abreisendmachung*', Beatrix Hoffmann-Holter reconstructs the experience of these refugees in exhaustive detail, basing her account on an impressively thorough trawling of Austrian government archives. She focuses on the refugees as 'objects of government welfare' (p. 75) and on the responses of the authorities and the populace at large to their sudden influx and continued presence. Her verdict is overwhelmingly negative: the refugees, she argues convincingly, were the objects of antipathy and outright hatred from almost every sector of Viennese society.

Hoffmann-Holter is relentlessly critical of the Austrian authorities, excoriating the role of the central government and the Viennese Gemeinderat (dominated by the Christian Social party) during the war, and the Social Democratic Party in the immediate post-war years. The Social Democrats' treatment of the refugees, for example, is called a 'dark stain' upon the movement's history (p. 209). She depicts Austrian officialdom, at all levels, as heartless and overly bureaucratic, mostly devoid of humanitarian concern for the refugees' plight. While wartime governments saw them as an unwelcome and barely tolerable burden, post-war governments repeatedly attempted to expel them, and were thwarted in doing so only by international pressure. The experience of the refugees in this telling is a story of unremitting deprivation, poverty, hunger and a constant struggle to cope with an unforgiving and hostile environment.

All this is dealt with in exemplary fashion. Hoffmann–Holter is on less sure ground, however, when dealing with the internal aspects of the refugee saga. Their palpable impact on Jewish society in Vienna remains largely a closed book to her, because she confines herself to German-language sources. By leaning too heavily on a narrow source base, in terms of primary and of secondary literature, Hoffmann–Holter short-changes the Jewish context of the refugees' experience. Her lack of familiarity with the broader Jewish historical background leads her astray at various points: for example, in her summary dismissal of religiously based welfare (pp. 118–19), and in her misleading description of the youth movements and of the Socialist-Zionist movement, Poale Zion, in wartime Vienna (p. 107, pp. 120–24).

As intimated by her title, Hoffmann–Holter focuses throughout the book on anti-Semitism, and it is this that provides the conceptual glue for her narrative. Carefully documenting the creeping entry of the concept of race into Austrian political and legal praxis, she recounts in impressive (indeed, at times, overwhelming) detail the panoply of anti-refugee agitation. A visible alien presence in the city, they were branded as profiteers, smugglers, black-market traders, hoarders and draft-dodgers, to name but a few of the accusations. Although it should be noted that this intense anti-Jewish hostility remained mostly in the realm of rhetoric, Hoffmann–Holter insists that it was a prelude to, and a prefiguring of, the fate of Austrian Jewry in the post-Anschluss years.

This problematic and ahistorical claim, teleologically merging two distinct historical experiences into an undifferentiated whole, is asserted repeatedly; the author makes no attempt, however, to substantiate her view or develop her argument. While rightly pointing out that anti-refugee sentiment was soon directed at Viennese Jewry in general, her assessment that this was a crucial episode in the history of Viennese anti-Semitism remains open to question. Nonetheless, her detailed analysis of government policy towards the refugees, along with her comprehensive account of what was certainly a significant example of the long-standing and virulent Viennese dislike of Ostjuden, is a valuable addition to the literature on Viennese and Austrian anti-Semitism.

The presence of the refugees in wartime Vienna and in the first years of the interwar Austrian republic has long been noted, but has remained mostly unexplored. Beatrix Hoffmann–Holter, in telling the story of their troubled experience, greatly expands our knowledge of this difficult chapter in Austrian-Jewish history.

DAVID RECHTER

Anne C. Shreffler, *Webern and the Lyric Impulse: Songs and Fragments on Poems of Georg Trakl* (Oxford: Clarendon Press, 1994), 256 pp., £35.00.

A remarkable elective affinity exists between Webern and Trakl: the poet's laconic and frequently disjunctive utterances find their most appropriate manifestation in the music of Webern, that musician of the Second Viennese School whose sparse expressiveness conceals a passionate urgency. Professor Shreffler concentrates on Webern's Opus 14, the setting of six poems by Trakl, and demonstrates convincingly that Webern was a lyric composer who used vocal compositions as a way out of an impasse created by the radical brevity of previous instrumental work. Her first chapter reminds us that, although Webern has been associated with severity and control, he can also be seen (and Adorno was one of the first to do so) as a composer who is not simply a cerebral adherent of dodecaphony but as a champion of a lyrical genre: it is in the poetry of Georg Trakl that he will find a voice that most closely resembled his own, that 'detached, submerged inwardness' of which Adorno wrote. Chapter 2 provides the historical context, referring specifically to the Akademischer Verband für Literatur und Musik in Wien; Professor Shreffler speculates, plausibly, that Webern and Trakl must have heard of each other's existence through the Verband, and she notes that Trakl's acquaintanceship with Karl Kraus, Adolf Loos and Peter Altenberg must have furthered the links between the two men. She is correct in stressing that Webern was drawn more to Trakl's second anthology (*Sebastian im Traum*); Webern, she claims, was attracted by Trakl's portrayal of nature, the euphony of many of his lines, but also by the introspective remoteness and haunting ethical resonances of the poems. It was, Professor Shreffler writes, 'this shared belief in the sacrosanct nature of artistic creation [that] formed the largest common ground between poet and composer'.

Part II of the study is devoted to Webern's compositional process, the diversity of his sketches and the sense of urgency with which he composed his songs. There are many details here on pencil sketches, fair copy and paper. There are also many musical extracts, prepared with great skill and care. Part II deals with the Trakl fragments, particularly 'In der Heimat' and 'In den Nachmittag geflüstert': occasionally the translations sound odd (why is 'Reseda' not translated? And 'Spülicht' is not gutter but dishwater, a mistranslation that misses the powerful sexual overtones). The section on Webern's experiments with ostinato shows the indebtedness to Schoenberg's *Pierrot Lunaire*: there are references to 'Siebengesang des Todes' and 'Abendland III'. Discussion of other Webern fragments include those of 'Verklärung' and the prose poem 'Offenbarung und Untergang'. Part IV is a detailed analysis of Opus 14 No 4: most perceptive is the discussion of 'Gesang einer gefangenen Amsel' at which Webern worked longer and more intensely than on any other Trakl poem. The dense, four-part texture of 'Nacht' is also considered, as is 'Die Sonne'. A brief Afterword considers Opus 14 as a modernist work, a powerful musical language the primary strength of which is flexibility, a multiple reference that perfectly suits Trakl's use of remote and rarefied images. Webern's Trakl settings, Professor Shreffler concludes, represent 'a unique historical moment in a long association between poetry and song'. Her book is an excellent discussion, thoroughly convincing and a most important contribution to Trakl and to Webern scholarship.

R. S. FURNESS

Roger Paulin and Peter Hutchinson (eds), *Rilke's 'Duino Elegies': Cambridge Readings* (London and Riverside, CA: Duckworth and Ariadne Press, 1996), xii + 237 pp., £35.00.

This volume presents the lectures on Rilke's *Duineser Elegien* given by members of the Faculty of Modern and Medieval Languages at Cambridge on two occasions in the early 1990s. While most contributors come to the poems as professional Germanists, Professor Patrick Boyde reflects on the fourth elegy as a Dantist, and the commentary on the fifth is by the comparatist, Naomi Segal, Professor of French at Reading. The enterprise recalls, as a whole, earlier work that popularised Rilke in Britain; and, in many respects, Boyde's masterly summary of themes (angels, animals, lovers, saints, plants and heroes) suggests that, in the broad lines of Rilke interpretation here, little has changed.

The opening elegy is addressed by the late Peter Stern in a lecture revised for publication by his wife. Stern pursues a strategy of delimitation and exclusion in his account of the modernity of the elegies: not philosophy, not theology nor even *religio intransitiva* (we have Rilke's assurance for this), and certainly not the deconstructive 'exclusion of meanings' envisaged by Paul de Man. Rather, Stern suggests, the first poem, like the whole cycle, moves through a series of concrete 'scenes' by means of which the 'unitary nature of worldly and metaphysical experience' can be explored. This is to be achieved by a method of *allusion* to earlier elegiac forms, to the tradition of a 'common poetic practice' and, simultaneously, by *liberation* from its power.

Stern regards this double device as providing one definition of modern poetry, and a number of other contributors make more historical attempts to locate the Elegies. Terry Llewellyn (on VIII) looks to Yeats and to T. S. Eliot for similar 'high quality poetry'[!], while Professor Paulin is more precise in fixing the Elegies only 'at the threshold' of radical lyrical experimentation in the twentieth century. Professor Segal provides a full and richly illustrated account of the background to Elegy V in Picasso and some of his antecedents; in Karen Leeder's view, Rilke confronts 'the place of art in the age of technology' in the Ninth Elegy's pastoral of naming; Peter Hutchinson brings the Seventh close to the sociological tradition of Simmel and Tönnies, and Leeder identifies a similar 'anxious apprehension of the age of the Modern'. Elsewhere the co-presence is felt of Freudian and Jungian concepts such as self-therapy, individuation, the archaic – though it may come dressed up in the threadbare props of 'a third-rate production of Wagner' (Timms); while David Midgley, most tellingly, discerns the Great War in the context of the heroes of Elegy VI.

Such variable approaches to context indicate an anxiety felt by a number of these commentators in confronting the unprecedented extremity of Rilke's diction and imagery. Few resist the temptation to pick holes in his similes ('Rilke has lapsed somewhat here' (Llewellyn)), to find his shifts from lyric to discursive speech awkward (Leeder), or to worry about artificial elisions (in 'Fühlns überfülln' (Hutchinson)). This is the obverse of a general willingness to derive meaning from acoustic effects, which seems dangerously oblivious to Peter Stern's earlier interdiction against the kind of sound-and-sense criticism he parodied as 'ululating ü ü ü sounds'. Minden (p. 22) and Leeder (p. 168) find they have been 'carried away' in their expositions, but most of these Cambridge lectures remind us that 'Poetry ... must apply its resources to the resistances of real experience' (Minden): David Midgley paraphrases this larger project of the Elegies as 'the conversion of negative experience into affirmation', which will also include what Professor Paulin's fine reading of Elegy X calls Rilke's mythopoeia of the heart as well as the frankly Freudian drives identified by Professor Timms.

These lectures are generally helpful as they 'paraphrase the ideas', in Professor Boyde's phrase, and guide the reader through imagery, diction and rhythm. The new translation provided for each poem by its respective commentator is valuable, stimulating and only occasionally eccentric. Yet many contributors are aware, like Hutchinson, of 'straining on our part to produce sense'. The strain shows in certain anachronisms, as when Professor Segal identifies one of the figures in Elegy V with the 'Schwarzenegger type' who 'has the same simplicity as the hero of *The Twins* if not of *Terminator 2*' (p. 84) or when Professor Boyde draws a parallel between Rilke's poems and 'barrels of "real ale", alive and still in ferment unlike the lagers and keg bitters of today' (p. 55). This last remark is itself gently guyed by Professor Paulin's description of ' "Todlos", 'jenes bitteren Bieres', as 'that "unreal" ale' (p. 181). *Captatio* aside, such comments indicate an anxiety with regard to the continuing vitality of the *Duino Elegies*; and, for all their careful exposition, these commentators do not fully confront it. To measure the fate of the Elegies for contemporary readers, and therefore the conditions under which they continue to yield meanings, we would need some sense of their continuing transmission and survival in recent poetry. If, for instance, the ruinous world of Anne Duden's post-*Duino* cycle, *Steinschlag*, is anything to go by, the results might be less jocular – and certainly certainly less comfortable about Rilke's Sublime.

ANTHONY PHELAN

Elizabeth Boa, *Kafka: Gender, Class, and Race in the Letters and Fictions* (Oxford: Clarendon Press, 1996), x + 304 pp., £40.00.

Unlike many of the canonical modernists with whom he is often grouped, Kafka has generally escaped the dethroning gestures of feminist criticism, in part because of the anti-mimetic tendencies of his texts. Faced with female characters like Leni (of the webbed hand) in *The Trial* or the singing mouse Josephine, critics have understandably felt uneasy in applying such straight-forward terms as 'woman' or 'female character', preferring instead to empha-sise the fragmentation or subversion of identity in Kafka's work, gender included. To my knowledge (and given the bulk of Kafka criticism, it is an amazing fact), there is no serious book-length study of Kafka from a feminist perspective. To fill this remarkable lacuna Elizabeth Boa has written a book that fairly bristles with intelligence and new insights gleaned from this standpoint. Thus, when writing about the opening of *Der Proceß*, she begins by focusing on 'a man expecting to be served breakfast in bed by a woman' (187). Not that Joseph K.'s arrest or his subsequent eating of an apple are unimportant in the larger scheme of the novel's legal and religious symbolism. But this mundane fact of gender relations, and gender hierarchies, offers Boa the point of access for a sustained discussion of the 'decay' of patriarchy as it manifests itself in the protagonist's interactions with female characters – women who, as the priest says, don't offer 'true help' in K.'s search for the Law. Women do matter in Kafka, as Boa shows us, and they matter precisely when they are marginalised, trivialised, demonised or animalised.

The problem, of course, is not just the distortion but also the famously sparse quantity of realist setting in Kafka's fictions. Like Sander Gilman in his *Franz Kafka, the Jewish Patient* (New York, 1995), Boa responds by injecting Kafka's minimalist texts with a good dose of contemporary historical and cultural material that functions not so much as a biographical source for the work but as its imaginative correlative. Historical context becomes the vehicle for thinking productively about a textual moment, a coloured glass through which the critic shows us the text in a new and stronger light. Boa's opening reading of the two-paragraph text 'Auf der Galerie' is a case in point. The circus setting, the beautiful equestrienne and stern ringmaster, the 'hammer blows' of the spectators' applause – these figures enact a spectacle of female performance under male eyes that Boa (not coincidentally the author of *The Sexual Circus: Wedekind's Theatre of Subversion* (Oxford, 1987)) associates with the sexual tensions in Wedekind's 'Lulu' plays. 'The circus in the first paragraph is a voyeuristic spectacle', she claims. 'The equestrienne's body is forced through the motions of sexual appeal by a sadistic pimp [i.e. the ringmaster], to the pleasure of a paying audience.' Kafka's weak-lunged equestrienne is then linked with 'actual prostitutes in industrial cities [and] cultural heroines, most famously the lady of the camellias [in *La Traviata*]' (10). Is this Kafka or is it Wedekind? Are we dealing with verbal constructions or with 'real' historical subjects? The question is moot from Boa's perspective, because what ulti-mately matters for her, I suspect, is the intersection between social reality and artistic representation, the common ground where such distinctions tend to be effaced.

Unlike Gilman, however, who tends to avoid sustained literary readings, Boa is consistently attentive to formal questions. Thus the famous reversal in the second paragraph of 'Auf der Galerie', which exposes the scenario in the first paragraph as a male fantasy, leads to the claim that the text 'deconstructs as much as it constructs and leaves a male reader caught in a crisis of a split masculinity which tries and fails to define itself in opposition to a doubled feminine'. Nietzsche, Derrida, Peter Brooks and Kristeva are invoked in a complex series of arguments about the inaccessibility of truth, melodramatic narratives and the symbolic order of language. Such renderings, which oscillate between feminist critique and sophisticated deconstructive and psycho-analytic readings, between close textual analysis and broad speculative gener-alisations, are characteristic of the entire book, which includes an opening section on 'Modernity and its Discontents'; a persuasive comparison between *Die Verwandlung* and Charlotte Perkins Gilman's *The Yellow Wallpaper*; two chapters on the body in canonical stories such as 'Strafkolonie' and 'Hungerkünstler'; feminist readings of *Der Proceß* and *Das Schloß*; as well as two chapters on the correspondences with Felice Bauer and Milena Jesenská. (Regrettably, the book also contains numerous typographical errors.)

This oscillation is at once the book's strength and its weakness. In a telling remark about *Das Schloß*, Boa speaks of the 'actively gymnastic reading' that this novel invites which, in turn, produces a kind of critical 'exhilaration' (245) in the reader. Boa herself is clearly exhilarated by the range of readings she performs, a *salto mortale*, as it were, embodying the most recent theoretical paradigms. At the same time, in her desire to avoid the 'sins' of a naïve feminism that treats literature as a 'transparent window on to the world' (20), Boa often seems to be engaged in a game of critical one-upmanship that accumulates, but does not sufficiently distinguish between, conflicting inter-pretations. Rather than build to strong conclusions, her readings get bogged down in brief, associative insights and the need to touch all methodological bases. The book's all-inclusive subtitle, the meandering bulk of some chapters (her reading of *The Trial* is over sixty pages), as well as the absence of a concluding chapter, are symptomatic in this regard.

Why, in a book where patriarchy weighs so heavily, does Boa make only passing reference to Kafka's 'Letter to his Father', a text that he gave to Milena Jesenská to encourage her in her own struggle with her father? Why is there only brief mention of Kafka's desire to found a journal with the anarchist and renegade psychoanalyst, Otto Gross, entitled *Blätter zur Bekämpfung des Machtwillens*? Why is there so little acknowledgment of the homoerotic and homosexual fantasies structuring his writing, fantasies that impinge critically on the question of gender identity? As Boa remarks, Kafka's position on gender is surely not a 'closed system', but 'in turmoil, full of ludicrous contradictions' (16), including some negative stereotypes. But just as surely one can recognise a coherent desire in Kafka to expose and to subvert the structures of patriarchy and social normalisation that he experi-enced in his family, school and work-place. When he visits his father's asbestos factory, for instance, he comments on the female employees working 'in their unbelievably dirty and untidy clothes, their hair dishevelled ... they aren't people, you don't greet them, you don't apologise when you bump into them ... they stand there in petticoats, they are at the mercy of the pettiest power' (5 February 1912). How not to hear in this early diary entry, written *before* all his major fictions, the note of filial rebellion, bourgeois guilt, and sympathetic *Einfühlung* for women who have been rendered subhuman by factory conditions? And how not to ask the question of the relation between such sentiments and the 'acting out' of gender identities in the writing? Boa begins her study here, but in the theoretical escalation to the 'intercourse of ghosts' and the 'taboo' of the male body, these elementary questions fail to receive the full articulation they deserve.

MARK ANDERSON

Alexander Stillmark (ed.), *Joseph Roth: Der Sieg über die Zeit. Londoner Symposium*, Publications of the London Institute of Germanic Studies 65 (Stuttgart: Heinz, 1996), x + 181 pp., DM 35.00.

The centenary in 1994 of Joseph Roth's birth was used as an opportunity to reassess the work of this prolific writer. Born in the Galician town of Brody in the latter years of the Austro-Hungarian Empire, he died all too young in French exile, just months before the outbreak of World War II. He is known mainly as the author of *Radetzkymarsch* and, as such, he is often seen as a contemporary of Carl Joseph von Trotta, the novel's anti-hero who died with the Austro-Hungarian Empire; this obscures the fact that most of Roth's work was written in the 1920s and '30s, while working as a journalist for German papers, and during his exile in France. The most recent edition of his collected works (1991) allows us to study his literary and his journalistic work in context. Its wide range is reflected in *Joseph Roth: Der Sieg über die Zeit*, a collection of papers given at the 1994 London Symposium (with additional articles by Hackert and Ochse).

This book is proof that Roth was not a cosy *k.-und-k.* novelist, but Hitler's young contemporary, desperately warning in his writing of impending fascism, and desperate to find an autonomous artistic practice transcending individual powerlessness in the face of barbarism.

The contributions to the book are uneven. The article by Norbert Leser, 'Zeitgeschichtlicher Hintergrund des Werkes von Joseph Roth', does not really provide – as one would expect with its title – an historical, social or cultural background; the article discusses some of Lueger's and Hitler's anti-Semitic views in relation to Roth's work, and it is concerned with rejecting the hypothesis of continuity between Austrian anti-Semitism and Nazi anti-Semitism; but it fails to outline the real political, economic, social and racial conflicts in Austria and Germany experienced by Roth and his contemporaries. There is hardly any discussion of the political, socio-cultural and intellectual environment in which Roth grew up: why he was so keen to leave Brody for Vienna, his war, his move to Berlin, etc. Leser praises Roth for his 'prophetic' depiction of Hitler as Antichrist and sees the work of that name as an apt characterisation of Nazi rule. By claiming that Christian anti-Semitism in Austria considered Jews 'basically as objects of religious conversion, ... but not of deadly aggression' (5), he fails to discuss the historical conditions under which racism turned into a programme of physical annihilation.

That Roth indeed tried to make sense of his time through a mixture of political and theological thought is discussed explicitly in Edward Timms's contribution; Timms sees Roth's critique of German anti-Semitism as the central axis of his large journalistic work. As a Galician Jew himself, Roth was keenly aware of the dilemma of eastern Jews who, fleeing from revolution and persecution in the east, sought refuge in a 'civilised' west that was soon to do away with any vestiges of democracy in preparation for the Final Solution. But, as Timms says, Roth does not defend democracy against fascism; rather, he pleads for a Christian-Jewish symbiosis as defence against the fascist Antichrist; he also opposes Zionism in favour of a cosmopolitan, Jewish, transnational Austrianness.

Stefan H. Kaszyński discusses Roth's journalism during his travels among the people and regions of his birth, in particular his reports from the Polish-Bolshevik war in 1920, which seem coloured by the expectations of the editors and readers of the *Neue Berliner Zeitung*, rather than reporting historically objective reality. Karl Wagner considers the distinctive, sympathetic treatment of Galicia in Roth's work, contrasting it with the attitudes of 'cultural imperialism' of authors such as Franzos and Bahr.

Joseph Strelka interprets the novel *Der stumme Prophet* as a reflection of Roth's disappointment with the Soviet Union as a political and moral alternative; the author's painful experience of political powerlessness is programmatically transformed into stoic, proud 'muteness' of the solitary sage – an ideal state which, ironically, Roth himself endeavoured to attain through obsessive myth-making.

The tension between historical fact and fiction as a literary theme is considered in Joachim Beug's article, while Roth's deep concern with morality is central to the discussion in Alexander Stillmark's contribution. Stillmark analyses the late novel *Beichte eines Mörders* (1936) in the context of Dostoevsky's thought; the ironic style of the narrator confirms the moral values based in religion, thus transcending the temporal 'morality' of the confessor.

Aspects of Roth's *Radetzkymarsch* are considered by both John Margetts and by Peter Branscombe. By establishing parallels between the novel's anti-hero and the Emperor's son Rudolf, Margetts interprets the novel as a critique of masculinist attitudes, but this does not seem to take the narrative structure into account: far from being engaged in a 'search for the lost mother' (85), as Margetts maintains, Roth's (anti)-hero progresses towards individuation in his journey *away* from the female as infantile and infantilising, as corrupt and corrupting. The novel is a drama of *male* relationships where women appear only in the margins and are portrayed as diversions on the way to the male individual's ultimate destiny of self-determination; Carl Joseph finds autonomy in (objectively senseless) self-sacrifice for his men, by assuming the role of the 'nurturing father' whom Roth himself never had. In his discussion of the novel's symbolism, Branscombe sees the narrative development in a similar way: Carl Joseph risks his life to get water for his men, in a 'third attempt of breaking from *anonymity*'

Reviews

[emphasis added] (104). In taking on 'personal', 'paternal' responsibility, he finds – through death – his place in the genealogy of patriarchal power.

Fritz Hackert looks at Roth's use of travelling circus people, who symbolise a counter-world to dominant bourgeois conventionality: Roth's earlier, clichéd pictures of travellers in his journalistic work are superseded by increasingly empathetic depictions of clowns, artistes and social misfits; Roth sees their performances as art which, in its grotesque distortions and anarchic inventiveness, functions as a critique of bourgeois rationality while, at the same time, offering a safety valve to the 'rational' circus spectators. His affinity to society's losers and marginalised individuals, which finds expression in his later journalistic and literary work, reflects his increasingly painful awareness of his own precarious artistic position and rootlessness.

A related psychological theme is picked up by Katharina L. Ochse in the concluding article where she considers Roth's first trip to France in 1925: his writing is euphoric, as he feels freed from the restrictions of German political life, which he experiences increasingly as nationalistic; the South of France reminds him of his childhood dreams, of home; it takes on the romantically stylised features of a social, political and religious Utopia. Ochse argues convincingly that it is at this time – *before* his 'conversion' to the Habsburg myth – that Roth turns to Catholicism, which he sees then as a force capable of renewing a transnational Europe. Roth discovers his syncretic version of Catholicism without breaking with his eastern Jewishness; according to Ochse, Catholicism was for him – in contrast to Judaism – also a secular, political power, and thus his conversion becomes plausible 'as the attempt to compensate his powerlessness in the face of political developments in Germany, by identifying with a power which is also secular' (172). All in all, the volume is a valuable, if patchy, contribution to the growing Roth scholarship.

MARTHA WÖRSCHING

'It's Up to Us!' Collected Works of Jura Soyfer, selected and translated by Horst Jarka (Riverside, CA: Ariadne Press) 593 pp., $54.95.

Since 1977, when Horst Jarka published a first selection of his own translations of Jura Soyfer's writings with the Engendra Press in Montreal, he has become the leading translator and the leading exponent of this extraordinarily gifted Russo-Viennese writer. In 1980, Jarka produced a massive volume of Soyfer's collected works in German (Europaverlag, Vienna); four years later he edited the much more manageable – and affordable – three-volume paperback edition of prose, poetry and plays; a fine critical study followed in 1987; and finally Jarka edited and published Soyfer's letters in 1991. By returning now to the substance of his original project, adding to, elaborating on, and honing his previous translations for this latest volume, Jarka has, to quote his own editorial note, 'closed the circle'. As far as the works of Soyfer are concerned, he has opened them up once again in a way that is characteristic of his scholarship and flair for what is of more than passing interest.

250

Soyfer's fame, such as it was, rested for many years on his Dachaulied [Song of Dachau], a poem set to music by his fellow prisoner, Herbert Zipper, in the concentration camp where they were both interned; soon it was known and sung by the inmates throughout the camp. It is a wonderfully optimistic piece of writing and was translated, along with the poem 'Das Lied vom einfachen Menschen' [Song of the Simple Man] by the author and publisher John Lehmann, who had met and been taught Russian by Soyfer in Vienna – as he recounts in the volume of his autobiography entitled *The Whispering Gallery*. Soyfer's impact was such that Lehmann decided to publish sections of Soyfer's novel *So starb eine Partei* [Thus died a Party] in the magazine *New Writing*, necessarily under a pseudonym. As a tribute to Lehmann Jarka has left those two poems in their original 1930s version. In his lifetime, however, Soyfer had been best known for his short, politically uncompromising journalistic pieces and for the exuberant cabaret plays that he wrote for the fringe theatres.

This new volume of translations not only contains all the previously published plays, it also updates the earlier volume and carries a hitherto unpublished translation of *Broadway Melody 1492*, Soyfer's highly politicised and imaginative adaptation of the rather dull Hasenclever/Tucholsky collaboration *Christoph Kolumbus*. Jarka, very much in the spirit of Soyfer, produced his own prelude for the New York première of the play on the occasion of the Columbus quincentenary in 1992. This piece is included in the present selection. Embedded in it is one of the rare typographical errors in the volume: 'a fancy *sear fir* for royalty' for 'seat fit'. With his own surreal sense of humour, it is a line Soyfer might have appreciated. There are also additional chapters to the novel fragment, *So starb eine Partei*, a work that its author considered his most important achievement but which is of more interest to the historian, whereas many of the plays, poems and shorter prose pieces still have much to offer as literature. Although these are most definitely of their time, the warnings they contain, whether against faceless bureaucracy, fascist inhumanity or mindless slogan-mongering and linguistic doublespeak, have a freshness and a pertinence for the Old World and the New. As relevant today as it was in the 1930s is Soyfer's relentless exploration of the demoralisation brought about by poverty and unemployment.

Horst Jarka has included a lively and informative afterword, reproducing several of Soyfer's letters, which amplify the complex optimism of this young 'Nestroy who had read his Marx' in Edwin Zbonek's phrase. It is a pity that room has been found for only a small selection of the poems – 'Matuska Speaks' is a notable omission – but Jarka has in this selection made the humour, humanity and vigour of Jura Soyfer admirably accessible to the English-speaking reader.

IAN HUISH

Reviews

Christopher J. Thornhill, *Walter Benjamin and Karl Kraus: Problems of a 'Wahlverwandt-schaft'*, Stuttgarter Arbeiten zur Germanistik 319 (Stuttgart: Heinz, 1996), 192 pp., DM 35.00.

In German, there is a saying 'über seinen eigenen Schatten springen' ['to jump over one's shadow'] which means to overcome the limits of one's existence. Christopher J. Thornhill suggests that, in his essay 'Karl Kraus' of 1931, Walter Benjamin uses the figure of Karl Kraus to jump over his own shadow. By portraying Karl Kraus as the negative force that rejects everything, as the 'demon', Benjamin, who saw himself in a similar position, is able to escape his former position and to develop the idea of a new political-theological philosophy. In Karl Kraus, Benjamin historicises himself. Thornhill concludes that the 'demon', who exists in rejecting everything, bears in himself the possibility of pointing beyond himself, of departing from his own being, and entering into history. It is this entering into history out of the spirit of demonism that is the main topic of Thornhill's study.

Thornhill presents Benjamin's entering into history and into political action as a history of the subject. Using the subtitles of Benjamin's Kraus essay as models, Thornhill narrates a line of development of Benjamin's thought from the 'Dämon' to the 'Unmensch' and finally to the 'Engel'. What then is the driving force of this development? What in the 'demon' makes possible the 'pointing' beyond the demon and allows the leap over the shadow? Thornhill describes the 'demon' as a self that relates to its world only negatively by rejecting the world and society, and a being that is self-fixated and claims a god-like mythical existence. Because its existence and self-constitution derive from the negative rejection of the world, it exists only in destruction. As a destructive force, the demon does not exist as a transcendental being but only in action, the action of destruction that undermines, in turn, its own selfhood. 'The sole mode of self-constitution in this sphere is the collapse of the self' (44). The existence of the demon thereby leads into his collapse and marks an epoch.

In this context, Thornhill's text has a limit in his decision to organise his arguments around the opposition of subject and object. This leads him to articulate Benjamin's notion of destruction as a special ability of the 'subject'. Where Benjamin explicitly rejects notions that relate to the subject, Thornhill still insists on the centrality of the subject (for example, Benjamin's 'antipathy towards subjectivism is therefore an insistence on the renovation of the fundamental character of the subject' (88)). Even when he notes that, in the opposition of subject and object, Benjamin does not favour the one over the other and instead aims for an 'undifferentiation' (89) or 'unio mystica' (85), Thornhill's matrix remains the notions of subject and object. It is true that, for Benjamin, destruction is a third force that resists the separation of subject and object and that even precedes the possibility of experience. To derive destruction from the subject-object relationship, however, would take away the radicalness of Benjamin's thought. Indeed, there is a sphere that Benjamin is never willing to give up but this sphere is not the sphere of the subject,

252

rather that of destruction, caesura, history, redemption, justice, epic theatre, and Messianism.

Related to the question of destruction is one of the most hotly debated issues in the work of Benjamin: the status of theology. Some critics have suggested that Benjamin reaches a sphere where he deciphers theological implications in the constructions of politics; others treat Benjamin's use of theology as a mere mistake. Thornhill is one of the latter, viewing the emergence of theological and religious tropes in Benjamin's work as a symptom of naïvety and irrationality that, at best, one should overlook. 'It is difficult to ignore the obtrusive theological undercurrent in this construct' (83). Even when, later on, he devotes one subchapter to Benjamin's 'positive-negative theology', it is mainly to point out that Benjamin's position is 'clearly regressive in nature' (137). (It is almost disturbing how often Thornhill uses the phrase 'it is clear that' with regard to these complex texts. Often, he makes little attempt to comment on his quotation and their dimensions.) Thornhill works as critic who suddenly finds the ugly dwarf theology below the table and now criticises Benjamin for deception. Benjamin, however, is very explicit about the employment of theology and explains his notion of it. In *Über den Begriff der Geschichte*, Benjamin mobilises theology against the non-critical concepts of progress and conformism. Benjamin's basic assumption is that the individuality that could resist the conformism of National Socialism does not simply exist or have an ontological status. Rather, individuality comes into being only in the form of a claim – a theology. In the paradigm of progress, history would be reduced to a steady improvement of human existence by means of technology, not open to individual influence. History would be a mere waiting; a better future would come automatically. In Benjamin's game of chess, the automaton that seems to direct future moves turns out to be a hidden dwarf, an intentional being. And so Benjamin tries to individualise change by introducing a notion of personal intentionality into history, not an intentionality that structures a common future, but an intention or intensification that holds on to one's past. In this holding on to the past, in the hope deriving from the past for some future encounter and fulfilment, Benjamin finds the root of non-conformist individuality. Because the expectation of the individual to live one's own life with its own hopes is not grounded in any law, does not derive from any necessity, and might in fact be groundless, the claim of individuality implies something groundless. It is here that the 'theology' Benjamin speaks about resides. For Benjamin, theology is not a dogma or a naïve belief, rather theology is a necessary assumption involved in the claim of non-conformist individuality. In this way, theology is a strategic device necessary to fight the anti-individual concept of progress at work in National Socialism.

One of the achievements of Thornhill's book consists in finding many sources of Benjamin's terms and concepts. In addition to an extensive discussion of the correspondences of Benjamin, Kierkegaard, and Heidegger, Thornhill draws specific attention to striking affinities between the work of Benjamin and conservative and even anti-Semitic critics such as Ludwig Klages,

Theodor Lessing, and Alfred Baeumler, many of which have not been previously discussed. He situates Benjamin between the two different camps of 'orthodoxism' and 'gnosis'. While the orthodox camp of Cohen, Buber, and Rosenzweig seeks a community 'in which the individual subject constitutes itself in obedience to social ethics', the gnostic camp of Bloch and Lukács advocates 'the ethically autonomous, or socially negative, subject' (34). Thornhill suggests that Benjamin uses 'destructive action' as a third term that affects the gnostic certainties of the self and releases the self from its 'extra-temporal locus', thereby recalling it as a being within a historically defined community.

Nevertheless, the nature of Benjamin's affinity to regressive thought often remains unexamined. Does Benjamin automatically fall into regressive and conservative thought by using notions taken from Klages? Thornhill's discussion does not address this point sufficiently. A prominent example of this is the notion of origin (compare chapter 'Origin and Interior'). The notion of 'Ursprung' that Benjamin uses in the Kraus essay leads into dangerous terrain. It is dangerous, not simply because this term was often used by conservatives, but mainly because the concept of a given origin can become a line of demarcation between those who are of the same origin and those who are not. All concepts of race have to make reference to the notion of origin. But how does Benjamin use the word 'Ursprung'? Thornhill quotes one example (156) where Benjamin replaces the expected notion of 'Ursprung' with the notion of the 'Sprung', without commenting on the integral question of origin:

> Wovor werden die Phänomene gerettet? Nicht nur, und nicht sowohl vor dem Verruf und der Mißachtung in die sie geraten sind als vor der Katastrophe wie eine bestimmte Art ihrer Überlieferung, ihre 'Würdigung als Erbe' sie sehr oft darstellt. – Sie werden durch die Aufweisung des Sprungs in ihnen gerettet. (V, 591)

Instead of the origin [Ursprung], it is the rapture [Sprung] that 'saves' the phenomena from tradition [Überlieferung]. Rather than showing the true nature of the phenomena at some lost origin that has to be regained, Benjamin emphasises the origin as rapture (as an Ur-Sprung) that makes the phenomena structurally incomplete, and therefore blocks any return. Only because the phenomena contain a rapture and are incomplete, can they call for a completeness they never had, suspend the settling in a fulfilled time, and entertain the hope for a future. The Ur-Sprung, therefore, is not the goal but the condition of possibility of citation [and Benjamin does not aim for a 'restoration of intact language' (137)].

At the end of the book, Thornhill finds his own shadow to jump over. His shadow is Walter Benjamin, and he ends up with Karl Kraus, who served as Benjamin's shadow. While Thornhill accuses Benjamin of falling prey to a regressive theology and a suspicious positive ontology, the late Kraus seems to offer an alternative. Thornhill reads Kraus's bizarre political situation between Right and Left, between the Dollfuss regime and radical revolutionary movements, in the light of his attempt to save nineteenth-century values for his age (chapter 'Between Reaction and Revolution'). It is here that Thornhill's book most clearly succeeds in deriving a writer's political position from his theoretical and literary texts. Thornhill's readings of Kraus are a valid contribution to the debate on politics in the 1930s. Unlike other critics, Thornhill does not simply accuse the late Kraus of withdrawing from political engagement, but reconstructs the development of his political positions. According to Thornhill, Kraus recognises the 'impossibility' of political action under the totalitarian government of the Nazis. In consequence, Kraus becomes a 'mere desperate pragmatist' (162), who admits that 'even the oppositional negativity of language ... is dependent for its impact on a small area of communion' (169). In short, Kraus, and not Benjamin, documents 'the genuine and inevitable collapse of a political position' (163), its 'groundlessness' (162), and language's 'unsustainability' (163). The difference between Benjamin and Kraus, then, is that Kraus does not develop a theology on the basis of this groundlessness.

Thornhill's book, the first book-length study on the comparison of Benjamin and Kraus, does not exhaust its topic, but it offers many suggestions for an evaluation of both Kraus's and Benjamin's philosophical-political arguments.

FRITZ BREITHAUPT

Verspielte Zeit: Österreichisches Theater der 30er Jahre, ed. Hilde Haider-Pregler and Beate Reiterer (Vienna: Picus Verlag, 1997), 384 pp., 298 Sch/DM 39.80.

These twenty-three essays are the product of a symposium held in Vienna in June 1996, interspersed with short anecdotal memories of leading figures from the Austrian theatre in the 1930s, and arranged so that often an essay on a general aspect is followed by one on a leading figure just mentioned. This gives the volume a sense of continuity and purpose matched by such underlying themes as the struggle of Austrian theatre during the 1930s to retain its independence against Austrofascism from within and the threat of National Socialism from Germany, or overt and covert anti-Semitism, or the debt to earlier models such as Viennese popular theatre and Johann Nestroy. There is a strong sense of betrayal by traditional institutions and state authorities, and many forms of theatre are shown to have provided the forum for national awareness, for independence of thought and expression, and for outright protest. The volume has advantages and disadvantages of hindsight: the July agreement of 1938, distribution of Hitler's *Mein Kampf* in Austria from 1937, the increased attempts of the 'Brückenbauer' (e.g. Bishop Hudal) to bring closer together Catholicism and National Socialism, and the drift towards fascist thinking on the part of many leading writers and academics, are all seen as precursors to the Anschluss. This allows for a subtext of implicit contrast to, or parallel with, today's internal political situation in Austria.

In the first essay, Erika Weinzierl records affirmative attitudes towards fascist policies in Austrian cultural politics in the 1930s, including a damning quotation from the Christian-Social *Reichspost* in spring 1933 on the burning of books in Germany that sees no reason why the works of certain Austrian writers should not be dealt with in a similar fashion. Anton Staudinger examines the spread of the Catholic Church's influence and shows how National Socialism was prepared for in Austria by Austrofascism and Catholic anti-Semitism amounting to 'Vermittlungsideologie' (p. 44). Gabriele Volsansky names leading writers and academics who served on juries and who trimmed their sails to the wind.

Johann Hüttner's masterly exposé of the interrelationship of art and politics in the Burgtheater highlights the problems faced by its director Hermann Röbbeling in trying to use the theatre as a forum for Austrianism while treading the uneasy path between political correctness and independent bourgeois Catholic patriotism. His 'Überlebenstechnik' (p. 63) included financial prudence and a sensitivity to the at least latent anti-Semitism of his audiences. Julia Danielczyk neatly sums up the most successful Austrian dramatist of the 1930s, Hermann Heinz Ortner, by describing his combination of Blubo ideology with mystical and magical elements, together with a remarkable talent for ingratiating himself with the élite of National Socialism while remaining a leading member of apparently independent Austrian cultural organisations. This 'wankender Geselle' (Grete Urbanitzky) even managed to survive by posing as a member of the resistance in 1945 and yet remain the most performed Austrian dramatist from 1929 to 1955.

Robert Werba gives a partly anecdotal account of opera in Vienna and the Salzburg Festivals, concentrating on Toscanini's role from 1935 after his refusal to fall in with Hitler's wish that he should conduct Wagner at Bayreuth in 1933. The political significance of opera productions is also emphasised. Angela Eder records the development and series of crises at the Theater an der Wien under Arthur Hellmer's direction (1936–38). The essay on the 'Theater für 49' in Vienna 1934–38, derived from Ulrike Mayer's thesis, describes the setting up of small theatres with less than fifty seats (legally on a different footing from the main theatres), their repertoire of short forms and tendency towards protest or independence.

Karl Müller provides a masterly critical piece on 'Vaterländische und nazistische Fest- und Weihespiele in Österreich' especially from 1934 on. Rudolf Henz's *St Michael, führe uns!* is shown to be constructed over artificially fused contrasts to create a false modernism. The techniques of Karl Springenschmid's *Lamprechthausener Weihespiel* are ruthlessly laid bare. In a more general section, Müller shows how these plays and many other less well-known examples were used to form a homogeneous 'Erinnerungsgemeinschaft' (p. 166) through manipulation of the senses.

Johann Holzner analyses in detail Franz Kranewitter's *Todsünden* cycle and contrasts it with the fate of Jura Soyfer's *Weltuntergang*. Kranewitter's work reveals the fatal norms of behaviour in a hermetically sealed-off village community, and this interpretation is above all supported by his *Totentanz* that looks back to the past and forward into the future. The small world of the village was probably intended to stand for the larger world of Austria – an uncomfortable view that Holzner does not spell out.

Ulf Birnbauer defines the position of Jura Soyfer's dramas with reference especially to Erwin Piscator and to Friedrich Wolf. Soyfer's dialectical constructs and quests for syntheses, both social and theatrical, are shown to be based on a variety of traditions, his *Weltuntergang* a form of parody of the Viennese 'Besserungsstück'. Jürgen Doll produces an entertaining account of Viennese political cabaret (1926–33) as a renewal of the Altwiener Volksstück. He makes pertinent detailed comments on examples by the two main writers Robert Ehrenzweig and Jura Soyfer, revealing how much they owed to Nestroy, and how relevant and effective such early forms of epic theatre could become for a modern social democratic public.

Walter Rösler gives an excellent account of so-called 'Kleinkunst' in Vienna (1931–38), concentrating especially on the cabaret, the documents and texts of which have been mainly lost. He highlights three important facts: that there was no other time when so much cabaret with claim to literary value took place in Vienna; that theatrical forms were so important that one may speak of an invasion of the theatre into cabaret; that at a time of dictatorship, Viennese cabaret enjoyed its greatest success. He stresses the significance of the 'Mittelstück' and the links back to Nestroy and forward to the 'Laterndl' in London during World War II. The direct influence of Peter Hammerschlag's Berlin 'Katakombe' and of his so-called 'Blitz-Dichtungen' on 'Lieber Augustin' and the direct influence of Jura Soyfer on the sketches of the late 1930s is perhaps understated, although Soyfer's *Die Botschaft von Astoria* and his *Broadway-Melodie* are well quoted. Birgit Peter seeks to correct false legends about Stella Kadmon and Peter Hammerschlag as directors and actors in 'Der liebe Augustin'.

Hilde Haider-Pregler, in narrating the fates of writers, directors and actors from Germany who fled to Austria in the early 1930s, shows how the apparently comic aliases they put on soon became serious means of survival in an atmosphere of growing anti-Semitism. Walter Firner's 'Österreichische Bühne' provided employment for many émigrés. She contrasts the methods of disguise of Awrum Albert in the 'Jüdisches Kulturtheater' with those of Hans José Rehfisch for the Marton Verlag. Above all, she describes the successful deceptions of Leo Reuss, who was to experience the archetypal fate of the émigré.

Brigitte Dalinger gives an account of 'Melodram' and 'Zeitstück' in the Jewish theatres. Abisch Meisel's reviews are seen as proof of a close relationship between Yiddish theatre and Zionist societies. Ursula Stamberg shows how many theatre people found employment in the 1930s in Prague and how, from there, they interpreted the situation in Vienna. Wolfgang Duchkowitsch characterises theatre criticism in four periodicals: *Rote Fahne*, *Arbeiter-Zeitung*, *Wiener Morgenblatt* and *Reichspost*. Eckart Früh records the sadistic anti-Semitic attacks on the Viennese theatre in *Der Stürmer* and cites Karl Kraus in particular as a prophet of what was to come. Peter Roessler's analysis of the Viennese theatre is based on the development of reviews written by Oskar Maurus Fontana. He convincingly shows how close the two images are of the man with the clenched fist and the man with the cross. Finally, Fritz

Hausjell brings together and comments on several quotations from Ludwig Ullmann's theatrical reviews and commentaries.

Most of the volume is of a documentary nature with only three or four contributions reaching the level of critical analysis. As an introduction to the variety of theatrical expression at the time in Vienna and to the central themes that ironically encouraged such a forum for intellectual resistance, this is an essential book but neither easy to read nor fully satisfying. There are too many contributions, most of which are short, densely written and with frequent scholarly reference to sources easily accessible only to scholars in the field.

BRIAN KEITH-SMITH

Susanne Rode-Breymann, *Die Wiener Staatsoper in den Zwischenkriegsjahren: Ihr Beitrag zum zeitgenössischen Musiktheater.* Wiener Stadt- und Landesbibliothek, Schriftenreihe zur Musik 10 (Tutzing: Hans Schneider, 1994), 485 pp., DM 112.

Following World War I, Vienna suffered a disorienting loss of status. From being the political and cultural hub of a multi-ethnic empire, the city had become the capital of a small, shaky and increasingly provincial Alpine republic. As if in compensation for its loss of political prestige, the Austrian state laid great store in maintaining an international profile for its cultural institutions, pre-eminent among which was the Vienna Opera. It is against this backdrop of cultural crisis and uncertainty that Susanne Rode-Breymann examines twenty years of Staatsoper history from 1918 until the Anschluss of 1938. These were years of glorious performances, with stars of the magnitude of Lotte Lehmann, Maria Jeritza, Richard Mayr, and Richard Tauber, conductors such as Richard Strauss, Karl Böhm, Clemens Krauss, and Bruno Walter, and legendary productions of works by Wagner, Mozart, Bizet, Strauss, and Puccini. The focus of the present study, however, is upon the Staatsoper's cultivation of contemporary works, and here the record is considerably less brilliant, particularly when compared to the wealth of new stage works premièred in Berlin, Leipzig or Frankfurt, or on any of several dozen smaller stages in Germany.

Rode-Breymann has sifted through masses of primary documents relating to the internal administration of the Staatsoper, including its own archives, and the private papers of its leading personalities and of the composers and publishers who sought performances there, as well as surveying the extensive commentary in the contemporary press, to present a fascinating insider's look at a decision-making process caught between sometimes good, if cautious, intentions, the dead weight of bureaucracy and a political and economic climate that positively militated against novelty and innovation. Her discussion of Franz Schalk who, with Richard Strauss, co-directed the opera from 1918 to 1924 and thereafter reigned alone until 1929, shows clearly how administrative circumstances increasingly restricted his creative options. Similarly, worsening economic circumstances dashed the early hopes that Clemens

258

Krauss, who was opera director from 1929 to 1935, might continue the exciting programming of his first year (which included the first Viennese performance of Berg's *Wozzeck*) into subsequent seasons. Particularly valuable is a chapter on dance and choreography, with its sad tale of Staatsoper resistance to newer trends in expressive modern dance. A chapter on staging discusses in particular the contributions of the stage directors Josef Turnau and Lothar Wallerstein and set designers such as Emil Pirchan and, even more important, Oskar Strnad, who emerges as a true successor to the pre-war innovator, Alfred Roller.

The bulk of the book takes the form of a documentation of those new works actually performed at the Staatsoper. Here, in alphabetical order by composer or choreographer, Rode-Breymann gives an summary of the surviving documents relating to the acceptance of each work, with notes on the production and its reception, as well as interspersed playbill reproductions and a section of production stills. Two invaluable appendices explain the mechanics that governed submitting, reviewing, accepting or rejecting new works, and provide an overview of those works submitted to the Staatsoper during the period in question, as well as a summary of any commentary that survives. A third appendix provides a list of scores and librettos of performed works that have made their way from the Staatsoper archives to various Viennese libraries. Taken all together, this study is a fascinating, if sobering, look at a central moment of twentieth-century Austrian cultural history by a scholar who is in superb control of an extraordinarily broad array of sources.

CHRISTOPHER HAILEY

Jutta Raab Hansen, *NS-verfolgte Musiker in England. Spuren deutscher und österreichischer Flüchtlinge in der britischen Musikkultur* (Hamburg: von Bockel, 1996), 530 pp., DM 68.00.

Some time ago, Ernst Loewy introduced the concept of a 'paradigm shift' in exile research, by which he meant that, for far too long, antifascist activity had been the sole criterion by which every piece of exile work in whatever sphere had to be judged. Because most refugees from National Socialism had been forced to leave Germany simply because they were Jewish and not because of their political beliefs, this inevitably meant that any subsequent consideration of exile experience based on antifascist commitment alone was bound to be askew. In addition, the focus had been for too long on the United States and on the leading exile figures in that country. Countries such as Britain had been largely ignored as a result. Jutta Raab Hansen's book is a welcome demonstration of Loewy's paradigm shift, not only because the focus is not political, but also because her area of interest is music and musicians, rather than artistic or literary figures, and further because she focuses on Britain rather than on any other much-researched country. Early on, however, she admits that Britain did represent merely a transit stage in the lives of many of the refugee musicians she is interested in.

Hansen has obviously enjoyed a good grounding in the background (musical, historical, political) necessary for an undertaking such as the present one. She was, as she reports, a member of the Hamburg Project Group for Music and National Socialism, which was set up under the guidance of Professor Peter Petersen to plan an exhibition for 1988 with the title: 'Zündende Lieder – verbrannte Musik: Folgen des Nationalsozialismus für Hamburger Musiker und Muskerinnen'. For this group, Hansen volunteered to undertake the research on Berthold Goldschmidt. This led her on to the much wider study that became her present doctoral dissertation. The story of Berthold Goldschmidt in itself is one of the miracles of exile studies, for this remarkable man was, until very recently, still alive and well and living in London though, at his age of ninety-three, a little frail. He died on 17 October 1996. For some years Goldschmidt had been in quiet retirement until, in 1982, an unexpected commission for a Clarinet Quintet released a stream of creative works that, once again, drew the attention of music critics to his previous periods of creativity in Berlin and London, resulting in more than a dozen CDs. When his opera *Der gewaltige Hahnrei* – from his days in the Berlin of the Weimar Republic – was performed to acclaim after a delay of some fifty years, the professional press became even more aware of the consequences of exile in a case such as this. Thereafter Goldschmidt received invitations from all over Germany to conduct and to perform his works, and now Decca is bringing out *The Goldschmidt Album* in a series devoted to 'Entarte Musik of the Third Reich'.

Once she arrived in England to pursue her researches, Hansen was able to hold extended interviews with Berthold Goldschmidt and with other 'Zeitzeugen'. She is generous and appreciative in her expression of thanks to him and to those others who helped: Erika Storm, Milein Cosman (the widow of Hans Heinrich Keller), Maria Lidka, Sigmund Nissel and Peter Gellner. Apart from such interviews, she has visited all the archives in Britain and elsewhere. Clearly, she has also read all the British musical journals of the time including *The Listener*, noting, for instance, that the President of the Nazi Reichsschrifttumskammer, Hans Friedrich Blunck, was invited to write for it in 1933 to explain the cultural policies of the new German government.

Although the starting point of Hansen's investigation was Hamburg and Germany, obviously she very soon realised that her scope had to be extended to include Austrians as well as Germans. 'German' music meant music written and performed by Germans, Austrians, and also artists from Czechoslovakia. Any kind of artificial dividing line between them would have been meaningless. This extension inevitably made the numbers of musicians involved even greater. The first chapter of her dissertation/book covers the period before and immediately after 1933, while the close connections between Germany, Austria and Britain are immediately apparent from the many reciprocal orchestral visits and exchanges discussed in the second chapter. This is a useful reminder that orchestras from Nazi Germany were still visiting England to some acclaim after 1933, while exile musicians in the latter country were suffering considerable hardship. This kind of paradoxical situation is highlighted by the fate of Furtwängler's secretary, Berta Geissmar, who was forced to leave Germany because she was Jewish, but who could revisit Germany again with the London Philharmonic Orchestra, when she took up a similar position with Sir Thomas Beecham. Her book *The Baton and the Jackboot* (1938) must have made many aware at the time of the true situation for musicians inside and outside Germany. The sections that follow investigate in detail public reactions to the refugees and, in particular, the position adopted by George Dyson, the Incorporated Society of Musicians and by various other interest groups.

Exiles and native British musicians did manage to come together over the formation of the Committee for the Promotion of New Music, and certainly something of an institution developed out of the National Gallery lunchtime concerts launched by Myra Hess, at which exile musicians were encouraged to play a prominent part. In a book such as this, the 'internment of aliens' has to be dealt with but, as is now well known, even out of this ghastly blunder good things could come; musicians did meet and play together as a result; Brainin could meet the people who would become first the Brainin, then the Amadeus Quartet. One slight criticism of this otherwise excellent book is that the author sometimes underestimates the impact of such groupings on the national consciousness. So, for example, she lists Rawicz and Landauer *separately*, only for their cabaret work in internment but not as the national favourites they later became when playing together.

Very important at the time were the exile organisations set up, mainly in London, though generally there were also branches in the provinces. Hansen is very well informed on the structure of the communist-inspired Free German League of Culture and the even more important Austrian Centre. In most surveys of these organisations the literary and theatrical activities tend to be stressed. Here it is gratifying to have reminders of the magnificent musical programmes with performers of the highest quality that both organisations were able to offer to large and appreciative British audiences. The already existing love of 'German' music among the British public gave musicians far more immediate success than artists and writers. Although Hansen has limited her survey to the two main German and Austrian organisations, the Czechs and the Sudeten Germans had their own centre in the Rudolf Fuchs House in London, and, as she shows elsewhere in passing, musicians from these areas were also active in the exile musical activities of the period.

The last chapters of the book are devoted to the Ernst Henschel Collection of programmes, and the mine of information this source contains, and then to the possible support the International Society for New Music could have given to the refugees. The book finishes with three exemplary biographies – Berthold Goldschmidt, Ernst Hermann Meyer and the violinist, Maria Lidka. As a final encore Hansen then adds 298 'short' biographies of exile musicians in Britain. This appendix contains an extraordinarily rich harvest of information, and all future researchers will long remain in Hansen's debt for what it contains. As has been noted earlier, many of the musicians she has studied were Jewish. To gather the essential details about their lives, she has had to resort to Nazi sources such as the Brückner-Rock *Judentum und Musik* (1938) and to the Stengel/Gerick *Lexikon der Juden in der Musik* (1940) but, needless to say, much more research has been necessary. Some famous names immediately catch the eye. Adorno, for instance, was in Oxford for some years before leaving for America. Hans Gal landed in Edinburgh University; Egon Wellesz in Lincoln College, Oxford; and Hans Ferdinand Redlich became Professor and Head of Department in Manchester. The Redlich Collection, we gather, now forms the basis of the Lancaster University Music Department Library. Less well known than the careers of these musical luminaries is that of Erich Gross, who took an MA, M.Litt. and D.Mus. at King's College, Aberdeen, before moving on to an academic career in Sydney, Australia. Cambridge University Library, we are reminded has the Paul Adolf Hirsch Collection, but even more significant, needless to say, is the Stefan Zweig Collection of musical manuscripts in the British Library.

In her summing up, Hansen fairly assesses the negative aspects of the manner in which many of the musical refugees from Germany, Austria and Czechoslovakia were received in Britain. There were clearly many reasons why so many wanted to go on to the United States, quite apart from the imminent danger of invasion. Some of the most famous, like Kurt Weill, succeeded. But that does not mean that only second-raters were left behind. First, major figures such as Adorno were in Britain, at least for several years. In some cases, great careers were possible in Britain. Richard Tauber is still remembered as a singer but he, too, made films that reached mass audiences and he was also a conductor. Mischa Spoliansky was successful from the beginning in every sphere he entered, as, too, was Josef Zmigrod (alias Alan Gray) who composed music for some 100 films. Popular music seems to have been an area in which many cabaret artists and song-writers from the German-speaking world found they could work with success. Some of their songs such as *Red Sails in the Sunset*, are accepted as so British that their 'German' origin has been completely forgotten.

Do the successes outweigh the failures or vice-versa? Certainly, as this book (and especially its many 'short' biographies) demonstrates, there were successes. When the Gombrich family makes its appearance in the biographies, through Leonie and Dea, the story moves out of the world of music and into that of art history. The success of Ernst Gombrich's art books is also a further reminder that, though there may not have been many publishers of German literature in London, there certainly were 'German' publishers of art books and of music. The 'short' biography of Alfred Kalmus here should be read as one example among many of great music publishers. Conductors, too, could re-establish their careers. Karl Rankl conducted at Covent Garden and then became the conductor of the Scottish National Orchestra. He is still fondly remembered. Chamber music was obviously easier to accommodate than large-scale orchestral pieces, as the example of the Max Rosstal Chamber Orchestra demonstrates, while, for the solo artist, such as the pianist Louis Kenter, there was always a place. Altogether, there is no doubt that this was no musical 'invasion'. There is equally no doubt that, despite the difficulties of the time,

Reviews

the whole spectrum of British musical life benefited enormously from the arrival of these 400 or so excellent musicians from the German-speaking regions. Jutta Raab Hansen has exposed a rich vein in the musical life of this country. For this all music lovers in Britain owe her a great debt of gratitude.

J. M. RITCHIE

Waltraud Strickhausen, *Die Erzählerin Hilde Spiel oder 'Der weite Wurf in die Finsternis'*, Exil-Studien 3 (Frankfurt: Peter Lang, 1996), 486 pp., DM 110.

Waltraud Strickhausen's *Die Erzählerin Hilde Spiel oder 'Der weite Wurf in die Finsternis'*, published in a bilingual Exile Studies series by Peter Lang, is based on a doctoral thesis. The format finely balances biography, literary history and literary analysis of Hilde Spiel's fictional work. Its wide range is symptomatic of the subject herself. Born in Vienna in 1911, Spiel's literary life spans the eras of pre- and post-war literature, several genres and two languages, German and English. This language-switch originated from Hilde Spiel's move to Britain in 1936. Her exile was the decisive point of Spiel's career and it is also an important reason for her rediscovery in the wake of an upsurge of interest in exile literature in Austria and Germany and within German and Austrian studies in Britain.

Strickhausen distinguishes four phases in Spiel's career. The period from 1926 to 1938 she calls Spiel's first epic phase ('I. epische Phase', p. 61) defined by her early short stories, novellas and novels such as *Kati auf der Brücke* and *Flöte und Trommeln*. The latter was originally written in German and later translated by Spiel herself with help from her husband, Peter de Mendelssohn, and a friend, and published in 1938 in English. This work forms the junction with the second phase from 1939 to 1960 ('englische Phase', p. 62) defined by her language-switch as well as her move from fiction to essay. During the first half of this phase she wrote two longer works. 'The Fruits of Prosperity', though written in English, never found a British publisher and was published only in the German translation in 1981. 'The Streets of Vineta', based on a diary written by Spiel upon her brief visit to Vienna in 1946–47, was also published only in German years later (1968). Her journalistic career was more successful at the time; from 1944 onwards, Spiel regularly published in British magazines. Journalism influenced her: in the same way as weighing up opposing arguments in an essay, Spiel developed a narrative style that uses dialogue and leaves the reader room for interpretation. In *The Darkened Room*, her only novel thematising the exile experience explicitly, she manages brilliantly to portray different attitudes towards exile in this way.

The next phase ('essayistische Phase', p. 62), lasting from 1960 to 1984, is marked by numerous essays, mainly on cultural themes, first published in newspapers and magazines but later collected in volumes such as *Welt im Widerschein* (1961) und *kleine schritte* (1976). In the last phase from 1979 onwards Hilde Spiel realised her wish to return from her journalism, which she saw mainly as a bread-winning job, to fictional and autobiographical writing ('II. epische Phase'). Outstanding here are the two volumes of her memoirs, *Die hellen und die finsteren Zeiten* (1989) and *Welche Welt ist meine Welt?* (1990).

Strickhausen concentrates on the novels and novellas belonging to the four phases. Following a biographical chapter, she discusses Spiel's early novels within the parameters of the historical and cultural situation in Central Europe during the 1920s and early 1930s. The next chapter focuses on Jewish identity in *Fanny von Arnstein oder Die Emanzipation* and *Die Früchte des Wohlstands*. In both books Spiel describes periods where Jews and gentiles lived together tolerating and respecting one another as individuals and, in some instances, even as groups. Strickhausen sees Spiel's life-long project as examining past periods of tolerance and the advancing toward a future model of understanding and rationality: 'ein Modell, das – selbst wenn es nie verwirklicht werden sollte – die humanste und vernünftigste Lösung darstellt' ['a model that – even if it will never be fully realised – constitutes the most humane and reasonable solution'] (p. 190).

In the fourth chapter Strickhausen examines Spiel's move into exile, which forms the major theme in several of her essays as well as in one novel and in one play. Spiel and de Mendelssohn were not typical of the German and Austrian exile community living in London. They did not move exclusively within exile circles; they started writing in English; they tried to integrate as much as possible into British literary society, and they did not expect to return to continental Europe. This makes her an especially apt analyst of the exile situation as she was able to look at it from a more differentiated point of view. Through her children she re-lived the linguist and cultural acquisition process of a British-born person. From 1940 onwards she wrote her diary in English. When she returned to the Continent for the first time after the war, she was officially a war correspondent attached to the British forces, and the resulting diary entries were again written in English. The fact that 'The Streets of Vineta' was never published in Britain is an indication that the path to recognition, however well prepared, was fraught with difficulty. Spiel described her language-switch as schizophrenic in the negative sense and as multi-dimensional in the positive sense

Even more unusually for an Austrian exile, Spiel attempted to be a mediator of British culture on the Continent. During the war a number of exiled writers tried through their writing to explain the situation in Central Europe to the British public. Strickhausen makes clear that Spiel did not want this cultural exchange to be one way. Even after her eventual return to Austria in 1963, she kept up the connection with Britain and, in 1983, aged seventy-two, she returned to Britain to become a foreign correspondent for the *Frankfurter Allgeimeine Zeitung*. The resulting work has since been published as *Englische Ansichten*. Spiel has frequently been described as a true European. Strickhausen shows us her ambiguous attitude to her own life between two countries, cultures and languages. This ultimately ties in with her striving for multicultural tolerance. Her project needs to be continued, though: it is a sad fact that much of the literature written in English by exiles originating from Central Europe has less chance of being recognised than their works written in German. This is because there is no awareness of their significance, and even their existence, within English literary studies.

After Spiel's return, her life in Austria was never straightforward. She never fitted in completely. Strickhausen poignantly describes Spiel's ambiguous reception, shortly after the war and in the years to come, as 'die unbequeme Mahnerin' ['the inconvenient admonisher'] (p. 293) regarding a wide range of issues such as Cold War politics or environmental protection. The last chapter, 'Frauenbilder – Frauengestalten', attempts an interesting analysis of Spiel in the light of modern women's writing and feminism. It appears, however, slightly out of line with the other chapters which are based on a stage in Spiel's life. Perhaps it should be seen as a starting point for a future detailed study.

Waltraud Strickhausen should be credited with an inspired rediscovery of Hilde Spiel, a comprehensive analysis of a wide range of her work and the compilation of a useful bibliography. She makes the complexity of Hilde Spiel as an author and as a person clear. Criticised for being too left-wing in PEN circles, seen as too reactionary in her realist literary style by literary critics, Spiel was criticised for being culturally élitist at the same time as being rebuked for producing 'Unterhaltungsliteratur'. Waltraud Strickhausen shows that Hilde Spiel's realism was not that of the nineteenth century and that the 'diskursive[r] Charakter der Erzählweise' ['discursive character of her narrative style'] (p. 383) opens up space for the dialogue between the generations.

ANDREA HAMMEL

Steven W. Lawrie, *Erich Fried: A Writer without a Country*, Austrian Culture 24 (New York: Peter Lang, 1996), 407 pp., $55.95.

It is odd that comparatively little attention has been paid by British Germanists to the work and person of Erich Fried. He has, after all, been an influential figure: a major German poet (though very uneven in his vast output); an outstanding translator of English poetry and of Shakespeare into German: and a significant point of contact with Britain for a whole generation of younger German writers. Clearly he was an engaging and committed mediator between the literatures. After his flight from Austria in 1938 at the age of seventeen, he made a more or less permanent home in London, until his death in 1988.

Steven Lawrie's study, originally a doctoral thesis, is the first monograph in English, and it is to be welcomed. It is not, as the title might imply, a full review of the life and works: the emphasis is squarely on the earlier years. In consequence, there is some overlap with Volker Kaukoreit's recent book, *Vom Exil bis zum Protest gegen den Krieg in Vietnam: Frühe Stationen des Lyrikers Erich Fried*, (Darmstadt: Häusser, 1991), which evidently came out while the thesis was being written. Lawrie avoids substantial duplication, however, by adopting the very particular perspective of England and of the experience of exile, on which he has much that is new to report. His researches (especially Chapter VI and Appendix II) for example, into Fried's involvement with the BBC have uncovered some fascinating new material.

Lawrie weaves a skilful descriptive narrative in short sections, covering various aspects of Fried's circumstances, his public opportunities, his political involvements, and his literary influences and contacts. About one-third of the book is devoted to each of: the war years and Fried's early literary ventures among the exiles of London; the post-war work with the BBC and as a translator, during which there was only meagre contact with the German scene (and the publisher Claassen); and, finally, Fried's 'reintegration' into the German literary world, especially after the success of his translation of *Under Milk Wood* in 1956. A consequence of this structure is the decidedly hurried account of the more important collections (*Warngedichte*, ... *und Vietnam und...* and beyond) and the political and literary activities of the later 1960s and '70s in Chapters IX and X: by which time, we are told, the 'writer without a country' had at least found a function, as something of a father figure to the new generation. Here Lawrie's tale begins to peter out.

Throughout the book, the poems themselves, which are often quoted in full (some wonderful, some truly awful), are used to reinforce the historical narrative. There is only ever sketchy analysis, and Lawrie betrays a distinctly unsteady hand on the occasions when he ventures into literary criticism or poetics. When, for example, we are told of the sacrifice of 'intended meaning' which apparently accompanies the use of rhyme, we may begin to think that the nature of poetic utterance is being quite seriously mistaken.

Fried is an exceptional subject. It is hard to think of another writer-exile from National Socialism who managed, at such a young age, to find a voice and to maintain (or rediscover) a grounded sense of identity, that permits even his earliest poems those glimpses of a humanity so characteristic, despite all the protest and gloom, of Fried's poetic legacy. There is only a handful of prominent writer-exiles (though there are many in other professions) who opted, throughout their careers, to pursue their negotiations with 'German' culture at arm's length, remaining 'in exile' and yet writing in German (Celan, Lasker-Schüler, Weiss are others). Although Lawrie gives us a very full account of the outward circumstances of all this, he can give us only occasional insights into the inner workings, the mental conditions and points of departure. Erich Fried must have been an extraordinary person to know (we have many testimonies of that), and it is a pity that this careful and precise (if rather oddly proportioned) study fails to capture more of the real energies of the man. Notwithstanding, this was clearly a good Ph.D. thesis, and it remains a very valuable addition to the critical literature on Fried.

TOM KUHN

Wolfgang Fleischer, *Das verleugnete Leben. Die Biographie des Heimito von Doderer* (Vienna, Kremayr & Scheriau, 1996), 576 pp., DM 67.00.

_____

In this year of centenary hoop-la one might approach another book on Doderer, especially one this length, with some scepticism. But in close to twenty-five years of reading and writing about Doderer, I have not found a book so full of detailed, carefully researched observations, and so well written that I found it hard to put down. The book is much more than a biography of one writer; almost coincidentally Fleischer has drawn the history of a family, a city, a coterie of writers, painters, academics, as well as a portrait of Doderer as a child, son, pupil, soldier and POW, student, disciple, 'master', lover, soldier and POW again, sadist, screwball mystic, posturing windbag, loyal and helpful friend, political opportunist, celebrated novelist, and finally stoic sufferer in the throes of disease and death.

What emerges in the end is a sense of a man prone to excesses of all sorts, some sympathetic, some less so, focused with obsessive discipline on writing, to the exclusion of virtually everything else. Success came, essentially because of the support of Horst Wiemer, reader for the C. H. Beck Verlag, in the late and politically very murky 1930s, while Doderer was living at Dachau. A measure of fame started to build in the late 1940s and early 1950s but it was not until the last decade of his life that Doderer reached financial security.

Fleischer, who served as his 'secretary', and later co-executor of his literary estate in the last three years of Doderer's life, is painstakingly truthful. The bulk of the book, until the success of *Die Strudlhofstiege,* is the story of failures. Fleischer draws a portrait of a spoiled minor aristocrat with middling success in school or university, who is irresponsible, vengeful, and impulsive in his private life. Together with a goodly number of friends – Albert Paris Gütersloh among them – he is infatuated with Nazism and later haunted by this (not uncommon) infatuation, only awkwardly covered up by his self-serving tendency to lie about his past (also not uncommon). In odd tandem with his exemplary early twentieth-century life, he develops an obsession to become a writer during his years in Russian POW camps. Whatever circuitous course his life took, this determination seems to have been the one thing he held onto with monomaniacal insistence. With some exceptions, he ran roughshod over personal relationships. Yet the compassionate picture Fleischer draws of the toothless, impotent, generous celebrity, sitting on the floor of his apartment searching for a couple of espresso cups to help his secretary and his friend set up an apartment, is as real as that of the voyeur with omnivorous sexual appetites.

There is no doubt about the truthfulness and eloquence of this biography the title of which, it seems to me, should really be *Das verlogene Leben.* But a legitimate question is whether this, or any other literary biography, no matter how rich in accurate detail, is necessary, or whether it contributes to a more truthful and balanced understanding of Doderer's published texts. If it is revealed that Author X was prone to a large measure of the weaknesses that flesh is heir to, does it matter to our understanding, liking, valuing the fictional world in published texts? In Doderer's case the answer to this question seems to depend on whether we look for history in the panoramas of his huge novels, or for philosophical coherence in his theoretical works, diaries, or 'sententiae'.

Fleischer has carefully shown the ways in which people from Doderer's surroundings emerged or submerged in his fiction, mostly having undergone considerable changes, and he has shown the hasty, and often hotchpotch, ways of his theorising and philosophising. Those who read Doderer's novels as *romans-à-clef* or as historical accounts will have to reassess their reading. Similarly, anyone who has taken Doderer's 'theory of the novel' as a serious scholarly enterprise will now have to think afresh in the light of Fleischer's portrait of the *ad hoc* theorist, bent mostly on demonstrating the validity of *his own* writing.

Luckily, for those of us who have considered primarily Doderer's rich and humorous fiction, for those of us who were captured by the freshness and eccentricity, the subtlety and poetic beauty of his descriptions, and the warmth and humour of the 'crotchety, gossipy voice' of the story-teller, far removed from the unsavoury aspects of the politics of the real Vienna, we can enjoy Doderer as before. But we must be warned, and warn all others, that splendid fiction is all he gives us. Not history, not theory, not philosophy. Again, luckily, that is plenty.

MICHAEL BACHEM

Die 'britische' Steiermark 1945–1955, ed. Siegfried Beer, Forschungen zur geschicht-lichen Landeskunde der Steiermark 38 (Graz: im Selbstverlag der Historischen Landeskommission für Steiermark, 1995), 763 pp.

This collection provides much new information about provincial life and politics in post-war Austria. Four main sections (Steirische Politik und Verwaltung; die Britische Militärregierung; Nachkriegsalltag und Wiederaufbau; Kultus, Bildung und Kultur) are followed by British and Austrian eyewitness ac-counts, photos and a chronology. The semi-official status of the publication is shown in the glossy format and in the introductory thanks of the Styrian governor, Landeshauptmann Krainer, to 'alle steirischen Landsleute [...], die mit ihrer Zuverlässigkeit, mit Zähigkeit und unbeirrbarem Willen, dieses Land aus Trümmern wieder aufgebaut haben'. This (self-)congratulatory note is echoed in some, but fortunately not all, of the subsequent contributions. Most are scholarly and informative.

Three major issues emerge, hinted at rather than addressed directly. The first is Austrian experience of the Russians, and the comparisons with the British, who succeeded them as occupying power in the summer of 1945. This is a topic that requires sensitive handling. The depredations of the Red Army and the operations of Soviet secret police and counter-intelligence are undeniable facts. But their interpretation – especially in a region which had by and large supported a National Socialist regime – has to avoid any suggestion of confirming Nazi stereotypes. Sensitivity is more evident in some accounts (e.g. Ella Hornung's and Gertrud Kerschbaumer's interviews with prisoners from Russian captivity) than others (e.g. Stefan Karner's contribution, which lumps together Cossacks who had fought in the Wehrmacht, the Vlasov army and the kidnap victims of Soviet counter-intelligence).

This leads to the second question – the degree of continuity with the Third Reich. Here, too, different positions are hinted at though, again, not drawn out. Thus, Otmar Pichl endorses what he terms (without any other corroboration) the 'objektive und kluge Schilderung' of a local Major of the reserve in the Mürztal. This states, *inter alia*, that 'in der NS-Zeit hatte sich die Bevölkerung fast einhellig zum Regime bekannt' but also that 'aus dem Mürztal fast ausschliesslich kriminelle Elemente in Haft genommen wurden.' Furthermore: 'die Ungerechtigkeiten hielten sich in erträglichen Grenzen'. Pichl closes with a – far from objective – tirade against antifascism (citing the dubious Ernst Topitsch). On the other side, Dieter Binder sarcastically confesses his inability as 'präpotenter Nachgeborener' to comprehend the level of anti-Semitic vitriol in pre-war Styria and notes its continuance in coded form in the post-war period when 'die Steiermark kehrt gleichsam in einen antisemitischen Bewusstseinszustand "vor Auschwitz" zurück'. Whereas Pichl (and Edith Marko-Stöckl) speak approvingly of the 'Versöhnungspolitik' adopted by the main parties towards former Nazis, Binder places the term in inverted commas. Wolfgang Muchitsch is similarly critical of the People's Courts in dealing so leniently, not merely with the proverbial small 'Parteigenosse', but with serious criminals. In this context, it is a pity that the continuities of the Styrian Grenzland – not least of Graz University – were not given an airing (though they are touched on by Christian Klösch and Hans-Peter Weingand's account of the Graz student body and the revival of the duelling Korps).

Thirdly, how 'British' was British Styria? The dust-jacket has the outline of the province cut out of the Union Flag, as if Cecil Rhodes had continued into Central Europe. Elsewhere there are references to British tutelage (Bevormundung) and 'constitutional dictatorship'. On the other hand, we also learn of the British concern to keep out of Austrian politics (in the 1945 election campaign) and of student life and of their lack of ambition to restructure the education system. In my view, this is closer to the truth. The mere facts of unconditional surrender and occupation, or the language of British military decrees or ordinances, do not prove anything like 'total control'. The voluminous files of British Military Government and Civil Affairs, now available in the Public Record Office, which have been profitably used by many of the contributors to this volume, may have the drawback of fostering the illusion that the British made more difference than they did.

ROBERT KNIGHT

Gudrun Kuhn, *Ein philosophisch-musikalisch geschulter Sänger. Musikästhetische Überlegungen zur Prosa Thomas Bernhards* (Würzburg: Königshausen & Neumann, 1995), 265 pp., DM 68.00.

No monograph on Thomas Bernhard is complete without at least a mention of the affinity of his prose style to music. In the majority of cases to date, the reference has hardly gone beyond the metaphorical level, probably because the authors of such studies have all been literary scholars. Now, it seems, the first book devoted entirely to Bernhard's relationship to music by an author versed in music aesthetics has appeared. This erudite volume, based on a doctoral thesis for the University of Erlangen, appears to deal with Bernhard's musical style in a truly all-encompassing way. A detailed and critical discussion of research published so far is followed by a lengthy presentation of just about every conceivable aspect of musical association in Bernhard's work. Starting from a post-structural point of view, in particular that of Roland Barthes who, as the author points out, not only shared Bernhard's medical problems but also Kuhn's views on music, proceeds to explicate Bernhard's work in terms of the music aesthetics of philosophers to whose names and works Bernhard repeatedly refers: Novalis, Schopenhauer, Wittgenstein. There is the obvious question of the validity of such an undertaking: can we really assume that Bernhard has actually read all these books simply because he mentions their titles? In the case of Schopenhauer's *Die Welt als Wille und Vorstellung*, Kuhn admits that Bernhard does not refer to the content of the work. By contrast, the whole of Franz Kafka goes unmentioned, despite its well-documented influence on Bernhard and the two writers' common view of music as a substitute for the unspeakable.

Kuhn interprets Bernhard's prose works in terms of '(singing) voices', which seems convincing for a narrative style that distances the actual story by having it reported by, sometimes, two narrators who, in addition, utter views that Bernhard took over from the above-mentioned philosophers. Kuhn describes this method in terms of a singer impersonating a character. A notable – if not new – heuristics is the idea of Bernhard's language as a signifier without a signified, a phenomenon that facilitates a comparison between his style and music. Bernhard's prose not only is largely self-referential but also contains 'supersigns' such as the ubiquitous (and usually italicised) *naturgemäß* which section the text in a graphical way but do not have any obvious 'meaning'. It seems odd in this context that Kuhn does not refer to Jacques Lacan and his theory of the 'signifying chain' ('The Agency of the Letter in the Unconscious'), according to which the signifiers no longer point to objects in the outside world but to each other. This seems to me a fitting and rather more straightforward way of describing Bernhard's prose than what Kuhn does, especially as her elaborate theoretical discussions typically lead to quite trivial conclusions.

Kuhn's pugnacious language is emotional, and at times it assimilates the tone of its subject. What is particularly irritating is the discussion of the same phenomenon in different works of Bernhard in terms of its 'musical' quality, as if this were unique to the text in question: for example, she mentions *Gehen* and *Billigesser* as two separate examples, in which Bernhard's quotation technique changes the quality of the narrated time in the reader's perception. In doing so she disregards the fact that this technique not only has the same effect in both texts but that it constitutes the hallmark of Bernhard's style throughout his work.

Extensive parts of Kuhn's book, especially towards its end, deal with philosophical problems that have little relationship to musical style or aesthetics. This brings up the question: for whom is this book intended? The paucity of music examples excludes the literature-versed musicologist. The literary scholar will be put off by the confusion of the literary and the factual (Kuhn repeatedly quotes the five volumes of Bernhard's autobiography as though it were a repository of safe facts – which is not advisable for any author, least of all for Bernhard).

So what remains after a demanding read? The volume yields some good ideas and many references worth following up, together with a great deal of irrelevant information that threatens to obscure the problem more than it can elucidate it.

ANDREA REITER

Herbert Zeman (ed.), *Literaturgeschichte Österreichs: Von den Anfängen im Mittelalter bis zur Gegenwart* (Graz: Akademische Druck- und Verlagsanstalt, 1996), 600 pp., 480 Sch. / DM 69.00.

There have already been three histories of Austrian literature: Joseph Toscano del Banner's incomplete effort in 1849; Nagl and Zeidler in 1889; Nadler in 1949. This is now the fourth and, no doubt, the fullest. It runs to 600 pages, and its aim is to give its subject the fullest possible coverage. Was there ever a history of literature so full of authors' names? Lists of them – from *Vormärz* political writers to operetta librettists, Aufklärung rationalists to the contributors to *Die Botschaft* – pass before the reader's eye. No wonder the index is so long, yet also so tantalisingly full of single *passim* references. Fortunately this rather irritating feature is less in evidence in the first four sections (by Alois Wolf, Fritz Peter Knapp and Werner M. Bauer). These unfold the literature of the areas first called Austria in AD 996 during those medieval centuries that saw them produce most of the major Middle High German writers. They form the solid basis for the more speculative enterprise that begins on page 185, and which time and again prompts the question: has there ever really been such a thing an 'Austrian' literature during the post-medieval centuries, a literature, that is, that can be read and understood in isolation from the 'German' one? Herbert Zeman, the authority behind this whole proud undertaking, thinks there is. He defines it as an amalgam of *Kulturregion* and *staatliches Gebilde*, and, in answer to his reader's nagging question, is careful to remind us that its literature has often interacted with, or reacted to, that other one that shares the same language.

Austria produced little or nothing of great note during the two centuries that in Germany were dominated by Luther and the Opitzian seventeenth-century renewal. Nevertheless, Erich Trunz and Dieter Breuer find much of interest to say about literary activity during this long period, though without ever outrightly addressing the leading question: why did Roman`Catholicism have such a discouraging effect on literary creativity in Austria when, in Catholic Spain and Italy, prose and poetry flourished? The eighteenth century, ably handled by Herbert Zeman, tells the story of a literature that, if Blumauer and Hofbauer were its greatest ornaments, deserves to be overshadowed by what was taking place in the other German states, and in Switzerland, too. Yet, perhaps paradoxically, it was a literature capable of withstanding the joint impacts of Jacobinism and Romanticism and of achieving distinction in the post-Napoleonic period of Metternichian reaction, and a complex voice of its own. Was this achievement connected in some way with the emergence of a Roman Catholic readership during the first half of the nineteenth century? Or was it, as Zeman suggests in pages that form the heart and centre of this history, because in Mozart, Raimund and Grillparzer Austria achieved a rare balance between high art and popular entertainment? The balance may have been short-lived; but it was long enough to shape and permeate the years of decadent greatness that terminated in 1918.

At this point, the pace of the narrative begins to slacken, much to its advantage. The cosmopolitan make-up of Austrian imperial civilisation and the consolidation of Vienna's metropolitan artistic and literary culture now become its central themes, and there are many moments when the reader's interest is aroused and directed to names, works and issues that may not always be familiar, but that are, nonetheless, always integral to the difficult task of presenting Austrian literature as an integrated and evolving whole. The sudden reversal of optimism into *Weltschmerz*, that quintessentially Austrian version of late Romantic spleen, soon leads, for example, to an unexpected but entirely justifiable emphasis on Feuchtersleben's seminal *Zur Diätetik der Seele* (1838) as perhaps the most significant product of the first wave of interest in theoretical and clinical psychology in Vienna, while the Schiller centenary festivities there, and the first Mozart festival in Salzburg three years earlier, are discussed as barometers of an ongoing change in civic and public attitudes to the cultural heritage which was to have far-reaching effects on the direction of literature, too, by enhancing the status of a new classical canon, much to the dismay of Sebastian Brunner, leading Catholic critic of the new cult of Weimar classicism, whose pet aversions give us, in Zeman's view, a good idea of the literary climate of mid-nineteenth-century Austria. Thus, the work of Stifter, so often studied in isolation, is given a more accurate context and takes on new dimensions of meaning.

On the debit side, it cannot be denied that this new *Literaturgeschichte Österreichs* sometimes suffers from the fact that, though it is masterminded by Herbert Zeman, it is also the work of other hands, and that these seem to be in tacit agreement to play down the presence and influence of non-Austrian German literature and to ignore the awkward moments when, for good or ill, the histories of both nations have coincided. There is another omission graver and sadder still. Though their names are given, most of the many women who contributed so much to Austria's literary achievement prior to 1945 – Caroline Pichler, Betty Paoli, Enrica von Handel-Mazzetti, Rosa Mayreder, Bertha von Suttner, Maria Grengg – are not discussed and their artistic aims and achievements are ignored. But why? This serious omission must surely tell us something important about the conflicting and contradictory attitudes that underlie the production and the consumption of literature in Austria and its subsequent critical evaluation. Even the great Catharina von Greiffenberg receives scarcely more than a mention. But this neglect would be no great surprise to the great Austrian Protestant baroque religious poet who had to turn to Nuremberg to find assistance and a warm welcome for her remarkable work from her male contemporaries on the banks of the Pegnitz.

Finally, modern times are reached. The chapter by Joseph Strelka on Austrian exile literature since 1938 (pp. 475–510) will be widely welcomed and should be carefully read by all those interested in what was being produced outside Austria during the Third Reich as well as in what was being written and read within. Lastly Werner M. Bauer takes on the post-war age, adopting a more text-oriented approach to do so. The passages he quotes in his wonderfully succinct survey provide a welcome break from the narrative style of the remainder of the book, and should do much to encourage students of the post-war period to consult it. No doubt it is not for nothing that it brings this new history of Austrian literature to an end with a quotation from Thomas Bernhard's *Heldenplatz* of 1988. Apart from three volumes edited by Donald Daviau and one written by W. E. Yates, the bibliography of useful reading contains nothing written in English.

PETER SKRINE

Notes on Contributors

LOUISE ADEY HUISH has published numerous articles on Nestroy, Keller, Horváth and others, and is one of the editors of the new critical edition of Nestroy (HKA).

MARK ANDERSON is Professor of German at Columbia University and author of *Kafka's Clothes* (Oxford University Press, 1992).

MICHAEL BACHEM is Professor of German at the University of Miami, Ohio. He wrote the volume on Doderer in the Twayne World Authors Series and is currently working on the fairy-tale with particular reference to Hofmannsthal.

ALAN BANCE is Professor of German at Southampton University and author of *Theodor Fontane* (Cambridge University Press, 1982). He has recently written the introduction to the Everyman edition of Joseph Roth's *Radetzky March*.

ANDREW BARKER is Professor of Austrian Studies at Edinburgh University. He is author of *Telegrams from the Soul: Peter Altenberg and the Culture of Fin-de-Siècle Vienna* (Camden House, 1996) and co-author, with Leo A. Lensing, of *Peter Altenberg: Rezept die Welt zu sehen* (Braumüller, 1995).

PETER BRANSCOMBE is Emeritus Professor of Austrian Studies at the University of St Andrews. His most recent book is *Mozart: Die Zauberflöte* in the Cambridge Opera Handbooks series (1991), and he is one of the editors of the HKA.

FRITZ BREITHAUPT is Assistant Professor of Germanic Studies at Indiana University, Bloomington. Besides his forthcoming book *Eidolatrie: Das Trugbild und die Revision des Bildlichen bei Goethe* he has published essays on Goethe, Kleist, Brecht, Celan, and the comic strip.

ANITA BUNYAN is a Fellow of Gonville and Caius College, Cambridge, and author of numerous articles on nineteenth-century German literature.

GILBERT J. CARR is Senior Lecturer in Germanic Studies at Trinity College, Dublin, and the author of numerous articles on Kraus and his contemporaries. He has recently edited the correspondence of Kraus and Otto Stoessl (Deuticke).

ANNE FUCHS is Lecturer in German at University College, Dublin, author of *Dramaturgie des Narrentums: Das Komische in der Prosa Robert Walsers* (Fink, 1993), and co-editor (with Theo Harden) of *Reisen im Diskurs: Modelle der literarischen Fremderfahrung von den Pilgerberichten bis zur Postmoderne* (Winter, 1995) and (with Florian Krobb) of *Ghetto Writing: Traditional and Eastern Jewry in German-Jewish Literature* (Camden House, 1998). She is working on a book to be entitled *A Space of Anxiety: a Study of Five German-Jewish Writers (Freud, Kafka, Roth, Drach and Hilsenrath)*.

R. S. FURNESS is Professor of German at the University of St Andrews. His publications include *Wagner and Literature* (Manchester University Press, 1982) and (with Malcolm Humble) *A Companion to Twentieth-Century German Literature* (Routledge, 1991).

CHRISTOPHER HAILEY is director of the Franz Schreker Foundation and author of *Franz Schreker (1878–1934): A Cultural Biography* (Cambridge University Press), editor of the correspondence between Paul Bekker and Franz Schreker (Rimbaud Verlag), co-editor of *The Berg–Schoenberg Correspondence* (Norton), and co-translator of Theodor Adorno's monograph on Alban Berg (Cambridge University Press).

ANDREA HAMMEL is a research assistant at the Centre for German-Jewish Studies, University of Sussex. She has published 'Remembering and Forgetting: Hilde Spiel's *Rückkehr nach Wien* in 1946' in *Austria 1945–55* (University of Wales Press, 1996). She is completing a doctoral thesis on women's exile literature, especially Anna Gmeyner, Martina Wied and Hermynia Zur Mühlen, and is one of the editors of a forthcoming volume of essays on Jakov Lind.

JÜRGEN HEIN, Professor of Modern German Literature at the University of Münster, has published widely on Viennese popular theatre, particularly Raimund and Nestroy, as well as on comedy and dialect literature. He has been a general editor of the HKA since 1977, and has edited a number of the plays.

IAN HUISH is a psychotherapist and former teacher of German at Westminster School, London. He has published a study of Ödön von Horváth, editions of several Horváth plays, and articles on Soyfer, Mann and Härtling.

BRIAN KEITH-SMITH has recently retired as Reader in German at Bristol University and now holds the title of Senior Research Professor at Mellen University. He has edited a ten-volume anthology, *German Women Writers*

1900–1933 (Edwin Mellen Press), and is preparing for the same publisher a twenty-volume edition of the published and unpublished works of the Expressionist Lothar Schreyer.

ROBERT KNIGHT is a Lecturer in the Department of European Studies at Loughborough University and editor of '*Ich bin dafür, die Sache in die Länge zu ziehen*': *Die Wortprotokolle der österreichischen Bundesregierung von 1945 bis 1952 über die Entschädigung der Juden* (1988).

TOM KUHN is Fellow in German at St Hugh's College, Oxford. He has published numerous articles on German drama from the 1920s to the present, and (with Karen Leeder) an English edition of memoir and source material, *The Young Brecht* (Libris, 1992). He is a general editor of the Methuen Brecht edition.

JILL LEWIS is a Lecturer in History at University College of Swansea. She is the author of *Fascism and the Working Class in Austria 1918–1934* (Berg, 1991) and is now working on the Austrian General Strike of 1950.

JOHN R. P. MCKENZIE is Senior Lecturer in German at Exeter University, and author of *Social Comedy in Austria and Germany 1890–1930*, in the series 'British and Irish Studies in German Language and Literature' (Lang, 1992). He is one of the editors of the HKA.

VICTORIA MARTIN is a Fellow of St Anne's College, Oxford, and University Lecturer in German Linguistics; she has a particular interest in the German language as spoken in Austria.

WALTER OBERMAIER, Librarian of the Vienna City Library and head of its Manuscript Department, has published widely on the cultural history of nineteenth-century Austria. In 1992 he became one of the HKA's general editors. He has edited Nestroy's letters and is preparing editions of four plays for the HKA.

ANTHONY PHELAN is a Senior Lecturer in German Studies at the University of Warwick. He has published a critical guide to Rilke's *Neue Gedichte*, contributed (with Stephen Lamb) the chapter on the Weimar Republic to *German Cultural Studies* (Oxford University Press, 1996), and is currently completing a study of Heine.

DAVID RECHTER is Clore Fellow in Modern Jewish History at the Oxford Centre for Hebrew and Jewish Studies. He is working on a history of Viennese Jewry and World War I.

ANDREA REITER, Research Fellow at the University of Southampton, has a doctorate from Salzburg and has published many articles on Kafka, Bernhard, Aichinger, Austrian anti-modernity, and concentration camp memoirs. Her book on the latter subject, '*Auf daß sie entsteigen der Dunkelheit*'. *Die literarische Bewältigung von KZ-Erfahrung*, was published by Löcker Verlag in 1995.

J. M. RITCHIE is President of the Research Centre for German and Austrian Exile Studies located at the Institute of Germanic Studies in London. He has published numerous studies and translations, mostly of twentieth-century German literature, including *German Literature under National Socialism* (Croom Helm, 1983).

RITCHIE ROBERTSON is Reader in German and Fellow of St John's College, Oxford, and author of *Kafka: Judaism, Politics, and Literature* (Oxford University Press, 1985). He contributed a chapter on literature 1890–1945 to the *Cambridge History of German Literature*, edited by Helen Watanabe-O'Kelly (1997).

IAN F. ROE is Senior Lecturer in German at Reading University and author of studies of Grillparzer (Edwin Mellen, 1991) and Grillparzer's reception (Camden House, 1995).

LESLEY SHARPE is Professor of German at Exeter University and author of numerous studies of eighteenth-century literature, including *Friedrich Schiller: Drama, Thought and Politics* (Cambridge University Press, 1991) and *Schiller's Aesthetic Essays: Two Centuries of Criticism* (Camden House, 1995).

PETER SKRINE is Professor of German at Bristol University. His books include *Hauptmann, Wedekind and Schnitzler* (Macmillan, 1989). His most recent book (written jointly with Eda Sagarra) is *A Companion to German Literature* (Blackwell, 1997).

MARTIN SWALES is Professor of German at University College, London. His many books include *Arthur Schnitzler: A Critical Study* (Clarendon Press, 1971) and, most recently, *Epochenbuch Realismus: Romane und Erzählungen* (Erich Schmidt, 1996).

ROBERT VILAIN is a Lecturer in German at Royal Holloway, University of London. He is at work on a study of Hofmannsthal and is also editing a book of essays on Yvan and Claire Goll.

FRIEDRICH WALLA, Professor of German at the University of Newcastle, New South Wales, Australia, has published many articles on Austrian literature, especially Nestroy. He has been involved with the HKA since its inception, editing some eighteen plays.

JOHN WARREN has recently retired from teaching German at Oxford Brookes University. He is co-editor, with Kenneth Segar, of *Austria in the Thirties: Culture and Politics* (Ariadne Press, 1990).

HELEN WATANABE-O'KELLY is Fellow and Tutor in German at Exeter College, Oxford. She has published *Triumphall Shews: Tournaments at German-speaking Courts in their European Context 1536–1730* (Gebr. Mann Verlag, 1992) and numerous studies of baroque literature and Adalbert Stifter, and is the editor of *The Cambridge History of German Literature* (Cambridge University Press, 1997).

MARTHA WÖRSCHING is Lecturer in German at Loughborough University and author of several articles on Joseph Roth.

DAGMAR ZUMBUSCH-BEISTEINER has recently completed an MA and is a doctoral candidate in musicology at the University of Bonn. Besides publishing a number of articles on music and drama, she is closely involved in the production of the HKA, as reader for the publishers and as author of the sections on music in Nestroy's plays that have appeared in several volumes of the edition.

Austrian Studies

Acknowledgements: The Editors gratefully acknowledge the support of the Austrian Institute in London. Thanks are also due to the colleagues listed below for their willingness to serve on the Advisory Board.

Advisory Board: Andrew Barker (Edinburgh), Peter Branscombe (St Andrews), Amy D. Colin (Pittsburgh), R. J. W. Evans (Oxford), Sander L. Gilman (Cornell), Murray G. Hall (Vienna), Jacques Le Rider (Paris), Eda Sagarra (Dublin), W. G. Sebald (East Anglia), Joseph Peter Strelka (New York), Robert Wistrich (Jerusalem), W. E. Yates (Exeter).

Books for review should be sent to Dr Judith Beniston, Department of German, University College London, Gower Street, London WC1E 6BT.

Typescripts for publication should be submitted in duplicate to Edward Timms, Arts Building, University of Sussex, Brighton BNI 9QN, England.

Guidelines: Articles should be written in English and should not exceed 7,500 words. They should be typed double-spaced, using endnotes (not a numbered bibliography) to identify the source of quotations. Quotations should normally be given in the original language, followed by an English translation. A detailed style sheet is available from either of the Editors, on request.

Austrian Studies may be ordered through any bookshop. Since it is an annual publication, it may also be obtained by subscription direct from the publishers, Edinburgh University Press, 22 George Square, Edinburgh EH8 9LF, Scotland.